The Mysterious
and the Foreign
in Early Modern England

Adriaen Brouwer, Flemish, 1605/6–38. *Taste,* c. 1635–38. Oil on plywood. Gift of Herman Levy Esq., O.B.E. McMaster University Collection, Hamilton, Canada. © McMaster Museum of Art, McMaster University, 2006. 1984.007.0012.

Contents

Introduction   9
    HELEN OSTOVICH, MARY V. SILCOX,
    AND GRAHAM ROEBUCK

Part I: The Foreign Journey

"An Habitation of Devils, a Domicill for Unclean Spirits,
and a Den of Goblings": The Marvelous North in
Early Modern English Literature   27
    COLLEEN FRANKLIN

Headless in America: The Imperial Logic of Acephalism   39
    SCOTT OLDENBURG

Slavery, Sex, and the Seraglio: "Turkish" Women and
Early Modern Texts   58
    BINDU MALIECKAL

To Russia without Love: George Turberville as
Resistant Traveler   74
    JANE FARNSWORTH

Jack Wilton and the Jews: The Ambivalence of
Anti-Semitism in Nashe's *The Unfortunate Traveller*   89
    MATHEW MARTIN

Part II: Profiting from the Mysterious

"These Recreations, which are strange and true":
Wit, Mathematics, and Jonson's *The Magnetic Lady*   107
    HELEN OSTOVICH

Usurers of Color: The Taint of Jewish Transnationality
in Mercantilist Literature and *The Merchant of Venice*   124
    JONATHAN GIL HARRIS

Speaking the Language, Knowing the Trade: Foreign Speech
and Commercial Opportunity in *The Shoemaker's Holiday*   139
    MARIANNE MONTGOMERY

The Subject of Smoke: Tobacco and Early Modern England 153
  SANDRA BELL

Sassafras 170
  GRAHAM ROEBUCK

Othello the Liar 187
  PHILIP D. COLLINGTON

Part III: The Domestication of the Mysterious and Foreign

Was Illyria as Mysterious and Foreign as We Think? 209
  PATRICIA PARKER

"We are yet strangers in our own country": Foreign and
Mysterious Elements in the Elizabethan Settlement of Religion 234
  STEPHEN BUICK

Pirates, Merchants, and Kings: Oriental Motifs in English Court
and Civic Entertainments, 1510–1659 249
  LINDA MCJANNET

The Strange Finding Out of Moses his Tombe: News, Travel
Narrative, and Satire 266
  KATE LOVEMAN

Strangely Familiar: Emblems in Early Modern England 281
  MARY V. SILCOX

Notes on Contributors 299
Index 303

The Mysterious
and the Foreign
in Early Modern England

Introduction

Helen Ostovich, Mary V. Silcox, and Graham Roebuck

THE *RELAZIONE* OF AN ANONYMOUS VENETIAN AMBASSADOR PROVIDES A vivid sketch of the English just before the upheavals of the Reformation. It recounts the rather mysterious customs of a foreign people measured against the standards and expectations of the most sophisticated and widely traveled inhabitants of the European world: "The English are, for the most part, both men and women of all ages, handsome and well-proportioned . . . [they] are great lovers of themselves, and of everything belonging to them; they think that there are no other men than themselves, and no other world but England; and whenever they see a handsome foreigner, they say that 'he looks like an Englishman,' and that 'it is a great pity that he should not be an English-man;' and when they partake of any delicacy with a foreigner, they ask him, 'whether such a thing is made in *their* country?'"[1] Parsimonious with wine at their otherwise sumptuous feasts, they wear very fine clothes and speak a language which, though derived from the German, is pleasing, having lost its harshness. They are pious enough in their religious observance, omitting nothing incumbent upon good Christians; yet, ominously, they harbor "various opinions concerning religion" (23). They also "have an antipathy to foreigners, and imagine that they never come into their island, but to make themselves masters of it, and to usurp their goods" (23–24). This observation naturally prompts the Italian to note that they do not trust people "as we do in Italy," and that they "keep a very jealous guard over their wives, though any thing may be compensated in the end, by the power of money" (24).

Not, perhaps, an entirely flattering portrait of the English, but there is admiration, mixed with a tincture of envy, for their wealth and self-sufficiency: "The riches of England are greater than those of any other country in Europe, as I have been told by the oldest and most experienced merchants, and also as I myself can vouch, from that I have seen" (28). Their wealth lies in the fertility of the soil, the value of their exports, especially tin and wool, the near absence of imports, with the exception of wine, and their fiscal policy which prohibits gold and silver from leaving the country. Their riches are displayed in silver plate and dishes both domestically by every innkeeper, "however poor and humble he may be," and ecclesiastically, "for there is not a parish church in the kingdom so mean as not to possess

9

crucifixes, candlesticks, censers, patens, and cups of silver" (29). The report rounds out the topic of English wealth with the information that many English monasteries "possess unicorns' horns of extraordinary size" (29).

Why would a nation so richly endowed, so self-sufficient in almost every regard—if we are to believe the Venetian observer—become concerned with, even obsessed by, what lies outside their familiar surroundings, as the essays collected in this volume attest? A difficult question to answer. No doubt, in addition to the continent-wide religious ferment, and economic advantages, the upsurge of philosophical skepticism played its part in unsettling English complacencies. Montaigne's restlessly speculative *Essais,* published in French from 1580 to 1595 and made available to readers of English in John Florio's masterly translation of 1603, extended intellectual horizons in a manner calculated to induce cultural vertigo: "If whatsoeuer has come vnto us by report of what is past were true, and knowne of anybody, it would bee lesse then nothing, in respect of that which is vnknowne. And even of this image of the world, which while wee liue therein, glideth and passeth away, how wretched, how weake, and how short is the knowledge of the most curious?"[2] From these deflating *sententiae* Montaigne leads the reader to the specific case of European "wonder at the miraculous inuention of our artilerie and . . . the rare deuice of Printing" (510) to point out that, unknown to Europeans, these wonders were commonplace a thousand years before in China. Then to the New World and the "never-like seen cities of Cuzco and Mexico" (511) whose civilizations were so thoroughly subdued by European force of arms. Is this not cause for pride? Not at all, is Montaigne's answer, for these people were betrayed by their own thirst for the mysterious: "over-taken by the curiosity to see strange and vnknowne things" (512)—horses, steel, and shot.

The curiosity of the English of the early modern period was, perhaps, no less naive than that of the New World inhabitants with whom they came into contact. Yet it is informed by a self-confidence such as that noted by the Venetian ambassador. Francis Bacon, though indebted to Montaigne in several respects, does not hesitate to prescribe rules for travelers abroad intended to make experience of the foreign a useful and codified commodity: "The Things to be seene and obserued are: The Courts of Princes, specially when they giue Audience to Ambassadors: The Courts of Iustice, while they sit and heare Causes; and so of Consistories Ecclesiasticke: The Churches, and Monasteries, with the Monuments which are therein extant: The Wals and Fortifications of Cities and Townes; And so the Hauens & Harbours: Antiquities, and Ruines: Libraries; Colledges."[3] And so on for a further thirty or so categories, "And, to conclude, whatsoeuer is memorable in the Places, where they go" (102). The traveler must keep a diary and must throughout his foreign travel take care to retain the manners of his native country, not adopt those of foreign parts (102). What he has learned abroad should be brought back like exotic flowers to be planted in his native soil (92).

Like Bacon, Sir Thomas Browne, also an heir to the sceptical tradition, holds practical knowledge in highest esteem: "For my owne part, besides the *Jargon* and *Patois* of severall Provinces, I understand no lesse than six Languages; yet I protest I have no higher conceit of my selfe than had our Fathers before the confusion of *Babel.*"[4] Thus provisioned, Browne regards himself as quite unflappable. The French taste for "frogges, snails, and toadstooles" does not provoke wonder, nor does that of the Jews for "Locusts and Grasse-hoppers, but being amongst them, [I] make them my common viands; and I finde they agree with my stomach as well as theirs; I could digest a Sallad gathered in a Church-yard, as well as in a Garden" (133). Browne goes on to explain how and why he has no prejudice against other people: "Those national repugnances doe not touch me, nor doe I behold with prejudice the *French, Italian, Spaniard,* or *Dutch;* but where I finde their actions in ballance with my Countreymens, I honour, love, and embrace them in some degree; I was borne in the eighth Climate, but seeme for to bee framed, and constellated unto all; I am no Plant that will not prosper out of a Garden. All places, all ayres make unto me one Countrey; I am in *England,* every where, and under any meridian" (133–34).

Another great traveler, and theorist of travel, James Howell, rejoicing in Englishness (although he is frequently enormously proud of being Welsh) gives *Instructions for Forreine Travell,* written when the idea of foreign travel was a sustaining memory for him, incarcerated for his Royalist sympathies in the English Civil Wars. The traveler, he writes, may not improperly be termed "a *moving Academy,* or the true *Peripatetique Schoole,*"[5] none more so than the English variety: "Amongst the other Nations of the World the *English* are observed to have gained much, and improved themselves infinitely by voyaging both by Land and Sea, and of those foure *Worthies* who compassed about the Terrestriall Globe, I find the major part of them were *English*" (14). But Howell cautions against the traveler's "excessive commendation and magnifying of his own Countrey; for it is too much observed, that the *English* suffer themselves to be to much transported with this subject, to undervalue and villifie other Countreys, for which I have heard them often censured" (61). The Venetian ambassador would probably recognize the portrait. Finally, in Baconian spirit, Howell recommends that "one should evertuate himselfe to bring something home, that may accrue to the publique benefit and advantage of his Country" (203).

The English of the early modern period were as fascinated by stories of the unnatural, the mysterious, and the criminal, as by the foreign, sometimes to moralize their own lives, and sometimes, apparently, out of a desire to imagine how other places, regimes, languages, and customs compared to their own—how other worlds of desperation, deprivation, hope, or delight might open their eyes to a truth about the English experience. A title teased prospective buyers with sensory and intellectual promises, like this collection of crime stories with both sensationalist lures and Latin indicators of learning: *A vvorld of vvonders. A masse of murthers. A couie of cosonages. Containing many of the moste notablest wonders, horrible murthers and detestable cosonages that haue beene within this land. Not imagined* **falso** *to delight vaine heads* **ociose,** *not practised* **trans mare** *to breed trueth* **cum ambiguitate,** *but commited euen at home* **re vera,** *and may be prooued* **cum honestate.** *A matter moste fit to be knowen, well wayed and considered of all men* (1595). Tales of horror, even if they took place at home, were certain sellers in a bookshop, and were filled with quasi-scientific or quasi-ecclesiastical hints of controls that should be exercised over family life: consider the anonymous "news" broadsheet retailing *Gods handy-vvorke in vvonders. Miraculously shewen vpon two women, lately deliuered of two monsters: with a most strange and terrible earth-quake, by which, fields and other grounds, were quite remoued to other places: the prodigious births, being at a place called Perre-farme, within a quarter of a mile of Feuersham in Kent, the 25. of Iuly last, being S. Iames his day* (1615). Stories of monstrous births, distressing diseases, and natural disasters, like modern television newscasts, delivered dire warnings about human behavior and its impact on the environment. God's contempt for foreigners is the subject of *A true relation of the birth of three monsters in the city of Namen in Flanders; As also Gods iudgement vpon an vnnaturall sister of the poore womans, mother of these abortiue children, whose house was consumed with fire from heauen, and her selfe swallowed into the earth. All which hapnd the 16. of December last. 1608* (1609). Such punishment would also fall upon papists, royalists (the court had moved to France by 1642), and, by implication, witches, as asserted (with woodcut illustration) in *A declaration of a strange and wonderfull monster: born in Kirkham parish in Lancashire (the childe of Mrs. Haughton, a Popish gentlewoman) the face of it upon the breast, and without a head (after the mother had wished rather to bear a childe without a head then a Roundhead) and had curst the Parliamnet* [sic] (1646).

Like the woodcut of the Lancashire infant torso with a face on its chest, visual evidence also seems to support the argument of Dr. Edward May's medical tract, *A most certaine and true relation of a strange monster or serpent found in the left ventricle of the heart of Iohn Pennant, Gentleman, of the age of 21. yeares* (1639), which comes complete with an enfolded diagram of the heart and what looks like a snake coiled into it, on which diagram the doctor lists the witnesses at the autopsy as evidence of his accuracy. May's ultimate point is that medical dissection should be allowed on all bodies, so that diseases can be apprehended, arrested, and destroyed before they kill others. His theory has merit, although not in the very literal sense he argues. Other medical theorists of the period discuss cures that seem oddly modern, like Edward Jorden's influential analysis of hysteria, *A briefe discourse of a disease called the suffocation of the mother: Written vppon occasion which hath beene of late taken thereby, to suspect pos-*

session of an evill spirit, or some such like supernaturall power: Wherein is declared that diuers strange actions and passions of the body of man, which in the common opinion, are imputed to the Diuell, have their true naturall causes, and do accompanie this disease (1603).

Of course, books attempted to explore other mysteries beyond the threat of ill health, inviting readers to examine the foreign from various perspectives. Often the object was to improve communication skills. Dictionaries of various kinds offered comprehension for ordinary folk, for example, John Florio's *Florio his firste fruites: which yeelde familiar speech, merie prouerbes, wittie sentences, and golden sayings. Also a perfect induction to the Italian, and English tongues, as in the table appeareth. The like heretofore, neuer by any man published* [1578], or Thomas Blount's *Glossographia: or A dictionary, interpreting all such hard vvords, whether Hebrew, Greek, Latin, Italian, Spanish, French, Teutonick, Belgick, British or Saxon; as are now used in our refined English tongue. Also the terms of divinity, law, physick, mathematicks, heraldry, anatomy, war, musick, architecture; and of several other arts and sciences explicated. With etymologies, definitions, and historical observations on the same. Very useful for all such as desire to understand what they read* (1656).

Another object of publication was to disseminate information about foreign lands, although protestations of veracity need careful weighing. Journals about voyages of discovery, tales of war or captivity, and news reports from foreign correspondents indicate the scope and proliferation of such adventurous experiences: for example, Edward Webbe's *The Rare and most wonderful thinges which Edward Webbe an Englishman borne, hath seene and passed in his troublesome travailes, in the Citties of Jerusalem, Dammasko, Bethlem, and Galely: and in the Landes of Jewrie, Egipt, Grecia, Russia, and in the Land of Prester John. Wherein is set foorth his extreame slaverie sustained many yeres togither, in the Gallies & wars of the great Turk against the Landes of Persia, Tartaria, Spaine, and Portugall, with the manner of his releasement, and comming into Englande in May last* (1590). The word "strange" appears again and again as a selling point in the titles of travel books: *Strange, fearful & true newes, which hapned at Carlstadt, in the kingdome of Croatia: Declaring How the Sunne did shine like Bloude nine dayes together . . . And how also a Woman was deliuered of three prodigious sonnes . . . All which happened the twelfth of Iune, last* (1605/6), Henry Timberlake's *A True and straunge Discourse of the Travailes of two English Pilgrimes: what admirable accidents befell them in their journey towards Jerusalem, Gaza, Grand Cayro, Alexandria, and other places. Also, what rare Antiquities, Monuments, and notable memories (according with the auncient remembrances in the holy Scriptures) they sawe in Terra Sancta* (1611), *Strange Newes from Antvvarpe, which happened the 12. of August last past* (1612), *Newes from Holland, true, strange, and wonderfull: A true relation of the strange floating of ice; and the great inundation*

which hath broken downe many dikes (1624), and Thomas Scott's *Sir VVal-
ter Ravvleighs ghost, or Englands forewarner. Discouering a secret con-
sultation, newly holden in the Court of Spaine. Together, with his torment-
ing of Count de Gondemar; and his strange affrightment, confession and
publique recantation: laying open many treacheries intended for the sub-
uersion of England* (1626). Possibly the most famous of the voyages of discovery was told in Captain John Smith's leather-bound folio, *The Generall
Historie of Virginia, New-England, and the Summer Isles with the names
of the Adventurers, Planters, and Governours from their first beginning
AN 1584 to this present* (1626), including the story of the lost colony of
Roanoke, the birth of Virginia Dare, the marriage and conversion of Poca-
hantas, a mini-dictionary of native words (thus introducing the Christian
world to "Mockasins, Shooes; Tomahacks, Axes," and even the word for
"cookold"), and the observations of Thomas Harriot, whose mathematical
instruments impressed the First Nations tribesmen: "Most things they saw
with us as Mathematicall Instruments, Sea-Compasses; the vertue of the
Loadstone, Perspective Glasses, burning Glasses: Clocks to goe of themselves; Bookes, writing, Guns, and such like; so far exceeded their capacities, that they thought they were rather the workes of gods then men; or at
least the gods had taught us how to make them, which loved us so much
better then them; & caused many of them give credit to what we spake concerning our god" (C2). In instances like these, Englishmen not only observed
what was strange to themselves in their travels, but they also observed the
effects of the strange on others.

An interesting sidelight on the Englishman abroad appears in the scientific detail supplied by William Davies in *The True Relation of the Travailes
and most miserable Captivitie of William Davies, Barber-Surgion of London, under the Duke of Florence. Wherein is tryly set downe the manner of
his taking, the long time of his slaverie, and meanes of his deliverie, after
eight yeeres, and ten moneths Captivitie in the Gallies. Discovering many
mayne Landes, Ilandes, Rivers, Cities, and townes, of the Christians and
Infidels, the condition of the people, and the manner of thier Countrey; with
many more strange things, as in the Booke is briefely and plainely expressed* (1614). Despite his many hardships, Davies held on firmly to his
English prejudices and very English desire to control and somehow marshal
his knowledge into columns of data that would demonstrate his victory
over adversity. He began with a lengthy A to Z compilation of all the places
he saw, from Alexandria, through parts of Barbary, Greece, Italy, Spain,
and the West Indies, to Zumbula, an island in Turkey. He excluded France,
the Netherlands, and Ireland as too familiar and close to home. Then he offered a list of the top twelve destinations, to which he devoted a few pages
each. He frequently expressed suspicion of the foreigners he met, rarely
finding anything complimentary to say, and usually objecting to their style
of dress and their women. Of Livorno, he commented: "These Italians are

very deceitful people, for when they laugh in a mans face, they will seeke to kill him, yet they are very cowards being naturall Italians: the women are altogether wicked and lewde" (C1); in Naples, "They are altogether Papists, and their women very audacious, especially in the sinfull use of their bodies, by reason they have as well their pardon as privilege from Rome" (D1), thus explaining the purpose of confession; in Malta, "their women are altogether lascivious and lewdly given" (D3); in the heat of Morocco, he objected to the way men and women wear only thin pieces of linen, exposing their bodies to view in a way the Englishman found uncomfortable. Yet the nudity of natives living along the Amazon River horrified him less than the insects: "This Countrey is full of Muskitas, which is a small Flie, which much offends a stranger comming newly into the Countrey" (D2).

In such a rich and variegated set of historical circumstances, the essays collected in this volume take their place. We have quite deliberately left the mysterious and foreign as broad categories. Our interest has not been prompted by a desire to formulate a strict definition of these terms that will please modern sensibilities; rather, we have been fascinated by the range of effects and responses that the unfamiliar elicited from early modern English men and women. The mysterious and foreign were concepts against which the known could be judged: "Where the modern structuralist understanding of the world tends to sharpen its sense of individuation by meditating upon the normative, the Renaissance tended to sharpen its sense of the normative by meditating upon the prodigious."[6] All the texts that the essays gathered here examine are driven by the relationship between the familiar and the unfamiliar, and the intellectual and emotional responses engendered by that relationship. Whether the response to the mysterious and foreign is one of wonder or horror, they function as mirrors, reflecting back upon the English viewers and altering them.

Early modern travel and discovery literature has received much attention over the past few years, particularly since theories of postcolonialization and orientalism elicited reexaminations of colonialization itself. While interesting studies were certainly produced before 1990, Stephen Greenblatt's *Marvelous Possessions: The Wonder of the New World* (1991) and Richard Helgerson's *Forms of Nationhood: The Elizabethan Writing of England* (1992) led this most recent wave, followed by a number of studies that extended and elaborated their work.[7] A virtual flood of articles and books on the relationship between the New World and Britain has resulted. Sixteenth- and seventeenth-century travel to and relations with the Middle East, particularly the Ottoman empire, have also received attention in studies such as Nabil Matar's *Turks, Moors and Englishmen in the Age of Discovery,* Daniel Goffman's *Britons in the Ottoman Empire 1642–1660,* and the volume edited by Ivo Kamps and Jyotsna G. Singh, *Travel Knowledge: European "Discoveries" in the Early Modern Period.*[8] As Gerald MacLean points out in the latter book: "For the insular British, personal and national

desires and identities were no longer constructed only from within the local, the familiar, and the traditional, but increasingly became inseparably
connected to the global, the strange, and the alien," beginning in the early
modern period.[9] The more critics have examined the foreign in relation to
England, the more obvious it has become that we must recognize the nu-
ances in those relations and shape our discussions of them accordingly.
Discourses of colonization used in studies of the New World and England,
for example, are not suitable when considering England and the Middle East.
Colonization of the Ottoman empire by the English was not a consideration at the time—on some occasions Elizabeth sought military/diplomatic
aid from the Ottomans—and as the above critics point out, early modern
writers employed distinctly different discourses for the Middle East than
for the New World. Edward Said's concept of Orientalism cannot be applied to the early modern period without significant revision: the notion
of the English dominating the Turks would have been an absurdity. Similarly, modern notions of racial otherness cannot be transferred naively to
the period: "As the seventeenth century began in England, there was,
strictly speaking, no such thing as 'race.' There was instead a volatile
mixture of xenophobia and openness, as the insular kingdom struggled to
assimilate its bewildering new encounters with human diversity."[10] Joan
Pau Rubies's caution that we need to recognize the complexity of representations of "the other" as ranging from negative to positive, to ambiguous or to simply defying categorization is fully supported by the articles in
this present collection.[11]

While the volumes discussed above largely concentrate on travel literature, others have taken up Richard Helgerson's perspective and have considered more closely what effect encounters with other cultures and peoples
had upon the literature of early modern England. While Claire McEachern's
The Poetics of English Nationhood, 1590–1612 is not directly focused on
the foreign, it is an important study that recognizes English conceptions of
"the other" were not entirely xenophobic. The good qualities of other cultures were thought worthy of imitation, and representations of "the other"
can be described as the "simultaneous play of repulsion and attraction" that
do not necessarily negate one another.[12] Claire Jowitt's *Voyage Drama and
Gender Politics 1589–1642: Real and Imagined Worlds* examines the sexualization of exploration discourse in these dramas and the use of foreignness to both critique and idealize the domestic. Gillian Brennan agrees with
McEachern that "the portrayals of foreigners in literature were not as hostile
as one would expect had the cultural ethos been saturated with nationalism
[as opposed to patriotism]. Their role as the outsider meant the national
stereotype could be used for moral or comedic purposes, and in more realistic portrayals of foreigners' class, religion or individual characteristics
continued to be more important than ethnic origin."[13] More recently Andrew
Escobedo has concluded in *Nationalism and Historical Loss in Renais-*

sance England: Foxe, Dee, Spenser, Milton that "English identity was constituted not from within but rather on its periphery, in terms of the heterogeneity of a multinational context that the idea of Englishness both relied on and sought to repress."[14]

Other areas of the unfamiliar and mysterious that critics have published in, while also functioning to constitute both normalcy and identity, are too broadly based to review here—witches, ghosts, the supernatural, monsters, unusual natural phenomena, antiquities, even in some instances animals. Curiosity and its companion, collecting, are one related area that has received concerted attention. Barbara Benedict argues that early modern "English culture portrays curiosity as the mark of a threatening ambition, an ambition that takes the form of a perceptible violation of species and categories: an ontological transgression that is registered empirically. Curiosity is seeing your way out of your place. It is looking beyond."[15] The danger and the value of looking beyond the known are registered in the articles in this collection. Our subheadings contextualize the groups of essays in a way that may help readers to see how ideas, fears, and wonder speak to one another across the pages, as early modern writers face their expanding world.

THE FOREIGN JOURNEY

Part I reveals the multidirectional interests of the English, who were rapidly becoming oriented to the world just unfurled to their gaze by the new cartography and the renewed enthusiasm for exploration. The essays examine the ominous North, the tropical jungles of South America, the wild and frigid wastes of Russia, and the forbidding lands under Ottoman sway that separated Western Europe from the East and posed a mighty threat to Christendom. Christian Europe is the final destination of this section, with an essay on violence and anti-Semitism in Nashe's Italy.

Colleen Franklin examines the early modern literature of the "marvellous North"—a region filled with inexplicable phenomena, frequently regarded as the location of hell. This idea, derived from the patristic writers, is tested by empirical knowledge of the region's geography, as it unfolded during the drive to discover the Northwest Passage. From the frozen North, we proceed to the tropical "Empire of Guiana." In considering Ralegh's travel narrative of the headless Ewaipanoma, whose eyes are in their shoulders and mouths in the middle of their breasts, Scott Oldenburg investigates the appeal of this image as well as Ralegh's anxiety about its credibility.

A quite different travel narrative, situated in the fearful strangeness of Russia, is Jane Farnsworth's subject. George Turberville wrote *The literary responses of George Turberville,* drawn from his experience on a diplomatic mission to Muscovy, including love poems and verse epistles, to make Russia comprehensible to himself and to his readers. His "responses" reveal an authentic voice, creating a distinct way of dealing with foreignness and difference. If the snowy wastes of Russia seemed remote and impossibly alien, the harems of the Ottoman empire, although "other" and remote, embodying the supposed sexual depravity of Islam, aroused both the indignation and the envy of some English writers. Several travelers, such as William Biddulph and Thomas Dallam, expressed their admiration for the Turkish way. Bindu Malieckal explores the dichotomies that epitomize the early modern English observer's experience of the Sultan's world.

From Islam we pass to Christian Europe, where Mathew Martin, in his study of Jack Wilton and the Jews, examines Nashe's depiction of anti-Semitism. Filled with representations of bodies in pain, Nashe's work, unlike Foxe's martyrology, withholds any historical significance from these depictions. Nashe's anti-Semitism, Martin argues, is ambivalent, but *The Unfortunate Traveller* is, in the end, both comic and destructive in its treatment of the meaninglessness of pain.

PROFITING FROM THE MYSTERIOUS

The essays in Part II, in quite different modes, examine how the English writer, audience, and reader assimilated foreignness to turn it to their own advantage, beginning with the revolutionizing role of mathematics. New and accessible means of computing profit and loss invigorated England's expanding trade, which in turn made more urgent the pressing problem of accurate navigation beyond the relatively safe bounds of Europe. The calculation of direction and risk in mercantile voyages became increasingly the concern when expensive goods arrived from a great distance; this part investigates two such profitable "far-fetched" commodities of mysterious and foreign origin. The exotic also fed tastes of a more personal kind, as Othello discovered when he acquired success as a self-exploiter, the shaper of his own tales.

Helen Ostovich places Jonson's *The Magnetic Lady* within the context of early modern mathematics as a phenomenon recently arrived in England from the continent, bringing new ways of seeing business practice (especially in the computation of interest), scientific advances in navigation, dimensions in art, encounters with the exotic, and entertainment by way of problem-solving connected with logical, verbal, arithmetical, and physical tricks. The English middle class enthusiastically participated in furthering this new knowledge, which provided them with a kind of compass for understanding national and personal goals using a "strange" but "true" methodology that would transform English life through accurate assessment.

Jonathan Gil Harris looks at the use of "foreign" notions in discourses of anti-Galenic pathology and English mercantilism. New iconoclastic languages of disease mediate the traditional "sin" of usury as an amoral practice of "Jewish" transnational identity and economy. *The Merchant of Venice*'s discourse of usury is shown to parallel that of the contemporary economist, Gerard Malynes, who figures usury as a mysterious, "tainted" dragon, stitched from Turkish and English components, yet associated with Jewishness. This essay provides a new reading of *Merchant* in which neither "usury" nor "Jew" seems quite as fixed as assumptions have hitherto taken for granted. Marianne Montgomery analyzes the representation of foreign speech on the English stage with special reference to Dekker's *The Shoe-maker's Holiday*. In Dekker's hands, English anxieties about the influence of foreign languages and of foreign labor and goods on the economy become a fantasy in which the English wittily laugh at and profit from foreign circumstances. While affirming England's ability to assimilate foreign labor and goods, the play acknowledges London's openness to alien culture.

The assimilation of tobacco to the English way of life is an especially dramatic story. Few other foreign imports (with the radical fashions it spawned) occasioned such controversy. Sandra Bell studies the associations of the American import with the Galenic medical views of the period, with the "uncivilized" savages, the influence of Spain, and, in due course, with treason. Bell captures the complex, often contradictory representations of and responses to the growth of tobacco culture. Another exotic import from the Americas, which temporarily eclipsed tobacco in market value, is Graham Roebuck's subject: sassafras. How did this now innocuous plant come to have such wild claims made for its efficacy? Roebuck traces the answer to this question to a deeply seated European habit of mind which expected that the divine arrangement of life would provide New World substances to replace those lost in the old world, and that the cure for terrible diseases, especially syphilis, would be discovered in the supposed locus of those diseases' origins.

If the claims for these commodities seem outrageous, so too, in Philip D. Collington's analysis, do Othello's "fantasticall lies" in the context of how Shakespeare's audiences might have interpreted available information on Africa and its peoples. By 1604, he argues, decades of English readers were acquainted with balanced and revisionary accounts, often by eyewitnesses, and were thus equipped to spot the general's charlatan storytelling, unlike the naïve Venetians of the play. Using Bacon's categories of Secrecy, Simulation, and Dissimulation, Collington shows Othello as a cynical manipulator of truth. He "sells" his stories to the otherwise "super subtle" Venetians.

THE DOMESTICATION OF THE MYSTERIOUS AND FOREIGN

The domestic, exposed to the mysterious and the foreign, may suddenly change its spots. In Part III, the essays deal with how the threat of foreignness changes perspectives on the familiar, and the ways in which the domestic adapts.

Patricia Parker investigates the common belief that Illyria in *Twelfth Night* was an imaginary country for Shakespeare's original audience and finds a surprising number of references to the country were published in England prior to the play's appearance. It was considered to be the dividing line between East and West, a site of romance and retirement, part of Roman and New Testament history, and threatened by the expanding empire of the Turks. While Illyria was certainly foreign, and certainly rendered exotic by Shakespeare, it was not unknown to early modern readers. In another unusual approach to the foreign, Stephen Buick focuses on the return of the Marian exiles to England from continental Europe where they sought refuge from persecution. To their surprise, they found England an alien land in which, as John Jewel remarked, "we are all of us hitherto as strangers at home." Whereas traditional historiography has concentrated on the Reformation as an intellectual movement, this study concentrates on the experience of dislocation caused by changes to the externals of religious customs and practices. In their turn, the former exiles were accused of foreignness.

In her discussion of Oriental motifs in court and in city entertainments, Linda McJannet poses two questions: How were "orientals" distinguished from one another in these works, and what significant differences emerge from how court and city employed these exotic signifiers? Unlike some other analyses, this essay points to the likelihood that civic audiences were more comfortable than courtly audiences in encountering these exotic others on a relatively equal footing. In another surprising view of English comfort zones, Kate Loveman studies a pamphlet that created "a great noise," purporting to reveal the location of the tomb of Moses in Palestine and recounting the foiling of a villainous Jesuit plot to steal the patriarch's remains. This hoax, perpetrated by the witty Thomas Chaloner through manipulated travel narratives, plays upon English preconceptions of Turks, Jews, and Jesuits and satirizes the ignorance and credulity of English readers. Here, complacency, rather than either toleration or fear of the exotic, is the crucial factor.

The beneficial assimilation of the foreign into English literature appears clearly in one of the earliest and most influential English emblem books, Geffrey Whitney's *A Choice of Emblemes* (1586). Mary V. Silcox argues that the emblem in England, and Whitney's work in particular, exploits the unfamiliar. Whitney's book not only adapts emblems from earlier continental emblem books, and takes part in the delicate and complex foreign relations of England during the 1580s, but also reveals how the emblem form itself transforms the strange and exotic into the familiar and morally universal. The very images of apes and lions, strange lands, and ancient figures all create the excitement and wonder of the other, while interpretation leads readers to assimilate the meaning in ways both comprehensible and personal. This analysis of *A Choice of Emblemes* reveals how the mysterious and the foreign affected both literary practice and production in early modern England.

As we can see from these articles, the mysterious and the foreign for early modern readers and writers encompass a broad and diverse range of subjects, from the frigid wastes of Russia to hysteria, monstrous births, and tobacco. The reasons for such a seeking out of the mysterious and foreign, for writing about it, displaying it, and using it, are various and complex, and seemingly odd when considered in light of the English self-sufficiency so clearly described by the Venetian ambassador. Perhaps only when a nation or people feel secure and powerful can they turn to the unsettling "other," the strange and unknown around them, observe it and go beyond the simple, instinctive response of fear and attack to finding pleasure, wonder, and use in it. These more complicated responses may have both positive and negative effects. As Steven Mullaney writes, "Difference draws us to it; it promises pleasure and serves as an invitation to first hand experience, otherwise known as colonization."[16] Colonization, one of the significant results of this interest in the mysterious and foreign, obviously creates hardship and resentment in the colonized who are feeling its effects, but it may also end up being a positive force for growth in early modern societies. Complex responses to the unknown "other" lead, ultimately, to the transformation of that "other" into the familiar, to the assimilation of that which was mysterious and foreign into the very definition of what it means to be English in the early modern period.

NOTES

1. Anon., *A Relation, Or Rather a True Account, of the Island of England*, trans. from the Italian by Charlotte Augusta Sneyd (London: Camden Society (Old Series, Vol. 37), 1847; repr. New York: Johnson Reprint Corporation, 1968), 20–21. All subsequent page references will be cited parenthetically in the text.

2. "Of Coaches," *Essayes Written in French By Michael Lord of Montaigne, Knight of the Order of S Michael, Gentleman of the French Kings Chamber. Done into English according to the last French edition, by Iohn Florio Reader of the Italian tongue vnto the Soueraigne Maiestie of Anna, Queene of England* [etc], (London: Melch. Bradwood for Edward Blount and William Barret, 1613 [the 2nd edition]), 510. All further page references will be cited parenthetically in the text.

3. "Of Trauaile," *The Essayes or Covnsells, Civill and Morall, of Francis Lo. Uervlam, Viscovnt Sr Alban*, (London: Iohn Haviland for Hanna Barret, 1625), 101. All subsequent page references will be cited parenthetically in the text.

4. *Religio Medici: A true and full coppy of that which was most imperfectly and Surreptitiously printed before under the name of: Religio Medici* (London: Andrew Crooke, 1643), 159–60. All further page references will be cited parenthetically in the text.

5. *Instructions for Forreine Travell. Shewing by what cours, and in what compasse of time, one may take an exact Survey of the Kingdomes and States of Christendome, and arrive*

to the practicall knowledge of the Languages to good purpose (London: T. B. for Humphrey Mosley, 1642), 8. All subsequent page refereces will be cited parenthetically in the text.

6. Stephen Greenblatt, "Fiction or Friction," in *Shakespearean Negotiations: The Circulation of Social Energy in Renaissance England* (Berkeley: University of California Press, 1988), 77.

7. Stephen Greenblatt, *Marvelous Possessions: The Wonder of the New World* (Oxford: Clarendon Press, 1991); and Richard Helgerson, *Forms of Nationhood: The Elizabethan Writing of England* (Chicago: University of Chicago Press, 1992).

8. Nabil Matar, *Turks, Moors and Englishmen in the Age of Discovery* (New York: Columbia University Press, 1999); Daniel Goffman, *Britons in the Ottoman Empire 1642–1660* (Seattle: University of Washington Press, 1998); and Ivo Kamps and Jyotsna G. Singh, eds., *Travel Knowledge: European "Discoveries" in the Early Modern Period* (New York: Palgrave, 2001).

9. Gerald MacLean, "Ottomanism Before Orientalism? Bishop King Praises Henry Blount, Passenger in the Levant," in Kamps and Singh, *Travel Knowledge,* 86.

10. Christopher Hodgkins, *Reforming Empire: Protestant Colonialism and Conscience in British Literature* (Columbia: University of Missouri Press, 2002), 114.

11. Joan Pau Rubies, "Travel Writing and Ethnography," in *The Cambridge Companion to Travel Writing,* ed. Peter Hulme and Tim Youngs, 242–60 (Cambridge: Cambridge University Press, 2002).

12. Claire McEachern, *The Poetics of English Nationhood, 1590–1612* (Cambridge: Cambridge University Press, 1996) 26.

13. Claire Jowitt, *Voyage Drama and Gender Politics 1589–1642: Real and Imagined Worlds* (Manchester, UK: Manchester University Press, 2003); Gillian E. Brennan, *Patriotism, Power and Print: National Consciousness in Tudor England* (Pittsburgh: Duquesne University Press, 2003), 24. See also Daniel J. Vitkus, *Turning Turk: English Theater and the Multicultural Mediterranean, 1570–1630* (New York: Palgrave Macmillan, 2003); Jonathan Burton, *Traffic and Turning: Islam and English Drama, 1579–1624* (Newark: University of Delaware Press, 2005); David J. Baker and Willy Maley, eds., *British Identities and English Renaissance Literature* (Cambridge: Cambridge University Press, 2002); and Mark Netzloff, *England's Internal Colonies: Class, Capital and the Literature of Early Modern English Colonialism* (New York: Palgrave Macmillan, 2003).

14. Andrew Escobedo, *Nationalism and Historical Loss in Renaissance England: Foxe, Dee, Spenser, Milton* (Ithaca, NY: Cornell University Press, 2004): 147.

15. Barbara Benedict, *Curiosity: A Cultural History of Early Modern Inquiry* (Chicago: University of Chicago Press, 2001), 2. See also Lorraine Daston and Katharine Park, *Wonders and the Order of Nature 1150–1750* (New York: Zone Books, 1998).

16. Steven Mullaney, "Strange Things, Gross Terms, Curious Customs: The Rehearsal of Culture in the Late Renaissance," *Representations* 3 (1983): 44.

BIBLIOGRAPHY

Bacon, Francis. "Of Trauaile." In *The Essayes or Covnsells, Civill and Morall, of Francis Lo. Uervlam, Viscovnt S^r. Alban.* London: Iohn Haviland for Hanna Barret, 1625.

Baker, David J., and Willy Maley, eds. *British Identities and English Renaissance Literature.* Cambridge: Cambridge University Press, 2002.

Benedict, Barbara. *Curiosity: A Cultural History of Early Modern Inquiry.* Chicago: University of Chicago Press, 2001.

Brennan, Gillian E. *Patriotism, Power and Print: National Consciousness in Tudor England.* Pittsburgh, PA: Duquesne University Press, 2003.

Browne, Thomas. *Religio Medici: A true and full coppy of that which was most imperfectly and Surreptitiously printed before under the name of: Religio Medici.* London: Andrew Crooke, 1643.

Burton, Jonathan. *Traffic and Turning: Islam and English Drama, 1579–1624.* Newark: University of Delaware Press, 2005.

Daston, Lorraine, and Katharine Park. *Wonders and the Order of Nature 1150–1750.* New York: Zone Books, 1998.

Escobedo, Andrew. *Nationalism and Historical Loss in Renaissance England: Foxe, Dee, Spenser, Milton.* Ithaca, NY: Cornell University Press, 2004.

Goffman, Daniel. *Britons in the Ottoman Empire 1642–1660.* Seattle: University of Washington Press, 1998.

Greenblatt, Stephen. *Marvelous Possessions: The Wonder of the New World.* Oxford: Clarendon Press, 1991.

———. *Shakespearean Negotiations: The Circulation of Social Energy in Renaissance England.* Berkeley: University of California Press, 1988.

Helgerson, Richard. *Forms of Nationhood: The Elizabethan Writing of England.* Chicago: University of Chicago Press, 1992.

Hodgkins, Christopher. *Reforming Empire: Protestant Colonialism and Conscience in British Literature.* Columbia: University of Missouri Press, 2002.

Howell, James. *Instructions for Forreine Travell. Shewing by what cours, and in what compasse of time, one may take an exact Survey of the Kingdomes and States of Christendome, and arrive to the practicall knowledge of the Languages to good purpose.* London: T. B. for Humphrey Mosley, 1642.

Hulme, Peter, and Tim Youngs, eds. *The Cambridge Companion to Travel Writing.* Cambridge: Cambridge University Press, 2002.

Jowitt, Claire. *Voyage Drama and Gender Politics 1589–1642: Real and Imagined Worlds.* Manchester, UK: Manchester University Press, 2003.

Kamps, Ivo, and Jyotsna G. Singh, eds. *Travel Knowledge: European "Discoveries" in the Early Modern Period.* New York: Palgrave, 2001.

Matar, Nabil. *Turks, Moors and Englishmen in the Age of Discovery.* New York: Columbia University Press, 1999.

McEachern, Claire. *The Poetics of English Nationhood, 1590–1612.* Cambridge: Cambridge University Press, 1996.

Montaigne, Michel. "Of Coaches." In *Essayes Written in French By Michael Lord of Montaigne, Knight of the Order of S Michael, Gentleman of the French Kings Chamber. Done into English according to the last French edition, by Iohn Florio Reader of the Italian tongue vnto the Soueraigne Maiestie of Anna, Queene of England* [etc]. London: Melch. Bradwood for Edward Blount and William Barret, 1613 [the 2nd edition].

Mullaney, Steven. "Strange Things, Gross Terms, Curious Customs: The Rehearsal of Culture in the Late Renaissance." *Representations* 3 (1983): 40–67.

Netzloff, Mark. *England's Internal Colonies: Class, Capital and the Literature of Early Modern English Colonialism.* New York: Palgrave Macmillan, 2003.

A Relation, Or Rather a True Account, of the Island of England. Translated from the Italian by Charlotte Augusta Sneyd. London: Camden Society (Old Series, Vol. 37), 1847. Reprint, New York: Johnson Reprint Corporation, 1968.

Vitkus, Daniel J. *Turning Turk: English Theater and the Multicultural Mediterranean, 1570–1630.* New York: Palgrave Macmillan, 2003.

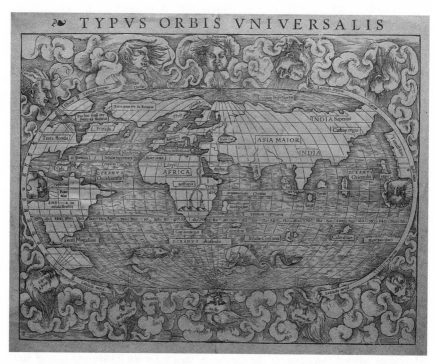

Sebastian Munster, Swiss, 1489–1522. *Typus Orbis Universalis*. nd. (Probably from Ptolemy's 1548 edition.) Woodcut. Gift of Herman Levy, Esq., O.B.E. McMaster University Collection, Hamilton, Canada. © McMaster Museum of Art, McMaster University, 2006. 1984.007.0003. Photo credit: Jennifer Pettiplace.

I
The Foreign Journey

"An Habitation of Devils, a Domicill for Unclean Spirits, and a Den of Goblings": The Marvelous North in Early Modern English Literature

Colleen Franklin

THE SEARCH FOR THE NORTHWEST PASSAGE BECAME A PARTICULARLY English concern in the early modern period. Driven by the religious and political threat from Spain, expansionist considerations, and the desire for experiential knowledge, sixteenth-century merchants, courtiers, and scholars lamented their belatedness in the "New World" and clamoured for an English presence in the northwest. Expansionist aims merged with developments in the study of natural philosophy, and those who were interested in the north began to demand experiential accounts of the region to replace or augment classical and medieval theories. Those who actually traveled north in the late sixteenth and early seventeenth centuries, however, struggled with the demands of their countrymen for empirical accounts of the region, for early modern explorers had no mode of perception available for experiencing the north in any other way but as malevolent. Unarmed with scientific method or an aesthetics of landscape that could provide them with an alternative mode for representing this entirely unfamiliar region, explorers were forced to negotiate with the medieval structures of belief that had constructed the north as a locus of evil. Because the monopoly of the Hudson's Bay Company effectively prevented further incursions into the area for several hundred years, the early modern explorers' accounts of the northern reaches of North America achieved a rare status. They remained the primary sources for information about the continent's subarctic and arctic until the British Admiralty renewed the search for the Northwest Passage in 1818. Even then, the early modern accounts continued to be consulted by scientists, geographers, explorers, and poets, and they continue to figure in representations of the Canadian landscape today.

Early modern accounts of the north were indebted to the medieval notion of the north as the location of hell, a belief that was authorized by the exegeses of the patristic writers of the early Church, who cited key passages from the biblical books of Isaiah, Jeremiah, Job, and Ezekiel[1] to situate the throne of Lucifer in the north.[2] The patristic insistence on the fall of Lucifer into the north acted in concert with the belief that demons were materially present on earth, and that they were responsible for a multitude of sublunar afflictions, such as drought, poor crops, hail, thunder, lightning, and storms.[3] The known north experienced particularly bad weather, and so, naturally, was assumed to contain a high complement of evil spirits. In *Our Ladye's Mirroure,* for example, the author explains: "The second part of the ayre is darke & colde for the reflecyon of the sonne beames may not come so hye. And in this parte of the ayre dwelle fendes unto the day of doume, and there are gendered tempestes of weder and hayle and snowe and thonder and lyght-nynge and such other. And therfore in nyghtes tyme when the lower parte of the ayre ys darke by absence of the sonne, and in tempestes of weder, the fendes come downe to the erthe more homly than in other tymes."[4]

The idea that demonic agency determined weather conditions was initially discouraged by the Church, and most scholars likewise believed that Nature was permeated by and subject to God's will.[5] But the belief that foul weather was indicative of the presence of demons persisted, as did the belief in *maleficium,* the supernatural agency that allowed witches to promote disorder, including the ability to practice "weather magic." According to Wolfgang Behringer, *maleficium* was popularly considered to be the cause of the agrarian disasters that befell Europe during the Little Ice Age of 1569–1625.[6]

The trope of the evil north is ubiquitous in the literature of medieval England.[7] Anglo-Saxon writers employed the patristic literature in responding to the Scots and Viking raids of the seventh to ninth centuries,[8] and later writers such as Langland, Chaucer, and Skelton, among others, engaged with the trope in more sophisticated ways.[9] Evidently because of its topicality, various early modern playwrights explored or referred to the practice of weather magic. The winds, fogs, floods, rotted crops, sickly flocks, frosts, and ice of Shakespeare's *A Midsummer Night's Dream* (c. 1596; first published 1600) are said by the Fairy Queen Titania to be the result of her quarrel with the Fairy King, Oberon: "We are their parents and original" (2.1.17).[10] The wretched weather of *Macbeth* (c. 1602–6; first published 1623) is associated with the witches and with the evil Macbeth does with their encouragement, but the Weird Sisters openly practice weather magic when they conjure up seastorms to injure the husband of a goodwife who has denied the First Witch some of her chestnuts (1.3.1–37).[11] In Christopher Marlowe's *The Tragicall History of Dr. Faustus* (c. 1588; first published 1604), Faustus longs to master the black arts that will allow him to command "All things that move between the quiet poles" (1.56).[12] Even emperors and kings, says Faustus, "are but obeyed in their several provinces";

they cannot "raise the wind, or rend the clouds" (1.57–59). The audience is privy to Faustus's first lesson in weather magic: "The framing of this circle on the ground, / Brings whirlwinds, tempests, thunder and lightning" (5.159–60). A bad angel tempts Faustus to be lord of the earthly elements, as Jove is lord of the sky (1.74–78). Since the earth is already the province of Lucifer, the metonymic relationship between the two overreachers is established while the audience becomes aware that all the promises made to Faustus will be empty ones. Robert Greene's *Friar Bacon and Friar Bungay* (c. 1590, first published 1594) rehearses all the medieval notions of the north at once, with explicit reference to the patristic account of the fall of Lucifer.[13] Shakespeare, too, invokes the patristic account in Joan la Pucelle's speech (5.3.1–7) in *The First Part of Henry VI* (c. 1589–91, first published 1623).[14]

The Little Ice Age, the height of the witchhunt craze, and the fascination of the early modern theaters with witchcraft, devils, and the patristic account of Lucifer's rebellion and fall occurred simultaneously with England's interest in the Northwest Passage, and the call for experiential accounts of the north by such courtiers and scholars as Sir Humphrey Gilbert and John Dee.[15] The search for the Passage began in earnest with the first of Martin Frobisher's three voyages, in 1576. These voyages (in 1576, 1577, and 1578) generated several published accounts and a healthy spate of related publication.[16] Dionyse Settle's *A True Reporte of the last Voyage . . . by Captaine Frobisher* (1577) explicitly identifies demystification of the north as an objective of exploration and, by extension, of Settle's own purpose in writing.[17] In "The Epistle Dedicatorie" to the *True Reporte*, Settle writes: "*I have both boldly passed the limittes of my duetie, and also unlearnedly taken upon me to set foorth some thing worthie notice, in this last voyage of our Capteine and Generall, Master Martine Frobisher. . . . By his great diligence, the voyage is worthily finished: whereby I am persuaded, that he will refell the rehearsall of those opprobrious wordes, namely, that,* All evill cômeth from or hath originall in the North [emphasis in text]: *not onely he, but many worthie subjectes more.*"[18] Settle's empirical stance, however, does not hold throughout the document that follows. His attempt to provide the reader with descriptions of Meta Incognita leaves him without any language but that of the marvelous north: "Who so maketh navigations to these Countreies, hath not onely extreame windes, and furious seas, to encounter withall, but also many monstrous and great Islands of yce: a thing both rare, wonderfull, and greatly to be regarded."[19] Although Settle provides several pages of dispassionate observations of the Inuit people he encountered, the capture of two Inuit women, one young and nursing a child, the other "an olde wretch, whom divers of our Saylers supposed to be eyther a divell, or a witch," becomes (North America's first?) witch trial, when the elderly woman "had her buskins plucked off, to see if she were cloven footed."[20] Settle is only one of the first English explorers to declare the Inuit "witches," "devils," and "idolaters."

Within fifty years of Martin Frobisher's voyages, "the relations and reports" of forty Englishmen who had traveled north, including Settle's, could be collected by Samuel Purchas in his *Purchas his Pilgrimes* (1614).[21] The Reverend Samuel Purchas, DD, was most emphatically an armchair traveler and is thus an important figure in the assessment of the reception of the marvelous north in early modern exploration literature. His four books of travels, three editions of *Purchas his Pilgrimages* (1613, 1614, and 1626) and one of *Hakluytus Posthumus, or, Purchas his Pilgrimes* (1625), self-consciously follow the lead of Richard Hakluyt, the magisterial editor of English voyage collections.[22] Hakluyt was concerned to vindicate the reputation of English navigators in the eyes of the rest of Europe, and to impress upon his countrymen the importance of supporting further exploration to spread Christianity and improve trade.[23] Purchas shared Hakluyt's ideological aims, but he expanded on them vigorously with the enthusiastic commentaries that introduce each section of his collections. In outlining the political and religious agenda he claimed for his work, he argued that much of the world was languishing in the "withered and fouler hue of passed out-worne rites" and "Irreligious Religions, not washed with the purer streames of sacred Baptisme." His book was a "Historie of Religion"[24] in which the sacred nature of discovery would be revealed.

Like Dionyse Settle before him, Purchas dismisses medieval accounts of the north, suggesting that the patristic writers were "more zealous than learned."[25] "Eyewitnes" [*sic*] accounts will displace the inherited wisdom of the ancients. For example, in reporting on Henry Hudson's 1610 voyage past Mount Hecla, traditionally one of the possible locations of Hell, Purchas carefully refutes the "Purgatory fables" that "others conceive themselves and [with which they] deceive others" through the testimony of "Arngrin Ionas [Arngrímr Jónsson], an Islander . . . who reproveth this and many other dreames related by Authors."[26] Again, as in the case of Settle, Purchas's empiricist rhetoric collapses as he launches into a paean to those who have attempted to navigate northern waters. The north is again a place of evil, where "Nature . . . is most unbridled." Purchas personifies the "monstrous icie islands," "the snows and cold" that continually beat "the rigid ragged face of the broken lands," "the unequal seas," and "the horrible earth-quakes," and grants them the agency to "amaze the hearer, and amaze the beholder," to cause the Tritons and Neptune "to quake with chilling fear," and to engage in a "continuall civill war." Purchas reports indignantly that "Boterus [Giovanni Botero], a zealous and slanderous Catholike, useth these speeches of this Discovery [the Hudson voyage] *Ma pare, che la Natura si fia opposta a gli heretici, e a disse [o]gni loro* [it seems to me, that it is Nature that is opposed to the heretics, and spoke to each of them]."[27] The Roman Catholic Church "that Adultresse [. . .] vanteth her selfe to be the only Darling of God and Nature." For Purchas the opposite is true. The evil present in the natural world of the north will be brought under control by further incursions by Englishmen. Because the light of true religion has been granted to the English, Purchas argues that it will be English navigators who will "subdue [Nature] to that Government and Subjection, which God over all blessed for ever, hath imposed on all sensible Creatures to the Nature of Man."[28]

In 1633, at the request of Charles I, Thomas James of Bristol published *The Strange and Dangerous Voyage of Captaine Thomas James,* an account of his journey through Hudson Bay in search of the Northwest Passage, and his overwintering in 1631–32 in what is now known as James Bay.[29] The narrative of James's discovery is surrounded by paratextual documents that are clearly informed by the new philosophy. These include a treatise on the search for a method to determine longitude by Henry Gellibrand, a Reader at Gresham College; an early salvo in the war between the ancients and moderns by William Watts, a Doctor of Divinity at Cambridge, who comes down clearly on the side of the moderns in respect to the knowledge of the natural world lately gained by exploration; and tables of astronomical observations taken by James during his overwintering. However, the narrative itself is a record of James's unease with the north, signaled immediately to his readers by the use of the word "strange" in the title. James feared for both his body and his soul, and wrote that he was "steering against the tyde of Satans malice."[30] An anomaly in exploration literature, James's narrative is a record of his encounter only with the landscape of Hudson Bay, and not the people. Though he actively attempted to seek out the people of the area, James again and again found only the deserted campsites of the "salvages," the natives eerily present only by their absence. He found the region "barren of all goodnesse";[31] like Purchas, James personified the elements, who appeared in the narrative as his personal enemies: "The fift in the morning, the winde shifted South-West, but changed not his condition; but continued in his old anger and fury. In the afternoone, it shifted againe to the Northwest, and there showed his uttermost malice; and in that tearing violence, that nor I, nor any that were then with me, ever saw the Sea in such a breach. . . . If this storme had continued Easterly, as it was at first, without Gods goodnesse we had all perished."[32] James concludes his narrative, not surprisingly, by arguing against continuing the search for the Northwest Passage.

Settle, Purchas, and James referred only elliptically to Satan's presence in the north, focusing mainly on the evil of his servants, that is, the native people and the elements. However, the belief in the presence of demons in the north could still be articulated, even after philosophers such as Bacon,

Descartes, and Hobbes had dismissed a demonic role in the ordering of the natural world. In 1676, John Storpin devoted some pages of his *Færoæ, & Færoa Referata* to the "Specters" of the Faeroe Islands: "these islands of *Feroe* . . . have been nothing but an habitation of Devils, a Domicill for unclean spirits, and a Den of Goblings, it being sufficiently known in History what power the Devil had antiently in the Countreys of the *North Island, Finland, Varmeland,* and *Lapland;* and many know how powerful they are there to this very day."[33] Although demons can live anywhere, the landscape of the Faroes was particularly hospitable to evil spirits: "Besides the solitariness of *Feroe,* there are not only found great Chinks, and long dark holes above in the Mountains; but also below underneath some places, quite through the Land . . . and when men took in the Country to possess it, those spirits could not be driven out by Fighting, force, or Weapons . . . for iron is like straw, and brass as a rotten wood, as the Lord saith, *Job, Chap. 41. ver 17.* against the strength of . . . the Divel."[34]

The reports of the early modern explorers stood nearly alone until the British Admiralty renewed the search for the Northwest Passage in 1818. This dearth of information was due to the fact that the Hudson's Bay Company, which held a monopoly over much of what is now known as Canada,[35] discouraged publication of its factors' reports as well as further exploration in the northwest (famously, the Company was said to have "slept beside the frozen sea").[36] The later seventeenth- and early eighteenth-century response to the north was to ignore the marvelous elements of early modern accounts and to harvest them for whatever empirical information they contained.[37] For example, Robert Boyle depended heavily on the "philosophicall and mathematicall [Rarities]"[38] recorded in James's *Voyage* for his scientific treatise, *New Experiments and Observations Touching Cold* (1665); and the editor of the second edition of James's *Voyage, The Dangerous Voyage of Capt. Thomas James* (1740), not only deleted the word "strange" from the title, but excised the poetry, the clearest expression of James's supernatural encounter with the north, from the narrative.[39] Editors of the tremendously popular genre of the travel collection edited early modern accounts of the north gathered from Hakluyt and Purchas in a similar fashion, focusing in their introductory essays on the heroism of the explorers and their roles in building the nation. Later in the century, however, as interest increased in the aesthetic of the sublime, Gothic writers seized eagerly on early modern accounts for their representations of the north. As I have argued elsewhere, the productions of these writers, for example, Samuel Taylor Coleridge's "Rime of the Ancient Mariner," which depended on both Purchas's and James's works,[40] and Mary Shelley's *Frankenstein,* fed the vilification of the north that occurred in the wake of the Franklin expedition, and helped to assure the survival of the trope of the evil north for another century.[41] England's fascination with the north began to lessen considerably by the early twentieth century, as the Northwest Passage was finally mapped and the North and South Poles conquered.[42] However, the representation of Canada, all of which was figured as "north," became a preoccupation with British settlers as they struggled to define themselves in relation to the land and climate of their new country, so utterly unlike England. The Canadian landscape remained a central concern of English Canadian writers, many of whom have represented the north as evil. This circumstance has not gone unnoticed by critics, from Northrop Frye's 1943 assessment of Canadian poetry as "a poetry of incubus and *cauchemar*"[43] to Margaret Atwood's 1991 Clarendon Lectures, published in 1995 as *Strange Things: The Malevolent North in Canadian Literature.*[44] Only recently have Canadians begun to argue that postmodern representations of the north must begin with an acknowledgment of the layers of European representations that have preceded them.[45] John Moss, a writer and critic who has forged an intensely personal relationship with the Arctic, writes: "The men . . . we think of as explorers were discovering known territory, imposing their own history, their own notion of geography, on lands and landscape, waterways and open seas, known to the people of those places for hundreds of generations. They were exploring, then, the limits of their own ignorance."[46]

The word "explore," which Moss invites his readers to unpack, has historically connoted the appropriation of the otherness of the Canadian north to the expansionist, imperialist, and finally the nationalist aims of Britain and descendants of the British in Canada, as we have seen. For Canadians of non-native descent, the accounts of the early modern explorers to the subarctic and Arctic are only now being seriously challenged by the accounts of those who have begun to deem themselves merely visitors to these regions, and, slowly, by the work of Inuit writers and artists.[47] And an understanding of the north as a land teeming with life, which supports an indigenous people and its rich culture, is finally superseding the representation of the north as "an habitation of devils, a domicill for unclean spirits, and a den of goblings."[48]

NOTES

1. For example, Isa. 14:12–14: "How art thou fallen from heaven, O Lucifer, son of the morning! How art thou cut down to the ground, which didst weaken the nations! For thou hast said in thine heart, I will ascend unto heaven, I will exalt my throne above the stars of God: I will sit also upon the mount of congregation, in the sides of the north. I will ascend above the heights of the clouds; I will be like the most High." See also Jer. 1:13–15; Ezek. 32:30; Job 38:22–23; 29–30 (King James Version).

2. *In Numeros homilia XII* (Origen), *Septuplum, Tractatus de septem viciis principalibus* (a paraphrase of Origen), *Ennarrationes in Psalmos,* Erfurst MS Amplon Q. 21, and well represented in the manuscript versions of the *Commentary on the Fables of Avianus*

(Augustine), *Summa Theologica* supp. 3.2.97 (Aquinas), *Commentaria in Isaiam* VI (Jerome), *Homilioe in Ezechielem* I (Gregory), *Expositio Veteris et Novi Testamenti* III (Paterius), *Hexameron* (Basil).

3. See Valerie J. Flint, *The Rise of Magic in Early Medieval Europe* (Princeton, NJ: Princeton University Press, 1991), 20.

4. Quoted in P. E. Dustoor, "Legends of Lucifer in Early English and in Milton," *Anglia* 54 (1930): 262.

5. Rudolf Simek, *Heaven and Earth in the Middle Ages: The Physical World before Columbus* (Woodbridge, UK: Boydell Press, 1996), 99.

6. See Wolfgang Behringer, "Weather, Hunger and Fear: Origins of the European Witch-hunts in Climate, Society and Mentality," in *The Witchcraft Reader,* ed. Darren Oldridge, 69–86 (London: Routledge, 2002).

7. Classical, Germanic, and Eastern sources also undoubtedly influenced the representation of the north as a locus of evil in the English literature of the Middle Ages. For example, the Teutonic "frost giants" are associated with the Vanir, the gods of the underworld and of death, who leaned toward evil and destruction. See Jeffrey Burton Russell, *Lucifer: The Devil in the Middle Ages* (Ithaca, NY: Cornell University Press, 1984), 64–65. Derek Pearsall records that "Germanic mythology . . . also placed Hell in the north (Mount Hecla, in Iceland, according to some ecclesiastical historians)" in *Piers Plowman: An Edition of the C-Text,* ed. Pearsall, 48 n. 110a (London: Edward Arnold, 1978). See also Dustoor, "Legends"; Malcolm Godden, "Biblical Literature," in *The Cambridge Companion to Old English Literature,* ed. Malcolm Godden and Michael Lapidge 227–42 (Cambridge: Cambridge University Press, 1991); and P. Salmon, "The Site of Lucifer's Throne," *Anglia* 81 (1963): 118–23.

8. See Eugene Green, "Aelfric," in *The Dictionary of Literary Biography 146: Old and Middle English,* ed. Jeffrey Helterman and Jerome Michell, 11–21 (Detroit, MI: Gale, 1994); Godden, "Biblical Literature," 218–23. See also Aelfric's *Sermo de initiae creaturae* and the anonymously authored poems *Genesis A, Genesis B, Christ and Satan,* and *Genesis and Exodus. Beowulf* appears to resonate here as well.

9. All variants of *Piers Plowman* refer to the fall of Lucifer into the north, but the C-text contains Langland's most engaged, and engaging, response to the trope. See Pearsall, *Piers Plowman,* I.103–32. For Chaucer, see "The Freres Tale," in *The Riverside Chaucer,* ed. Larry Benson (Boston: Houghton Mifflin, 1987), (D) l. 1412–13; for Skelton, see "Collyn Clout," in *The Complete English Poems,* ed. John Scattergood, 246–78 n. 345 (Harmondsworth, UK: Penguin, 1983).

10. All quotations from Shakespeare's plays are taken from *The Riverside Shakespeare,* eds. G. Blakemore Evans and J. J. M. Tobin, 2nd ed. (Boston: Houghton Mifflin, 1997).

11. Scotland is, of course, north of England, and northern Scotland in particular was represented through reference to hell. See Arthur H. Williamson, "Scots, Indians and Empire: The Scottish Politics of Civilization 1519–1609," *Past and Present* 150 (February 1996): 46–56. As late as 1814 Sir Walter Scott made use of the trope in *Waverley,* employing Miltonic allusion to a northern hell to evoke a Satanic rebelliousness in the (northern) Highlands during the Jacobite Rebellion of 1745.

12. Christopher Marlowe, *The Tragicall History of Dr. Faustus,* in *The Complete Works of Christopher Marlowe, Vol. 2,* ed. Roma Gill (Oxford: Clarendon Press, 1990).

13. Robert Greene, *Friar Bacon and Friar Bungay,* ed. W.W. Greg (Oxford: Oxford University Press, 1926), 8.1171–78, 8.1260, 10.1169, 10.1593–94, 14.2052–54.

14. Note also Mary Floyd-Wilson's work on climate theory in early modern England. In her *English Ethnicity and Race in Early Modern Drama* (Cambridge: Cambridge University Press, 2003), Floyd-Wilson argues that the English of the sixteenth and seventeenth centuries, uneasy with their status of "northerners," reinterpreted classical geohumoral theory to claim for themselves a special status within the category.

15. Humphrey Gilbert, *A Discourse of a Discoverie for a New Passage to Cataia* (London, 1576); John Dee, *The Mathematicall Praeface,* ed. Allen G. Debus (New York: Science History Publications, 1975).

16. See James McDermott, "Frobisher's 1578 voyage: early eyewitness accounts of English ships in Arctic seas," *Polar Record* 32, no. 183 (1996): 325–34.

17. Dionyse Settle, *A True Reporte of the last Voyage [. . .] by Captaine Frobisher* (London: Henrie Middleton, 1577).

18. Ibid., 5–6.

19. Ibid., 30.

20. Ibid., 35. Cf. the words of the Clown, in Marlowe's *Dr. Faustus:* "I'll tell you how you shall know [he devils and she devils]: all he devils has horns, and all she devils has clefts and cloven feet" (4:54–46).

21. These range from conversations Purchas had with whalers, sailors, and neighbors of seamen (Robert Salmon), to peeps at manuscripts and logbooks (Josias Hubert, William Baffin, Abacuck Prickett), to accounts culled from previously published material (especially the voyage collections of Richard Hakluyt).

22. Although Richard Eden's *Decades of the Newe Worlde* (London, 1555) is considered the first travel collection in English, Richard Hakluyt's three books of voyages, *Divers Voyages* (London, 1582), *The Principall Navigations of the English Nation* (London, 1589) and *The Principal Navigations of the English Nation* (London, 1598–1600) are such comprehensive works that they must be considered the *terminus a quo* for the genre of the English travel collection.

23. Hakluyt, "The Epistle Dedicatorie" to *The Principall Navigations,* 3.

24. Samuel Purchas, *Hakluytus Posthumus, or Purchas his Pilgrimes* (London, 1625), ¶2[b].

25. Ibid., 719.

26. Purchas, *Purchas his Pilgrimages* (London, 1614), 744.

27. I am indebted to the combined efforts of Dr. Linda Morra, Mrs. Jessie Morra, and Dr. and Mrs. Dominic Manganiello for their assistance with the translation of this sentence.

28. Purchas, *Pilgrimages,* (1614) 746.

29. Thomas James, *The Strange and Dangerous Voyage of Captaine Thomas James* (London: John Leggatt for John Partridge, 1633).

30. Ibid., 39.

31. Ibid., 18.

32. Ibid., 29.

33. John Storpin, *Færoæ, & Færoa Referata* (London, 1676), 376.

34. Ibid., 376–77.

35. The Hudson's Bay Company's control over the region extended from the time of its charter in 1670 to the establishment of Lord Selkirk's Red River settlement in 1812. The rival Northwest Company had challenged the Hudson's Bay Company's domination of the fur trade in the early nineteenth century, but Selkirk's settlers were the first to threaten the Company's monopoly of the land. The Hudson's Bay Company had held 1.5 million square miles of land without any serious contest for 142 years. See Peter C. Newman, *The Company of Adventurers* (Markham: Penguin, 1985), 338.

36. Newman, *Company,* 141.

37. This response was undoubtedly influenced by contemporary aesthetics as well as by the medieval structures of belief I have outlined. Marjorie Hope Nicolson, in her study of pre-Romantic poetry, *Mountain Gloom and Mountain Glory: The Development of the Aesthetics of the Infinite* (1959; New York: Norton, 1977), suggests that the topographic poetry of the Renaissance and eighteenth century was informed by an aesthetic of landscape heavily indebted to both the classical norms of order and form and a widely held belief that the earth, once a perfect sphere, had been restructured at the Flood as a consequence of God's anger at the sinfulness of human beings.

38. James, *Voyage,* title page.

39. Thomas James, *The Dangerous Voyage of Captain T. James* (London: O. Payne, 1740).

40. See Ivor James, *The Source of "The Ancient Mariner"* (Cardiff, UK: Daniel Owen, 1890), and John Livingston Lowes, *The Road to Xanadu: A Study in the Ways of the Imagination* (1927; London: Constable, 1955).

41. Colleen Franklin, "Northern Gothic: *The Strange and Dangerous Voyage of Captaine Thomas James,"* in *Worlds of Wonder: Readings in Canadian Science Fiction and Fantasy Literature,* eds. Camille La Bossière and Jean-François Leroux, 147–54 (Ottawa, ON: University of Ottawa Press, 2004). See also Maurice Hodgson, "The Literature of the Franklin Search," in *The Franklin Era in Canadian Arctic History, 1845–1859,* ed. Patricia D. Sutherland (Ottawa, ON: National Museums of Canada, 1985) and Margaret Atwood, *Strange Things: The Malevolent North in Canadian Literature* (Oxford: Clarendon Press, 1995).

42. The South Pole, long only imagined, was routinely figured through northern tropes.

43. Northrop Frye, *Mythologizing Canada: Essays on the Canadian Literary Imagination,* ed. Branko Gorjup, 35 (New York: Legas, 1997).

44. Other critics have noted that Frye and his ilk have been unnecessarily limiting, arguing that writers and artists of the early twentieth century, intent on realizing a national culture, claimed a beneficent animism for Canada's north. See, for example, Susan Glickman, *The Picturesqe and the Sublime: A Poetics of the Canadian Landscape* (Montreal, QC: McGill-Queen's University Press, 1998), and Linda Morra, "Re-viewing the Canadian Landscape: Representations of Canada in Ralph Connor, Tom Thomson, The Group of Seven, and Emily Carr" (PhD diss., University of Ottawa, 2002). This consciously counterimperial move was still, however, infused with a European aesthetic, based as it was on the Burkean formulation; in effect, this nationalist north remained in many ways a realm of the marvelous. NB: Morra offers a thorough survey of the critics of the Frygian school in her first chapter.

45. See, e.g., John Moss, *Enduring Dreams: An Exploration of Arctic Landscape* (Concord, ON: Anansi, 1994), and Sherrill Grace, *Canada and the Idea of North* (Montreal, QC: McGill-Queen's University Press, 2001).

46. John Moss, "Preface: Landscape Writing Landscape," *The Northern Review* 17 (Winter 1996): 12.

47. See, e.g., Grace, *Canada;* Shelagh D. Grant, "Arctic Wilderness—And Other Mythologies," *Journal of Canadian Studies* 32, no. 2 (Summer 1998): 27–41.

48. I am grateful to the Social Sciences and Humanities Research Council of Canada, the American Society for Eighteenth-Century Studies, and the William Andrews Clark Library, Los Angeles, for their support of my research.

BIBLIOGRAPHY

Atwood, Margaret. *Strange Things: The Malevolent North in Canadian Literature.* Oxford: Clarendon Press, 1995.

Behringer, Wolfgang. "Weather, Hunger and Fear: Origins of the European Witch-hunts in Climate, Society and Mentality." In *The Witchcraft Reader.* Edited by Darren Oldridge, 69–86. London: Routledge, 2002.

Chaucer, Geoffrey. "The Freres Tale." *The Riverside Chaucer.* Edited by Larry Benson, 123–28. Boston: Houghton Mifflin, 1987. III (D).

Dee, John. *The Mathematicall Praeface.* Edited by Allen G. Debus. 1570. Reprint, New York: Science History Publications, 1975.

Dustoor, P. E. "Legends of Lucifer in Early English and in Milton." *Anglia* 54 (1930): 213–68.

Eden, Richard. *The Decades of the Newe Worlde.* London, 1555.

Flint, Valerie J. *The Rise of Magic in Early Medieval Europe.* Princeton, NJ: Princeton University Press, 1991.

Floyd-Wilson, Mary. *English Ethnicity and Race in Early Modern Drama.* Cambridge: Cambridge University Press, 2003.

Franklin, Colleen. "Northern Gothic: *The Strange and Dangerous Voyage of Captaine Thomas James.*" In *Worlds of Wonder: Readings in Canadian Science Fiction and Fantasy Literature.* Edited by Camille LaBossière and Jean-François Leroux, 147–54. Ottawa, ON: University of Ottawa Press, 2004.

Frye, Northrop. *Mythologizing Canada: Essays on the Canadian Literary Imagination.* Edited by Branko Gorjup. New York: Legas, 1997.

Gilbert, Humphrey. *A Discourse of a Discoverie for a New Passage to Cataia.* London, 1576.

Glickman, Susan. *The Picturesque and the Sublime: A Poetics of the Canadian Landscape.* Montreal, QC: McGill-Queen's University Press, 1998.

Godden, Malcolm. "Biblical Literature." In *The Cambridge Companion to Old English Literature.* Edited by Malcolm Godden and Michael Lapidge, 206–26. Cambridge: Cambridge University Press, 1991.

Grace, Sherrill. *Canada and the Idea of North.* Montreal, QC: McGill-Queen's University Press, 2001.

Grant, Shelagh D. "Arctic Wilderness—And Other Mythologies." *Journal of Canadian Studies* 32, no. 2 (Summer 1998): 27–41.

Green, Eugene. "Aelfric." In *The Dictionary of Literary Biography 146: Old and Middle English.* Edited by Jeffrey Helterman and Jerome Michell, 11–21. Detroit, MI: Gale, 1994.

Greene, Robert. *Friar Bacon and Friar Bungay.* Edited by W. W. Greg. Oxford: Oxford University Press, 1926.

Hakluyt, Richard. *Divers Voyages.* London, 1582.

———. *The Principal Navigations of the English Nation.* London, 1598–1600.

———. *The Principall Navigations of the English Nation.* London, 1589.

Hodgson, Maurice. "The Literature of the Franklin Search." In *The Franklin Era in Canadian Arctic History, 1845–1859.* Edited by Patricia D. Sutherland, 1–11. Ottawa, ON: National Museums of Canada, 1985.

James, Ivor. *The Source of "The Ancient Mariner."* Cardiff, UK: Daniel Owen, 1890.

James, Thomas. *The Dangerous Voyage of Capt. Thomas James.* London: O. Payne, 1740.

———. *The Strange and Dangerous Voyage of Captaine Thomas James.* London: John Leggatt for John Partridge, 1633.

Langland, William. *Piers Plowman: An Edition of the C-Text.* Edited by Derek Pearsall. London: Edward Arnold, 1978.

Lowes, John Livingston. *The Road to Xanadu: A Study in the Ways of the Imagination.* 1927. London: Constable, 1955.

Marlowe, Christopher. *The Tragicall History of Dr. Faustus.* In *The Complete Works of Christopher Marlowe,* Vol. 2 Edited by Roma Gill, Oxford: Clarendon Press, 1990.

McDermott, James. "Frobisher's 1578 voyage: early eyewitness accounts of English ships in Arctic seas." *Polar Record* 32, no. 183 (1996): 325–34.

Morra, Linda. "Re-viewing the Canadian Landscape: Representations of Canada in Ralph Connor, Tom Thomson, The Group of Seven, and Emily Carr." PhD diss., University of Ottawa, 2002.

Moss, John. *Enduring Dreams: An Exploration of Arctic Landscape.* Concord, ON: Anansi, 1994.

———. "Preface: Landscape Writing Landscape." *The Northern Review* 17 (Winter 1996): 11–18.

Newman, Peter C. *The Company of Adventurers.* Markham, ON: Penguin, 1985.

Nicolson, Marjorie Hope. *Mountain Gloom and Mountain Glory: The Development of the Aesthetics of the Infinite.* 1959. New York: Norton, 1977.

Pearsall, Derek, ed. *Piers Plowman: An Edition of the C-Text.* London: Edward Arnold, 1978.

Purchas, Samuel. *Hakluytus Posthumus, or Purchas his Pilgrimes.* London, 1625.

———. *Purchas his Pilgrimage.* London, 1613.

———. *Purchas his Pilgrimage.* London, 1614.

———. *Purchas his Pilgrimage.* London, 1626.

Russell, Jeffrey Burton. *Lucifer: The Devil in the Middle Ages.* Ithaca, NY: Cornell University Press, 1984.

Salmon, P. "The Site of Lucifer's Throne." *Anglia* 81 (1963): 118–23.

Settle, Dionyse. *A True Report of the last Voyage* [. . .] *by Captaine Frobisher.* London: Henrie Middleton, 1577.

Shakespeare, William. *The Riverside Shakespeare,* 2nd ed. Edited by G. Blakemore Evans and J. J. M. Tobin. Boston: Houghton Mifflin, 1997.

Simek, Rudolf. *Heaven and Earth in the Middle Ages: The Physical World before Columbus.* Woodbridge, UK: Boydell, 1996.

Skelton, John. "Collyn Clout." *The Complete English Poems.* Edited by John Scattergood, 246–78. Harmondsworth, UK: Penguin, 1983.

Storpin, John. *Færoæ, & Færoa Referata* (London, 1676).

Williamson, Arthur H. "Scots, Indians and Empire: The Scottish Politics of Civilization 1519–1609." *Past and Present* 150 (February 1996): 46–83.

Headless in America:
The Imperial Logic of Acephalism

Scott Oldenburg

TOWARD THE END OF HIS *DISCOVERY OF GUIANA,* SIR WALTER RALEGH writes, "This empire is made known to her majesty by her own vassal, and by him that oweth to her more duty than an ordinary subject, so that it shall ill sort with the many graces and benefits which I have received to abuse Her Highness, either with fables or imaginations."[1] Ralegh wants to differentiate his travel narrative from the many popular travel narratives that mixed documentary with fanciful fiction. Indeed, throughout the description of Guiana, Ralegh reminds his readers of how careful he is in distinguishing fact from fiction. Ralegh writes, "but my intelligence was far from truth . . . afterwards understanding to be true . . . . Many and most of these I found to be true."[2] Ralegh even ceases listing the names of the islands of the area out of fear that his narrative will look too much like the more fictive travel narratives that had gained popularity in England at the time.[3]

In addition to proving the existence of an Edenic Guiana, Ralegh's claims to truth were part of a strategy for reclaiming Elizabeth's favor: "The primary aim of *The Discoverie of Guiana,*" writes Walter S. H. Lim, "is to convince Elizabeth I of the trials experienced and undergone by the courtier in the service of his queen."[4] Joyce Lorimer suggests that Ralegh was intent on seeming truthful because he was especially "sensitive to ridicule" and so, "to counter the arguments of those disposed to dismiss his entire enterprise as the product of an over-active imagination, Ralegh pointed out the growing level of French interest in the Amazon."[5] As Mary C. Fuller has pointed out, however, Ralegh's claims to truth did not help him avoid accusations of fabrication nor did the genre of discovery in which Ralegh related a non-discovery, the mere hope of a city of gold. Some even suspected that Ralegh had travelled no further than Cornwall, that his "discovery" was no more truthful than any work of fiction written to gain (or here regain) the Queen's favor.[6] Given that Ralegh never found the City of Gold (El Dorado) he set out to claim, it makes sense that he would be at greater pains to appear more truthful than the average narrator of discovery.

Ralegh, then, writes his narrative to get out from under the gaze of skepticism and disfavor. Such a motive accounts for his efforts to name names, to corroborate information, to dispel rumors that his narrative is largely full of "fables or imaginations." However, as any reader of the *Discovery* knows, Ralegh included a healthy dose of those "fables or imaginations" in his description of Guiana. Ralegh may well have believed in the existence of El Dorado, but that legendary city is not the only fabulous element in the *Discovery*. Indeed, the more fanciful parts of the narrative captured early modern readers' imaginations, for illustrations of several wonders mentioned in Ralegh's narrative are featured prominently on the cover of many editions of *The Discovery of Guiana,* yet Ralegh describes such fictive elements as a form of "abuse." Since early modern readers accepted, and even desired this particular form of "abuse," they must have found something valuable and pleasurable in it, a story that they at least wanted to believe in. Whether readers recognized these elements of Ralegh's narrative as myth or fact, the passages about Amazons and the Ewaipanoma—headless people—seem to have been nonetheless important to readers.

Ralegh, no doubt, knew how appealing "fables and imaginations" were for his readers, but for all the fabulous elements in his narrative he is, throughout the *Discovery,* careful in emphasizing which elements were based on his own observations and which were based on information re-

Detail of Jodocus Hondius the Elder's 1599 map of Guiana. © British Library Board. All rights reserved (Maps.184.g.2).

ceived from others. Still, if Ralegh wanted to appear truthful, why would he devote more attention to the fantastic headless Ewaipanoma than to El Dorado and Amazons? As will be seen, the headless people of Ralegh's narrative inspired illustrations and found their way into popular theater, while the City of Gold received much less attention from Ralegh's readers. About the headless Ewaipanoma, Ralegh writes,

> Next unto Arvi there are two rivers Atoica and Caora, and on that branch which is called Caora are a nation of people, whose heads appear not above their shoulders; which though it may be thought a mere fable, yet for mine own part I am resolved it is true, because every child in the provinces of Arromaia and Canuri affirm the same: they are called Ewaipanoma: reported to have their eyes in their shoulders, and their mouths in the middle of their breasts, and a long train of hair groweth backward between their shoulders. The son of Topiawari, which I brought with me into England, told me, that they are the most mighty men of all the land, and use bows, arrows, and clubs, thrice as big as any of Guiana or of the Oroonokoponi, and that the Iwarawakeri took a prisoner of one of them the year before our arrival there, and brought him into the borders of Arromaia, his father's country: and further, when I seemed to doubt of it, he told me that it was no wonder among them; but that they were as great a nation, and as common, as any other in all the provinces, and had of late years slain many hundreds of his father's people, and of other nations their neighbors. But it was not my chance to hear of them till I was come aways; and if I had but spoken one word of it while I was there, I might have brought one of them with me, to put the matter out of doubt. Such a nation was written of by Maundeville, whose reports were held for fables for many years, and yet since the East Indies were discovered, we find his relations true of such things as heretofore were held incredible: whether it be true or no, the matter is not great, neither can there be any profit in the imagination; for mine own part, I saw them not, but I am resolved that so many people did not all combine or forethink to make the report.[7]

The description of the Ewaipanoma is perhaps the oddest passage in all Ralegh's narrative. Stephen Greenblatt has noted the narrative's affinity with epic, but Ralegh's epic search for the City of Gold and revenge upon Antonio de Berrío are here interrupted by a fantastic digression owing much to the genre of romance, a generic element furthered by Ralegh's description of the river as a "labyrinth."[8] David Quint has observed that such romantic digressions within epics give voice to "Epic's losers" and therefore often bring about a "collapse of narrative."[9] The passage indeed causes problems; regarding Ralegh's claims to the documentary truth of his epic travel narrative and, in that sense, causes a "collapse of narrative," but if epic is, as Quint among others asserts, the genre of empire, how might Ralegh's Ewaipanoma be construed as "losers" given that they are never defeated because they are never contacted? The relationship between the headless people, made so much of in Ralegh's *Discovery* and England's (as well as all of Europe's) imperial aspirations, is a complex one which occupies the rest of this article. The headless antecedents of the Ewaipanoma found in other travel narratives, subsequent descriptions of headless people influenced by Ralegh's *Discovery,* and the fundamental issue of anatomical deformity form a constellation that appealed to early modern Europeans' sense of a right and duty to conquer, colonize, or otherwise profit from the New World.

Although Ralegh does not invest this passage with his own eyewitness authority, his credulousness marks him as perhaps not a very reliable evaluator of what he is told. By Ralegh's logic—"must be true because children say so"—one may equally believe in any number of folkloric figures. It may be that the allusion to children was meant to be a wink to the reader, a kind of inside joke regarding the fantastic subject matter commonly found in travel narratives of the period.[10] However, such passages in Ralegh's narrative do seem to have been received, if not as documentary, then, at the very least, as the most meaningful and interesting element in the narrative: the Ewaipanoma were soon to find their way onto several maps of the Americas; they are portrayed in subsequent editions of the *Discovery;* and, as we shall see, other narratives of exploration of the Americas refer to the Ewaipanoma with no apparent irony. As Gonzalo tells his fellow castaways in *The Tempest:*

> Faith, sir, you need not fear. When we were boys,
> Who would have believed that there were mountaineers
> Dewlapped like bulls, whose throats had hanging at 'em
> Wallets of flesh? Or that there were such men
> Whose heads stood in their breasts? Which now we find
> Each putter-out of five for one will bring us
> Good warrant of. . . .[11]

(3.3.43–49)

Gonzalo, like Ralegh, suggests that repeated reports corroborate the existence of headless men and the like.

Even stranger than the length of Ralegh's description of the Ewaipanoma is his immediate dismissal of the topic. He writes "the matter is not great," but he very soon after tries to corroborate the existence of the Ewaipanoma through a conversation "with a Spaniard not far from thence, a man of great travel" who had seen many Ewaipanoma.[12] Lest the reader suspect this Spaniard to be a teller of tall tales, Ralegh assures readers that he is "esteemed a most honest man of his word," but Ralegh "may not name him, because it may be of his disadvantage."[13] This corroborating evidence is suspiciously anonymous. If the "matter is not great," why does Ralegh devote so much time to it, and if Ralegh is at great pains to appear accurate and truthful in his narrative, why even mention what he knows looks like

the "fables or imaginations" he tries to avoid? If the names of the many islands seem too incredible to mention, surely the Ewaipanoma are more incredible, and more likely to undermine the perceived, truthful value of his
narrative. There are, I argue, several reasons the Ewaipanoma may have
been important to Ralegh and his readers.

Possibly, Ralegh wanted to align himself with one of the most famous
of travel narratives of his day, *Mandeville's Travels.* This motive would
explain his use of that text as support of the existence of the Ewaipanoma.
Mandeville's Travels was certainly widely read, having been translated into
at least ten languages by the end of the sixteenth century.[14] While it was
not until the late nineteenth century that the author of *Mandeville's Travels*
would prove as elusively anonymous as Ralegh's witness to the Ewaipanoma, it was already a text received as fictive as often as documentary.[15]
Aligning the *Discovery* with *Mandeville's Travels,* then, may suggest
Ralegh's anticipation of fame, but it does not seem to be a very sound approach to ensuring his readers' credulousness.

There must be some reason Ralegh would devote so much of his narrative to precisely that which would call its veracity into question. Attempting to find a reason or reasons places the critic in much the same position
as Ralegh in his search for El Dorado, but, along the way, one might be able
to come to grips with the ostentatiously speculative and fictive moments
which occur in so many early modern travel narratives. That is, the passage
on the Ewaipanoma does not readily fit the categories Greenblatt finds
balanced in the *Discovery:* "history, speculation on Spanish intentions, anthropological observations, military strategy, topographical description,
patriotic appeals, prophecy, and straightforward narrative."[16] On the contrary, Ralegh's description of the Ewaipanoma seems purely speculative,
suspiciously so since Ralegh simultaneously dismisses the Ewaipanoma as
a "matter . . . not great" but devotes considerable space to it and corroborates
it with the tales of children, an anonymous Spaniard, and a text of much
renown but questionable authority.

To be fair to Greenblatt's assessment, the Ewaipanoma may be part of
Ralegh's genuine attempt at accumulating anthropological data, of recording exactly what the people he encounters told him. Neil Whitehead claims
that the "trope of the monstrous, used as an expression of alterity, was already present in native thought before the European arrival."[17] The son of
Topiawari, argues Whitehead, may have been projecting the dehumanizing
image of the Ewaipanoma onto their rivals along the Caura river.[18] Conversely, Whitehead suggests that the image of the Ewaipanoma may have
a basis in fact: the image may be less a matter of imagined monstrosity, as
it is perhaps an account of actual "cranial deformation" among the Taruma,
a practice used to differentiate themselves from their neighbors.[19] Arthur
O. Friel and Raleigh Trevelyan have similarly speculated that the inhabitants

in question may have worn headgear or painted faces on their chests in such a way as to confuse onlookers.[20] It may also be that the Ewaipanoma were an invention of the son of Topiawari designed to strike fear in the hearts of the European visitors. Such a strategy of misinformation was employed in Europe by Lombards who, when faced with the prospect of war, spread rumors that they were allies with a race of vicious Cynocephali, or dog-headed people.[21] Finally, given the linguistic gap, headlessness may have been a misinterpretation of statements made by Ralegh's informants.

Nonetheless, Ralegh's translation of the image of the Ewaipanoma, with its appeal to the authority of *Mandeville's Travels,* notes Whitehead, dis-torts it so that, despite Ralegh's efforts at ethnography, the image resonates more strongly with the European version of acephalism.[22] Even without Ralegh's explicit reference to Mandeville, many of his readers would no doubt have remembered the passage from *Mandeville's Travels* or other pre- and early modern authorities. To get at how the image of the headless Ewaipanoma may have been full of meaning for Ralegh's European readers, a look at the acephalic peoples, described in texts prior to Ralegh's, is nec-essary because those earlier texts informed the reading of the Ewaipanoma.

Ralegh explicitly refers his readers to *Mandeville's Travels.* As he enters the East Indies, the narrator of *Mandeville's Travels* encounters an island where "the Fadre eteth the Sone, the Sone, the Fadre, the Husbonde the Wif, and the Wif the Husbonde."[23] Despite the horror of this initial de-scription of impossible cannibalism, the island appears to have some order and is ruled by a king who "hathe under him 54 grete Yls" inhabited vari-ously by "folk of grete Stature, as Geauntes," "lityle folk, as Dwerghes," "folk that han Hors Feet," "folk that ben bothe Man and Woman," "folk that gon alle weyes upon here Knees," and "many other dyverse folk of dyverse natures."[24] The narrator explains that "in another Yle, toward the Southe, duellen folk of foule Stature and of cursed kynde, that han no Hedes: and here Eyen ben in her Scholdres."[25] Later, he explains that those "withouten Hedes" and other "Monstres, and folk disfigured" are the progeny of Noah's cursed son, Cham or Ham, who took over all of Asia.[26] As the connection to Ham suggests, acephalic deformity here signifies a cursed or depraved state.

A well-read early modern reader of *Mandeville's Travels* would very likely have recognized the description of the "dyverse folk" of Asia as largely plagiarized from or at least strikingly similar to Pliny's description of inhabitants of Africa who, according to him, "have fallen below the level of civilization."[27] Among these are a tribe that is always naked, Satyrs, "Strapfoots" who crawl rather than walk, speechless "Cave-dwellers," a people who have no concept of marriage but "live with their women promis-cuously," and, important for the purposes of this essay, "[t]he Blemmyae [who] are reported to have no heads, their mouth and eyes being attached to their chests."[28] Later, in drawing connections between Africa and India, Pliny explains that the places have in common people "with their feet turned backward," a one-legged people, "a tribe of human beings with dogs' heads," and again "some people without necks, having their eyes in their shoulders."[29] For Pliny headlessness and other anatomical anomalies indicate a lack of civilization, a lack of human social relations. It is possible, too, that both Pliny and the narrator of *Mandeville's Travels* were drawing on Herodotus, who describes western Libya as populated by "dog-faced creatures, and the creatures without heads, whom the Libyans declare to have their eyes in their breasts."[30] Whether one looks to Herodotus, Pliny, Mandeville, or Ralegh, the monstrous figures appear in largely unknown areas outside of Europe, always on the horizon of "discovery."

It is difficult if not impossible to assess whether early modern readers were credulous of these descriptions found in Herodotus, Pliny, and *Mandeville's Travels,* but Ralegh seems to be using the dubiousness of *Mandeville's Travels* to his advantage by situating himself as a new Mandeville. According to Ralegh, Mandeville's "reports were held for fables for many years" until the East Indies came to be better known so that "we find his relations true of such things as heretofore were held incredible." Similarly, implies Ralegh, doubters and nay-sayers will come to trust the veracity of *The Discovery of Guiana* as Guiana is further explored and exploited. Whatever verification *Mandeville's Travels* had received is transformed into a promise of verification of Ralegh's claims.

Still, to claim the validity of an encounter (or near encounter) in the New World by referring to an East Indies encounter narrative has certain critical implications. Anthony Pagden's concept, "the principle of attachment," may be of use here.[31] When confronted by the newness of the New World, argues Pagden, early modern Europeans invariably attempted to detach an aspect of the encounter from its context and reattach it to a European context: "nakedness," for example, was frequently detached from its context as a cultural norm in specific areas of the New World and recontextualized in a culture that takes nakedness as a sign of either Edenic innocence or absolute lasciviousness—in either case, a deviation from a European norm and a glaringly wrong-headed interpretation of New World cultures. As Ralegh situates his unique New World encounter in the context of a widely disseminated European's encounter with the East Indies, the Ewaipanoma lose their cultural specificity and come to be associated with the disorder and cannibalism described in *Mandeville's Travels.* Ralegh's description of the Ewaipanoma discourages readers from understanding the New World encounter on its own terms, that is, as simply new, and instead compels readers to think of the Ewaipanoma (and by extension all encounters in the narrative) in terms of European traditions of monstrosity.[32] That tradition, as has been seen in Herodutus, Pliny, and *Mandeville's Travels,* associated monsters, specifically headless people, with cannibalism, a cursed state inherited from Noah's son, Cham or Ham, and a lack of civilization.

However, just as Ralegh's description of the Ewaipanoma was structured by headless antecedents, so the description of the Ewaipanoma came to structure subsequent descriptions of the New World. The text of Captain Lawrence Kemys's 1596 account of the exploration of Guiana is revealing in this respect. Kemys explains that his interpreter "certified me of the headlesse men, and that their mouths in their breasts are exceeding wide. The name of their nation in the Charibes language is Chiparemai, and the Guianans call them Ewaipanomus. What I have heard of a sorte of people more monstrous, I omit to mention because it is no matter the difficultie to get one of them, and the report otherwise will appear fabulous."[33] Here we have new details about the Ewaipanoma—they have big mouths and are also called "Chiparemai," and these details suggest that Kemys is not so much following Ralegh as reinforcing his narrative by relating another encounter with a native account of the Ewaipanoma. But Kemys does borrow from Ralegh the narrative strategy of describing the image while worrying about the reader's perception of its "fabulousness," of combining in Robert Applebaum's words "a rigorous skepticism . . . with a vigorous credulity."[34] In doing so, both Kemys and Ralegh present themselves as acutely conscious of what might go through the skeptical reader's mind, as partially participating in the reader's skepticism. I would go so far as to say that Ralegh and Kemys bring up the potential for interpreting their narratives as fictive so as to dispel such a notion; that is, in anticipating, even co-opting the reader's objections, they attempt to present themselves as already having gone through a skeptical, scrutinizing examination of the material for the reader.

In both Kemys's and Ralegh's narratives, the description of the Ewaipanoma is made prominent. Ralegh devotes roughly two pages of text to the description whereas Kemys's text is accompanied by a marginal gloss that draws the reader's attention to the passage. The gloss next to the passage on the Ewaipanoma explains, "They have eminent heads like dogs, & live all day time in the sea. They speake the Charibes language."[35] Robert H. Schomburgck assumes that the marginal gloss was written as supplemental information by Kemys himself.[36] This seems unlikely not only because authors rarely prepared their own glosses, but because this particular gloss seems to run counter to Kemys's fear that his narrative "will appear fabulous." Moreover, none of the other glosses in the text offer supplemental information as this one does. Given the tendency for the marginalia to be summary and given the echo of "Charibes language" from main text to margin, I suspect that the description of dog-headed people indicates both a printer's desire for sensationalism and the degree to which prior narratives—like Pliny's *Natural History*, which included a description of dog-headed people—structured the reading of new narratives of exploration. Rather than clarifying matters, as most marginal glosses are wont to do, this note turns the reader's eye to murky waters: the acephali become cynocephali, a dog's head is placed on the headless shoulders of the Ewaipanoma.

The author of this marginal note not only buys into Ralegh's appeal to the authority of *Mandeville's Travels,* but seems to have mistaken one narrative for another, the East for the West Indies. The narrator of *Mandeville's Travels,* again perhaps drawing on Pliny, writes of an island near Java called Nacumera where "alle the men and women of that Yle han Houndes Hedes: and they ben clept Cynocephali: and thei ben ful resonable and of gode undirstondynge, saf that thei worschipen an Ox for here God." In addition to idol worship, accounts of Native Americans which emphasized nakedness and cannibalism may have reminded early modern Europeans of the Cynocephali who, the narrator reports, "gon alle naked," and "zif thei taken ony many in Batayle, anon thei eten him."[37] The popularity of earlier travel narratives seems to have dominated the way in which the author of the marginalia read Kemys, and this tendency of reading new texts in terms of previous ones seems to have been prevalent among many early modern readers.

In addition to the disorder that the headless people likely recalled for readers of Kemys's and Ralegh's narratives, readers might have remembered that in *Mandeville's Travels* the Cynocephali are "fulle riche." *Mandeville's Travels* emphasizes the enormous wealth of the Cynocephali whose king wears "abouten his Nekke 300 Perles oryent, gode and grete [along with] a Rubye oryent, noble and fyn, that is a Fote in lengthe, and fyve fingres large."[38] The Cynocephali not only recall the fabulous Ewaipanoma in Kemys's and Ralegh's narratives, but the fantastic wealth both Kemys and Ralegh promise but never deliver in their accounts of a search for El Dorado.

The connection between the two missed encounters (one with the Ewaipanoma, the other with El Dorado) are combined in Domingo de Vera Ibargoyen's account of Guiana, which was delivered to Ralegh in 1594, before Ralegh's own journey to Guiana, by the privateer Captain George Popham. Upon seeing the Indians feasting on numerous hens, de Vera investigated where the hens were to be found. He explains the results of the inquiry: "They were brought from a mounatine not passing a quarter of a league thence, where were many Indians, yea so many as grasse on the ground, and that those men had the pointes of their shoulders higher then the Crownes of their heades, and had so many hens as was wonderfull, and if we would have any we shoulde send them Iewes harpes for they woulde give for every one two hens, we tooke an Indian and gave him 500 harpes, the hens were so many that he brought us, as were not to be numbred. Wee said we woulde goe thither, they told us they were now in their Borrachera and would kill us, we asked the Indian, that brought the hens if it were true, he said it was most true." The *borrachera,* or drunken celebration, as described by one Indian, involves "many Eagles of Gold hanging on their breasts and pearls in their eares, and that they daunced being al covered with Gold."[39] The Ewaipanoma of de Vera's narrative combine, like the Cynocephali of *Mandeville's Travels,* monstrousness, brutality, and immense wealth. To ensure that his description of the Ewaipanoma was read in terms of de Vera's, Ralegh appended de Vera's letters to the 1596 editions of the *Discovery.*

The Indian informer, of course, could not have known that he had uttered the buzzword of European avarice, gold. The Spanish offered a hatchet for which they were given "an Eagle that wayed 27 pounds good Gold." Later on that night, de Vera learned that "the Indians with the high shoulders meane . . . to kill vs for our marchandize."[40] De Vera's narrative seems to be the source of Ralegh's belief that the immense wealth of the legendary city El Dorado was located just beyond the explored territory of Guiana. Indeed, de Vera's letters with their promise of gold and the prospect of undermining the Spanish presence in the Americas seem to have prompted Ralegh's expedition.[41] For Ralegh, then, the story of a "nation of people, whose heads appear not above their shoulders" and who danced "covered with Gold" was a sign that he was close to his goal. In his imagination the Ewaipanoma and El Dorado were intimately linked by de Vera's letter. This perhaps explains Ralegh's emphasis on the existence of the Ewaipanoma in a narrative that otherwise seems strained to avoid "fables or imaginations." Ralegh, after all, included de Vera's letters in all of the 1596 editions of his *Discovery,* probably in the hope that his readers would come to the same conclusion he had, that El Dorado was just beyond the horizon where the Ewaipanoma dwelled and that he had served his Queen well in locating it.

Ralegh's use of the Ewaipanoma as a sign of the proximity of El Dorado, however, seems to have been lost on his readers. The Spanish letters appended to his narrative bolstered his opponents' claims that Ralegh never left England; that is, the similarities between his narrative and those of the letters Popham seized in 1594 allowed for the belief that he had in fact plagiarized the journey. Still, many of the texts prior to Ralegh's that mention headless people do seem to have contributed to the fascination with the Ewaipanoma: from the earlier texts readers may have associated the Ewaipanoma with exotic, unexplored lands, extraordinary violence, a fallen state, a lack of civilization, and immense wealth.

More important than how *Mandeville's Travels* and other such texts structured early modern readers' experience of Ralegh's *Discovery* is how the Ewaipanoma become such a prominent aspect of the text in subsequent publications. A 1599 map of the Guiana region, for example, features just beyond Guiana at roughly the center of the map, two Ewaipanoma.[42] Two translations of Ralegh's *Discovery,* one in Latin and the other in German, feature illustrations of the Ewaipanoma by Theodore de Bry and Levinus Hulsius,[43] and numerous scholars claim that the aforementioned passage from *The Tempest* and Othello's description of "The Anthropophagi, and men whose heads / [Do grow] beneath their shoulders" (1.3.143–44) are attributable to Ralegh's influence.[44] Ralegh's description of the Ewaipanoma, rather than the City of Gold, seems to have resonated most strongly with the reading public.

The image of the Ewaipanoma, then, does not seem to function exclusively as a sign of proximity to El Dorado in these subsequent representations, but proximity in general is important. John Gillies argues that in the early modern period distance and difference were intimately linked.[45] In *Mandeville's Travels* and Pliny's *Natural History,* the number of marvels increases with the narrator's distance from his home. Especially in *Mandeville's Travels,* it is as if Europe were the center for normative civilization and all other peoples were somehow deviations from the "human." Insofar as Ralegh is attempting to portray himself as the good courtier, the Ewaipanoma indicate the distance he has gone for his Queen. Following Gillies, Applebaum suggests that these figures exist at the limit of human knowledge of geography, as markers of the infinite possibilities of the terra incognita, what he calls "anti-geography."[46] Ralegh seems to make such use of the Ewaipanoma, placing them at the horizon of his expectation of the City of Gold he cannot quite locate, and this certainly seems to be the case with the 1599 map which features the Ewaipanoma at the edge of the explored area.

Acephali, cynocephali, and so forth stand not only at the edge of the blank spots on the map, however, but at the border of natural categories.[47] Saint Augustine, for example, is confounded as to whether to believe that "certain men with no necks, who have their eyes in their shoulders" and other "monstrous races of men described in pagan history were descended from the sons of Noah."[48] In short, Augustine wants to know what constitutes the category "human." Despite his promise of resolving the question, Augustine sidesteps the issue, declaring "if such races do exist, they are not human; or, if they are human, they are descended from Adam."[49] The narrator of *Mandeville's Travels* believed that they were definitely human but of the "Generacioun of Cham," the cursed son of Noah;[50] that is, in *Mandeville's Travels,* acephali are human but of a substandard type. Pliny more subtly attempts to present a continuum: he begins by describing the isolationist but fully human Gamphasantes, then the Blemmyae who lack some human anatomy, and then the Satyrs who mix the human with the clearly nonhuman.[51] In any case, acephali were understood to be difficult to categorize as fully human.

To return to Gillies's equation that distance equaled difference in the early modern period, the early modern fantasy that acephali, cynocephali, and similar deviations from known beings existed in the New World affirmed the notion that Native Americans were somehow further from human status than Europeans. That is, if the Ewaipanoma stand at the border of the human, their neighbors, the other tribes in and around Guiana, are fairly close to them in terms of distance and difference from a European norm, whereas Europeans are, according to this imperial fantasy, literally and figuratively oceans apart. The texts that informed early modern readers' reading of the Ewaipanoma and their neighbors, then, associated headlessness not only with violence, chaos, and wealth, but also with a group of beings of dubious humanity and therefore questionable rights.

As Whitehead points out, the image of acephali symbolized alterity for both the Europeans and the son of Topiawari.[52] In its distortion of normal anatomy, the image denies a group of people humanity or at least a level of humanity. Indeed, some three hundred years later, when confronted by a patient who envisioned his father as having no head, but with "facial features on the abdomen," Sigmund Freud suggested that while the image has mythological antecedents, the intention was to debase the patriarch.[53] While I am tempted to put Ralegh on the analyst's couch, I wish here only to suggest that a similar debasement of a people is at work in the recurring image of the headless people be it Pliny's Blemmyae or Ralegh's Ewaipanoma.

The dehumanization of the inhabitants of the City of Gold is important for Ralegh and his readers, for it makes conquest much less complicated. This takes the rhetoric of vagabondage, which sought to compare Native Americans to landless peasants, a step further, according to James Boon. He finds in descriptions of New World inhabitants the idea that Native Americans were vagabonds may have limited Europeans' perception of Native American property rights, but the association of Native Americans with the subhuman made empire even easier.[54] Ralegh and others could relish the ambiguity Augustine found in descriptions of headless people, for it provided a serious stumbling block for theological or moral objections to the destruction of a civilization for the sake of profit. Only humans had the right to property, after all, and one need not negotiate with nor justify the killing of sub- or nonhumans. The image of the Ewaipanoma offered up a fantasy of an uninhabited and rich place in the New World where no competing land claims existed—not that actual land claims led Europeans to cease their colonization of the Americas—but the fantasy may have helped rationalize conquest in the minds of Ralegh and others who objected to the "Black Legend" of Spanish bloodlust.[55]

More important than the implication that the inhabitants of the New World were somehow less human, and therefore less entitled to natural rights, early modern notions of acephalism relate to the idea of the head as the seat of rational thought, as that which restrains bodily instincts, hence the current phrase "losing one's head" as describing someone who has momentarily lost control of rational faculties. Much worse than "losing one's head," however, is never having had a head in the first place; the image of headless people conjures up the idea of a people without restraint or the ability to reason, and many of the accounts of the Ewaipanoma as brutal, ready to kill those they traded with, and so forth reinforce the image. This provides yet another reason for the appeal of the image of headless people in the Americas. From the imperialist or colonialist point of view, if the inhabitants of a desired piece of land lack rationality, one can more easily explain away their humanity or fantasize that colonization will be a great benefit in that it will bring the advances of European rational thought. Keeping in mind Gillies's formulation of distance relating to difference, it must be supposed that for early modern readers, the rest of the tribes of the Americas were more similar to the Ewaipanoma than they were to Europeans; the Ewaipanoma, after all, are presented as representative figures on the cover of the *Discovery* and several maps.

The individual body, moreover, stands in as a symbol for the larger political body. As Jonathan Gil Harris has shown, "writers of the period conceived of social structure and process through the prism of the human body."[56] Thomas Hobbes, for example, anatomizes the Commonwealth: "by art is created that great LEVIATHAN called a COMMONWEALTH, or STATE, in Latin CIVITAS, which is but an artificial man; though of greater stature and strength than the natural, for whose protection and defence it was intended; and in which the sovereignty is an artificial soul, as giving life and motion to the whole body; the magistrates, and other officers of judicature and execution, artificial joints; reward and punishment, by which fastened to the seat of the sovereignty every joint and member is moved to perform his duty are the nerves, that do the same in the body natural."[57] Likewise, in his own political treatise, *Maxims of State,* Ralegh writes, "for that commonwealths (as natural bodies) are preserved by avoiding that which hurteth the health and state thereof, and are also cured by contrary medicines."[58] In fact, in the preface to *The Discovery of Guiana,* Ralegh writes, "whatsoever kingdom shall be forced to defend itself may be compared to a body dangerously diseased, which for a season may be preserved with vulgar medicines."[59]

The human body is the model by which Ralegh and his contemporaries conceptualized society. Invariably the head figured metaphorically as the locus of proper rule, and the appearance of a monster or a bodily deformity could signify a problem in the body politic.[60] Thus, rebellions were often characterized as a "many headed Hydra."[61] By the same token, the body politic of the improperly led or anarchic state was sometimes described as headless. This point is emphasized in John Knox's 1558 *The First Blast of the Trumpet against the Monstrous Regiment of Women.* According to Knox, God

> hath set before our eyes two other mirrors and glasses, in which he will, that we should behold the order, which he hath appointed and established in nature: the one is the natural body of man, the other is the politic or civil body of that commonwealth, in which God hath appointed an order, that the head shall occupy the uppermost place. And the head hath he joined with the body, that from it doth life and motion flow to the rest of the members. In it hath he placed the eye to see, the ear to hear, and the tongue to speak, which offices are appointed to none other member of the body. The rest of the members hath every one their own place and office appointed: but none may have neither the place nor the office of the head. For who would not judge that body to be a monster, where there was no head eminent above the rest, but that the eyes were in the hands, the tongue and mouth beneath the belly, and the ears in the feet. Men, I say, should not only pronounce this body to be a monster: but assuredly they might conclude that such a body could not long endure. And no less monstrous is the body of that commonwealth where a woman beareth empire.[62]

A body politic with "no head eminent" and its "mouth beneath the belly" evokes an image not unlike that of the Ewaipanoma, and if the social structure is a microcosm of the body of its members, then the body politic of the New World may have been thought of as anarchic or headless, like the Ewaipanoma who became the central image associated with Ralegh's narrative. Of course, Ralegh was not looking to revive Knox's antifeminist rant, but the image of the headless Ewaipanoma certainly suggests the European perception of the disorderly society Knox feared, one in which the carefully regulated gender and class system of Europe simply did not apply.

Part of the imperial fantasy of acephali in the Americas is that the Native Americans, who might otherwise complicate colonization, lived in a headless body politic; they were "headless" literally and politically. This is in part why Ralegh attempts to bring about admiration for his "great cassique of the north," Elizabeth I, by showing inhabitants a miniature of her head.[63] Ralegh supposed that Elizabeth could institute a proper body politic for the Americas. As with the dehumanization of the native, the idea that the Ewaipanoma lacked governance paved the way for the legitimation of conquest. Thus, the image of the Ewaipanoma appearing on the title page and held up as representatives of Guiana in subsequent publications of Ralegh's *Discovery* invites particular colonial-imperial fantasies of justified, even much needed, conquest.

Jeffrey Jerome Cohen suggests that the monstrous, in which the acephali are included, emerge as "an embodiment of a particular cultural moment" and are produced by the psychological mechanism of projection.[64] The Ewaipanoma are certainly no exception. Whether they are a creation of the son of Topiawari or not is immaterial, for they took on a life of their own in the European imagination, mentioned in popular plays and appearing on maps and books. But as a product of projection, they reveal something about the colonial imagination of Europeans and the rhetoric they used to legitimate conquest. Bartolome de Las Casas, in his description of the forced labor Bahamians were put to, explains, "their backs come out in great salt sores, so that they look more like deformed monsters than men."[65] In his long descriptions of colonial cruelty, Las Casas reveals the nature of this kind of projection, for the monsters of European travel narratives are the products of a European imagination set on conquest. The monster is not the Native American in forced servitude whose body suffers as a result of exploitation, but the imperialist who brings that social relation about, who in turn projects his own monstrous quality onto those he exploits. As the colonizer displaced one group of humans, he displaced onto them his own inhumanity, brutality, and lack of civil behavior. For Ralegh to make this fiction work for his readers, however, he had to claim his narrative as documentary rather than fiction, truth rather than "fables and imaginations."

NOTES

1. Sir Walter Ralegh, *The Discovery of Guiana,* in *The Works of Sir Walter Ralegh, Kt.,* vol. 8 (New York: Burt Franklin, 1829) 391–478, 466.

2. Ralegh, *Discovery,* 396, 418.

3. Ibid., 383.

4. Walter S. H. Lim, *The Arts of Empire: The Poetics of Colonialism from Ralegh to Milton* (Newark: University of Delaware Press, 1998), 44.

5. Joyce Lorimer, *English and Irish Settlement on the River Amazon* (London: Hakluyt Society, 1989), 14.

6. Mary C. Fuller, "Ralegh's Fugitive Gold: Reference and Deferral in *The Discovery of Guiana,*" in *New World Encounters,* ed. Stephen Greenblatt, 218–40, 226 (Berkeley and Los Angeles: University of California Press, 1993).

7. Ralegh, *Discovery,* 444.

8. Stephen J. Greenblatt, *Sir Walter Ralegh: The Renaissance Man and His Roles* (New Haven, CT: Yale University Press, 1973), 107; Ralegh, *Discovery,* 420.

9. David Quint, *Epic and Empire: Politics and Generic Form from Virgil to Milton,* (Princeton, NJ: Princeton University Press, 1993), 45.

10. This possibility was suggested to me by Professor Phillip Collington of Niagara University.

11. William Shakespeare, *The Norton Shakespeare,* eds. Stephen Greenblatt, Walter Cohn, Jean E. Howard, and Katharine Eisaman Maus (New York: W. W. Norton, 1997). All subsequent Shakespeare citations refer to *The Norton Shakespeare.*

12. Ralegh, *Discovery,* 445.

13. Ibid., 445.

14. Stephen J. Greenblatt, *Marvelous Possessions: The Wonder of the New World* (Chicago: University of Chicago Press, 1991), 30.

15. Greenblatt, *Marvelous Possessions,* 34.

16. Greenblatt, *Sir Walter Ralegh,* 106.

17. Neil Whitehead, "The Discoverie as Ethnological Text," in *The Discoverie of the Large, Rich, and Bewtiful Empyre of Guiana. By Sir Walter Ralegh.* Transcribed, annotated, and introduced by Neil Whitehead (Manchester, UK: Manchester University Press, 1995), 60–116, 93.

18. Whitehead, "Discoverie," 94.

19. Ibid., 114.

20. Arthur O. Friel, *The River of Seven Stars* (New York: Harper and Brothers, 1924), 378–80; Raleigh Trevelyan, *Sir Walter Raleigh* (London: Penguin, 2002), 244.

21. Jeffrey Jerome Cohen, "Monster Culture (Seven Theses)," in *Monster Theory, Reading Culture,* ed. Jeffrey Jerome Cohen, 3–25, 131–2 (Minneapolis: University of Minnesota Press, 1996).

22. Whitehead, "Discoverie," 94.

23. Sir John Mandeville, *The Voiage and Travaile of Sir John Maundeville which Treateth the Way to Hierusalem; and Other Marvayles of Inde, with Other Ilands and Countryes.* (1725; repr., London: J. Davy Printers, 1866), 201. Throughout I shall be referring to this text by its shorter and more common name, *Mandeville's Travels.*

24. Mandeville, *Mandeville's Travels,* 202–6.

25. Ibid., 203.

26. Ibid., 222–23. For a discussion of the significance of the story of Noah in the early modern period, see the following: Colin Kidd, *British Identities before Nationalism: Ethnicity and Nationhood in the Atlantic World, 1600–1800* (Cambridge: Cambridge University Press, 1999); and Scott Oldenburg, "The Riddle of Blackness in England's National Family Romance," *The Journal for Early Modern Cultural Studies* 1, no. 1 (2001): 46–62.

27. Pliny, *Natural History,* vol. 2, trans. H. Rackham, 5.8.45 (Cambridge, MA: Harvard University Press, 1942).

28. Ibid., 5.8.46.

29. Ibid., 7.2.21–24.

30. Herodotus, *The Persian Wars,* in *The Greek Historians: Herodotus, Thucydides, Xenophon, and Arrian,* vol. 1, trans. George Rawlinson, 4.191 (New York: Random House, 1942).

31. Anthony Pagden, *European Encounters in the New World: From Renaissance to Romanticism* (New Haven, CT: Yale University Press, 1993), 17–49.

32. For an extensive discussion of early modern Europe's fascination with "monsters," see Mark Thornton Burnett, *Constructing 'Monsters' in Shakespearean Drama and Early Modern Culture* (New York: Palgrave, 2002).

33. Lawrence Kemys, *A Relation of the Second Voyage to Guiana* (London: Thomas Dawson, 1596), 14.

34. Robert Applebaum, "Anti-Geography," Special Issue 3, *Early Modern Literary Studies* 4, no. 2 (1998), http://www.shu.ac.uk/emls/04–2/appeanti.htm.

35. Kemys, *Relation,* 14.

36. Robert H. Schomburgck, introduction to *Discovery of the Large, Rich, and Beautiful Empire of Guiana with a Relation of the Great and Golden City of Manoa (Which the Spaniards Call El Dorado) Etc. Performed in the year 1595. By Sir Walter Ralegh* (New York: Burt Franklin, 1970), xiii–lxxv, 86 n. 2.

37. Mandeville, *Mandeville's Travels,* 196–97.

38. Ibid.

39. Qtd. in Ralegh, *Discovery,* 473–74.

40. Ibid., 474.

41. Stephen Coote, *A Play of Passion: The Life of Sir Walter Ralegh* (London: Macmillan, 1993), 231–33.

42. Ferdinand von Langegg, *El Dorado* (Austria: Akademische Druck Universität Verlagsanstalt, 1973), 7.

43. Langegg, *El Dorado*, 3–4; Charles Nicholl, *The Creature in the Map: A Journey to El Dorado* (New York: Morrow, 1996), 5–7; Schomburgck, *Discovery*, lxv–lxvi.

44. Coote, *Play of Passion*, 251; Nicholl, *Creature*, 280.

45. John Gillies, *Shakespeare and the Geography of Difference* (Cambridge: Cambridge University Press, 1994).

46. Applebaum, "Anti-Geography."

47. This reading of the monstrous is discussed more generally in Cohen, "Monster Culture."

48. Saint Augustine, *The City of God Against the Pagans*, vol. 5, trans. Eva Matthews Sanford and William McAllen Green, 19.8.41; 43. (Cambridge, MA: Harvard University Press, 1965).

49. Ibid., 19.8.49.

50. Maundeville, *Mandeville's Travels*, 223–24.

51. Pliny, *Natural History*, 5.8.45–46.

52. Whitehead, "Discoverie," 93–94.

53. Sigmund Freud, "A Mythological Parallel to a Visual Obsession," in *Character and Culture*, trans. C. M. J. Hubback, 152–54 (New York: Collier Books, 1963).

54. James Boon, *Other Tribes, Other Scribes: Symbolic Anthropology in the Comparative Study of Cultures, Histories, Religions, and Texts* (Cambridge: Cambridge University Press, 1982), 168–73.

55. On the so-called Black Legend, see William Maltby, *The Black Legend in England: The Development of Anti-Spanish Sentiment* (Durham, NC: Duke University Press, 1971). Since Maltby's book there have been number of reassessments of the Black Legend; see, e.g., Jay P. Corrin, "Revising the Black Legend," *Chesterton Review: The Journal of the Chesterton Society* 2 (1976): 158–83; Roberto Fernandez-Retamar and John Beverley, "Against the Black Legend," *Ideologies and Literature: A Journal of Hispanic and Luso-Brazilian Studies* 2, no. 10 (1979): 16–35; and J. H. Forse, "How 'Black' was the 'Black Legend' in Elizabethan England?" *Shakespeare and Renaissance Association of West Virginia Selected Papers* 25 (2002): 13–33.

56. Jonathan Gil Harris, *Foreign Bodies and the Body Politic: Discourses of Social Pathology in Early Modern England* (Cambridge: Cambridge University Press, 1998), 1.

57. Thomas Hobbes, *Leviathan* (Harmondsworth, UK: Penguin, 1968), 81.

58. Sir Walter Ralegh, *Maxims of State*, in *The Works of Sir Walter Ralegh, Kt.*, vol. 8 (New York: Burt Franklin, 1829) 1–36, 10.

59. Ralegh, *Discovery*, 389.

60. See, e.g., Burnett's discussion of Richard's various deformities as relating to the succession crises in Shakespeare's *Richard III*; Burnett, *Constructing 'Monsters,'* 65–94.

61. For an early and brilliant exposition of the many-headed hydra motif, see Christopher Hill, "The Many-Headed Monster," in *Change and Continuity in 17th-Century England* (Cambridge, MA: Harvard University Press, 1975). For a more recent discussion of the image, see Peter Linebaugh and Marcus Rediker, *The Many-Headed Hydra: Sailors, Slaves, Commoners, and the Hidden History of the Revolutionary Atlantic* (Boston: Beacon Press, 2000).

62. John Knox, *The First Blast of the Trumpet Against the Monstrous Regiment of Women* (1558), ed. Edward Arber, 27–28 (London: English Scholar's Library, 1878).

63. Ralegh, *Discovery*, 395, 430.

64. Cohen, "Monster Culture," 4.

65. Bartolome de Las Casas, *A Short Account of the Destruction of the Indies,* trans. Nigel Griffin, 94 (New York: Penguin, 1992).

BIBLIOGRAPHY

Applebaum, Robert. "Anti-Geography." Special Issue 3. *Early Modern Literary Studies* 4, no. 2 (1998):12.1–17.

Augustine. *The City of God Against the Pagans.* Vol. 5. Translated by Eva Matthews Sanford and William McAllen Green. Cambridge, MA: Harvard University Press, 1965.

Boon, James. *Other Tribes, Other Scribes: Symbolic Anthropology in the Comparative Study of Cultures, Histories, Religions, and Texts.* Cambridge: Cambridge University Press, 1982.

Burnett, Mark Thornton. *Constructing 'Monsters' in Shakespearean Drama and Early Modern Culture.* New York: Palgrave, 2002.

Cohen, Jeffrey Jerome. "Monster Culture (Seven Theses)." In *Monster Theory, Reading Culture.* Edited by Jeffrey Jerome Cohen, 3–25. Minneapolis: University of Minnesota Press, 1996. 3–25.

Coote, Stephen. *A Play of Passion: The Life of Sir Walter Ralegh.* London: MacMillan, 1993.

Corrin, Jay P. "Revising the Black Legend." *Chesterton Review: The Journal of the Chesterton Society* 2 (1976): 158–83.

Fernandez-Retamar, Roberto, and John Beverley. "Against the Black Legend." *Ideologies and Literature: A Journal of Hispanic and Luso-Brazilian Studies* 2, no. 10 (1979): 16–35.

Forse, J. H. "How 'Black' was the 'Black Legend' in Elizabethan England?" *Shakespeare and Renaissance Association of West Virginia Selected Papers* 25 (2002): 13–33.

Freud, Sigmund. "A Mythological Parallel to a Visual Obsession." In *Character and Culture.* Translated by C. M. J. Hubback, 152–54. New York: Collier Books, 1963.

Friel, Arthur O. *The River of Seven Stars.* New York: Harper and Brothers, 1924.

Fuller, Mary C. "Ralegh's Fugitive Gold: Reference and Deferral in *The Discovery of Guiana.*" In *New World Encounters.* Edited by Stephen Greenblatt, 218–40. Berkeley and Los Angeles: University of California Press, 1993.

Gillies, John. *Shakespeare and the Geography of Difference.* Cambridge: Cambridge University Press, 1994.

Greenblatt, Stephen J. *Marvelous Possessions: The Wonder of the New World.* Chicago: University of Chicago Press, 1991.

———. *Sir Walter Ralegh: The Renaissance Man and His Roles.* New Haven, CT: Yale University Press, 1973.

Harris, Jonathan Gil. *Foreign Bodies and the Body Politic: Discourses of Social Pathology in Early Modern England.* Cambridge: Cambridge University Press, 1998.

Herodotus. *The Persian Wars.* In *The Greek Historians: Herodotus, Thucydides, Xenophon, and Arrian.* Vol. 1. Translated by George Rawlinson, 3–566. New York: Random House, 1942.

Hill, Christopher. "The Many-Headed Monster." In *Change and Continuity in Seventeenth-Century England,* 181–203. Cambridge, MA: Harvard University Press, 1975.

Hobbes, Thomas. *Leviathan.* Harmondsworth, UK: Penguin, 1968.

Kemys, Lawrence. *A Relation of the Second Voyage to Guiana.* London: Thomas Dawson, 1596.

Kidd, Colin. *British Identities before Nationalism: Ethnicity and Nationhood in the Atlantic World, 1600–1800.* Cambridge: Cambridge University Press, 1999.

Knox, John. *The First Blast of the Trumpet Against the Monstrous Regiment of Women.* 1558. Edited by Edward Arber. London: English Scholar's Library, 1878.

Langegg, Ferdinand von. *El Dorado.* Austria: Akademische Druck Universität Verlagsanstalt, 1973.

Las Casas, Bartolome de. *A Short Account of the Destruction of the Indies.* Translated by Nigel Griffin. New York: Penguin, 1992.

Lim, Walter S. H. *The Arts of Empire: The Poetics of Colonialism from Ralegh to Milton.* Newark: University of Delaware Press, 1998.

Linebaugh, Peter, and Marcus Rediker. *The Many-Headed Hydra: Sailors, Slaves, Commoners, and the Hidden History of the Revolutionary Atlantic.* Boston: Beacon Press, 2000.

Lorimer, Joyce. *English and Irish Settlement on the River Amazon.* London: Hakluyt Society, 1989.

Maltby, William. *The Black Legend in England: The Development of Anti-Spanish Sentiment.* Durham, NC: Duke University Press, 1971.

Mandeville, Sir John. *The Voiage and Travaile of Sir John Maundeville which Treateth the Way to Hierusalem; and Other Marvayles of Inde, with Other Ilands and Countryes.* 1725. Reprint, London: J. Davy Printers, 1866.

Nicholl, Charles. *The Creature in the Map: A Journey to El Dorado.* New York: Morrow, 1996.

Oldenburg, Scott. "The Riddle of Blackness in England's National Family Romance." *The Journal for Early Modern Cultural Studies* no. 1, 1 (2001): 46–62.

Pagden, Anthony. *European Encounters in the New World: From Renaissance to Romanticism.* New Haven, CT: Yale University Press, 1993.

Pliny. *Natural History.* Vol. 2. Translated by H. Rackham. Cambridge, MA: Harvard University Press, 1942.

Quint, David. *Epic and Empire: Politics and Generic Form from Virgil to Milton.* Princeton, NJ: Princeton University Press, 1993.

Ralegh, Sir Walter. *The Discovery of Guiana.* In *The Works of Sir Walter Ralegh, Kt.* Vol. 8, 391–478. New York, 1829.

———. *Maxims of State.* In *The Works of Sir Walter Ralegh, Kt.* Vol. 8, 1–36. New York: Burt Franklin, 1829.

Schomburgck, Robert H. Introduction. In *The Discovery of the Large, Rich, and Beautiful Empire of Guiana with a Relation of the Great and Golden City of Manoa (Which the Spaniards Call El Dorado) Etc. Performed in the year 1595. By Sir Walter Ralegh.* New York: Burt Franklin, 1970.

Shakespeare, William. *The Norton Shakespeare.* Edited by Stephen Greenblatt, Walter Cohn, Jean E. Howard, and Katharine Eisman Maus. New York: W. W. Norton, 1997.

Trevelyan, Raleigh. *Sir Walter Raleigh.* London: Penguin, 2002.

Whitehead, Neil. "The Discoverie as Ethnological Text." In *The Discoverie of the Large, Rich, and Bewtiful Empyre of Guiana. by Sir Walter Ralegh.* Edited by Neil Whitehead. Manchester, UK: Manchester University Press, 1995.

Slavery, Sex, and the Seraglio:
"Turkish" Women and Early Modern Texts

Bindu Malieckal

IN 1717, AFTER SEVERAL WEEKS OF TRAVEL WITHIN THE OTTOMAN EMPIRE, Lady Mary Wortley Montagu reached Adrianople and wrote to her sister, Lady Mar, about the women she observed in a Turkish bath. While Montagu describes the ladies' beautiful appearance and the comforting milieu of the *hamam,* she also comments on the women's sovereignty: "Upon the whole, I look upon the Turkish women as the only free people in the empire. The very Divan pays respect to 'em; and the Grand Signior himself, when a pasha is executed, never violates the privileges of the harem (or women's apartment), which remains unsearched entire to the widow."[1] Montagu's assertion that Turkish women are the "only free people in the empire"—perhaps more so than their female counterparts in England—implies that the women possessed political influence, social equality, and domestic agency, privileges overlooked by previous male authors whom Montagu calls "our voyage writers."[2] Those travelers, Billie Melman clarifies in *Women's Orients: English Women and the Middle East, 1718–1918,* portray the harem, or seraglio, as the "*locus* of an exotic and abnormal sexuality."[3] Thus, a certain body of critics have heralded Montagu's commentary as her appreciation of female space and a validation of gender parity in the Ottoman Empire. Cynthia Lowenthal's influential assessment is typical of this trend: "Lady Mary is pleased to see high-ranking Turkish women living a life of ease which would be the envy of many of her countrywomen, not locked away in the drudgery of a slavery that their husbands impose on them."[4]

Montagu, however, does not address the fact that many "Turkish" women and almost all the inhabitants of the Ottoman Sultan's seraglio were slaves and that these odalisques endured certain restrictions because of their status. The term "Turkish" has been placed in quotation marks because slave women of the Ottoman harem were not ethnic Turks but Europeans, Central Asians, and Africans. Such was the case especially in the seraglios from Sultan Mehmed II (1444–46, 1451–81) to the last Ottoman, Sultan Mehmed VI (1918–22). Even so, Leslie P. Peirce, in her outstanding work, *The Im-*

perial Harem: Women and Sovereignty in the Ottoman Empire, argues that favorites of the Sultan held power unacknowledged by Western and even contemporary Turkish scholars, like Ahmed Refik, who first used the uncomplimentary phrase "the Sultanate of Women" to describe the favorites' authority.[5] Many slave women felt honored to be included in the royal harem, a place where they could learn to read, write, entertain, gain wealth, and from where, as Carla Coco points out in *Secrets of the Harem,* they could be manumitted in nine years and marry well.[6] By all accounts, the seraglio was an elite institution for "Turkish" women, but despite the "opportunities" it provided, more than a few would not have chosen slavery as a profession. Slave women could not abandon the harem and could not choose whom to love. As Ehud Toledano posits in *Slavery and Abolition in the Ottoman Middle East,* "While we should note the privileged position of *kuls* [military slaves] and *harem* women, we must not overlook the unhappy side of their lives,"[7] specifically the "involuntary" nature of their presence and activity in the seraglio.[8]

Travel narratives, letters, and plays from England and Europe in the sixteenth and early seventeenth centuries depict "Turkish" slave women as both "white" European and Asian women, and "black" African women, of the Ottoman seraglio.[9] Early modern documents show the seraglio to be a shadowy realm: an "oriental" and alluring institution as well as an enclosure where women were confined to slavery. Yet, for early moderns, the presence of "white" European women in the harem diminishes some of the seraglio's mystery, for the slaves were foreigners in Turkey and therefore "familiars," if not "family." When "Turkish" women whom the Sultan preferred gained political clout and promoted trade with the West, the women were seen as insiders and allies. Similarly, while "Turkish" women of early modern drama often tempt Venetian, Maltese, and English men to "turn Turk," some "Turkish" women are portrayed positively when they convert to Christianity and immigrate to the continent. "Turkish" women do not always fit nicely into racial or religious dichotomies, the reason why they might be the least examined of all such "others" in early modern literary criticism, which has inspected conflicts between "white" Christians, Turkish and Moorish men, and "black" women.[10] In summary, "Turkish" women in early modern texts present a combination of contradictory characteristics: they are slaves and queens; Christians and Muslims; European, African, and Ottoman; defeated yet decisive.

THE TRAFFIC IN "TURKISH" WOMEN

From the reign of Mehmed II onward—Mehmed II conquered Constantinople in 1453—aristocratic marriages for Ottoman heirs were discouraged so that the political complications of showing favoritism toward any foreign or domestic power could be avoided.[11] Other Islamic empires, such as the Mughals of India and the Safavids of Persia, possessed slave women or concubines in their seraglios, but the Mughals and Safavids continued to broker conjugal alliances, unlike Ottoman royalty. Mehmed's directive ensured that only slave women would inhabit the harem, a practice followed by his successors. Since fellow Muslims could not be enslaved, harem women were usually Christians or pagans acquired from outside Turkey and forced to convert to Islam as they entered the harem (though the conversion did not guarantee freedom). Slave women deemed unworthy to join the Ottoman seraglio were distributed to the harems of lesser Ottoman officials. Mehmed appears to have taken advantage of his own pronouncement. John Freely, in *Inside the Seraglio: Private Lives of the Sultans of Istanbul,* writes that Mehmed's eldest son was Bayezid or Beyazid II, whose mother, Gülbahar, was probably a Greek concubine.[12] Mehmed's decree came into full force only with the accession, in the sixteenth century, of his great grandson, Süleyman I. André Clot, author of *Suleiman the Magnificent,* notes that Süleyman's harem consisted solely of slave women, mostly Tartars, Georgians, Circassians, Serbs, Italians, and Greeks.[13]

While it is unlikely that male travel writers from the sixteenth and seventeenth centuries directly interacted with Ottoman women, the men's narratives possess some accuracy with regard to the harem's population. Nicolas de Nicolay, royal geographer to King Henry II of France, was part of an official embassy to Istanbul in 1551. In his travelogue, *The Nauigations Into Turkie* (translated into English by T. Washington in 1585), de Nicolay writes that harem women are not of Islamic origin and are slaves: "Being the most part daughters of Christians, some beyng taken by courses on the seas or by land, aswel from Grecians, Hongarians, Wallachers, Mingreles, Italians as other christian nations, some of the other are bought of merchants, and after wardes by Beglierbeis, Baschas and Captaines presented vnto the great Turke."[14] Ottaviano Bon was the Venetian *bailo* to Istanbul between 1604 and 1607. In *The Sultan's Seraglio: An Intimate Portrait of Life at the Ottoman Court* (published in English in 1625), Bon provides a similar picture of the harem's ethnic and religious compositions and mentions that non-Turkish courtesans are trained in household arts and entertainment skills: "Now, those which are kept up for their beauties, are all young virgins taken and stolen from foreign nations, who after they have been instructed in good behavior, and can play upon instruments, sing, dance, and sew curiously; they are given to the *Grand Seignor,* as presents of great value: and the number of these increaseth daily, as they are sent and presented by the *Tartars,* by the *Bashaws,* and other great men, to the King and Queen."[15]

Both de Nicolay and Bon provide a few details about the daily activities of slave women. According to de Nicolay, the Sultan "keepeth them within this Sarail, wel apparrelled, nourished & entertained vnder streight keeping of the Eunuches, and euery ten of them haue a Matrone, too instruct, gouerne, and teach them too woorke all sorts of needle woorkes."[16] Bon names the "Matrone" or overseer, "*Kahiyah Cadun,* that is, as we say, the mother of maids,"[17] and of a concubine's education, reports, "There are other places likewise for them, where they go to school, to learn to speak and read, if they will, the *Turkish* tongue, and to sew also, and to play on divers instruments: and so they spend the day with their mistresses, who are all ancient women; some hours, notwithstanding, being allowed them for their recreation, to walk in their gardens, and use such sports as they familiarly exercise themselves withall."[18] In addition to learning Turkish language and manners, slave women were required to convert to Islam. The process of the women's conversion, Bon indicates, is quite simple: "These virgins, immediately after their coming into the *Seraglio,* are made *Turks:* which is done by using this ceremony only; to hold up their forefinger, and say these words; *law illawheh illaw Allawh, Muhammed resoul Allawh. That is, there is no God but God alone, and *Mahomet* is the messenger of God."[19] Regarding the Sultan's selection of women to have sex with, the "Kahiyah Cadun" diligently prepares the chosen slave, "attiring, painting, and perfuming her,"[20] and afterward, the Sultan pays the woman with money and gifts.[21] Despite his depiction of the Ottoman seraglio as a strict and controlled environment, Bon asserts that concubines are waited upon by other slaves (usually African women, as I will elaborate later) and that they live in relative comfort and leisure: "nor do they want any thing whatsoever, that is necessary for them."[22]

Like de Nicolay and Bon, many English and Europeans reported on "Turkish" women and/or the Ottoman harem—travelers and diplomats such as Michel Baudier, Ogier Ghiselin de Busbecq, Hans Dernschwam, Paul Rycaut, and others.[23] The accounts are analyses aimed at showing the "mysterious and foreign" nature of the seraglio, as well as impassioned criticisms of the practice, especially since the harem's inhabitants, in the words of both de Nicolay and Bon, had been kidnapped, or "taken," from Christian nations. The narratives implicitly indict Turks for the crime of theft, and in the transformation of Christian women to "Turkish" slaves, the suggestion is made that religious, ethnic, and national identities were also "taken" away and subverted.[24] According to early modern travel writers, "Turkish" women move from being "subjects" in their homelands to "objects" in the seraglio. Thus, "Turkish" slave women were "baptised" with "suggestive" new names such as Safiye (Pleasing One), Perestu (Little Swallow), and Gülbahar (Rose of Spring),[25] all indicative of their standing as commodities worth only as much as they might appeal to the Sultan's attention and desire.

Another factor to take into consideration when assessing the commodification of "Turkish" women for the Sultan's pleasure—a factor implied in early modern travel narratives—is that the seraglio's concubines were required to be "white." Early modern English texts and critical studies on those texts usually describe "whiteness" as a feature of Anglo-Saxon authors or "fair" characters in conflict with "black" Africans.[26] In John Fletcher's *The Knight of Malta* (1618), for example, the "white" Oriana is pitted against the "black" Zanthia, who in turn is the antithesis to Miranda, the virginal knight of Malta.[27] The black woman's skin is contrasted with the white woman's body and a white man's spiritual and physical "purity" to depict "whiteness," which is defined not by what it is but what it isn't. "Whiteness," then, for the Ottomans, was the nonappearance of a black complexion and a requirement for true "Turkish" identity. From the perspective of the expansive Ottoman Empire, however, "whiteness" was not limited to Western Europeans but was possessed by all Europeans, from Albanians to Russians, and even Eurasians, including Ukrainian, Turkic, Tartar, Circassian, and Georgian peoples, though "girls" with "blue eyes" and "blond hair" seem to have been preferred.[28] Since Ottomans equated "whiteness" with beauty, "white" female slaves were sought after for the seraglio. In *Race and Slavery in the Middle East,* Bernard Lewis writes that Ottoman harems were supplied with "white" women by the Tartar Khanate of Crimea, whose raiders regularly seized "white" women from all over Europe and Asia.[29] Halil Inalcik and Donald Quataert state in *An Economic and Social History of the Ottoman Empire* that these women were sent, via the Black Sea, to slave markets in Istanbul and other Ottoman cities.[30] One source informs that at times, families in Circassia, Georgia, and other parts of the Caucasus sold their daughters to Ottoman slave traders.[31] "White" slave women were also acquired through corsair raids along the coasts of Greece, Italy, Spain, and even up to Iceland.[32] Once at the slave market, "white" women commanded high prices (but not as high as eunuchs, who were rarer) and entered the harems of the wealthy, for only the rich could afford to purchase them.[33]

In addition to "white" women, slave markets of the Ottoman Empire carried African women, who were sold for either concubinage or labor. Murray Gordon, in *Slavery in the Arab World,* finds that African slave women came from Egypt, Sudan, Ethiopia, and Somalia.[34] Joseph Harris points out in *The African Presence in Asia: Consequences of the East African Slave Trade* that with the onset of European colonization in the Maghrib, which slowed the slave trade, African women were gathered from as far south as Kenya and Tanzania.[35] Throughout the Islamic world, Ethiopian and other slave women from the Horn of Africa became the concubines of men who could not afford to buy a "white" woman, who cost three times as much as an Ethiopian.[36] Though not "white," Ethiopian women were considered the "'second best'" option because their facial features and skin tone were seen as somewhere between "white" and "black" and therefore marginally acceptable.[37] In *Islam's Black Slaves: The Other Black Diaspora,* Ronald Segal records that "black" women from sub-Saharan Africa, such as the Sudanese (the least expensive of slaves), were present as menials in almost every Ottoman household, rich or otherwise.[38] Some were used as sexual partners and had children with their owners, but sources give no indication that any African woman, whether Ethiopian or Sudanese, was a concubine in the Ottoman imperial harem; rather, these "Turkish" women functioned purely as waiting women, slaves of slaves.[39]

CONCUBINES AND QUEENS

Although English and European travel writers were aware of the enslavement of "Turkish" women, they also knew that some Ottoman women held great power. William Biddulph, in *The Travels of Certain Englishmen into Africa, Asia and to the Blacke Sea* (1609), praises the freedoms enjoyed by the Sultan's sisters and female relatives, who were not considered slaves, in spite of being born to slave mothers. Biddulph states, "the daughters and the sisters of the great Turke are more free than all other men and women."[40] Similarly, Bon clarifies, "The King's daughters, sisters, and aunts, have their lodgings also in the same *Seraglio;* being royally served, and very sumptuously appareled, and live together by themselves, in continual pleasures; until such time as, at their request, the King shall be pleased to give them in marriage."[41] Despite Biddulph's and Bon's assertions, the seraglio's most powerful were the Sultan's chosen slaves, who would advise the Sultan on political and personal matters, acquire wealth, and advance the fortunes of their offspring. Certain events could elevate a concubine to an elite position: if she became the Sultan's favorite (*haseki*); if she married the Sultan, whereby she would be known as the Sultan's wife (*kadén*); if she was appointed Queen Mother and thereby head of the harem (*valide sultan*).[42] Bon declares that women who give birth to the Sultan's sons are celebrated, rewarded, and permitted a degree of independence: "The King likewise alloweth her a large revenue, that she may give away, and spend at her pleasure, in whatsoever she may have occasion; and all they of the *Seraglio* must, and do acknowledge her for Queen, shewing all the duty and respect that may be, both to herself, and to them that belong unto her."[43] One should remember that such supremacy was accorded only to a privileged few. In the sixteenth and seventeenth centuries, hundreds of women were present in the Ottoman imperial seraglio (both the Old Palace and the New Palace): in total, 122 women in 1575; 250 women in 1581–82; 583 women in 1600–1601; 610 women in 1603–4; and 705 women in 1622.[44] Since favoritism and reproductive politics were intertwined, Peirce writes, "Sex in the imperial harem was necessarily surrounded with rules, and the structure of the harem was aimed in part at shaping, and thus controlling, the outcome of the sultan's sexual activity"—the percentage of slave women who rose to be powerful (as favorites) or free (through marriage) was minimal.[45]

Three Ottoman Sultans who ruled between 1520 and 1603, Sultans Süleyman I (1520–66), Selim II (1566–74), and Murad III (1574–95), each had a beloved "Turkish" slave. Süleyman's *haseki* was Hurrem, popularly known in the West as Roxelana. Hurrem was born Alexandra Lisowska in Poland. She was kidnapped by Tartars and later given to Süleyman by Ibrahim, the Grand Vizier.[46] Hurrem soon supplanted Süleyman's previous favorite, Mahidevran, mother of his oldest son, Mustafa, and, in 1534, she married Süleyman.[47] After a fire destroyed part of the Old Palace, Hurrem and her retinue moved to Topkapi Palace, and as Andrew Wheatcroft notes in *The Ottomans,* "the character of the palace was altered irrevocably."[48] While Wheatcroft refers to the shift in power from the chief white eunuch to the chief black eunuch, the transfer of the harem from the Old Palace to Topkapi allowed Hurrem to participate in political intrigues, such as the assassinations of Mustafa and Ibrahim.

After Hurrem's death in 1558 and Süleyman's in 1560, one of their sons, Selim II, was crowned Sultan, and he favored Nur Banu, the mother of the future Murad III. Nur Banu's origins seem to be in dispute. According to one source, Nur Banu was really Kalè Kartánou, a Cypriot.[49] The more accepted perspective is that she was born, in 1525, as Cecelia Vernier-Baffo, the illegitimate daughter of Nicolo Vernier, Lord of Paros, and Violante Baffo, a Venetian noblewoman, and at the age of twelve was kidnapped from Paros by Barbarossa, who presented her to Selim.[50] Nur Banu became Selim's "legal wife" in 1571,[51] but it was during the reign of Murad III, beginning in 1574 and as *valide sultan* that Nur Banu became all-powerful. Nur Banu corresponded with Catherine de' Medici,[52] promoted good relations with Venice, Persia, and the Hapsburgs,[53] and single-handedly prevented an Ottoman invasion of Crete, a Venetian colony.[54] Nur Banu might have been murdered by Safiye, her own son's concubine.[55] Susan Skilliter believes that Safiye was from the Balkans and that in 1563, at thirteen years of age, entered Murad III's harem.[56] Four years later, she gave birth to a son, the future Sultan Mehmed III (1595–1603). Safiye functioned as intercessor for the Venetian ambassador appointed to Istanbul,[57] but she had a particular interest in England's Elizabeth I (1558–1603), to whom she sent two letters, in 1593 and 1599. In the first letter, Safiye offers to advance Elizabeth and English interests before Murad: "I can repeatedly mention Her Highness's gentility and praise at the footdust of His Majesty, the fortunate and felicitous Padishah, the Lord of the fortunate conjunction and the sovereign who has Alexander's place, and I shall endeavor for Her aims."[58] By the time Safiye sent her second letter, Mehmed III had been crowned Sultan, and Safiye was *valide sultan*. She responds to a note that Elizabeth sent to Mehmed requesting assistance to obtain freedom for English slaves in North Africa, a Turkish regency. Safiye thanks Elizabeth for bringing to her attention the plight of the English slaves: "Your letter has arrived and reached (us); whatsoever you said became known to us. God willing, action will be taken according to what you said."[59] She promises to remind Mehmed not to enslave English citizens: "We do not cease from admonishing our son, His Majesty the Padishah, and from telling him: 'Do act according to the treaty!' Be of good heart in this respect!"[60]

Safiye's letter of 1593 became famous because Richard Hakluyt published it in his *Principall Navigations* (1598), and the second letter must have received attention as well.[61] The news of Safiye's correspondence would have aroused curiosity about the enigmatic Ottoman queen, but some might have recalled that Safiye, like her predecessors Nur Banu and Hurrem, were in fact "Turkish" women of Christian and European origins. Safiye's missives reveal that she saw Elizabeth as a friend and ally—a fascinating connection that Bernadette Andrea skillfully explores in her forthcoming book[62]—yet Safiye was completely loyal to the Ottoman Empire. Likewise, Nur Banu and Hurrem had a vested interest in the business affairs of European officials in Istanbul, but they never undermined Turkey. They worked hard to maintain good relations between Ottomans and others. Safiye, Nur Banu, and Hurrem had more than a passing interest in the West, but it is important to remember that they were first and foremost Ottoman agents. As Muslim royalty not by birth but through coercion, their rise and empowerment reflect the successful appropriation of Ottoman identity, so much so that Safiye, Nur Banu, and Hurrem should be seen as truly "Turkish," and given their unique, elevated status, they are, to borrow Montagu's words, literally "the *only* free people in the empire" (italics mine).

Additionally, Ottoman harem women with financial resources funded numerous institutions in Istanbul. Yvonne J. Seng reveals that in 1543, Süleyman's manumitted slave, Gülfem, established the financial groundwork to build a "timber-frame mosque" in "downtown" Istanbul.[63] In 1557, in Istanbul, Süleyman's daughter, Mihramah, financed an expansive complex consisting of a mosque, bath, school, library, and soup kitchen; another member of the imperial harem, a *valide sultan*, Büyük, funded a food bank for lepers.[64] Thus, some women transcended their status as slaves to participate in the domestic scene and in the international arena and afford another angle from which to consider "Turkish" women in the early modern period.

"These Turkish Dames . . . if lust once fire their blood . . . enjoy their wanton ends"

Besides commenting on the lives of "Turkish" women in the Ottoman seraglio, early modern writers express physical appreciation of the slaves. In *Description of the Turkish Empire* (1615), George Sandys gushes, "They be women of elegant beauties, for the most part ruddy, clear, and smooth as polished ivory."[65] Thomas Dallam provides another complementary perspective. In 1599, Dallam installed an organ for Mehmed III and wrote of his experiences in *The Diary of Thomas Dallam*. Mehmed was so pleased with Dallam and the organ, a present from Elizabeth I, that he wanted Dallam to remain in Turkey. Mehmed made Dallam an offer that Dallam did indeed refuse: "Than they toulde me that yf I would staye the Grand Sinyor would give tow wyfes, either tow of his Concubines or els tow virgins of the beste I Could Chuse my selfe, in Cittie or contrie."[66] About a month later, Dallam was invited to court and given a tour of some of the Sultan's private chambers. He saw the sword of Osman and caught a glimpse of about thirty harem women. At first, Dallam thinks that the concubines are men, but he soon figures out, from their hair and clothes, that they are women, and extols "verie prettie ones in deede."[67] Dallam stares at the women for so long that he angers his guide. Forced to avert his gaze, Dallam says sadly, "the which I was very lothe to dow, for that sighte did please me wondrous well."[68]

Sandys's and Dallam's fascination parallels Christian characters' attraction for "Turkish" women in early modern drama. John Fletcher's *The Knight of Malta* (1616), Phillip Massinger's *The Renegado,* and William Daborne's *A Christian Turned Turk* (1612) all contain a beautiful "Turkish" woman who either inadvertently or willfully persuades Christian men to apostatize.[69] In *The Knight of Malta,* the "white" Luscinda (3.4)—whose Latinized name might indicate that she is "Turkish"—has been captured by the Knights of Malta and is a modest woman with a propensity for Christianity; however, her mere presence almost causes Miranda, an Italian knight, to break his vow of chastity. Miranda refers to Luscinda and to Islam implicitly as "tempting" (3.3). In *The Renegado* (1624), Vitelli, a Venetian, is warned about "Turkish" women:

> You are young
> And may be tempted, and these Turkish dames
> (Like English mastiffs that increase their fierceness
> By being chained up), from the restraint of freedom,
> If lust once fire their blood from a fair object,
> Will run a course the fiends themselves would shake at
> To enjoy their wanton ends.
>
> (1.3.7–13).

He describes Donusa, the "fair" (1.1.99) Ottoman princess, as "this second siren" (3.5.22) and has sex with her but rejects her invitation to convert to Islam. In *A Christian Turned Turk,* John Ward, an English pirate, calls the "Turkish" Voada, who is also "fair" (7.149), a "sorceress" (11.32) and comments on her allure:

> Here comes an argument that would persuade
> A god turn mortal. Until I saw her face,
> I never knew what men term beauty was.
>
> (7.90–92)

Voada tells Ward that if he wants to marry her, he must "turn Turk—I am yours" (7.127). Ward heeds Voada's recommendation.

The image of "Turkish" women presented in early modern drama corresponds to Irvin Cemil Schick's argument, regarding Western literature's consistent "eroticization" of Turkish women and their designation "as key markers of place, and hence as determinants of identity and alterity."[70] In other words, the sexualization of "Turkish" women and by extension the harem in early modern drama is a "territorialization" of the "Orient"— English and European authors' efforts to define the parameters of their own self and space.[71] Schick's argument applies to Luscinda, Donusa, and Voada because the degree of each character's sexuality determines the spiritual integrity of her corresponding Christian admirer. Luscinda's passive sensuality matches Miranda's; therefore, Miranda can resist Luscinda and adhere to his vow of chastity. Donusa's and Voada's aggressive pursuit, however, parallels respectively Vitelli's and Ward's strong inclination to adopt Islam: Ward converts, but Vitelli escapes to Venice with Donusa, who embraces Christianity. In a ground-breaking article, Patricia Parker discovers that early modern treatises, narratives, and fiction "routinely linked" the Turk, "turning Turk," and witchcraft, which explains why terms like "siren" and "sorceress" are used to describe "Turkish" women in *A Christian Turned Turk* and *The Renegado;*[72] however, Parker brilliantly proves that "turning Turk" was also conflated with a series of perceived "preposterous" activities that Turks were accused of, such as sodomy.[73] Likewise, in early modern drama, the renegade and "Turkish" woman are sometimes conflated: "Turkish" women's beauty or "whiteness" and marginality (compared to Turkish men) exemplify the Christian renegade. Ward finds that his conversion has disenfranchised, emasculated,[74] and even feminized him, so that rather than permanently transforming into the "raging Turk," he experiences regression and reversal so that he mirrors the object of his affection, the "Turkish" woman.

Alternately, early modern drama presents a "Turkish" woman who is not defined by sexuality and conversion but rather by her affiliations to enslavement and loss: Zabina, Bajazeth's Queen in Christopher Marlowe's *Tamburlaine, Part I* (1588).[75] After Tamburlaine defeats Bajazeth, Zabina is reduced to slavery: she becomes the slave of Anippe, maid of Zenocrate, herself Tamburlaine's concubine. The real Bayezid I (1389–1403) was married to Maria, a Serbian, the only spouse of the Sultan mentioned in Ottoman chronicles.[76] Marlowe conflates Maria with the "Turkish" women of the Ottoman seraglio to create Zabina, who bemoans her loss of sovereignty and blames the Prophet and Islam for her suffering:

> Then is there left no Mahomet, no God,
> No fiend, no Fortune, nor no hope of end
> To our infamous, monstrous slaveries?

(5.1.239–41)

However, like her historical counterparts Hurrem, Nur Banu, and Safiye, Zabina is also a woman with authority and honor. Thus, while Luscinda, Donusa, and Voada function primarily as foils to Christian characters and are the exaggerated products of playwrights' impressions of "Turkish" women, Zabina is an independent character who can be evaluated on her own merits and who elicits the kind of sympathy and admiration that early moderns would have felt for the "Turkish" women of the seraglio, whether concubines or queens.

CONCLUSION

"Turkish" women in early modern texts play a variety of roles: they are mistresses, mothers, mediators, and missionaries. They might be merchandise or merchants and elicit either sympathy or submission. Nabil Matar, in *Turks, Moors and Englishmen in the Age of Discovery,* and Daniel Vitkus, in an article, indicate that early moderns regarded the Ottoman Empire and Turkish men with terror.[77] The frightening reputation did not fully transfer to "Turkish" women. Matar offers one explanation: he conjectures that English and European authors "credit the military power of Muslims to their ascendancy over their women."[78] However, as early modern texts reveal, "Turkish" women are from differing religious and ethnic backgrounds and possess varying degrees of power or subjugation. They impart both the multiplicity within and hegemony of the Ottoman Empire and are therefore a truer representation of "the Turk" and perhaps even "the Muslim" in the sixteenth and seventeenth centuries. The "diversity" that one finds among "Turkish" women then corresponds to a compelling argument made by Jonathan Burton in a valuable essay. Burton contends that the "reciprocative commerce" between England and the Ottoman Empire shows that "westerners" did not simply consider Turks as "immovable stereotypes" but as part of "a rather elastic set of representations."[79] Such is true for depictions of "Turkish" women as well. Ottoman connections to slavery, sex, and the seraglio instigate authors to portray "Turkish" women as victims of "mysterious and foreign" institutions, which render the women as "other," but "Turkish" women are also seen as recognizable and known individuals with real intentions. Thus, collectively, "Turkish" women in early modern texts are surprisingly complex and complicated, and merit further study.

NOTES

I thank Bernadette Andrea for her comments on the final draft of this essay, and I thank Christian Bednar, my research assistant, for his help. As always, I am indebted to the Research Center at the New Hampshire Institute of Politics for providing a wonderful space to work.

1. Mary Wortley Montagu, *The Turkish Embassy Letters*. Edited by Malcolm Jack (London: Virago, 2000), 72.

2. Ibid.

3. Billie Melman, *Women's Orients: English Women and the Middle East, 1718–1918* (Ann Arbor, MI: University of Michigan Press, 1992), 60.

4. Cynthia Lowenthal, "The Veil of Romance: Lady Mary's Embassy Letters," *Eighteenth-Century Life* 14, no. 1 (1990): 69. I am grateful to Bernadette Andrea for informing me of other scholars whose readings "complicate" Lowenthal's approach, such as Joseph W. Lew, "Lady Mary's Portable Seraglio," *Eighteenth-Century Studies* 24, no. 4 (1991): 432–50; Bridget Orr, "'The Only Free People in the Empire': Gender Difference in Colonial Discourse," in *De-Scribing Empire: Post-Colonialism and Textuality,* ed. Chris Tiffin and Alan Lawson, 152–68 (London: Routledge, 1994); Mary Jo Kietzman, "Montagu's Turkish Embassy Letters and Cultural Dislocation," *SEL* 38 (1998): 537–51; Teresa Heffernan, "Feminism Against the East/West Divide: Lady Mary's Turkish Embassy Letters," *Eighteenth-Century Studies* 33, no. 2 (2000): 201–15.

5. Leslie P. Peirce, *The Imperial Harem: Women and Sovereignty in the Ottoman Empire* (New York: Oxford University Press, 1993), 289 n. 4.

6. Carla Coco, *Secrets of the Harem* (New York: Vendome, 1997), 72; Peirce, *The Imperial Harem,* 31.

7. Ehud R. Toledano, *Slavery and Abolition in the Ottoman Middle East* (Seattle: University of Washington Press, 1998), 54.

8. Ibid., 4.

9. This article's focus concerns mostly "Western" observations and conclusions about "Turkish" women, which tell only one side of the story. Another essay on the voices of "Turkish" women themselves needs to be written.

10. See Bindu Malieckal, "'Hell's Perfect Character': The Black Woman as The Islamic Other in Fletcher's *The Knight of Malta,*" *Essays in Arts and Sciences* 28 (1999): 53–68.

11. Coco, *Secrets of the Harem,* 156.

12. John Freely, *Inside the Seraglio: Private Lives of the Sultans of Istanbul* (New York: Penguin, 2000), 9.

13. André Clot, *Suleiman the Magnificent* (New York: New Amsterdam, 1992), 216. See also Coco, *Secrets of the Harem,* 63.

14. Nicolas de Nicolay, *The Nauigations Into Turkie* (Amsterdam: Da Capo, 1968), 53.

15. Ottaviano Bon, *The Sultan's Seraglio: An Intimate Portrait of Life at the Ottoman Court.* Edited by Godfrey Goodwin (London: Saqi, 1996), 46.

16. de Nicolay, *The Nauigations Into Turkie,* 53.

17. Bon, *The Sultan's Seraglio,* 47.

18. Ibid.

19. Ibid., 46.

20. Ibid., 48.

21. Ibid., 49.

22. Ibid., 47.

23. For a complete list of European commentators, see Peirce, *The Imperial Harem,* 349–50; N. M. Penzer, *The Harem* (London: Spring Books, 1965), 27–52.

24. For more on the Ottomans, colonization, theft, and identity, see Bindu Malieckal, "'Bondslaves and Pagans Shall Our Statesmen Be': Moors, Turks, and Venetians in *Othello,*" *Shakespeare Yearbook* 10 (1999): 162–89.

25. Coco, *Secrets of the Harem,* 66.

26. See Peter Erickson, "Representations of Blacks and Blackness in the Renaissance," *Criticism* 35 (1993): 499–528; Kim F. Hall, "Beauty and the Beast of Whiteness: Teaching Race and Gender," *Shakespeare Quarterly* 47, no. 4 (1996): 461–75.

27. Malieckal, "'Hell's Perfect Character,'" 59.

28. Toledano, *Slavery and Abolition,* 36.

29. Bernard Lewis, *Race and Slavery in the Middle East* (Oxford: Oxford University Press, 1990), 12, 72. See also Goodwin, *The Sultan's Seraglio,* 148 n. 4.

30. Halil Inalcik and Donald Quataert, eds., *An Economic and Social History of the Ottoman Empire* (Cambridge: Cambridge University Press, 1994), 597. See also Lewis, *Race and Slavery,* 12.

31. Bon, *The Sultan's Seraglio,* 148 n.3.

32. Lewis, *Race and Slavery,* 13.

33. Ibid., 90.

34. Murray Gordon, *Slavery in the Arab World* (New York: New Amsterdam, 1989), 80.

35. Joseph Harris, *The African Presence in Asia: Consequences of the East African Slave Trade* (Evanston, IL: Northwestern University Press, 1971), 7.

36. Gordon, *Slavery in the Arab World,* 82.

37. Ibid.

38. Ronald Segal, *Islam's Black Slaves: The Other Black Diaspora* (New York: Farrar, Straus and Giroux, 2001), 115.

39. Lewis, *Race and Slavery,* 90.

40. William Biddulph, *The Travels of Certain Englishmen into Africa, Asia and to the Blacke Sea* (1609; Amsterdam: Da Capo, 1968), 56.

41. Bon, *The Sultan's Seraglio,* 51.

42. Peirce, *The Imperial Harem,* 107–9.

43. Bon, *The Sultan's Seraglio,* 49.

44. Peirce, *The Imperial Harem,* 122.

45. Ibid., 3.

46. Clot, *Suleiman the Magnificent,* 69.

47. Peirce, *The Imperial Harem,* 62.

48. Andrew Wheatcroft, *The Ottomans* (New York: Viking, 1993), 34.

49. Coco, *Secrets of the Harem,* 58.

50. Ibid., 58.

51. Peirce, *The Imperial Harem,* 93.

52. Coco, *Secrets of the Harem,* 58.

53. Ibid., 165.

54. Peirce, *The Imperial Harem,* 223.

55. Clot, *Suleiman the Magnificent,* 216; Coco, *Secrets of the Harem,* 58.

56. Susan Skilliter, "Three Letters from the Ottoman 'Sultana' Safiye to Queen Elizabeth I," in *Documents from Islamic Chanceries, First Series,* ed. S. M. Stern, 144 (Columbia: University of South Carolina Press, 1965).

57. Peirce, *The Imperial Harem,* 223.

58. Skilliter, "Three Letters," 132–33.

59. Ibid., 139.

60. Ibid., 140.

61. Ibid., 119.

62. Bernadette Andrea, *Women and Islam in Early Modern English Literature* (Cambridge: Cambridge University Press, 2007).

63. Yvonne J. Seng, "Invisible Women: Residents of Early Sixteenth-Century Istanbul," in *Women in the Medieval Islamic World: Power, Patronage, and Piety,* ed. Gavin R. G. Hambly, 245 (New York: St. Martin's Press, 1998).

64. Ibid., 245.

65. George Sandys, *Description of the Turkish Empire* (1615; Amsterdam: Da Capo, 1973), 67.

66. J. Theodore Bent, ed., *Early Voyages and Travels in the Levant: I. The Diary of Master Thomas Dallam, 1599–1600. II. Extracts from the Diaries of Dr. John Covel, 1670–1679* (London: Hakluyt Society, 1893), 73.

67. Ibid., 74.

68. Ibid., 75.

69. A. R. Waller, ed., *The Works of Beaumont and Fletcher,* Vol. 7 (Cambridge: Cambridge University Press, 1909); Daniel J. Vitkus, ed., *Three Turk Plays From Early Modern England: Selimus, A Christian Turned Turk, and The Renegado* (New York: Columbia University Press, 2000). All subsequent references to Fletcher's *The Knight of Malta,* Massinger's *The Renegade,* and Daborne's *Turned Turk* will be cited parenthetically in the text.

70. Irvin Cemil Schick, "The Women of Turkey as Sexual Personae: Images From Western Literature," in *Deconstructing Images of "The Turkish Woman,"* ed. Zehra F. Arat, 84 (New York: St. Martin's Press, 1998).

71. Ibid., 85.

72. Patricia Parker, "Preposterous Conversions: Turning Turk and its 'Pauline' Rerighting," *Journal for Early Modern Cultural Studies* 2, no. 1 (2002): 8.

73. Ibid., 9.

74. For an investigation of the connections between apostasy and emasculation, see Bindu Malieckal, "'Wanton Irreligious Madness': Conversion and Castration in Massinger's *The Renegado,*" *Essays in Arts and Sciences* 31 (2002): 25–43.

75. Christopher Marlowe, *Tamburlaine The Great,* eds. J. S. Cunningham and Eithne Henson (Manchester, UK: Manchester University Press, 1998). All subsequent act, scene, and line numbers shall be cited parenthetically in the text.

76. Peirce, *The Imperial Harem,* 32.

77. Nabil Matar, *Turks, Moors, and Englishmen in the Age of Discovery* (New York: Columbia University Press, 1999), 19. See also Daniel J. Vitkus, "Turning Turk in *Othello:* The Conversion and Damnation of the Moor," *Shakespeare Quarterly* 48.2 (1997): 145–76. Vitkus writes that early modern literature produced "demonizing representations of 'the Turk,' not from the perspective of cultural domination but from the fear of being conquered, captured, and converted" (147).

78. See Nabil Matar, "The Representation of Muslim Women in Renaissance England," *The Muslim World* 86, no. 1 (1996): 56.

79. Jonathan Burton, "Anglo-Ottoman Relations and the Image of the Turk in *Tamburlaine*," *Journal of Medieval and Early Modern Studies* 30, no. 1 (2000): 126, 125.

BIBLIOGRAPHY

Andrea, Bernadette. *Women and Islam in Early Modern English Literature.* Cambridge: Cambridge University Press, 2007.

Bent, J. Theodore, ed. *Early Voyages and Travels in the Levant: I. The Diary of Master Thomas Dallam, 1599–1600. II. Extracts from the Diaries of Dr. John Covel, 1670–1679.* London: Hakluyt Society, 1893.

Biddulph, William. *The Travels of Certain Englishmen into Africa, Asia and to the Blacke Sea.* 1609. Amsterdam: Da Capo, 1968.

Bon, Ottaviano. *The Sultan's Seraglio: An Intimate Portrait of Life at the Ottoman Court* (From the Seventeenth-Century Edition of John Withers). Edited by Godfrey Goodwin. London: Saqi, 1996.

Burton, Jonathan. "Anglo-Ottoman Relations and the Image of the Turk in *Tamburlaine*." *Journal of Medieval and Early Modern Studies* 30, no. 1 (2000): 125–56.

Clot, André. *Suleiman the Magnificent.* New York: New Amsterdam, 1992.

Coco, Carla. *Secrets of the Harem.* New York: Vendome, 1997.

de Nicolay, Nicolas. *The Nauigations Into Turkie.* Amsterdam: Da Capo, 1968.

Erickson, Peter. "Representations of Blacks and Blackness in the Renaissance." *Criticism* 35 (1993): 499–528.

Freely, John. *Inside the Seraglio: Private Lives of the Sultans of Istanbul.* New York: Penguin, 2000.

Gordon, Murray. *Slavery in the Arab World.* New York: New Amsterdam, 1989.

Hall, Kim F. "Beauty and the Beast of Whiteness: Teaching Race and Gender." *Shakespeare Quarterly* 47, no. 4 (1996): 461–75.

Harris, Joseph. *The African Presence in Asia: Consequences of the East African Slave Trade.* Evanston, IL: Northwestern University Press, 1971.

Heffernan, Teresa. "Feminism Against the East/West Divide: Lady Mary's Turkish Embassy Letters." *Eighteenth-Century Studies* 33, no. 2 (2000): 201–15.

Inalcik, Halil, and Donald Quataert, eds. *An Economic and Social History of the Ottoman Empire.* Cambridge: Cambridge University Press, 1994.

Kietzman, Mary Jo. "Montagu's Turkish Embassy Letters and Cultural Dislocation." *Studies in English Literature:* 38 (1998): 537–51.

Lew, Joseph W. "Lady Mary's Portable Seraglio." *Eighteenth-Century Studies* 24, no. 4 (1991): 432–50.

Lewis, Bernard. *Race and Slavery in the Middle East.* Oxford: Oxford University Press, 1990.

Lowenthal, Cynthia. "The Veil of Romance: Lady Mary's Embassy Letters." *Eighteenth-Century Life* 14, no. 1 (1990): 66–82.

Malieckal, Bindu. "'Bondslaves and Pagans Shall Our Statesmen Be': Moors, Turks, and Venetians in *Othello*." *Shakespeare Yearbook* 10 (1999): 162–89.

———. "'Hell's Perfect Character': The Black Woman as The Islamic Other in Fletcher's *The Knight of Malta*." *Essays in Arts and Sciences* 28 (1999): 53–68.

―――. "'Wanton Irreligious Madness': Conversion and Castration in Massinger's *The Renegado*." *Essays in Arts and Sciences* 31 (2002): 25–43.

Marlowe, Christopher. *Tamburlaine The Great*. Edited by J. S. Cunningham and Eithne Henson. Manchester, UK: Manchester University Press, 1998.

Matar, Nabil. "The Representation of Muslim Women in Renaissance England." *The Muslim World* 86, no. 1 (1996): 50–61.

―――. *Turks, Moors, and Englishmen in the Age of Discovery*. New York: Columbia University Press, 1999.

Melman, Billie. *Women's Orients: English Women and the Middle East, 1718–1918*. Ann Arbor: University of Michigan Press, 1992.

Montagu, Mary Wortley. *The Turkish Embassy Letters*. Edited by Malcolm Jack. London: Virago, 2000.

Orr, Bridget. "'The Only Free People in the Empire': Gender Difference in Colonial Discourse." In *De-Scribing Empire: Post-Colonialism and Textuality*. Edited by Chris Tiffin and Alan Lawson, 152–68. London: Routledge, 1994.

Parker, Patricia. "Preposterous Conversions: Turning Turk and its 'Pauline' Righting." *Journal for Early Modern Cultural Studies* 2, no. 1 (2002): 1–34.

Peirce, Leslie P. *The Imperial Harem: Women and Sovereignty in the Ottoman Empire*. New York: Oxford University Press, 1993.

Penzer, N. M. *The Harem*. London: Spring Books, 1965.

Sandys, George. *Description of the Turkish Empire*. 1615. Amsterdam: Da Capo, 1973.

Schick, Irvin Cemil. "The Women of Turkey as Sexual Personae: Images From Western Literature." In *Deconstructing Images of "The Turkish Woman."* Edited by Zehra F. Arat, 84. New York: St. Martin's Press, 1998.

Segal, Ronald. *Islam's Black Slaves: The Other Black Diaspora*. New York: Farrar, Straus and Giroux, 2001.

Seng, Yvonne J. "Invisible Women: Residents of Early Sixteenth-Century Istanbul." In *Women in the Medieval Islamic World: Power, Patronage, and Piety*. Edited by Gavin R. G. Hambly, 245. New York: St. Martin's Press, 1998.

Skilliter, Susan. "Three Letters from the Ottoman 'Sultana' Safiye to Queen Elizabeth I." In *Documents from Islamic Chanceries, First Series*. Edited by S. M. Stern. Columbia: University of South Carolina Press, 1965.

Toledano, Ehud R. *Slavery and Abolition in the Ottoman Middle East*. Seattle: University of Washington Press, 1998.

Vitkus, Daniel J., ed. *Three Turk Plays From Early Modern England: Selimus, A Christian Turned Turk, and The Renegado*. New York: Columbia University Press, 2000.

―――. "Turning Turk in *Othello*: The Conversion and Damnation of the Moor." *Shakespeare Quarterly* 48, no. 2 (1997): 145–76.

Waller, A. R., ed. *The Works of Beaumont and Fletcher*. Vol. 7. Cambridge: Cambridge University Press, 1909.

Wheatcroft, Andrew. *The Ottomans*. New York: Viking, 1993.

To Russia without Love:
George Turberville as Resistant Traveler

Jane Farnsworth

> By this time our men had learned that this Countrey was called Russia
> or Moscovie, and that Evan Vasilivich (which was at that time their
> kings name) ruled and governed farre and wide in those places. And the
> barbarous Russes asked likewise of our men whence they were, and
> what they came for; whereunto answere was made, that they were Eng-
> lishmen sent into those coastes, from the most excellent King Edwarde
> the Sixt, having from him in commaundement certaine things to deliver
> to their King, and seeking nothing els, but his amitie and friendship,
> and trafique with his people, whereby they doubted not, but that great
> commoditie and profite would growe to the subjects of both kingdomes.
> —Richard Chancellor, "The newe Navigation and discoverie
> of the kingdome of Moscovia 1553"[1]

"GREAT COMMODITIE AND PROFITE" WAS THE PRIME MOVER FOR TUDOR
explorers who began traveling to Russia in the 1550s. By the end of the sixteenth century trade with Russia centered on the expanding Muscovy Company and diplomatic relations were well established.[2] Travelers to Russia
were merchants and traders and wrote about Russia in those terms; Richard
Chancellor, Anthony Jenkinson, and Jerome Horsey, for example, were all
trading company agents, and Thomas Randolph and Giles Fletcher were
both agents of the Queen seeking trade agreements. Their accounts of their
Russian travels focus on trade and encourage readers to make voyages of
their own: "The piece of writing returned to the Muscovy Company was to
reproduce the voyage, and thus to make the material of experience durable,
accessible, useful."[3] And it is not just the content of their reports that is
affected by their trade with Russia. As T. J. Cribb in "Writing up the Log:
The Legacy of Hakluyt" says, "this practical purpose . . . informs [Hakluyt
and these other writers'] method" of describing their travels.[4] Even more,
"The authenticity of the experience is further guaranteed by the style of
writing, which is anti-literary in its eschewal of adornment."[5] Among all
these practical, plain, prose narratives and logs printed from 1550 to 1590,
however, we find an anomaly—three verse epistles and eight poems by a
young gentleman named George Turberville. Turberville was not a merchant

or agent, but a young man who, acting as secretary to Sir Thomas Randolph, accompanied him on his diplomatic mission to Russia/Muscovy in 1568–69 in hopes of improving his personal prospects. Before this trip to Russia, Turberville was already a published poet of *Epitaphes, Epigrams, Songs and Sonets* (1567) and a translator of Ovid and Mantuan. It is perhaps not surprising, then, that, instead of commercial and geographical reports, he produced, as Anthony Cross points out, "England's first poetic response to Russia."[6]

Turberville's poems on Russia are found in a collection of his verse printed with a group of Italian stories translated by him and published as the *Tragicall Tales.*[7] Although the edition of the *Tragicall Tales* here discussed is dated 1587, Hankins, in *The Life and Works of George Turbervile,* persuasively argues that there was an earlier edition of the *Tales* in 1574 which places it and this verse collection much closer to the time of the Russia trip.[8] An interesting note in *The Dictionary of National Biography* says that during his trip to Russia, Turberville wrote "his first volume, entitled 'Poems describing the Places and Manners of the Country and People of Russia, Anno 1568.' No copy of this work, as cited by Wood, appears to be known, but some of the contents were evidently included among his later verse ('Tragical Tales')" (1248). On the title page to the collection attached to his *Tragicall Tales,* Turberville sets out its contents in detail: "Epitathes and Sonnettes annexed to the tragical histories, by the author. With some other broken pamphlettes and Epistles, sent to certaine his frends in England, at his being in Moscovia, Anno 1569." Such a variety of verse and metrical forms presents the kind of eclectic collection familiar to readers in the mid-sixteenth century, for example, in *Tottel's Miscellany (1557–1587).* Very likely, then, Turberville composed at least some of these poems while actually in Russia and certainly he wishes his reader to believe that version of events.

Few of the modern critics writing on the sixteenth-century English expeditions to Russia mention Turberville at all. Those who do focus exclusively on his three verse epistles to his friends Dancie, Spencer and Parker, perhaps because they were printed in Hakluyt's *Principal Navigations,* and completely ignore his shorter poems.[9] Hakluyt's use of the epistles signals that they were more closely aligned to the descriptive, informative and "urgently practical"[10] prose of the typical travelers' reports he gathered together in the *Principal Navigations,* whereas Turberville's short poems move dramatically away from the purpose and style of the log and travel narrative. Even Turberville's verse epistles, however, were sometimes at cross-purposes with the interests of the English travelers and merchants. Lloyd Berry points out that Hakluyt "omitted the most vituperative of Turberville's attack on the morals of the *muzhiki* or peasants," found in lines 19–24 of the epistle "To his especiall friend Master Edward Dancie," in his 1589 and 1598–1600 editions of *Principal Navigations.*[11] Berry reasonably suggests that Hakluyt feared the Tsar might be offended and retaliate with economic reprisals against the Muscovy Company. Obviously, Turberville did not concern himself at all with the possible political or economic ramifications of his work.

Turberville's short poems on Russia would not persuade anyone to travel there—their focus is very different from that of the other English writings on that "strange and barbarous realm."[12] In fact, difference itself lies at the heart of his poems. When confronting new and foreign lands and people, a society or an individual must somehow deal with the differences so obviously apparent between the known and the unknown. They must find a category or place in which to situate these differences and make them comprehensible. Michael Ryan terms this "assimilation of the new worlds . . . [a] domestication."[13] Faced with unnerving difference, Europeans sought familiarity; there were many different conceptual strategies that they could employ to ease the strangeness. Ryan, for example, mentions a number of possibilities, including theological beliefs that diversity arose from "the fullness of the divine being" or from the "natural tendency of earthly things to degenerate over time," that "the unbaptized exotic was just that—a heathen," and that new pagans were actually linked to classical antiquity.[14] Ultimately, Europeans could tame new worlds by making them into very old worlds and "reduce their uniqueness to similarity."[15] In his poetry, Turberville seeks to make Russia comprehensible, to, in a way, tame it, but contrary to Ryan's findings, Turberville does this by emphasizing and exploiting difference rather than diminishing it. As Kamps and Singh remark, "The travel *writer* calls on language to bridge the cultural divide, to explain the other. But that very instrument—language—is also an essential reason that the distance exists in the first place."[16] Turberville's English and his ordered deployment of it based on specific cultural traditions are essentially alien to Russia and constantly keep alive the difference that exists between the speaker and his subject. At the same time, poetic forms and conventions, in particular Petrarchism, provide Turberville with the means to contain, even attack, the threat of the foreign.

His first and most obvious literary tactic is the use of verse instead of prose, and forms such as songs and sonnets (at least what mid-century writers called sonnets)[17] instead of travel narratives, lists, and logs. Although there are irregularities in his verses, most of the poems are carefully structured and have a definite shape and obvious rhyme scheme. Turberville thus transforms the strange into a recognizable literary shape. Unlike the generally looser structure of prose narrative, such poetic forms create the illusion of a firm control over and a fixed limit to the content of the poem—here, Russia. As well, the use of a particularized, self-dramatizing speaker further creates a sense of control over the subject of the poems. While there is certainly a voice describing things seen and done in travel narratives, the speaker is at the heart of a lyric, ordering the experience of the poem more obviously and emotionally for the reader. By setting the writing of these poems in Russia itself, Turberville appears to guarantee the reliability and authenticity of his speaker, as well as adding to the personal quality of the verse. How the speaker feels and how he views Russia and its people comes from immediate experience and intimate knowledge. His speaker, introduced in the first poem of the collection as a devoted son, develops into the faithful lover of the following poems. In fact, the speaker becomes the recognizable and familiar self-conscious poet-lover of the Petrarchan tradition.

In *Unrequited Conquests: Love and Empire in the Colonial Americas,* Roland Greene has made some interesting connections between Petrarchism and the colonial/discovery literature of the New World. He suggests that "Petrarchism, the convention of writing about unrequited love derived from the work of . . . Petrarca, is one of the original colonial discourses,"[18] and that the earliest explorers, like Christopher Columbus, set a pattern of response for others who confronted strange new worlds by writing of exploration in Petrarchan terms: "[Columbus] represents himself as the searching, emotionally volatile, chronically unfulfilled lover of an other [the new lands and/or peoples] that in part is his own creation and in another part ferociously resists him."[19] Mid-century writers like Wyatt, in Greene's view, continue this pattern, widening "the import of love to take in the problems of exploration, conquest, and rule," and beginning the discussion of imperialism in English literature.[20] Turberville certainly uses the discourse of Petrarchism to respond to the strange new land of Russia, and he does want to domesticate the foreign. But, far from longing for Russia as the Petrarchan beloved, Turberville and his speaker express resistance to this frightening other land.

One of the effects of exploration for Englishmen like Turberville was, of course, facing many "others," of being forced to reflect "on one's own identity and culture which will inevitably transform the writer concerned —and quite possibly the reader—and will call into question received assumptions, inducing a sense of wonder at the magnificence of the other, or reaffirming deeply felt differences with a vengeance."[21] Greenblatt argues in *Marvelous Possessions* that wonder is "the central figure in the initial European response to the New World [and the unknown], the decisive emotional and intellectual experience in the presence of radical difference."[22] He also sees it as shifting from the medieval "sign of dispossession to . . . [the renaissance] agent of appropriation . . . : the colonizing of the marvelous."[23] In that sense there is very little wonder in Turberville's response to Russia; his speaker emphatically rejects the other of Russia in his songs and sonnets and expresses only a wish to leave behind that strange land. He uses Petrarchan form and rhetoric to reaffirm the great difference he sees between barbarous Russia and England, and to confirm the superiority of England and Englishmen in the face of a powerful, disturbing "other" who could not be colonized and who was geographically far closer than the Americas. Petrarchism gives Turberville a language with which to talk about Russia and a form in which even a young, relatively powerless man like himself could contain and control this exotic new land.

The opening poem of Turberville's collection is "A farewell to a mother Cosin, at his going towardes Moscovia." The third person "his" in the title is typical of mid-century writers, suggesting a universal or generic aspect to the situation of the speaker in the poem, as well as a personal one.[24] The use of the term "Cosin" and of "mother" underscores the intimacy of the address and gives an affectionate tone to the poem right from the beginning.[25] This farewell to his mother puts the speaker's trip to Russia in a very personal perspective, or at least the illusion of one. It is difficult to tell how much biography is behind the speaker's description of his situation, but, in many ways, that is very much to the point. Turberville is not writing a factual account of his trip (we can find that in Thomas Randolph's account published in Hakluyt), but rather a poem about the feelings of a young man on leaving home to seek his fortune. The speaker believes his mother will be upset at the news that her son is going off on a dangerous sea voyage "where winter wyndes do . . . rore." He addresses the paper and warns it that "doubtlesse she with trembling handes / will you in sunder teare." This description is a typical Petrarchan opening which establishes the self-consciousness of the speaker as poet. The rest of the poem is an explanation of why he must go on this potentially dangerous journey.

He paints this trip as a desperate attempt by him to improve his circumstances. Ironically, his trip to Russia had the same practical, monetary purpose as those of other travelers who wrote up their experiences in logs or narratives. He speaks of cares, expenses that nip him near, lost love, lack of friendship, and the failure of his studies to make him successful. He hopes that he will "returne with gaine" and says he would be no better than a "sotted dolt" or "slouthfull Groome" if he did not try to better himself. In some ways the speaker's characterization here prepares us for the critical view of Russia which we find throughout his poems. He traveled to Russia not out of curiosity or love of adventure, but because he had to, because his own country was not affording him opportunities to succeed. These pragmatic ends are softened by his concern for his mother's worry about him. Her fears may have been rooted not only in fears concerning the physical harshness of the land, but also in the early modern notion that the north was the location of hell, a place of evil wherein demons resided.[26] He makes light of the reputed deadly cold of Russia: "They say the country is too colde [but all that means is] the whotter is the fire." The usual hot and cold oppositions of Petrarchan verse are present here, serving a very different purpose than expressing the contrary states of love. This opposition of fire and ice is found in many contemporary and later accounts of Russia. As Daryl Palmer suggests, "Here was a Russian world whose climate modeled the unstable psychologies of its inhabitants."[27] Turberville himself in his verse epistles uses the trope this way, but not in his short poems. He reassures her even more with gentle mockery:

> Moscovia is the place,
>> where all good furres be sold
> Then pray thee (mother) tel me how
>> thy sonne shall dye with colde.

He says her prayers will keep him safe and when he returns he will tell her all about his "harde mishappes." The sense of urgent necessity, the resentment at having to leave his country to succeed, the jokes to conceal possible fears about the trip, and the expectation of tales to tell on return all reveal a familiar state of mind, that of a young man setting sail from England to make his fortune in a foreign land. But significant differences are also revealed. Although Russia is the object of his journey and there are expectations of wonders ("whatsoever straunge / or monstrous sight") to be seen, Russia is also very clearly not the object of his desire. Instead, it is a barrier separating the speaker from those he loves and from his native land.

In the seven poems on Russia that follow, this complaining son becomes the easily recognizable, complaining Petrarchan lover who is separated from the object of his desire: his mistress and England. These love poems in the Petrarchan tradition are addressed to a mistress, or "friend" in sixteenth, and seventeenth-century usage (*OED*). Given Turberville's earlier writing of a loose poetic sequence in honor of a mistress ("a Discourse of the Friendly affections of Tymetes to Pyndara his Ladie," 1567), his knowledge of Ovid and other classical authors, and the great influence of *Tottel's Miscellany* upon his work, it is not necessary to seek a real woman as the recipient of his poems from Russia. As a matter of fact, Turberville warns the readers of his earlier Petrarchan-inspired sequence against taking his writings about love at face value and says his poems are the "meere fiction of these Fantasies."[28] The significance of these later songs and sonnets (as for his earlier sequence) is in the poetic fiction of love he creates, not in the identity of the mistress. But even more, it is in how and for what purposes he employs that fiction to confront the difference of Russia. Through a subtle and cumulative development of Petrarchan strategies in these little-known poems, Turberville presents his early and distinctive response to Russia.

In the first love poem, "That nothing can cause him to forget his frend, wherein is toucht the hardnes of his travayle," the difficulties and strangeness of his Russian journey are transformed by the speaker into a typical

Petrarchan test of his love for his mistress. The poem is tightly structured into a logical "if . . . then" argument. The first seventeen lines each begin with "if" and use the land and people of Russia as negative examples:

> If boystrous blasts of fierce and froward wynde,
> If weltring waves, and frothie foming Seas,
> If shining Sunne by night against his kinde,
> If lacke of lust to meate, and want of ease,

and so on through coldness, frozen rivers, lack of sleep, hard beds, poor food, stinking stoves, and savage men. Turberville creates a vivid and uncomfortable picture that strengthens the affirmation of constant love that his speaker swears to his mistress at the end of the poem:

> If these (I say) might make a man forget
> So true a frend, then thou art out of minde.
> But in good fayth, my fancie firme was set,
> No Russie mought the true love knot unbinde.

Russia becomes the strongest test of love possible and the land becomes understandable through its conformity to a familiar poetic strategy. In many ways, Russia becomes a kind of anti-*locus amoenus,* a *locus horribilis* to the speaker. The last two lines of this poem, "Venus be judge, and Cupid in this case, / Who did pursue me aye from place to place," use images from classical myth in sharp contrast to the previous natural images of Russia— civilization in contrast to the wilderness. The poem has a very strong element of closure with its final rhyming couplet that differs sharply from the "if" construction of its first seventeen lines. One could even see this poem as a kind of loose sonnet—the rhyme scheme is six quatrains and a couplet. Russia is enclosed and contained within the poetic structure and erased by the generalized word "place" in the very last line: "Who did pursue me aye from place to place." The fear that a strange land and people may lead to his forgetting of his beloved and England is almost ritually exorcised through the repetitious structure of the poem. The speaker is adamant that Russia will not affect him or his heart and makes clear his resistance to and rejection of the foreign. Russia is never the desired object but only an unwanted obstacle in his Petrarchan fiction.

Turberville goes even further in his next poem and develops Russia as an image of imprisonment. The title sets up the comparison—"He declares that albeit he were imprisoned in Russia, yet his minde was at libertie, & did daily repaire to his friend." Sir Thomas Randolph and his expedition party spent a great deal of its time waiting to be seen by the Tsar, and the frustration engendered by the seventeen weeks of virtual house arrest in Moscow may lie behind this poem. As Randolph later wrote:

We were brought to a house built of purpose by the Emperour for Embassadours, faire, and large, after the fashion of that Countrey.

Two gentlemen were appointed to attend upon me, the one to see us furnished of victuals, and that we lacked nothing of the Emperours allowance: the other to see that we should not goe out of the house, nor suffer any man to come unto us, in which they left nothing undone that belonged to their charge. But specially he that looked to our persons so straightly handled us, that we had no small cause to doubt that some evill had bene intended unto us. No supplication, suite, or request could take place for our libertie, nor yet to come to his presence.[29]

The use of Russia to express bondage and imprisonment may have seemed a natural move because of the English perception of it as a land of physical constrictions and of a society of tyrants and slaves.[30] However, rather than deal with these restrictions in political terms, Turberville uses it as another proof of his speaker's love for his lady, and, of course, the overcoming of obstacles by the lover is all part of the Petrarchan mythos. Although his body is in Russia, his soul is free to fly to his love: "I finde the proofe in me, / Who captive am, and yet at libertie." Russia is not mentioned specifically in the body of the poem although the words "churles checke" and "Tyrants threat" bring to mind the social structure of the country. Again, he ends the poem with a classical reference, this time to Daedalus, his waxen wings and Icarus:

> I doe desire no ayde of Dedalus,
> By feate to forge such waxen winges anew
> As erst he gave his sonne young Icarus,
> When they from Crete for feare of Mynos flew.

The speaker does not desire to end as Icarus does in self-destruction, but he may feel a similar fear of violence from a tyrant. Instead of faulty waxen wings, however, the speaker concludes that he will flee Russia on the safer feathers of Dame Fancy. These familiar classical images, especially at the end of the poem, blunt the fearful strangeness of Russia and leave the speaker and reader in familiar territory, poetically speaking. The "posie" at the end of this poem, "Il desire non bariposo," which roughly means "He desires no barrier," emphasizes again the speaker's sense of being trapped in Russia and separated from his mistress and England.

The poetic matter of the third love poem is comfortingly familiar and obviously Petrarchan, with elements of the blazon: "A comparison of his mistresse, with a brave Lady of Russia." The speaker here creates a relationship between the strange (the Russian lady) and the known (his mistress) through comparison, but he does so to deny any similarity between them. He opens by describing the lady of Russia in vague terms; her face is "fair" and her looks "lovely." Her clothing, however, appears in sensual

detail—"Rich be thy robes," he says and goes on to itemize her silver ear-
rings, her boots, her sable-trimmed and embroidered clothing, and her pearl
necklace. The reader would certainly find her attractive so far. The next
stanza opens, though, with a negative turn: "The Russies rude doe deeme
right wel of thee, / Mine English eye no paynted image seekes." The reader
has been put in the uncomfortable position of judging incorrectly, of thinking like a foreigner not an Englishman, of going by outside appearances.
The speaker then describes his mistress in terms of her physical attributes,
her body rather than her clothes. The made-up Russian lady is but a simu-
lacrum, not true beauty. The phrases, "kindly shape" and "kindly coloured
cheekes," suggest the proper and natural quality of the mistress's beauty
in opposition to the artificial beauty of the lady. He moves on to use the
typical Petrarchan attributes of feminine beauty—hair like golden wires,
eyes like diamonds, lily cheeks, ruby lips, and pearly teeth. The description
suggests that the mistress's beauty is inherent and superior to the Russian
lady's contrived appearance. The mistress's pearls are a natural part of her,
unlike the borrowed pearls of the Russian lady's necklace. He ends with a
challenge to the reader—"Now judge of both which is the braver dame."
The structure of this poem suggests that foreignness can initially be intriguing, that difference can be attractive, but the ending makes it clear that it is
only a false perception. His comparison is essentially between the Russian
lady's clothing and the English mistress's body, clearly emphasizing the
difference between assumed, external beauty and inherent, natural beauty.
As well, the description of the Russian lady could be seen as appealing
more to the sense of touch than to that of the mistress, whose description
is strongly visual, for example, in its use of the color and sparkle of gem-
stones. Touch was seen as an inferior and more morally dangerous sense than
sight. The inferiority of the Russian may also be marked by the speaker's
use of the familiar form ("thy," "thine," and "thee") in addressing her. His
direct address to the Russian lady in contrast to his use of the third person
for his mistress also subtly underscores the presence of the one and the absence of the other. The speaker is always aware and makes the reader aware
of the distance between him and his mistress. The Italian "posie" that follows the poem emphasizes again the moral line being drawn here: "La mia
donna bella e buona" (My lady beautiful and good). The exotic in this poem
is both expressed and repressed through traditional Petrarchan rhetoric, defeated by superior and familiar English beauty.

Also structured around contrasts is "From the citie of Mosqua, to his
friend in England." Here the contrast is between the speaker's presence in
Russia and his mistress's in England. England is called "Brutus land," which
firmly ties it to civilized antiquity and heightens the difference between it
and wild, wintry Moscow. But even more significant for Turberville's appropriation of Petrarchism is the contrast drawn between the cold of Rus-

sia and the fires of love. The typical conceits of love sighs like winds and desire like flames are redirected both metaphorically and literally to battle the frigid climate of Moscovy: "Go burning sighes, and pierce the frozen skie, / Slack you the snow with flames of fancies fire." Once again, the speaker's love is tested by the Russian landscape, and the harsh climate of Russia is potentially dangerous to the soul or character as well as to the physical body. The speaker tries to reassure his beloved, his "friend," whom he describes as his "phoenix" and "saint," that "no winters force in Russia [will] binde / My heart so heard, or alter so my minde" that he will forget her. The impact of these common images is strengthened and made fresh by their localized appropriateness. At the same time, the harsh and unforgiving Russian landscape is tamed by its association with conventional poetic images. The particular situation of the speaker is nicely summed up in the Petrarchan "posie" to this poem, "ardo e ghiaccio" (I burn and freeze).

In all these love poems, being far away with the limitless tracts of frozen land and sea between the speaker and all he knows and loves is constantly emphasized. Such isolation creates a certain sympathy for the speaker and makes understandable, even reasonable, his critical stance toward Russia and his anxious reassurances to his mistress that he has not forgotten her even though he is so far away. In the fifth poem to deal with Russia and love, "That though he may not possible come or send, yet he lives mindfull of his mistresse in Moscovia," the speaker compares himself to Leander, another lover who found himself far away from his mistress. Yet Leander was happier than the speaker because he could swim to his love, whereas the speaker cannot:

> For swimming wil not serve my turne
>   to bryng me to my loving mate.
> The clouds are frozen round about,
>   the snow is thick on every side:
> The raging Ocean runnes betwixt
>   my frend and me with cruel tide.

He goes on and describes actual rivers, the Volga, Suchan, and Dwina, that now are frozen solid and afford "no way for any barge, / much lesse for any man to goe." He is trapped by the Russian winter and cannot be a Leander to his Hero. Turberville has used a classical story to try to convey his speaker's situation, a common technique in Renaissance poetry. However, the classical comparison does not ultimately work—the Russian winter makes it impossible—and suggests by that failure that Russia is incompatible with the cultural myths of Europe. Difference is highlighted, yet at the same time rendered comprehensible, because of the familiarity of the comparison. And again, Russia becomes the ultimate test of a lover's fidelity:

In Russia where I leade my life,
and long againe at home to be,
No force shall cause me to forget
or lay the care of love aside.

Turberville clearly means this poem to read as if the speaker were in Russia. As in many Petrarchan poems and sequences, the speaker feels that if his mistress could read his lines the pain of love would be eased: "If I might have conveid my lines, / unto thy handes, it would have easde, / My heavy heart of divers doubts." Unlike most other Petrarchan situations, however, it is not possible for the mistress to read the speaker's words of love because he is far away in a foreign land. His direct address to his mistress in expressing this desire for physical connection between them adds to the intensity of his need. Russia is an impediment to love. The poem concludes with an emphasis on his fidelity and his eventual return to her and England. Turberville here, as elsewhere in these poems, inextricably mixes Petrarchan love and patriotic love. The unspoken equation between the speaker's fidelity to his English mistress and his fidelity to England and its culture is easily made by the reader. This poem is perhaps the most unsettling of the love poems because it reveals the huge distance, both physically and culturally, between Russia and England.

In the next love poem, however, Turberville presents a slightly different perspective on the speaker's relationship with his mistress. Here the landscape of Russia is not so much a test of constancy in love as a means to forget the pains of love—as the title says, "Unable by long and hard travell to banish love, returnes hir friend." Russia's snows here are a hoped-for remedy for the fires of desire: "Wounded with love . . . Of your faire face, I left my native land / With Russia snow to slacke mine English fire." Again, the foreign landscape of Russia is placed within the familiar Petrarchan metaphoric structure of the heat and cold of love—not even Russian cold can quench the coals of Cupid. The poet actually places Cupid, a classical god and a conventional figure from Petrarchan love poetry, in the Russian landscape and has him triumph over it:

The Ocean sea for all his fearefull flood,
the perils great of passage not prevaile,
To banish love the rivers do no good,
the mountains hie cause Cupid not to quaile.

Again, the speaker mentions actual rivers, the Dwina and Suchan, not as aids for the future navigation of the reader, but as poetic intensifiers. Not even the power of these rivers can wash away the love of the speaker for his mistress. The poem ends with a look beyond Moscovy, to a time when the speaker will be home: "From Mosqua I thy frend will home retire." The strange and dangerous land will soon be just a memory for the speaker, who says repeatedly that he will not change in any way because of this journey and who tells his mistress directly that he will return as faithful to her as when he left. Turberville's speaker is a resisting traveler whose eyes are always turned back to the familiar. Difference is recognized, but ultimately dismissed as a temporary concern.

The last poem in this group once again juxtaposes Russia with classical myth, here the figure of Echo. The title of this poem emphasizes the harshness of the Russian landscape: "Travailing the desert of Russia, he complayneth to Eccho, with request that she comfort his afflicted state." The speaker asks Echo to help him in his pain by allowing him to hear his mistress's name resounding through the hills and valleys. It seems his mistress has found another lover while the speaker has been away. There is, however, no specific mention of Russia in the poem itself, only generalized allusions to a vague landscape. The title of the poem would seem to operate metaphorically—the desert of Russia equals the desert of the speaker's heart. The strange land has again become a way of exploring the speaker's feelings. The foreign has been fully internalized into a landscape of the heart in desolation—Russia essentially disappears. The poem turns to the speaker's future plans to seek out his mistress when he finally returns and to a praise of her beauty. This praise is expressed through the classical tale of Paris's choice between the goddesses, Venus, Pallas, and Juno. His mistress, the speaker asserts, would have put them all to shame with her matchless beauty. The speaker laments his forfeited love, the result of his absence and a rival, and his use of the third person to speak *of* his mistress and not *to* her reinforces the emotional as well as the physical distance between them. Such a loss of his English mistress points to the dangers of being in a foreign land, of losing connections to home and of being overcome by difference.

This short Petrarchan narrative, sustained over seven poems, is not a happy one, and Moscovy is the villain of the piece, even though it is domesticated and contained through Petrarchan poetic strategies. Russia's foreignness in these eight poems is both revealed and denied by Turberville's poetic manipulation of it. While some of Turberville's descriptions and comments about Russia—for example, the cold and the wintry harshness of the land—may seem clichéd, they are only so in the context of future observations and literary depictions of Russia. Athough most critics agree with Hankins's assessment of Turberville's works in general, that they are "almost entirely derivative . . . with a lack of any marked originality," Turberville has done something very original in these particular poems.[31] Not only does his use of Petrarchism, one of the most familiar poetic traditions of his day, render the strangeness of Russia comprehensible, but his use of Russian themes and details revitalizes that familiar tradition in return. Unlike most of his contemporary travelers (and most future travelers to Russia and beyond), Turberville presents a speaker who does not find wonder in the new or desire its possession, but who resists difference and desires only home. Turberville's poems about love and Russia present an original and innovative approach to (or perhaps a retreat from would be the more accurate phrase) the mysterious and the foreign.

NOTES

1. Richard Chancellor, "The newe Navigation and discoverie of the kingdome of Moscovia 1553," in Richard Hakluyt, *The Principal Navigations Voyages and Discoveries of the English Nation,* vol. 1, (Cambridge: Cambridge University Press, 1965), 283–84.

2. Numerous books and articles describe and interpret the English experience in Russia and their rather difficult trading relationship. Some useful sources are Marshall Poe, *Foreign Descriptions of Muscovy: An Analytic Bibliography of Primary and Secondary Sources* (Columbus, OH: Slavica Publishers, 1995); John Michael Archer, *Old Worlds: Egypt, Southwest Asia, India, and Russia in Early Modern English Writing* (Palo Alto, CA: Stanford University Press, 2001); Francesca Wilson, *Muscovy: Russia Through Foreign Eyes 1553–1900* (New York: Praeger, 1970); Charles J. Halperin, "Sixteenth-Century Foreign Travel Accounts to Muscovy: A Methodological Excursus," *Sixteenth Century Journal* 6 (1975): 89–111; Lloyd E. Berry and Robert O. Crummey, *Rude & Barbarous: Russia in the Accounts of the Sixteenth-Century English Voyagers* (Madison: University of Wisconsin Press, 1968), and, of course, Hakluyt, *The Principal Navigations.*

3. Mary C. Fuller, *Voyages in Print: English Travel to America, 1576–1624* (Cambridge: Cambridge University Press, 1995), 6.

4. T. J. Cribb, "Writing up the Log: The Legacy of Hakluyt," in *Travel Writing and Empire: Postcolonial Theory in Transit,* ed. Steve Clark, 102 (London: Zed Books, 1999).

5. Cribb, "Writing up the Log," 103, in Clark, *Travel Writing and Empire.*

6. Anthony G. Cross, *The Russian Theme in English Literature from the Sixteenth Century to 1980: An Introductory Survey and Bibliography* (Oxford: William A. Meeuws, 1985), 3. There were instances of Russian themes and characters used in sixteenth- and early seventeenth-century literature, but, in all cases, these examples, from Shakespeare's *Love's Labor's Lost* (1594) to John Fletcher's *The Loyal Subject* (1647), postdate Turberville's poems.

7. George Turberville, *Tragicall Tales* (London: Abell Jeffs, 1587). All quotations of Turberville's poetry come from this edition unless otherwise noted.

8. John Erskine Hankins, *The Life and Works of George Turbervile* (Folcraft, PA: Folcraft Library Editions, 1971), 36–37, 70.

9. These critics are Archer, *Old Worlds:* 114–16; Lloyd E. Berry, "Richard Hakluyt and Turberville's Poems on Russia," *Bibliographical Society of America* 61 (1967): 350–51; Berry and Crummey, *Rude & Barbarous,* 71–84; and Halperin, "Sixteenth-Century Foreign Travel Accounts to Muscovy," 102, 105, 108.

10. Cribb, "Writing up the Log," 102, in Clark, *Travel Writing and Empire.*

11. Berry, "Richard Hakluyt," 350.

12. Berry and Crummey, *Rude & Barbarous,* xvii.

13. Michael T. Ryan, "Assimilating New Worlds in the Sixteenth and Seventeenth Centuries," *Comparative Studies in Society and History* 23 (1981): 523.

14. Ibid., 524–25.

15. Ibid., 533.

16. Ivo Kamps and Jyotsna G. Singh, *Travel Knowledge: European "Discoveries" in the Early Modern Period* (New York: Palgrave, 2001), 4.

17. In the introduction to his edition of *Tottel's Miscellany (1557–1587)* (Cambridge, MA: Harvard University Press, 1966), Hyder Baker Rollins writes that "poets like Googe and Turberville christened their verse 'songs and sonnets' but no genuine sonnets can be found among them; and for a time the word 'sonnet' meant nothing but a brief lyric" (1:108).

18. Roland Greene, *Unrequited Conquests: Love and Empire in the Colonial Americas* (Chicago: University of Chicago Press, 1999), 1.

19. Ibid., 17.

20. Ibid., 136.

21. Andrew Hadfield, *Literature, Travel, and Colonial Writing in the English Renaissance 1545–1625* (Oxford: Clarendon Press, 1998), 1.

22. Stephen Greenblatt, *Marvelous Possessions: The Wonder of the New World* (Chicago: University of Chicago Press, 1991), 14.

23. Ibid., 24–25.

24. Anne Ferry, *The "Inward" Language: Sonnets of Wyatt, Sidney, Shakespeare, Donne* (Chicago: University of Chicago Press, 1983), 18–19.

25. According to the *OED*, "cosin" was used as "a term of intimacy, friendship, or familiarity," and "in legal language formerly often applied to the next of kin."

26. See Colleen Franklin's chapter in this collection.

27. Daryl W. Palmer, "Jacobean Muscovites: Winter, Tyranny, and Knowledge in *The Winter's Tale*," *Shakespeare Quarterly* 46 (1995): 328.

28. George Turberville, *Epitaphes, Epigrams, Songs and Sonets* (London: H. Denham, 1567).

29. Thomas Randolph, "The Ambassage of the right worshipfull M. Thomas Randolfe Esquire, to the Emperour of Russia, in the yeere 1568," in Hakluyt's *The Principal Navigations,* 1:401.

30. See Archer, *Old Worlds,* "Chapter Three: Slave-Born Muscovites," 101–210.

31. Hankins, *The Life and Works of George Turbervile,* 71–72.

BIBLIOGRAPHY

Archer, John Michael. *Old Worlds: Egypt, Southwest Asia, India, and Russia in Early Modern English Writing.* Palo Alto, CA: Stanford University Press, 2001.

Berry, Lloyd E. "Richard Hakluyt and Turberville's Poems on Russia." *Bibliographical Society of America* 61 (1967): 350–51.

Berry, Lloyd E., and Robert O. Crummey. *Rude & Barbarous: Russia in the Accounts of the Sixteenth-Century English Voyagers.* Madison: University of Wisconsin Press, 1968.

Campbell, Mary B. *The Witness and the Other World: Exotic European Travel Writing, 400–1600.* Ithaca, NY: Cornell University Press, 1988.

Clark, Steve. Ed. *Travel Writing and Empire: Postcolonial Theory in Transit.* London: Zed Books, 1999.

Cross, Anthony G. *The Russian Theme in English Literature from the Sixteenth Century to 1980: An Introductory Survey and Bibliography.* Oxford: William A. Meeuws, 1985.

Ferry, Anne. *The "Inward" Language: Sonnets of Wyatt, Sidney, Shakespeare, Donne.* Chicago: University of Chicago Press, 1983.

Fuller, Mary C. *Voyages in Print: English Travel to America, 1576–1624.* Cambridge: Cambridge University Press, 1995.

Greenblatt, Stephen. *Marvelous Possessions: The Wonder of the New World.* Chicago: University of Chicago Press, 1991.

Greene, Roland. *Unrequited Conquests: Love and Empire in the Colonial Americas.* Chicago: University of Chicago Press, 1999.

Hadfield, Andrew. *Literature, Travel, and Colonial Writing in the English Renaissance 1545–1625.* Oxford: Clarendon Press, 1998.

Hakluyt, Richard. *The Principal Navigations Voyages and Discoveries of the English Nation.* Vol. 1, 1589. Cambridge: Cambridge University Press, 1965.

Halperin, Charles J. "Sixteenth-Century Foreign Travel Accounts to Muscovy: A Methodological Excursus." *Sixteenth Century Journal* 6 (1975): 89–111.

Hankins, John Erskine. *The Life and Works of George Turbervile.* Folcroft, PA: Folcroft Library Editions, 1971.

Kamps, Ivo, and Jyotsna G. Singh. *Travel Knowledge: European "Discoveries" in the Early Modern Period.* New York: Palgrave, 2001.

Palmer, Daryl W. "Jacobean Muscovites: Winter, Tyranny, and Knowledge in *The Winter's Tale.*" *Shakespeare Quarterly* 46 (1995): 323–39.

Poe, Marshall. *Foreign Descriptions of Muscovy: An Analytic Bibliography of Primary and Secondary Sources.* Columbus, OH: Slavica Publishers, 1995.

Rollins, Hyder Baker, ed. *Tottel's Miscellany (1557–1587).* Cambridge, MA: Harvard University Press, 1966.

Ryan, Michael T. "Assimilating New Worlds in the Sixteenth and Seventeenth Centuries." *Comparative Studies in Society and History* 23 (1981): 523.

Turberville, George. *Epitaphes, Eppigrams, Songs and Sonets.* London: H. Denham, 1567.

———. *Tragicall Tales.* London: Abell Jeffs, 1587.

Wilson, Francesca. *Muscovy: Russia Through Foreign Eyes 1553–1900.* New York: Praeger, 1970.

Jack Wilton and the Jews:
The Ambivalence of Anti-Semitism in Nashe's
The Unfortunate Traveller

Mathew Martin

AN "OUTLANDISH" CHRONICLE OF THE EUROPEAN MISADVENTURES OF the page Jack Wilton told to a fictional audience of English pages and an implied audience of English readers, Thomas Nashe's *The Unfortunate Traveller* (1594) stands beside such better-known literary works as *The Faerie Queene* as a participant in the late sixteenth-century project of defining English national identity in relation to the foreign.[1] The Jews occupied a prominent and vexing position in the development of this project. "Englishness," James Shapiro writes, "would not be the same as it is without the existence of Jewishness. . . . This is especially so because the first and only story of mass deportation of people from England—what has come to be known as 'the Expulsion of the Jews in 1290'—has meant that Englishness has in part defined itself by the wholesale rejection of that which is Jewish."[2] As Jonathan Gil Harris argues in his essay in this volume, however, rejection could quickly become "infection": analyzing the intersection of mercantilist and pathological discourses in *The Merchant of Venice,* Harris concludes that "even as the 'parti-coloured' hybridity of the Jew ostensibly functions as a foil to the economic and cultural purity of the Gentile, it can equally work to disclose the latter's own originary hybridity."[3] Moreover, the rejection of Jewishness was complicated by religious discourse: if, as Shapiro asserts, "by the late sixteenth century the Protestant English began to see themselves as having taken the place of God's first elect people, the Jews," then the Jews were not only the rejected other of English identity but also its mirror image.[4] Indeed, radical Protestant sects like the Traskites were often accused by their opponents of Judaizing, of completely collapsing the distinction between English Protestants and Jews.[5]

Nashe's engagement with the Jews' vexing duality is central to his attempt in *The Unfortunate Traveller* to define English identity. Although representations of Jewish characters are confined to a small section of the work, that section's anti-Semitism is crucial to the work's ideological project. Most critics, however, remark upon the work's anti-Semitism merely in passing. Those who do treat it at some length tend to conclude, with Laura Wheeler, that "although they are portrayed as some of the most disgusting characters, within the context of Nashe's narrative the Jews are incidental, little different from the Germans or Italians except perhaps in their repulsive physicality and inhuman nature."[6] Wheeler's qualifying phrase suggests the ambivalence of *The Unfortunate Traveller*'s anti-Semitism: the anti-Semitic stereotypes are little different from the work's other stereotypes, yet perhaps very different. Like the others with whom Wheeler groups them, the Jews in *The Unfortunate Traveller* possess an intertextuality whose excavation reveals the destabilizing interconvertibility of the English subject and its others. Yet the work's anti-Semitism positions the Jews at the extreme of otherness. The Jews are represented as paradigmatic exiles, rejected by the figure of the father. Grounded in the notion of England as the place of the father, the construction of Englishness at work in *The Unfortunate Traveller* must disavow the exile and locate in the exile its most intense fears and loathing.

As Wheeler and others have demonstrated, in *The Unfortunate Traveller* the English subject is the implied norm in contrast to which the foreign is represented as duplicitous and excessive.[7] The English traveler could find such otherness seductive as well as repulsive, however, and in sixteenth-century English travel literature the English traveler who succumbs to these seductions is often represented as losing his Englishness. In *Images of the Educational Traveller in Early Modern England,* Sara Warneke observes that "the clear association of the traveler with a loss of cultural and national identity and allegiance appeared throughout the sixteenth century in more general works, and it began appearing regularly in popular literature from the 1590s."[8] Nashe's fictional travel narrative follows this representational strategy, at several points presenting the reader with the traveling English subject's strange metamorphosis into the foreign others to which elsewhere it is opposed. Jack provides one example early in the work, returning from France with "my feather in my cap as big as a flag in a fore-top, my French doublet gelt in the belly as though, like a pig ready to be spitted, all my guts had been plucked out, a pair of side-paned hose that hung down like two scales filled with Holland cheeses" (225). Travel has transformed Jack into a motley of foreign fashions and foods. Later the banished English earl lectures Jack on such metamorphoses, denouncing travel's deformation of the English traveler's character. The English subjects who embark on the Odyssean project of seeing and knowing "The cities of a world of nations, / With all their manners, mindes and fashions" risk decentering and even effacing the Englishness that provides the vantage point for seeing and knowing, and thus for distinguishing themselves from, foreign others.[9] "What is there in France to be learned more than in England," the earl exclaims, "but falsehood in fellowship, perfect slovenry, to love no man but for my pleasure, to swear *Ah par la mort Dieu* when a man's hams are scabbed? . . . I have known some that have continued there by the space of half a dozen year, and when they come home they have hid a little wearish lean face under a broad French hat, kept a terrible coil with the dust in the street in their long cloaks of grey paper, and spoke English strangely. Naught else have they profited by their travel save learnt to distinguish of the true Bordeaux grape, and know a cup of neat Gascon wine from wine of Orleans. Yea, and peradventure, this also: to esteem of the pox as a pimple, to wear a velvet patch on their face, and walk melancholy with their arms folded" (285). The English traveler fares no better in Spain or Italy, returning a hybrid creature whose attempt to know the "manners, mindes and fashions" of more than one national culture has left him fully belonging to none. The text, however, works to contain the dangerous potential of these transformations. Its representations of the hybrid English traveler reinscribe its constructions of Englishness even while illustrating their transgression. Like French fashions or the French pox—which, as Margaret Healy claims became in the period "the disease *par excellence* of someone else, some other nation," affectation, duplicity, and immorality are figured as contaminants that come from without, that properly belong elsewhere.[10] The work's xenophobic discourses displace heterogeneity and corruption onto the foreign, thereby protecting the fiction of a unified and normative English subject.

The process of refiguring the inside as the outside leaves discernible intertextual traces in *The Unfortunate Traveller,* however. "Hear what it is to be Anabaptists, to be puritans" (236), Nashe declaims at the end of his account of the slaughter of John Leyden's followers at Munster, and in Nashe's sermonizing upon the Anabaptists' religious fanaticism can be heard the tones of the rhetoric Nashe in the Martin Marprelate controversy had directed against the internal threat of English religious radicalism. Indeed, many of the characters, scenarios, and stereotypes in the work appear in one of Nashe's earlier works, *Pierce Penilesse His Supplication to the Divell,* a satire on London. A first draft of the frenchified Jack appears there, as do Greedinesse and Dame Niggardize, in whom Nashe condenses what he considers to be the worst aspects of London's mercantile ethos and who are the models for *The Unfortunate Traveller*'s two main Jewish characters, Zadok and Dr. Zachary.[11] Similarly, the tournament in which Jack's Italian travels with the Earl of Surrey culminate functions to contrast the absurd Italians with the truly chivalrous Surrey, who alone "observed the true measures of honour" (267). Nonetheless, as Katherine Duncan-Jones notes, this episode's parodic target is one of the central works in English sixteenth-century literature, Sidney's *Arcadia,* whose author elsewhere Nashe calls "Englands Sunne."[12] The potential interconvertibility of English and foreign did not escape *The Unfortunate Traveller*'s first readers: in the prefatory epistle to the 1594 edition of *Christs Teares over Jerusalem,*

Nashe writes that "there be certaine busie wits abrode, that seeke in my *Iacke Wilton* to anagramatize the name of Wittenberge to one of the Vniversities of England."[13] The textual nexus in which *The Unfortunate Traveller* is embedded, then, belies the work's insistence on the distinction between "English" and "out-landish" (309), revealing the Englishness of precisely those elements the work repudiates in order to produce the fictions of a coherent English self and its foreign others.

To compensate for the instability of the distinction between the English subject and its foreign others, *The Unfortunate Traveller* represents those others as grotesque. If we accept Mary Russo's definition of the grotesque as "a deviation from the norm," then all the foreign others in *The Unfortunate Traveller* are potentially grotesque.[14] The work consistently associates the foreign with "the bodily lower stratum," the defining characteristic of the grotesque according to Bakhtin.[15] Bakhtin writes that "to degrade an object does not imply merely hurling it into the void of non-existence, into absolute destruction, but to hurl it down to the reproductive lower stratum, the zone in which conception and a new birth take place."[16] The grotesque in *The Unfortunate Traveller,* however, does not follow the Bakhtinian path from degradation to regeneration but rather to waste, sterility, and obliteration. Neil Rhodes observes that in Nashe's work "saturnalia drifts towards satire, and the festive violence which is so typical of Rabelais is charged with the purgatorial spirit of contemporary didactic literature."[17] However festive it may appear, Nashe's style typically moves from the satirical construction of otherness to the complete destruction of the satirized object. The description of the battle between the Swiss and the French, for example, moves from defining but degrading caricature to the complete fragmentation of bodies and identities: "Here the unwieldy Switzers wallowing in their gore like an ox in his dung, there the sprightly French sprawling and turning in the stained grass like a roach new taken out of the stream . . . the half-living here mixed with squeezed carcasses long putrified. Any man might give arms that was an actor in that battle, for there were more arms and legs scattered in the field that day than will be gathered up till doomsday" (228). Just as the description refuses to ennoble the combatants by adopting a heroic idiom, so too it refuses to grant their degradation the regenerative power Bakhtin locates in Rabelais's grotesque imagery. In Rabelais's images of the body's violent destruction, Bakhtin states, "blood is transformed into wine; ruthless slaughter and the martyr's death are transformed into a merry banquet; the stake becomes a hearth."[18] In contrast, in Nashe's battle description the ox and roach are not transformed into a feast, the putrid bodies do not fertilize, the arms and legs scattered on the field do not lead to a gathering or harvest. Here and elsewhere in *The Unfortunate Traveller,* Nashe's grotesque representations of foreign others complete only half the cycle of becoming, containing the boundary-dissolving potential of Rabelaisian fertility to freeze the foreign others in their otherness.

Significantly, the English subject does not actively participate at the level of representation in the violence of the grotesque. Once Jack has left Henry's camp in France and his status as carnival king behind, he, the English pages who constitute his fictional audience, and the English reader are positioned as spectators of acts of violence that are consistently framed as tragedy: the battle between the French and the Swiss is called "a wonderful spectacle of tragedy" (228), and subsequent battles, rapes, tortures, and executions are framed in variants of the phrase. Nashe's conception of tragedy, like Nick Bottom's, is hardly Aristotelian and is far crueller than in the rude mechanicals' "tragical mirth."[19] More important than its definition, though, are the generic label's framing and distancing functions. By reducing the English subject to the beholding eye, the text both posits that subject's unity in contrast to the heterogeneity and fragmentation to which the foreign objects of its gaze are degraded and transforms the potential anxiety of confrontation with and contamination by grotesque others into the pleasure of art, or at least entertainment.

The Imperial soldiers in Nashe's account of the slaughter of the Anabaptists illustrate the success, and the strain, of this strategy of displacement and containment. Associated with the "bodily lower stratum" by their use of such things as chamber pots and shoes for helmets and dung forks for weapons (229), the Anabaptists must be destroyed. Yet, as Stephen Greenblatt has argued, murdering defenseless peasants brings no honor to those soldiers assigned the task. Rather, it renders them as base as the peasants they are killing. "In the economy of honor," Greenblatt writes, peasants "are not simply a cipher but a deficit, since even a defeat at the hands of a prince threatens to confer upon them some of the prince's store of honor, while what remains of the victorious prince's store can be tarnished by the unworthy encounter."[20] Nashe solves this problem by aligning the eyes of the Imperial soldiers with the remote, aestheticizing gaze of the reader and displacing the agency for the massacre onto their hands and then their weapons: "The imperials themselves, that were their executioners, like a father that weeps when he beats his child, yet still weeps and still beats, not without much ruth and sorrow prosecuted that lamentable massacre. Yet drums and trumpets, sounding nothing but stern revenge in their ears, made them so eager that their hands had no leisure to ask counsel of their effeminate eyes. Their swords, their pikes, their bills, their bows, their calivers slew, empierced, knocked down, shot through, and overthrew as many men every minute of the battle as there falls ears of corn before the scythe at one blow" (236). The carnivalesque army of "illuminate botchers" (236) is destroyed, while the honor of the Imperials is preserved by their emotionally appropriate response to the tragedy they witness along with the other "indifferent eyes" (236) in the audience. Considerable rhetorical violence is necessary to effect this displacement of agency, and ultimately it is Nashe's rhetoric that does the dirty work. The serial synecdoches of the last quoted sentence completely remove the Imperial soldiers from the battle, and the lengthy paratactic sequence of nouns then verbs exerts an overwhelming pressure on the "many men" (236) who are the objects of the sentence, a pressure that by the end of the description of the battle has fragmented them into "mangled flesh hung with gore" (236). Tellingly, it is Nashe's narrative persona, not the Imperial soldiers, who is contaminated by his contact with the Anabaptists. Immediately after describing the massacre, the narrator states that "I would gladly rid my hands of it cleanly if I could tell you how, for what with talking of cobblers and tinkers and ropemakers and botchers and dirtdaubers, the mark is clean gone out of my muse's mouth" (236).The defilement of the narrator's hands and mouth—writing hand, speaking mouth—is the price of the detached beholding eye's victory over the grotesque others in its gaze.[21]

Insofar as it juxtaposes a detached English subject and a violently destroyed other, *The Unfortunate Traveller*'s anti-Semitism may be said to be a part of the general strategy of displacement and containment by which the work attempts to establish the fiction of a coherent English self in opposition to its foreign others. Yet the virulence of the anti-Semitism is symptomatic of a crucial difference between the work's Jewish characters and its other non-English characters. If, as Ann Rosalind Jones has argued, English writers constituted the foreign as a "field of fantasy" for the invention and vilification of ethnic others, Nashe's travel narrative marks out a unique and especially fantastic place in that field for the Jews.[22] The Jews' extreme vilification is a function of their paradigmatic status as exiles, a status that is not a deviation from but antithetical to the work's conception of Englishness. Describing to Jack the miseries of exile, the banished English earl invokes three figures: Cain, Lucifer, and the Jews, all rejected by a father figure and exiled from home. "God had no greater curse to lay upon the Israelites than by leading them out of their own country to live as slaves in a strange land" (283), the earl tells Jack, later advising him in contrast to "Get thee home, my young lad; lay thy bones peaceably in the sepulchre of thy fathers; wax old in overlooking thy grounds" (287). As the earl goes on to explain, rejection by the father immerses the exile in the grotesque. In exile "there is no liberty or freedom. It is but a mild kind of subjection to be the servant of one master at once, but when thou hast a thousand thousand masters, as the veriest botcher, tinker, or cobbler freeborn will domineer over a foreigner, and think to be his better or master in company, then shalt thou find there's no such hell as to leave thy father's house (thy natural habitation) to live in the land of bondage" (283). Given the patriarchal nature of early modern society, the Oedipal scenario is not surprising. Freedom depends on acceptance by the father, succeeding him as wielder of authority, and ultimately taking one's place in the line of fathers whose bones guarantee social identity and order. Rejection by the father, in contrast, leads to the loss of freedom—in the earl's case—a reversal of social status and subordination to precisely the botchers, cobblers, and tinkers whom the Imperial soldiers found so problematic. Indeed, the exile's position is always precarious: only through the constant repetition of the exile's rejection can the privileges of the Oedipal sons be defined and maintained.

The anti-Semitism of *The Unfortunate Traveller*'s representation of the Jewish community in Rome fully exposes and exploits their status as exiles. Although the two main Jewish characters have a place in the Roman community, Zadok as a merchant and Dr. Zachary as the pope's doctor and member of Rome's medical college, the Jewish community is represented as a community of internal aliens, exiles topographically, nationally, theologically, and physically. Confined to the quarter of Rome known as "the Old Jewry" (291), the Jews are represented as "the scattered children of Abraham" (289), the "cursed generation" (289), the "ill tree" of which "good fruit" (293) should not be expected, and "foreskin-clippers" (291). The text tropes this exiled status as a dangerously fluid physicality. Dr. Zachary converts his own bodily fluids, such as "snot and spittle" (290) and the excretions from his "rheumatic eyes" (290), not only into medicines but also into poisons. Julia Kristeva argues that such excremental fluids—examples of what Mary Douglas calls "matter out of place"—embody "the danger to identity that comes from without: the ego threatened by the non-ego, society by its outside."[23] Precisely because they embodied a danger from without, Jonathan Gil Harris observes, Jewish physicians were often given a privileged place in the courts of early modern popes and monarchs: "The Jewish physician in the Jewless state was frequently regarded as a kind of social inoculation, a 'necessary' poison ingested for the welfare of the bodies of ruler and state."[24] Such a privilege is insecure at best, however, and it is in response to the deadly potential of Dr. Zachary's medicine that the pope, having contemplated genocide, banishes the Jews. Zadok is even more grotesque than Dr. Zachary. Zadok's anger upon hearing the news of the expulsion transforms him into "a toad-fish which, taken out of the water, swells more than one would think his skin could hold, and bursts in his face that toucheth him" (294). Zadok's bursting takes the form of cursing those who "worship that crucified God of Nazareth" (294) and threatening to poison wells, cut children's throats and sell their processed bodies as food to the pope's navy, desecrate hosts, to convert his already corrupt body into poison then plague, and to set fire to the city. In response, the pope reiterates Zadok's status as exile by executing him in a brutal and sodomitical parody of Christ's crucifixion: "To the execution place was he brought, where first and foremost he was stripped, then on a sharp iron stake fastened in the ground has he his fundament pitched, which stake ran up along into his body like a spit. Under his armholes two of like sort" (298).

The anti-Semitism of the work's representation of the Jewish community has an hallucinated quality, however, in both crime and punishment. Dr. Zachary does not, in fact, attempt to poison the pope. Rather, as part of her plot to obtain Jack from Dr. Zachary, Juliana, the pope's mistress, plays on the pope's anti-Semitic fears and manufactures the fiction of Dr. Zachary's attempted poisoning, a fiction that leads directly to the Jews' expulsion. Similarly, in contrast to Barabas, Marlowe's Jew of Malta, who claims already to have done such things as poison wells and murder people out of hostility to Christianity, Zadok only imagines doing them. He does attempt to blow up Rome, but this crime, like Dr. Zachary's, is largely manufactured by Juliana, who "set men about him to incense and egg him on in courses of discontentment" (289). Once Zadok has done enough to incriminate himself, the same men prevent him from lighting the fuse and send him to his execution. Indeed, the fiction of the Jews as noxious, contaminating others is a disavowal and displacement of a greater threat. The train of events leading to the expulsion is set in motion when Zadok and then Dr. Zachary attempt to wield Roman law. Zadok claims the authority to dispose of Jack's body as he wishes by "the law in Rome that if any man had a felon fallen into his hands, either by breaking into his house, or robbing him by the highway, he might choose whether he would make him his bondsman or hang him" (288). Zadok chooses a variant of the latter and sells Jack and the legal power over Jack's life and death to Dr. Zachary, who intends to use Jack as a cadaver and refuses to give up his legal power over Jack at Juliana's request. The rest is fiction, anti-Semitic fiction that preserves Oedipal privilege and order by writing the Jews as dangerous, defiling, and therefore deserving of their punishment.

The punishments are equally the products of anti-Semitic fantasy. The Jews were not, historically, expelled from Rome in 1527, none of Nashe's sources records such an event, and the expulsion of the entire Jewish community is not necessary to the success of Juliana's plot (merely confiscating Dr. Zachary's goods, for example, would have sufficed).[25] The Jews' expulsion, then, is a fiction that exceeds both historical and narrative logic. Michael Keefer has linked this fiction to the expulsion of the Jews and Moors from Spain in 1492, but its excessiveness also suggests the trace of English history.[26] Moving from the intended murder of a young English boy by a Jew to the expulsion of an entire Jewish community, the narrative echoes English anti-Semitic fictions of the expulsion of the Jews from England in 1290, fictions which cited as justification a list of Jewish crimes including the ritual murder of such innocents as Hugh of Lincoln, the model for the "litel clergeon" in Chaucer's *The Prioress's Tale*.[27] And if we consider Dr. Zachary to be an allusion to Dr. Lopez, the Jewish physician who was executed in 1594 for attempting to poison Queen Elizabeth, then it becomes even clearer that the Oedipal privileges and order protected by the work's anti-Semitic fictions are not only Italian or Spanish but also ultimately English.[28]

Representational excess also characterizes Zadok's execution. The very presence of the description of the execution exceeds the work's narrative logic: Jack, the ostensible narrative eye, is at the time of the execution locked in Juliana's closet and could not have witnessed it. The English reader witnesses the execution, then, from a curiously disembodied, purely fictional vantage. This disembodiment is opposed to the execution's terrible insistence on Zadok's embodiment. In marked contrast to its treatment of the Italian revenger Cutwolfe, the text allows Zadok no last words. The description of the execution is a savage blazon whose rhetorical scheme mimics the work of the executioners as it breaks up into a list of Zadok's body parts and the particular tortures inflicted on each. The rhetoric even mimics the execution's cruel festivity, matching the "streaming fireworks" (299) that are tied to Zadok's genitals with a simile that compares the underpropping of Zadok's fingernails "with sharp pricks" (299) to "a tailor's shop half open on a holiday" (299). Having triggered the series of events that leads to the expulsion of the Jewish community by asserting his legal rights over another's body, Zadok is now stripped of any control over his own: he does not have a body but is a body. Yet, as Philip Schwyzer argues, "from a realistic point of view, the tortures applied to [Zadok's] living body preclude one another, go on longer than they could, and are hopelessly out of order. They go on as long as Nashe wants them to, and so could conceivably go on forever." Consequently, "the reality of execution seems to be annulled by the excess of its own representation."[29] This rhetorical excess returns us to the relationship between the implied author and the English reader, revealing the grotesque Jewish body to be a fantasy presented by Nashe the textual executioner for the pleasure of the fantastically disembodied—and therefore not vulnerable, not grotesque—English subject.

The Unfortunate Traveller, then, defines Englishness in opposition to Jewishness conceived as a condition of permanent exile and abject embodiment. The excessive, phantasmagorical nature of the work's construction of Jewishness, however, betrays the anxiety and insecurity at the heart of its construction of Englishness. "Lay thy bones peaceably in the sepulchre of thy fathers; wax old in overlooking thy grounds" (287), the banished English earl advises Jack, but how many English sons could say where their fathers' bones were or had grounds to wax old overlooking? The earl offers his construction of Englishness to the humble page as classless, but it is in fact aristocratic and gendered, implicitly exiling most English people, including Jack and Nashe, from the full assumption of English subjecthood.

Jack as a character is given no father, and Nashe as author never managed to secure the fatherly patronage he seemed to seek in such dedicatory epistles as the one to the earl of Southampton prefacing *The Unfortunate Traveller.* In response, Jack and Nashe attempt to exploit their fatherlessness as an opportunity for social mobility, profit, and pleasure, yet their attempts ultimately fail. Part of the pleasure Jack's creator offers the English reader is the pleasure of witnessing Jack's degradation as condemned criminal, Dr. Zachary's cadaver, and Juliana's disposable lover. Escaping these, at the end of the work he is "mortifiedly abjected" (308) by the execution of another rebellious son, Cutwolfe, and he hastens back to Henry's camp in France and thence presumably to England, where Nashe offers up his textual body, "certain pages of his misfortunes" (208), as "waste paper" (208). Nashe himself could not avoid mortification and abjection. Patronless, penniless, and on the run from London for his part in a "lewd plaie . . . contaynynge very seditious and sclanderous matter," four years after the publication of *The Unfortunate Traveller* Nashe in Yarmouth writes *Lenten Stuffe,* in which he imagines the production of the English author as an abjected body.[30] His excessive words having been interpreted by court spies as seditious, the English author is tortured by the monarch's agents until he confesses. But what he confesses to is not, or not just, treason: "The poor fellow so tyrannously handled would rather in that extremity of convulsion confess he crucified Jesus Christ than abide it any longer."[31] The English author confesses to crucifying Christ, the crime of which the Jews were accused in English anti-Semitic discourse from the twelfth-century Bishop of Lincoln, Robert Grosseteste, to Nashe in *Christs Teares over Jerusalem.* Under the violence of torture the distinction between the English author and the Jewish characters of *The Unfortunate Traveller* collapses.[32]

The political implications of this collapse are startling if we take into account that Nashe in *Lenten Stuffe* has expanded the category of author to include "some fool, some drunken man, some mad man in an intoxicate humour [who] hath uttered he knows not what"—in short, potentially any (male) English speaking subject.[33] The point of Nashe's satire in his description of the tortured English subject depends upon an implicit distinction between Englishness and Jewishness, on the apparent absurdity of the image of ordinary, implicitly English subjects confessing to crucifying Christ. Under scrutiny, however, the image's underlying distinction collapses. Jonathan Crewe comments that "within a Christian culture, there is a moral sense in which this confession is always a priori *true;* sin constitutes at least guilt by association with the crucifiers of Christ."[34] In a Good Friday sermon before King James, Lancelot Andrewes elaborates upon this moral sense: "It is we, that are to be found the principals in this acte; and those on whom we seek to shift it, to derive it from ourselves, Pilate and Caiaphis and the rest, but instrumental causes onely. . . . Sin onely is the murtherer and our sinnes the murtherers of the Sonne of God."[35] Far from reaching an absurdly false conclusion, then, the torture of the ordinary English subject discovers a theological truth that, as Andrewes points out, is repressed by early modern anti-Semitism. The same violence that in *The Unfortunate Traveller* creates the distinction between Englishness and Jewishness returns in *Lenten Stuffe* to efface that distinction. Indeed, the truth discovered by state torture falsifies the fiction of England as the elect nation ruled by Elizabeth under God: there are no loyal English subjects, torture reveals, only Christ-killers whose treason against the monarch of heaven justifies the violence directed against them for treason against the monarch of England.

NOTES

1. Thomas Nashe, *The Unfortunate Traveller,* in *An Anthology of Elizabethan Prose Fiction,* ed. Paul Salzman, 309 (Oxford: Oxford University Press, 1987). All subsequent references to the work are to this edition and will be cited parenthetically.

2. James Shapiro, *Shakespeare and the Jews* (New York: Columbia University Press, 1996), 4.

3. Jonathan Gil Harris, "Usurers of Color: The Taint of Jewish Transnationality in Mercantilist Literature," in this collection.

4. Shapiro, *Shakespeare and the Jews,* 44.

5. See David S. Katz, *Philo-Semitism and the Readmission of the Jews to England 1603–1655* (Oxford: Clarendon Press, 1982), 9–42.

6. Laura Scavuzzo Wheeler, "The Development of the Englishman: Thomas Nashe's *The Unfortunate Traveller,*" in *Christian Encounters with the Other,* ed. John. C. Hawley, 69 (New York: New York University Press, 1998).

7. See also the following: James Keller, "Thomas Nashe's *The Unfortunate Traveller:* Taming the Spirit of Discontent," *The Elizabethan Review* 1, no. 2 (1993): 7–17; John Wenke, "The Moral Aesthetic of Thomas Nashe's *The Unfortunate Traveller,*" *Renascence: Essays on Values in Literature* 34, no. 1 (1981): 17–33.

8. Sara Warneke, *Images of the Educational Traveller in Early Modern England* (New York: Brill, 1995), 61.

9. Homer, *The Odyssey,* trans. George Chapman, ed. Allardyce Nicoll, 1.5–6 (1956; repr., with a preface by Garry Wills, Princeton, NJ: Princeton University Press, 1984).

10. Margaret Healy, *Fictions of Disease in Early Modern England: Bodies, Plagues and Politics* (Houndmills, Basingstoke, UK: Palgrave, 2001), 132.

11. G. R. Hibbard makes this connection in *Thomas Nashe: A Critical Introduction* (London: Routledge and Kegan Paul, 1962), 171.

12. Katherine Duncan-Jones, "Nashe and Sidney: The Tournament in 'The Unfortunate Traveller,'" *Modern Language Review* 63 (1968): 3–6; Thomas Nashe, "Preface to Sidney's 'Astrophel and Stella,'" in *The Works of Thomas Nashe,* ed. R. B. McKerrow, 3:330 (Oxford: Blackwell, 1966).

13. Thomas Nashe, prefatory epistle to the 1594 edition of *Christs Teares Over Jerusalem,* in *The Works of Thomas Nashe,* ed. R. B. McKerrow, 2:182 (Oxford: Blackwell, 1966).

14. Mary Russo, *The Female Grotesque: Risk, Excess and Modernity* (New York: Routledge, 1994), 11.

15. Mikhail Bakhtin, *Rabelais and His World*, trans. Helene Iswolsky, 21 (Bloomington: Indiana University Press, 1984).

16. Ibid.

17. Neil Rhodes, *Elizabethan Grotesque* (London: Routledge and Kegan Paul, 1980), 16.

18. Bakhtin, *Rabelais and His World*, 211.

19. *A Midsummer Night's Dream*, Arden edition, ed. Harold F. Brooks, 5.1.57 (1979; repr., London: Routledge, 1988).

20. Stephen Greenblatt, "Murdering Peasants: Status, Genre, and the Representation of Rebellion," in *Learning to Curse: Essays in Early Modern Culture*, 109 (New York: Routledge, 1990).

21. Neil Rhodes in "Nashe, Rhetoric and Satire" comes to a similar conclusion about Nashe's rhetoric here ("Nashe, Rhetoric and Satire," in *Jacobean Poetry and Prose: Rhetoric, Representation and the Popular Imagination*, ed. Clive Bloom, 25–43 [Houndmills, Basingstoke: Macmillan, 1988]. See also David Kaula, "The Low Style in Nashe's *The Unfortunate Traveller*," *Studies in English Literature 1500–1900* 6 (1966): 43–57.

22. Ann Rosalind Jones, "Italians and Others," in *Staging the Renaissance: Reinterpretations of Elizabethan and Jacobean Drama*, ed. David Scott Kastan and Peter Stallybrass, 260 (New York: Routledge, 1991).

23. Mary Douglas, *Purity and Danger: An Analysis of the Concepts of Pollution and Taboo* (1966; repr., London: Routledge, 1995), 36; Julia Kristeva, *Powers of Horror: An Essay on Abjection*, trans. L. Roudiez, 71 (New York: Columbia University Press, 1982).

24. Jonathan Gil Harris, *Foreign Bodies and the Body Politic: Discourses of Social Pathology in Early Modern England* (Cambridge: Cambridge University Press, 1998), 86.

25. See Sam Waagenaar's *The Pope's Jews* (La Salle, IL: Library Press, 1974). The Jews were not expelled from Rome immediately before its sack in 1527. They were, however, ghettoized in 1555 by Pope Paul IV. Neither Thomas Cooper's *Chronicle* (Thomas Cooper, trans. and ed., *Cooper's Chronicle*, by Thomas Lanquet [London, 1560]) nor Sleidanus's *Commentaries* (Joannes Philippson, *A Famouse Chronicle of oure time, called Sleidanes Commentaries*, trans. J. Daus [London, 1560]), Nashe's two major historical sources, records an expulsion.

26. Michael Keefer, "Violence and Extremity: Nashe's *Unfortunate Traveller* as an Anatomy of Abjection," in *Critical Approaches to English Prose Fiction 1520–1640*, ed. D. Beecher, 183–218 (Ottawa, ON: Dovehouse, 1998).

27. Geoffrey Chaucer, "The Prioress's Prologue and Tale," in *The Riverside Chaucer*, ed. Larry Benson, 503 (Boston: Houghton Mifflin, 1987); see Bernard Glassman's *Anti-Semitic Stereotypes Without Jews: Images of the Jews in England 1290–1700* (Detroit, MI: Wayne State University Press, 1975), esp. chap. 1, "Genesis of a Stereotype."

28. The following critics and historians make the connection between Dr. Zachary and Dr. Lopez: Lewis Brown, "*The Unfortunate Traveller* by Thomas Nashe, " *Journal of Jewish Lore and Philosophy* 1 (1919): 241–54; Maria Gibbons, "Polemic, the Rhetorical Tradition, and *The Unfortunate Traveller*," *Journal of English and Germanic Philology* 63 (1964): 408–21; Glassman, *Anti-Semitic Stereotypes Without Jews*, 72; David Katz, *The Jews in the History of England 1485–1850* (Oxford: Clarendon Press, 1994). See chap. 2 of Katz's work, "The Jewish Conspirators of Elizabethan England," for a full account of the Lopez affair and the possible allusions to it in Nashe's works.

29. Philip Schwyzer, "Summer Fruit and Autumn Leaves: Thomas Nashe in 1593," *English Literary Renaissance* 24, no. 3 (1994): 596, 597.

30. Privy council document cited by Hibbard, *Thomas Nashe*, 235.

31. Thomas Nashe, *Lenten Stuffe*, in *The Unfortunate Traveller and Other Works*, ed. J. B. Steane, 449 (Harmondsworth: Penguin, 1972).

32. Glassman writes that Robert Grosseteste, twelfth-century bishop of Lincoln, "firmly

believed that the Jews, 'being guilty of murder in cruelly killing by crucifixion the Savior of the world,' were condemned to bear the mark of Cain and live a wretched life among Christian people" (*Anti-Semitic Stereotypes Without Jews,* 15). Nashe reiterates this belief at length in *Christs Teares Over Jerusalem.*

33. Nashe, *Lenten Stuffe,* 449.

34. Jonathan Crewe, *Unredeemed Rhetoric: Thomas Nashe and the Scandal of Authorship* (Baltimore: Johns Hopkins University Press, 1982), 100.

35. Cited in Glassman, *Anti-Semitic Stereotypes Without Jews,* 63.

BIBLIOGRAPHY

Bakhtin, Mikhail. *Rabelais and His World.* Translated by Helene Iswolsky. 1968. Reprint, Bloomington: Indiana University Press, 1984.

Brown, Lewis. *"The Unfortunate Traveller* by Thomas Nashe." *Journal of Jewish Lore and Philosophy* 1 (1919): 241–54.

Chaucer, Geoffrey. "The Prioress's Prologue and Tale." In *The Riverside Chaucer.* Edited by Larry Benson. Boston: Houghton Mifflin, 1987.

Cooper, Thomas, *Cooper's Chronicle,* trans. and ed. by Thomas Lanquet. London, 1560.

Crewe, Jonathan. *Unredeemed Rhetoric: Thomas Nashe and the Scandal of Authorship.* Baltimore: Johns Hopkins University Press, 1982.

Douglas, Mary. *Purity and Danger: An Analysis of the Concepts of Pollution and Taboo.* 1966. Reprint, London: Routledge, 1995.

Duncan-Jones, Katherine. "Nashe and Sidney: The Tournament in 'The Unfortunate Traveller.'" *Modern Language Review* 63 (1968): 3–6.

Gibbons, Sister Maria. "Polemic, the Rhetorical Tradition, and *The Unfortunate Traveller.*" *Journal of English and Germanic Philology* 63 (1964): 408–21.

Glassman, Bernard. *Anti-Semitic Stereotypes Without Jews: Images of the Jews in England 1290–1700.* Detroit, MI: Wayne State University Press, 1975.

Greenblatt, Stephen. "Murdering Peasants: Status, Genre, and the Representation of Rebellion." In *Learning to Curse: Essays in Early Modern Culture.* New York: Routledge, 1990.

Harris, Jonathan Gil. *Foreign Bodies and the Body Politic: Discourses of Social Pathology in Early Modern England.* Cambridge: Cambridge University Press, 1998.

Healy, Margaret. *Fictions of Disease in Early Modern England: Bodies, Plagues and Politics.* Houndmills, Basingstoke, UK: Palgrave, 2001.

Hibbard, G. R. *Thomas Nashe: A Critical Introduction.* London: Routledge and Kegan Paul, 1962.

Homer. *The Odyssey.* Translated by George Chapman. Edited by Allardyce Nicoll. 1956. Reprint, with a preface by Garry Wills, Princeton, NJ: Princeton University Press, 1984.

Jones, Ann Rosalind. "Italians and Others." In *Staging the Renaissance: Reinterpretations of Elizabethan and Jacobean Drama.* Edited by David Scott Kastan and Peter Stallybrass, 251–62. New York: Routledge, 1991.

Katz, David. *The Jews in the History of England 1485–1850.* Oxford: Clarendon Press, 1994.

———. *Philo-Semitism and the Readmission of the Jews to England 1603–1655.* Oxford: Clarendon Press, 1982.

Kaula, David. "The Low Style in Nashe's *The Unfortunate Traveller.*" *Studies in English Literature 1500–1900* 6 (1966): 43–57.

Keefer, Michael. "Violence and Extremity: Nashe's *Unfortunate Traveller* as an Anatomy of Abjection." In *Critical Approaches to English Prose Fiction 1520–1640*. Edited by D. Beecher, 183–218. Ottawa, ON: Dovehouse, 1998.

Keller, James. "Thomas Nashe's *The Unfortunate Traveller:* Taming the Spirit of Discontent." *The Elizabethan Review* 1, no. 2 (1993): 7–17.

Kristeva, Julia. *Powers of Horror: An Essay on Abjection.* Translated by L. Roudiez. New York: Columbia University Press, 1982.

Nashe, Thomas. *Christs Teares Over Jerusalem.* In *The Works of Thomas Nashe.* 5 vols. Edited by R. B. McKerrow, 2:7–186. Oxford: Blackwell, 1966.

———. *Lenten Stuffe.* In *The Unfortunate Traveller and Other Works.* Edited by J. B. Steane. Harmondsworth, UK: Penguin, 1972.

———. *Pierce Penniless his Supplication to the Devil.* In *The Unfortunate Traveller and Other Works.* Edited by J. B. Steane. Harmondsworth, UK: Penguin, 1972.

———. "Preface to Sidney's 'Astrophel and Stella.'" In *The Works of Thomas Nashe.* 5 vols. Edited by R. B. McKerrow. 3:327–33. Oxford: Blackwell, 1966.

———. *The Unfortunate Traveller.* In *An Anthology of Elizabethan Prose Fiction.* Edited by Paul Salzman. Oxford: Oxford University Press, 1987.

Philippson, Joannes. *A Famouse Chronicle of oure time, called Sleidanes Commentaries.* Translated by J. Daus. London, 1560.

Rhodes, Neil. *Elizabethan Grotesque.* London: Routledge and Kegan Paul, 1980.

———. "Nashe, Rhetoric and Satire." In *Jacobean Poetry and Prose: Rhetoric, Representation and the Popular Imagination.* Edited by Clive Bloom, 25–43. Houndmills, Basingstoke, UK: Macmillan, 1988.

Russo, Mary. *The Female Grotesque: Risk, Excess and Modernity.* New York: Routledge, 1994.

Schwyzer, Philip. "Summer Fruit and Autumn Leaves: Thomas Nashe in 1593." *English Literary Renaissance* 24, no. 3 (1994): 583–619.

Shakespeare, William. *A Midsummer Night's Dream.* Edited by Harold F. Brooks. 1979. Reprint, London: Routledge, 1988.

Shapiro, James. *Shakespeare and the Jews.* New York: Columbia University Press, 1996.

Waagenaar, Sam. *The Pope's Jews.* La Salle, IL: Library Press, 1974.

Warneke, Sara. *Images of the Educational Traveller in Early Modern England.* New York: Brill, 1995.

Wenke, John. "The Moral Aesthetic of Thomas Nashe's *The Unfortunate Traveller.*" *Renascence: Essays on Values in Literature* 34, no. 1 (1981): 17–33.

Wheeler, Laura Scavuzzo. "The Development of the Englishman: Thomas Nashe's *The Unfortunate Traveller.*" In *Christian Encounters with the Other.* Edited by John C. Hawley, 56–73. New York: New York University Press, 1998.

Albrecht Dürer, German, 1471–1528. *A Burgundian Standard-bearer,* c. 1502/3. Engraving. Gift of Herman Levy Esq., O.B.E. McMaster University Collection, Hamilton, Canada. © McMaster Museum of Art, McMaster University, 2006. 1984.007.0115. Photo credit: Jennifer Pettiplace.

II
Profiting from the Mysterious

"These Recreations, which are strange and true": Wit, Mathematics, and Jonson's *The Magnetic Lady*

Helen Ostovich

W HY DID JONSON CHARACTERIZE COMPASS, THE HERO OF *THE MAGNETIC Lady,* as a "scholar mathematic" from Oxford?[1] What kind of intelligence is he defining with this piece of information? The answer turns out to be both simpler and far more complicated than I imagined when I first wrote about the metaphor of the mariner's compass as controlling meaning in Jonson's play.[2] For one thing, Oxford University was not the center of mathematical learning in England; indeed, both Cambridge and Oxford were slow to appoint even a lecturer in mathematics. The subject was considered too new, too untheoretical, and perhaps too foreign, since the acknowledged seat of higher mathematics was in Italy. Cambridge had the advantage, however, of having professors nominally teaching Greek or other acceptable subjects, but actually inspiring their students with mathematical zeal. The history of English mathematics in the early modern period begins in the 1550s with Robert Recorde, a graduate of Oxford and Cambridge with a passion for algebra, geometry, and related empirical sciences. He essentially democratized learning by making it readily available in books and public lectures, arguing its value irrespective of class and gender. Although Recorde practiced medicine in London when he was not taking on government appointments as Comptroller of the Bristol mint (1549–51) and Surveyor of the Mines and Monies in Ireland (1551–53 and 1556), he nevertheless found time to write the first English mathematics texts on arithmetic, algebra, and geometry, as well as on astronomy, navigation, and surveying of various kinds, including the invention of a new quadrant. In his preface to *The Whetstone of Witte* (1557), he also set a standard for the intelligent study of practical mathematics by defending its application to other fields of knowledge as a kind of key to the "castle of knowledge" housing law, medicine, divinity, astronomy, and the weights and measures so necessary to the running of any business or governmental institution. Mathematics, in other words, gives access to truth and equity.[3] As a mathematical scholar, Compass is able to predict, subvert, or absorb the schemes of all the devious plotters, representing all classes and occupations, in Lady Lodestone's house, thus ensuring the ultimate success of his own superior plot. A study of logical principles and practical applications, mathematics prepares the mind for anything that requires the processing of relations and functions.

Intellectually, the chief problem with the study of mathematics was that it was seen as practical, rather than theoretical, and hence could be considered merely a mechanical skill, not worthy of higher study.[4] The experiments and writings of William Gilbert, Thomas Harriot, Copernicus, Galileo, Tycho Brahe, Johannes Kepler, and countless others were proving to the contrary that the brave new world of "empirics" was challenging thinkers at all levels of problem solving. Jonson himself was sneered at as an empiric, an epithet he embraced in his writings, even though he took pains to establish his more orthodox skills as a classicist. Many of the books on mathematics and navigation written in England between 1580 and 1635 were written by self-taught middle-class men whose new grasp of mathematics, acquired from Recorde's texts, enabled them to deduce principles that confirmed aspects of the new science; such men include Leonard Digges (who pioneered in applied geometry, devising astronomical and nautical tables and instruments), John Blagrave (who invented various surveying instruments), and Robert Norman (who announced the magnetic dip that made the unmodified compass unreliable outside of Europe, thus explaining one then insurmountable difficulty in defining longitude), to name a few. On the one hand, Protestants and Catholics alike were disturbed by the challenge to Genesis in the concept of an infinite universe that operated by scientific principles other than moral or divine injunction: Giordano Bruno was burned as a heretic; Galileo was locked up; and Robert Fludd, sometimes called the last alchemist, believed in Copernican cosmography, but at the same time could not relinquish fundamentalist beliefs about God's power. Lightning, for example, was simply not to be understood in physical terms, but rather as the naked will of God; that is why it struck people who did not run and hide when they saw it. Roger Ascham, in *The Scholemaster,* printed in the same year, 1570, as John Dee's *Mathematicall Praeface,* spoke only of the benefits of Latin studies for children, making no mention whatsoever of mathematics.[5]

John Dee was both a credulous alchemist/astrologist/conjuror and an extraordinary mathematician/astronomer/cartographer, to whom an explorer reputedly once offered to give Canada in exchange for his knowledge of maps![6] His *Mathematicall Praeface* justifies the study of mathematics by expanding on Recorde's preface of 1557. Dee argues that all knowledge and wisdom, all arts, are a form of mathematics: he repeats Recorde's contentions about the necessity of numbers in justice (arguing for proportion), battle strategy, administration of ships and armies, accounts, and reckonings;

theology is a kind of divine reckoning; and geometry as linking mathematics and philosophy: "Geometrie is the knowledge of that which is everlastyng" because it tells us "the Veritie" [Aii v].[7] In that sense, mathematics is the logic that informs our understanding of all things physical and metaphysical because we are looking for the lines, planes, and numbers that will allow us to connect concepts and apply a method of comprehension. Without geometry, we have no basis for measuring in geography, topography or topology, hydrography, war strategy, and the art of navigation, which is dependent upon mathematical tools for working out "the shortest good way, by the aptest Direction, & in the shortest time . . . betwene any two places" (Diiij) or, for that matter, perspective, astronomy, and music, all of which demonstrate God's glorious firmament. The mystery of mathematics is that it has the power to dispel mystery and reveal a greater truth.

Both Recorde and Dee point to an important mathematical process of thinking, a way of working out problems, a logical method that Jonson also explores in his art, with its careful measures, balances, and intersections, its ironies and complex trompe-l'oeil plotting. Although Thomas Greene has already argued that Jonson's poetic use of the center and the circle are important symbolically, I am arguing—both more broadly and more concretely—that mathematical figures and tools are important to thinking practically, as a process by which Jonson understands his universe. Jonson's world, for himself and others like him who were excited by the possibilities of mathematics, demands complicated responses to a series of unfolding facts that reveal the universe as scientifically and objectively knowable to the astute observer.

Alongside this mathematical quest among Jonson's contemporaries, especially after 1600, to comprehend the workings of the universe, was a simpler fascination with the mathematical tools themselves. The broken compass of Jonson's personal impressa is one well-known example, understood metaphorically as the impossible human quest for perfection. But the tool itself is a sign of the times. Although scientific tools were certainly used, many were objets d'art acquired and displayed for their beauty and curiosity value, for example, the astrolabe. Too elaborate for sailors, it was designed by Blagrave as a "Mathematicall Jewell" in 1585, made by Charles Whitwell in 1595, and purchased by Robert Dudley, who later bequeathed it to the Duke of Tuscany.[8] Similar is the diptych dial made of ivory and brass, and decorated with a colored map of England and Wales with the motto: "OF THESE THINGES FOLLOWINGE, THIS FAMOVSE ILE IS FVEL, MOVNTAYNES FOVNTAYNES BRIDGES CHVRCHES WOMEN & WOLL";[9] by the 1630s a compass had become, like a multifunctional cell phone, the kind of elegant and expensive object without which no well-to-do traveler would leave home.[10] Nor was it merely acquiring the tool as material object that people enjoyed. They also enjoyed building the tools—erecting sundials had been fashionable since 1599, when Sir Puntarvolo in Jonson's *Every Man Out of his Humour* demonstrated his acquisition of the art in an extended metaphor.[11] As well, people liked to work out problems, a mental challenge perhaps set first by Recorde, whose method in his mathematical texts was to explain the theory, give several practical demonstrations, and then pose problems or games, to which solutions would subsequently be given, after the readers had the fun of trying to figure the answers out themselves. Mathematics was a hobby. After twenty years of thinking about numbers while running his estate, John Napier, Baron of Merchiston, published (in Latin, 1614; translated into English, 1616) the key idea for the invention of logarithms. In 1615, Henry Briggs, first Gresham professor of geometry and soon to become the first Oxford professor of geometry in 1619—incidentally, the brother of Jonson's friend Richard Briggs—arrived in Scotland to discuss improvements and refinements to Napier's invention. In 1617, Briggs's first work on logarithms, *Logarithmorum Chilias Prima,* was published in London, and in 1624, Kepler (in Prague) published proof of how logarithms worked. By 1627, John Speidell published advances on Napier's work, along with a set of geometrical problems for which he showed shorter solutions, and Edmund Wingate, by 1630 in his *Arithmetick made easie, in two Bookes,* assumed that everyone could work with logarithms well enough to follow his solutions for the calculation of interest: "Deduct the logarithme of the principall out of the Logar, of the principall and interest added together: this done, if you divide their difference by the time, and lastly adde that Quotient to the Logarithme of 100, l. that summe is the Logarithme of 100, l and the Rate added together." He then offers the following problem:

> A having a Daughter of the Age of 3 yeares, delivers at the same time a thousand markes or 666,l.13,s.4d upon condition that B shall deliver unto his daughter at the Age of 15 yeares two thousand markes, or (which is all one) 1333,l. 6,s. 8,d. Now the question is, at what rate B enjoys the 666.13.4 that it may augment to 1333.6.8 in 12 yeares? Facit at the rate of 5.19 per centum. For here first I deduct 2,82390, the Logarithme of 1333.6.8; this done, their difference is 30103, which if I divide by 12, the quotient is 2508.6; this quotient if I adde to 2.00000, the Logarithme of 100, the summe is 2.02509, which is the Logarithme of 105,l, 19 s. I conclude therefore, that the 666.13.4 will increase in 12 yeares to 1333.6.8 at the rate of 5.19 percentum, which is the Facit, or resolution of the question propounded, as aforesaid.[12]

No wonder then that Jonson, in *The Magnetic Lady,* has Sir Moth Interest engaged almost constantly in the computation of interest on his niece's inheritance, working with more complicated numbers than Wingate's 5 percent, given that the interest rate was 10 percent up to 1624, and then changed to 8 percent. If £16,000 is left to an heiress for fourteen years, and she is born in 1616, how much money will she receive in 1631? I would guess that some of the gentlemen in the audience could calculate the answer, and, based on Wingate's solution, I would also guess that the result would be as much as triple the original sum. That is certainly the conclusion rapidly calculated by Jonson's lawyer Master Practice:

> PRACTICE.   But here's a mighty gain, sir, you have made
> Of this one stock. The principal first doubled
> In the first seven year, and that redoubled
> I'the next seven! Beside six thousand pound,
> There's threescore thousand got in fourteen year
> After the usual rate of ten i'the hundred,
> And the ten thousand paid.
>
> (2.6.29–35)

That is, the principal of £16,000 would double twice at 10 percent—"ten i'the hundred" —in fourteen years to approximately £64,000. If the rate were 10 percent for the first seven years, and only 8 percent for the next seven, nevertheless, the profit by 1632 would roughly fit Practice's rapid calculation. If Sir Moth then pays out £10,000 as the marriage portion, keeping £6,000 of the original trust for himself, he is left with £54,000 of interest + £6,000 = £60,000—as Practice says, "threescore thousand got in fourteen year." New mathematics books with charts for figuring interest make the numbers easier to work out; but at that rate, the trustee Sir Moth can certainly afford to fob off the eager political suitor Master Bias with a mere £10,000, while hoarding the rest for himself. Whether an audience could compute the calculations or not, they would respond to the fascinating sound of vast sums of money manipulated by wheeler-dealers who seem to know what they are saying. The rhetoric of mathematics embellishes its users with expertise that cannot be denied.

The popularity of mathematical problems appears in another phenomenon of the 1630s, the game book. *Récréations Mathématiques,* a hefty volume divided into three parts totaling 350 pages, not counting the many tables, first compiled in 1624 by Henry Van Etten, expanded in 1626, and then translated into various languages including English by 1633, offers a variety of problems, ranging from sophisticated mathematical skills to facetious logic.[13] I will give examples shortly from the 1633 English translation, which does not always follow the order, volume and page numbering, or exact wording of the French and omits problems without explanation. Generally, the translation echoes the original. Some problems are magic tricks: how can one balance a light object in a scale so that it seems to be of the same weight as a heavier object (1.75)? Some depend on geography: how to find the lattitude of countries (2.4); or geometry: how to draw an equilateral triangle; or how to construct parallel lines (2.10) or how to measure the height of a tree with two straws (2.15); or optics: how to use mirrors to make a small quantity appear a large amount (2.22); or physics: how to use a lever or a pulley to solve specific difficulties (how to make a ladder you can keep in your pocket [2.44] or how to empty a cistern with a syphon [2.5]2). One problem that seems to reflect Compass's wit concerns circles: the author notes in large letters, "C'est icy vne Question curieuse: Si c'est chose plus difficile & admirable, de faire vn cercle parfaict sans compas, que de trouuer le centre & le milieu du cercle?" (1.86) [Here's a curious question: If it's more difficult and astonishing to make a perfect circle without a compass, or to find the center and middle of the circle?] The answer is the former—as all of Compass's rivals discover, and as the end of Jonson's induction reveals about the playwright's intentions in completing the perfect circle of his career: "The author, beginning his studies of this kind with *Every Man in his Humour* and after, *Every Man Out of his Humour,* and since, continuing in all his plays . . . finding himself now near the close or shutting up of his circle, hath fancied to himself in idea this magnetic mistress . . . his centre attractive, to draw thither a diversity of guests, all persons of different humours to make up his perimeter."[14] The variety and complexity of game-book brainteasers give a very strong sense not only of what Jonson wanted to give his audience, but also of what his audience enjoyed and wanted to grapple with. As van Etten remarks in his preface to the 1624 French publication: "I took singular pleasure in certain problems no less ingenious than recreational, which our tutor ['notre Regent', perhaps better translated as 'our governor', the term Jonson used for Wasp in *Bartholomew Fair*] used in order to stimulate us in the study of other more difficult and serious demonstrations."[15]

The title page of the English translation, illustrated with drawings of scientific instruments, places the title in an elongated oval as *MATHEMATI-CALL / Recreations / Or a Collection, of / sundrie excellent / Problems / out of ancient & moderne / Phylosophers / Both Vsefull / and / Recreative /* London Printed for / Rich. Hawkins in / Chancery Lane / near Serjantes / Inne / 1633. The prefatory poem (unique to this early English edition, in which it is pasted onto the inside cover) asserts the superiority of intellectual puzzles as entertainment:

On the Frontispice and Booke
All Recreations do delight the minde
But these are best being of a learned kinde:
Here Art and Nature strive to give content,
In shewing many a rare experiment;
Which you may reade, and on their Schemes here looke,   5
Both in the Frontispice, and in the Booke,
Upon whose table new conceits are set
Like dainty dishes, thereby for to whet

And winne your judgement, with your appetite,
To taste them, and therin to take delight.   10
The Senses objects are but dull at best,
But Art doth give the Intellect a feast.
Come hither, then, and here I will describe,
What this same table doth for you provide.
Here Questions of Arithmeticke are wrought,   15
And hidden secrets unto light are brought,
The like it in Geometry doth descrie,
With Strange experiments in Astronomie,
And Navigation with each severall Picture,
In Musique, Opticks, and in Architecture;   20
In Staticke, Machanicks, and Chimistrie,
In Waterworkes, and to ascend more hie,
In Fireworkes, like to Jove's Artillerie.
All this i know thou in this Booke shalt finde,
And here's enough for to content thy minde.   25
For from good Authors, this our Author drew,
These Recreations, which are strange and true;
So that this Booke's a Center, and 'tis fit,
That in this Center, lines of praise should meete.

                                                                    W. S.

Using a particularly Jonsonian turn of phrase, the poet claims the superiority of games-playing as recreation, intellectualizing pleasure by locating it somewhere between jest-book wit and philosophy, and describing the table of contents as a feast of "dainty dishes" which tempt the appetite to further study, profiting the mind by feeding it delight. Some of the book's entertainment take the form of riddles, such as Problem 24: "How may a man stand at the same time having both his head and his feet up?" The answer depends on the reader's ability to break free of conventional paradigms and test other patterns: here, the answer is that he has to be in the middle of the earth where up and down no longer signify. In *The Magnetic Lady* (2.7), the riddle posed by the hero Compass challenges Pleasance to understand his use of metonymy and analogy, when he lets loose a flood of legal references to suits, retaining counsel, joining patentees, and keeping charge of the case:

COMPASS.   Stay, Mistress Pleasance, I must ask you a question:
              Ha' you any suits in law?
PLEASANCE   I, Master Compass?
COMPASS   Answer me briefly; it is dinner time.
              They say you have retained brisk Master Practice
              Here of your counsel, and are to be joined   5
              A patentee with him.

PLEASANCE   In what? Who says so?
          You are disposed to jest.
COMPASS   No, I am in earnest.
          It is given out i'the house so, I assure you.
          But keep your right to yourself and not acquaint
          A common lawyer with your case. If he   10
          Once find the gap, a thousand will leap after.
          I'll tell you more anon.   [*Exit.*]
PLEASANCE   This riddle shows
          A little like a love-trick, o' one face,
          If I could understand it. I will study it.   [*Exit.*]

What he really wants to know is whether Pleasance has fallen in love with
his rival, the lawyer, and permitted him any sexual intimacies or hopes for
the future. Pleasance recognizes the riddle as a "love-trick," but does not
commit herself yet to an answer, preferring, sensibly enough, to "study it"
first. And that, of course, is the object of the math-game book: to encourage readers to reject the immediate reactions of the senses, which may be
"dull," and instead to connect evidence imaginatively and speculatively
into a meaningful pattern: "But Art doth give the Intellect a feast" is the
prefatory claim.

The concept of intellectual games as an artistic banquet that increases
the appetite for learning is also part of the "Letter to the Reader," which argues that thinking about anything is better than the opposite alternative. In
a kind of Seinfeldian twist, the letter insists that minds both ancient and
modern "have sported and delighted themselves upon severall things of
small consequence, as upon the foote of a fly, upon a straw, upon a point,
nay, upon nothing; striving as it were to shew the greatnesse of their glory
in the smalnesse of the subject," and goes on to defend the math-game book
even "though perhaps these labours to some humorous persons may seeme
vaine, and ridiculous; for such it was not undertaken." The motive rather
was to be "an invitation and motive to the search of greater matters, and to
imploy the minde in usefull knowledge, rather than to be busied in vaine
Pamphlets, Play-bookes, fruitless Legends, and prodigious Histories that
are invented out of fancie, which abuse many Noble spirits, dull their wits,
& alienate their thoughts from laudable and honourable studies." The profit
and delight of this book is ultimately described as "manly," a Jonsonian
accolade.

Mathematicall Recreations offers several insights into the games-playing
of *The Magnetic Lady*. One problem, like Wingate's, deals with progres-
sion and multiplication; Problem 84, "Of Pigges," makes the following
proposition: "the great *Turke* with all his Revenues, is not able to maintaine
for one yeares time, all the Pigges that a sow may pigge with all her race,
that is, the increase with the increase unto 12 yeares: this seems impossible,

yet it is most true; for let us suppose and put the case that a Sow bring forth but 6, 2 males and 4 females; and that each female shal bring forth as many every yeare, during the space of 12 yeares," the result will be "33 millions of Pigges." If each pig cost 1 crown each year to maintain, that will require at least 33 million crowns—more than the Sultan has in his coffers (179–82)! The details are different from Wingate's investment problem, quoted earlier, but the computational and logical skills are similar, and reflect Jonson's coupling of economic increase with human gestation in the play.[16] Other problems involve testing counterfeit money: how does one correctly determine which box is full of gold and which full of lead, if they look identical from the outside and weigh the same (Problem 42, pp. 62–64)—a problem similar to Compass's deducing which girl is the true niece and heiress and which is the "slip" or false coin. The answer is not just a guess for a mathematician: if he can weigh the boxes first in air, and then in water, he can apply Archimedes' principle, which proves that gold weighs less by one-eighteenth and lead by one-eleventh. Or he might use compasses to clip each box and hold them in counterpoise over a piece of iron; the balancing of the weights in proximity to iron, according to this text, gives the correct answer, although one mathematician, perhaps the translator, commenting on this solution, spurned it as "False and absurd" when tested. One of the comic elements of *Mathematicall Recreations* is its habit of defending or spurning the solutions to its own problems. Nevertheless, these elements of gold and false gold are features in Jonson's play that when balanced and put to the test by Compass, in the proximity of his friend Ironside, reveal the right solution. Problem 39, "Of a Glasse very pleasant," is a practical joke on a related idea: create two glasses that fit together one within the other, put wine between the glasses, and seal them together. It will look like a glass of wine but will be empty when one tries to drink and "so will cause laughter to these that stand by" (58). The plot of *The Magnetic Lady* also plays games with the idea of the full glass and the empty glass in comparing the two girls, only one of whom can be the true heiress, and in inserting practical jokes that make fools of the less aware or skillful. The important factor is the perception of the observer.

The observer, or audience, has to be aware both of the pleasures of spectacle and of its deceits. Problem 44 explains "How to represent diverse sorts of Rainebowes here below" (66), a kind of blinding or seducing of spectators with fancy color and display, theoretically not unlike the contrasts developed in Jonson's play between the courtier's clothing, the soldier's uniform and swordplay, and the rhetoric or wordplay spouted by the lawyer, the merchant, and the politician in their fierce combat for control of the heiress and her estate. Spectacle, of course, is a key ingredient not only of drama, but also of magic and religion. *Mathematicall Recreations* tells a wonderful story as part of Problem 67, "Of the Adamant or Magnet, and the needles touched therewith" (103–7), which represents the power of a magnet as magic, permanently transforming needles to make them turn north and south. In commenting on the profound impression such scientific magic has on its beholders, the translator tells the history of a mosque, "one of the Turkish synagogues at Meca" in which "the sepulcher of that infamous *Mahomet* rests suspended in the aire" (104), because the magnet placed in the roof holds the massy substance of iron afloat without any support beyond the magnetic pull. The translator also cited Pliny's *Natural History* in claiming that the Temple of Arsinoë in Alexandria was vaulted in the roof with magnets "to produce the like deceit, to hang the sepulcher of that goddess in the aire" (104). All of these problems, as Problem 71 explicitly states, educate by encouraging the playing of games. Even tennis and bowls depend on the player's mathematical ability to calculate angles and probable motion as the ball rebounds: "The Angle is always equall to the Angle of reflection" (123), and this is a lesson that goes well beyond being good at sports. The mathematical genius of Compass, complemented by his best friend's astute comprehension of military strategy, wins them both, as the result of "reflection," love, not just rich wives, and defeats those who use mathematics only for the crass purpose of calculating and hoarding, never seeing pleasure beyond the number-crunching.

If mathematics had, by 1632, "now become a game" testing the skill of the players (so described in the dedicatory verse to Napier's *Rabdology*), it had also become a fierce battle to stake claims on intellectual and economic property.[17] Even *Mathematicall Recreations* has a tangled intellectual property argument attached to it. Trevor H. Hall argues that *Mathematicall Recreations* was plagiarized by Henry van Etten, a not very good student of mathematics at the University at Pont-a-Mousson in Lorraine, where the book was published first as *Mathematicall Recreation* (here singular, but plural in subsequent expanded editions). Van Etten studied under Père Jean Leurechon, SJ, a serious philosophy and mathematics scholar who entertained his classes with tricks from the 1612 book of mathematics games by Claude-Gaspar Bachet, sieur de Meziriac; van Etten never completed his degree, but he compiled the book and dedicated it to his wealthy uncle Seigneur Lambert Verreycken, probably hoping for financial support. The dedication appears only in the two Mousson editions of 1624 and 1626 and in the first two Paris issues of 1626 and 1627. Hall argues that Leurechon had nothing to do with the book; that van Etten copied, almost word for word in places, Meziriac's book, and that even Meziriac never claimed his games were original. Meziriac cites other scholars, Forcadel on Gemma Frisius (Dutch mathematician) and Gosselin's translation of Nicholas Tartaglia (Italian treatise published 1556). Meziriac's preface to his reprint says he wrote his book to test public interest in mathematics, as a prelude to his translation of Diophantus of Alexandria (Paris, 1621)—"And as he was afraid lest, since his Diophantus was already come abroad, people should be astonished that after he had written so serious a piece and one so full of profound speculations as his Diophantus, he should amuse himself in retouching his problems, he prepared in his preface the following answer among other. 'Books are the children of our souls and besides the natural inclination with fathers have to love their children in general, they bear a particular affection for their first-born.' Wherefore, as this book is the first which I have sent abroad and as it were the eldest born of my mind, it is but just that I should cherish it particularly, that not satisfied with having sent it into the world, I still choose to take care of its preservation and advancement."[18]

The question of intellectual property emerging in this period offers a sharply edged comment on the attachment to authority marked in other areas of early modern scholarship. Robert Recorde expressed consistent opposition to the dogmatic imitation of ancient authorities, including Aristotle, and appealed to reason and observation as surer guides;[19] so too Jonson wrote in *Timber* that the ancients "opened the gates, and made the way, that went before us; but as guides, not commanders."[20] Scientists of the time were having difficulty sorting out what was arrived at by predecessors, what by collaborators, and what by independent individual discovery. Two cases are pertinent here.[21]

First is the magnetic rivalry of Mark Ridley and William Barlow after the death of William Gilbert with whom they had both collaborated on magnetism, along with Edward Wright and Henry Briggs. Ridley published *A Short Treatise of Magneticall Bodies and Motions* in 1613, closely following Gilbert's *De Magnete* (1600) on the lodestone and magnetic needle, which Ridley followed up with his own experiments, paying special attention to instruments and methods of determining the magnetic variation at sea. Barlow published his *Magneticall Advertisements* first in 1616, also closely based on Gilbert and on Barlow's own experiments, and charged Ridley with plagiarism: in the dedication to Sir Dudley Digges, Barlow remarks, "Only this I am sure of that I have met with many portraitures of my Magneticall implements, and divers of my propositions set abroad in print in another mans name, and yet some of them not rightly understood by the partie usurping them" (A3). He blames the printer for stalling the publication of Barlow's work for three years, thus making Ridley seem to be the originator of the material. His reason for dedicating the book to Digges may have some bearing on Jonson's characterization of Compass as a natural regulator of events. Barlow writes: "First, because your rare learning join'd with so great pietie, accompanied with so pleasing a carriage of your selfe towards everie man is such, as causeth all goode men which know you, to love you, by force of a naturall sympathy not unlike the appetite of concourse & coniunction whereby our very Magnets doe affect their proper objects" (A3v). Barlow ends his book with a letter he received early in his career from Gilbert, praising Barlow's inventions, especially his explanation of double capping the lodestone with iron, and hoping Barlow will agree to contribute some of his inventions to a book Gilbert is currently writing (87–88). Ridley replied in 1617 with *Magneticall Animadversions. Upon certaine Magneticall Advertisements lately published by Maister William Barlow,* aggressively asserting his credentials as "Doctor of Physicke" and quibbling over Barlow's wording and content, claiming several times that Barlow plays fast and loose with magnetic principles, and that a mariner following Barlow's instructions would run aground. Barlow responded in *A Briefe Discovery of the Idle Animadversions of Marke Ridley Doctor in Phisicke upon a Treatise entituled, Magneticall Advertisements* (1618), appended to the second edition of his book, listing unequivocally all the places where Ridley copied Barlow. Given the evidence, if accurate, it is very peculiar that Ridley would dare to publicly "traduce" Barlow "so contemptuously in his frivolous *Animadversions*" (Barlow, *Briefe Discovery,* 3–4) and yet never acknowledge his debt to Barlow's work: "For except this Ridley had ploughed with my Heifor, hee had not knowne my riddle. *Sic vos non vobis,*" claims Barlow (4). But other scientists did not think the Barlow-Ridley quarrel could be so easily settled, first because both men borrowed heavily from Gilbert, who himself depended partly on the practical and mathematical experience of others; and second because Barlow's concept of the earth's rotation was at odds with recent discoveries of Jupiter's satellites as seen through a telescope and also with new views about the immense distance of the stars, and hence Barlow's claims for the uses of his improved compass were not entirely substantiated.[22] In any case, the history of science has many instances in which two men work on the same idea, each apparently unaware of the other, as was the case earlier with Robert Recorde and Peter Ramus. Evidence indicates that neither Ramus nor Recorde knew of each other; Recorde's work preceded Ramus's by ten to fifteen years in publication, but they read the same sources and had many of the same thoughts, working independently, one in English, the other in German and Latin. Ramus became established as the authority only in the decade after Recorde's death.[23]

The other intellectual property dispute occurred during the "mathematical explosion" of the 1620s, when almanacs advertised practitioners' services as teachers, land surveyors, gaugers, diallists, gunners, engineers, and promoted their skills in medicine, astronomy, horology, cosmography, and tidal predictions, many of them men without degrees, or working in other fields, who had learned their craft by experience.[24] William Oughtred was an Anglican minister and mathematics tutor who invented a slide rule and allowed his student William Forster to have the instrument made for sale. The problem was that another of his students, Richard Delamain, claimed to have invented the slide rule first. As it happened, this project, like the Barlow-Ridley case, was collaborative, in that both inventors employed Elias and John Allen as their instrument makers, and that may be how Oughtred's project got mixed up with Delamain's, with the Allens unconsciously leaking ideas. Delamain, unlike the well-reputed Oughtred, had no university degree (he learned his mathematics initially through the Gresham public lectures, and then took instruction privately with Oughtred and others), and was in the more precarious position when William Forster accused him of stealing the design for Oughtred's "Circles of Proportion" (as the slide rule was called). As in the Ridley-Barlow case, Delamain published his description of the slide rule first in *Grammelogia, or the Mathematicall ring* (1630), but Oughtred had described a slide rule in 1622, although he didn't describe the circular slide rule until *Circles of Proportion and the Horizontal Instrument* (1632). Meanwhile Delamain published a second book in 1631 on the quadrant, work which Oughtred also considered plagiarized from his own theories. The debate became heated: Oughtred sharply criticized Delamain for acting as though mathematical understanding was all in the use of instruments, not in the theory; Delamain countered that although theory reveals the highest level of understanding, most people prefer to know the answer quickly and accurately, and that is what instruments provide. The recent history of computers and calculators bears out Delamain's story. Certainly the ideal since the days of Robert Recorde had been to achieve a cooperation between theory and practice, and utility was not to be scorned. Oughtred continued to demonstrate his fertile scientific imagination by inventing a more accurate logarithmic gauge for wine vessels; Elias Allen built the instrument to sell along with Oughtred's book, and the only problem was that the instrument was sold before the book that explained its use, causing some anxiety among purchasers.[25]

In *The Magnetic Lady,* we have a broadly comparable situation: several people of different backgrounds and orientations attempt to attain the same goal (control of the heiress and her fortune), and most of them fail because their narrow understanding of relations and functions and of how to navigate through obscure or partly known territory limits them. The real competition, Mistress Polish, who stands for women's education, almost reaches the goal first, but she is hampered mostly by her lack of a strong theoretical position. She has the instruments and the practical authority to use them, but her grasp of the larger situation is inadequate, partly because of timing and partly because of miscalculations based on incomplete information. As Copernicus says of knowing the systematic procession of events and the harmony of the whole universe, you have to face the facts "with both eyes open."[26] Only Compass, the scholar mathematic from Oxford, has access to theory and practice in many fields—especially the theory and application of magnetism—and the ability to manipulate military strategy (Captain Ironside), divinity (Parson Palate), law (Master Practice), politics (Master Bias), finance (Sir Moth Interest), medicine (Dr Rut and his apothecary Master Item), and court diplomacy (Sir Diaphanous Silkworm). A former world traveler with the Loadstone merchant fleet, Compass is a risk-taker who can theorize his acquired knowledge and improve his status within the Loadstone domestic economy, increasing the power of the legitimate family business. His mathematical expertise ensures justice and good government by exposing the fraudulent "accounts" of Polish on the one hand and Interest on the other; in Poovey's terms, Compass improves his social and financial standing "precisely by stabilizing a system of rewards and risks and by codifying the behaviors that would be rewarded within this system".[27] As a result, Compass is able to control and compensate for all the competing directional pulls to arrive at the destination he seeks: a rich and virtuous wife. Pleasance Steel's name sums it up. She gives pleasure, and her maiden "steel," touched by Lady Lodestone's power, is strengthened magnetically, empowering both herself and her new husband to enjoy a secure future. Compass would certainly agree with Robert Recorde that "besides the mathematical arts there is no infallible knowledge, except that it be borrowed from them."[28]

NOTES

1. See "The Persons that act" (A2), in Ben Jonson, *The Magnetick Lady: Or Humors Recondil'd* (London, 1640). The text cited in this essay is the modernized text I prepared for the Cambridge Works of Ben Jonson, forthcoming from Cambridge University Press, 2008.

2. See Helen Ostovich, "The Appropriation of Pleasure in *The Magnetic Lady*," *SEL: Studies in English Literature* (Spring, 1994) 425–42; rev. and rept. in *Maids and Mistresses, Cousins and Queens: Women's Alliances in Early Modern England*, ed. Susan Frye and Karen Robertson, 134–55 (Oxford: Oxford University Press, 1999).

3. Mary Poovey, *A History of the Modern Fact: Problems of Knowledge in the Sciences of Wealth and Society* (Chicago: University of Chicago Press, 1998). Poovey traces a somewhat less optimistic picture of the democritizing spread of mathematical knowledge in this period by problematizing the cultural value accorded merchants, whose prestige increased as their bookkeeping practices demonstrated the justice of their profits. Reformed accounting practices provided evidence of mercantile expertise, subsequently acknowledged by late sixteenth-century political theorists as pivotal in ensuring the power of a state. Financial increase, in other words, or the breeding of money invested to make more money, became a type of gestation that produced reliable knowledge based upon the formal precision of double-entry bookkeeping and the moral rectitude or virtue of the merchant established thereby (see chap. 2, esp. 31–33). John Dee also struggled with this problem of whether to focus on democratic humanism in applied mathematics or on scholarly elitism in more abstract mathematical goals such as alchemy and occultism; see William Sherman, *John Dee: The Politics of Reading and Writing in the English Renaissance* (Amherst: University of

Massachusetts Press, 1995), 21–3. Sherman points out that the revision of Recorde's *Ground of Artes* in Dee's "Mathematicall Praeface" to Euclid "appealed to the mercantile and mechanical classes as much as to academics or adepts" (22).

4. See Henry Turner's forthcoming book, *The English Renaissance Stage: Geometry, Poetics, and the Practical Spatial Arts* (Oxford: Oxford University Press), for a discussion of the influence of traditions of practical knowledge on early modern drama.

5. For a short list of resources on early scientists, see *Epact: Scientific Instruments of Medieval and Renaissance Europe,* an electronic catalogue of medieval and renaissance scientific instruments from four European museums: the Museum of the History of Science, Oxford; the Istituto e Museo di Storia della Scienza, Florence; the British Museum, London; and the Museum Boerhaave, Leiden (http://www.mhs.ox.ac.uk/epact/ [accessed September 23, 2005]); J. J. O'Connor and E. F. Robertson, *The MacTutor History of Mathematics Archive,* School of Mathematics and Statistics, University of St Andrews, 2001 (http://www-groups.dcs.st-and.ac.uk/~history/index.html [accessed September 23, 2005]); E. G. R. Taylor, *The Mathematical Practitioners of Tudor & Stuart England* (Cambridge: Cambridge University Press, 1954); David W. Waters, *The Art of Navigation in England in Elizabethan and Early Stuart Times* (London: Hollis and Carter, 1958).

6. Sherman discusses Dee's prodigious contribution to the development of the British Empire through exploration and cartography, particularly his early participation in the search for the Northwest Passage, a project from which he withdrew without explanation (see *John Dee,* chap. 9, esp. 173–77), although he continued to advocate the spread of trade as a means of attaining English global supremacy (180–81). See also John H. Lienhard, "John Dee," in *Engines of Our Ingenuity* (http://www.uh.edu/engines/epi474.htm.

7. John Dee, *The Elements of Geometrie of the most aunccient Philosopher Euclide of Megara, With a very fruitfull Preface by M. I. Dee, specifying the chiefe Mathematicall Sciences* (London, 1570).

8. See *Epact,* 33.

9. Ibid., 218.

10. Ibid., 165.

11. See Ben Jonson, *Every Man Out of his Humour,* ed. Helen Ostovich, 2.1.207–11 (Manchester, UK: Manchester University Press, 2001).

12. Edmund Wingate, *Arithmetick made easie, in two Bookes* (London, 1630), 473–76.

13. My French source is the 1629 copy owned by the British Library: *Récréations Mathématiques Composées De plusieurs Problems, plaisans & facetiues, d'Arithmetique, Géométrie, Astrologie, Optique, Perspectiue, Méchanique, Chymie, & d'autres rares & curieux Secrets* (Pont-a-Mousson, Paris, 1629). The English translation, first published in London, 1633, is discussed below (I used the 1633 British Library copy and the 1653 copy owned by the Thomas Fisher Rare Book Library, University of Toronto). The 1653 and 1674 editions include William Oughtred's pamphlet on the double horizontal dial.

14. Induction (modernized); p. 7 in the 1640 folio.

15. Cited and translated in Trevor H. Hall, *Mathematicall Recreations: An Exercise in Seventeenth-Century Bibliography* (Leeds, UK: Leeds University School of English, 1969), 35.

16. Jonson's metaphor was an accepted contemporary view: see Poovey, *History of Modern Fact,* on financial increase as described in note 3 above. For other related views of economic expansion, see Douglas Bruster,*Drama and the Market in the Age of Shakespeare* (Cambridge: Cambridge University Press, 1992); David Glimp, *Increase and Multiply: Governing Cultural Reproduction in Early Modern England* (Minneapolis: University of Minnesota Press, 2003).

17. John Napier, *Rabdology* (1617), trans. William Frank Richardson; introd. Robin E. Rider (Cambridge, MA: MIT Press, 1990), 5.

18. Hall, *Mathematicall Recreations,* 33.

19. Francis R. Johnson, and Sanford V. Larkey, "Robert Recorde's Mathematical Teaching and the Anti-Aristotelian Movement," *The Huntington Library Quarterly* 7 (April 1935), 77–78.

20. George Parfitt, ed., *Ben Jonson: The Complete Poems* (London: Penguin, 1988), 379.

21. Many other pertinent cases exist. The pamphlet war between the economic theorists Gerard de Malynes and Edward Misselden, which often treated the issue of what constitutes the "center" of commerce, offers a link between Jonson's figure of the compass as the sign of his career and his use of mathematics in *The Magnetic Lady* to calculate interest and profit. Poovey, *History of Modern Fact* (69–78), discusses the pamphlet war as a contest between fixed values (Malynes) and free trade, in which risk is healthy, keeping the market vigorous (Misselden). See also Joseph Loewenstein, *The Author's Due: Printing and the Prehistory of Copyright* (Chicago: University of Chicago Press, 2002) on the problem of text as property, and *Ben Jonson and Possessive Authorship* (Cambridge: Cambridge University Press, 2002), on what a text means to an author, as opposed to its value to a publisher (64–68), on piracy and plagiarism (73–88), and, in chap. 5, on the personal investment of the author in his text.

22. Taylor, *The Mathematical Practitioners of Tudor & Stuart England,* 183.

23. Johnson and Larkey, "Robert Recorde's Mathematical Teaching," 81–85.

24. Taylor, *Mathematical Practitioners,* 57–58.

25. Ibid., 65.

26. O'Connor and Robertson, *MacTutor History of Mathematics Archive,* Copernicus entry.

27. Poovey, *History of Modern Fact,* 90.

28. O'Connor and Robertson, *MacTutor History of Mathematics Archive,* Recorde entry.

BIBLIOGRAPHY

Barlow, William. *Magneticall Advertisements.* London, 1616. Reprinted with a separately paginated Appendix containing *A Briefe Discovery of the Idle Animadversions of Mark Ridley,* London, 1618.

Bruster, Douglas. *Drama and the Market in the Age of Shakespeare.* Cambridge: Cambridge University Press, 1992.

Dee, John. *The Elements of Geometrie of the most anucient Philosopher Euclide of Megara. With a very fruitfull Preface by M. I. Dee, specifying the chiefe Mathematicall Sciences.* London, 1570.

Epact: Scientific Instruments of Medieval and Renaissance Europe. http://www.mhs.ox.ac.uk/epact/

Glimp, David. *Increase and Multiply: Governing Cultural Reproduction in Early Modern England.* Minneapolis: University of Minnesota Press, 2003.

Hall, Trevor H. *Mathematicall Recreations: An Exercise in Seventeenth-Century Bibliography.* Leeds, UK: Leeds University School of English, 1969.

Johnson, Francis R., and Sanford V. Larkey. "Robert Recorde's Mathematical Teaching and the Anti-Aristotelian Movement." *The Huntington Library Quarterly* 7 (April 1935): 59–87.

Jonson, Ben. *Every Man Out of his Humour.* Edited by Helen Ostovich. Manchester, UK: Manchester University Press, 2001.

———. *The Magnetick Lady: Or Humors Recondil'd.* London, 1640.

Lienhard, John H. "John Dee." In *Engines of Our Ingenuity*. http://www.uh.edu/engines/epi474.htm/ (Accessed September 23, 2005).

Loewenstein, Joseph. *The Author's Due: Printing and the Prehistory of Copyright*. Chicago: University of Chicago Press, 2002.

———. *Ben Jonson and Possessive Authorship*. Cambridge: Cambridge University Press, 2002.

Mathematical Recreations; or a Collection of Sundrie Excellent Problems out of Ancient & Moderne Phylosophers Both Usefull and Recreative. London, 1633.

Napier, John. *Rabdology*. 1617. Translated by William Frank Richardson. Introduction by Robin E. Rider. Cambridge, MA: MIT Press, 1990.

O'Connor, J. J., and E. F. Robertson. *The MacTutor History of Mathematics Archive,* School of Mathematics and Statistics, University of St. Andrews, 2001. http://www-groups.dcs.st-and.ac.uk/~history/index.html/

Ostovich, Helen. "The Appropriation of Pleasure in *The Magnetic Lady*." *SEL: Studies in English Literature* (Spring 1994): 425–42. Revised and reprinted in *Maids and Mistresses, Cousins and Queens: Women's Alliances in Early Modern England*. Edited by Susan Frye and Karen Robertson, 134–55. Oxford: Oxford University Press, 1999.

Parfitt, George, ed. *Ben Jonson: The Complete Poems*. London: Penguin, 1988.

Poovey, Mary. *A History of the Modern Fact: Problems of Knowledge in the Sciences of Wealth and Society*. Chicago: University of Chicago Press, 1998.

Recorde, Robert. *the Castle of Knowledge*. London, 1556.

———. *The Grounde of Artes*. London, 1542; enlarged 1552.

———. *The Pathwaie of Knowledge*. London, 1551.

———. *The Whetstone of Witte*. London, 1557.

Récréations Mathématiques Composées De plusieurs Problems, plaisans & facetiues, d'Arithmetique, Géométrie, Astrologie, Optique, Perspectiue, Méchanique, Chymie, & d'autres rares & curieux Secrets. Pont-a-Mousson, Paris, 1629.

Ridley, Mark. *Magneticall Animadversions*. London, 1617.

Sherman, William. *John Dee: The Politics of Reading and Writing in the English Renaissance*. Amherst: University of Massachusetts Press, 1995.

Taylor, E. G. R. *The Mathematical Practitioners of Tudor & Stuart England*. Cambridge: Cambridge University Press, 1954.

Turner, Henry. *The English Renaissance Stage: Geometry, Poetics, and the Practical Spatial Arts*. Oxford: Oxford University Press, forthcoming.

Waters, David W. *The Art of Navigation in England in Elizabethan and Early Stuart Times*. London: Hollis and Carter, 1958.

Wingate, Edmund. *Arithmetick made easie, in two Bookes*. London, 1630.

Usurers of Color: The Taint of Jewish Transnationality in Mercantilist Literature and *The Merchant of Venice*

Jonathan Gil Harris

IN KEEPING WITH THE TITLE OF THIS VOLUME, I ATTEND HERE TO BOTH THE mysterious and the foreign. My goal is to interpret a mysterious passage from Shakespeare's *Merchant of Venice:* Shylock's prolix justification of his money-lending practices through his parable about Laban and Jacob (1.3.69–80), which readers have struggled to make sense of as a commentary on usury.[1] But I am equally concerned with the foreign in a variety of guises. Supplementing the important work of James Shapiro, I examine the Jew as a special, problematic species of foreigner in early modern English literature.[2] I also argue that to understand Shakespeare's coding of the Jew's foreignness and to interpret Shylock's mysterious parable, we need to pay heed to two seemingly unrelated yet overlapping discourses of the foreign that are crucial to *The Merchant of Venice:* first, the English mercantilist critique of alienating domestic bullion to foreign factors; and second, an emergent paradigm of disease as residing in, and transmitted by, foreign bodies. It is the points of intersection between these two discourses of the foreign that I seek to illuminate in this essay.

SICK ECONOMIES

For all its suasive force in our own time, the notion of disease as an invasive foreign body is of comparatively recent provenance. So naturalized has this notion of disease become that it is easy to forget there once was a time when people's pathological fears were not figured in terms of viruses, bacteria, germs, or any other foreign body. At the beginning of the sixteenth century, the dominant English conceptions of health and disease looked decidedly different from our modern counterparts. Rather than an external, invasive entity, as it has overwhelmingly been understood since Louis Pasteur formulated his theory of germs and Robert Koch discovered the bacillus that causes tuberculosis, disease was imagined as a state of internal imbalance, or *dyskrasia,* caused by humoral disarray or deficiency. An excess of melancholy, phlegm, or choler, or a deficiency of blood, was understood as both the immediate cause *and* the form of illness. The goal of the Galenic physician was not to prevent entry of any determinate, invasive disease, therefore, but to restore the body to a condition of humoral homeostasis or balance.[3] Until and during the Tudor period, Galen retained a virtually uncontested monopoly in scholastic English understandings of disease and its transmission. Nearly all the academic and lay treatises on disease of the sixteenth century shoehorn illness into the glass slipper of humoralism. The Scottish physician Andrew Boorde's *Breuiary of Helthe* (c. 1540), for example, which was published in numerous editions in the sixteenth century, offers an exhaustive glossary of early modern diseases, every one of which it endeavors to explain in terms of humoral composition and imbalance.[4]

During the sixteenth and seventeenth centuries, the Galenic emphasis on the body's internal humoral balance was gradually if only partially supplanted by a new medical understanding of the body's vulnerability to invasion and infection by external foreign bodies. Regular outbreaks of epidemic illnesses such as plague, the sweating sickness and, in particular, syphilis revealed the inadequacy of the conventional, Galenic understanding of disease as an endogenous state. Although humoral understandings of disease retained currency into the eighteenth century, physicians increasingly began to propose that illness was a determinate thing transmitted from body to body. This new exogenous model of disease, which I have examined elsewhere, was formally outlined in the first decades of the sixteenth century by the Veronese physician Girolamo Fracastoro and the iconoclastic Swiss physician Paracelsus.[5] Neither Fracastoro nor Paracelsus dispensed entirely with the theory of the humors. In attempting to explain the transmission of epidemic illness, however, both radically reconfigured the very notion of disease itself. For Fracastoro and Paracelsus alike, disease was less an internal state of complexional imbalance than a determinate *semina,* or seed, an external entity that invaded the body through its pores and orifices. Other intellectual developments helped fuel the new exogenous models of disease. The renewed seventeenth-century interest in the Roman poet Lucretius and his doctrine of atomism helped writers like Margaret Cavendish to reimagine disease as an irreducibly small, migratory particle.[6] And the invention of the microscope, which prompted Antony van Leeuwenhoek's discovery of miniscule parasites, potentially pushed European medical science even further in the direction of a pathological microbiologism.

To understand the emergence of these new exogenous models of disease simply in the idealist terms of philosophical and scientific discoveries, however, is to conceal much. In particular, it neglects the seemingly unrelated

yet immensely formative nationalist and economic discursive horizons
within which the pathological objects of these new discoveries were first
conceived. In the sixteenth century, the names of dangerous diseases increasingly become nationalized to denote their putative point of origin.
Typhus fever, for example, was often called the *morbus Hungaricus;*
dysentry was known as the Irish disease. Such nationalized nomenclature
is particularly evident in the case of syphilis: "the Muscovites referred to
it as the Polish sickness, the Poles as the German sickness, and the Germans as the French sickness—a term of which the English also approved
(*French pox*) as did the Italians. . . . The Flemish and Dutch called it 'the
Spanish sickness', as did the inhabitants of North-West Africa. The Por-
tugese called it 'the Castillian sickness', whilst the Japanese and the people
of the East Indies came to call it 'the Portuguese sickness.'"[7] As this account hints, the global spread of syphilis prompted radically new etiologies
of the disease. It had begun to be seen not as a *state,* but as a *thing* that mi-
grates across national borders. This quotation makes clear, moreover, how
the perception of syphilis's migrations had an unmistakeably economic
tinge: the movement of the disease from Spain to Holland and North Africa,
and from Portugal to the East Indies and Japan, delineated new international
trade routes. Infection of the body politic by foreign bodies thus provided
a model for infection of bodies natural.

   This overlap of the economic and the pathological is nowhere more evident than in the English mercantilist literature of the early seventeenth century. Inasmuch as this corpus of writing displays unprecedented attention
to the vicissitudes of England's commerce with other nations—including the
pathologies of trade imbalances, international currency exchange, bullion
flows, and importation of exotic commodities–it displays a heightened interest in the foreign as the potential agent of both economic disease and
health. In the process, mercantilists repeatedly resorted to metaphors of disease as a foreign body or contamination that subtly displace the orthodox
Galenic conception of *dyskrasia.* In 1601, Gerard Malynes styled the continental banker who manipulated foreign exchange rates as the pathological
"canker" of England's commonwealth. In 1622, Edward Misselden coined
the term "hepatitis" to represent the loss of England's lifeblood, or money,
to evil foreign agents such as Turkish pirates or the Dutch East India company. And in 1630, Thomas Mun artfully recoded consumption as less a
disease of the natural and political bodies than a necessary evil—the inges-
tion of foreign luxury commodities—that ensures the health of the national
economy.[8] In all these examples, the language of disease works to make
visible the operations of transnational commerce; conversely, the move-
ments of global trade help refashion disease as a foreign body.

   In the remainder of this essay, I consider a related series of early modern
pathological terms that not only mercantilist writers, but also Shakespeare

reconceived as communicable disorders arising from foreign contamination. In *The Merchant of Venice,* the Jewish usurer Shylock brings a "plea so tainted and corrupt" against the Christian merchant Antonio (3.2.75). If modern readers tend to understand "taint" simply as a moral blemish, the term possessed a much wider array of meanings for Shakespeare and his audiences. In courts of law, a "taint" was a conviction for felony; hence when Antonio pronounces himself a "tainted wether of the flock" (4.1.113), he arguably accepts what he presumes will be the Venetian court's ruling against him. Yet as this example also demonstrates, "taint" additionally possessed a pathological meaning. The term could refer to an illness, especially of domesticated farm animals such as horses and sheep. In this pathological sense, its meaning shaded into that of "infection," whose etymology is almost identical to one of the senses of "taint"—a staining or contamination. I shall argue here that the pathological meaning of "taint" is central to the late Elizabethan mercantilist discourse of usury, which recodes the old sin as a new phenomenon endemic to early modern Europe: the alienability of money and identity across national borders.

   This recoding is evident in another "usury" text with which *The Merchant of Venice* is not normally associated: Gerard Malynes's *Saint George for England Allegorically Described* (1601). Malynes's treatise criticizes, from a recognizably mercantilist perspective, the depletion of England's bullion reserves. What is voiced in Malynes's fable is less the conventional Christian condemnation of usury as a sinful or unnatural practice of commerce, than a modern problematic of transnationality for which "the Jew" serves as a fixing yet highly unstable signifier. As I shall show, the mercantilist recoding of usury finds voice in Shakespeare's *Merchant of Venice.* Malynes and Shakespeare both produce the usurer as a foreign palimpsest, within which discrete categories of national and religious identity have been fused and confused. Crucial to the mercantilist recoding of usury is a chain of pathological signifiers that, although falling short of modern germs, viruses, and bacteria, provisionally fashion disease as a foreign body rather than an internal state of humoral imbalance.

Colored Money

As any student of *The Merchant of Venice* knows, the enduring association of Jews with usury stemmed from their temporary "welcome" into medieval European cities to practice a trade that Christians regarded as sinful. For Thomas Aquinas, the biblical proscription against charging interest on loans to "brothers" (Deuteronomy 23:20–21) meant that, thanks to the Christian ideal of universal brotherhood, no true believer could practice usury. But in the later Middle Ages, Europe's merchants increasingly needed ready sources of credit for capitalist ventures at home and abroad. To accommodate them, scholastics identified in the Deuteronomic proscription an ingenious, if xenophobic, loophole—*Christians* could not recoup interest on loans, but *Jews* could do so when lending to Christians, because Jews conveniently regarded gentiles as "others" rather than "brothers." This loophole was put into practice in England for only a relatively short time. But for centuries after the expulsion of Jews from England in 1290, English writers continued to regard the usurer as a synonym for "Jew."

Critical discussions of *The Merchant of Venice* tend to reference the conventional biblical arguments against usury. Hence analyses of Shylock's first scene customarily note Deuteronomy's proscriptions against charging interest on loans to "brothers." These references are frequently accompanied by citation of Francis Bacon's essay on usury and, in particular, one of the several "discommodities" that Bacon, following Aristotle, identifies with the practice: "They say . . . that it is against nature for money to beget money; and the like."[9] Yet such moral arguments do not provide the only framework for understanding Jewish usury in *The Merchant of Venice*. On the contrary, Shylock forcefully asserts his "thrifty" ability to make money breed as fast as did the biblical Jacob's "rams and ewes" (1.3.88):

> Mark what Jacob did:
> When Laban and himself were compromised
> That all the eanlings which were streaked and pied
> Should fall as Jacob's hire, the ewes being rank
> In end of autumn turned to the rams,
> And when the work of generation was
> Between these woolly breeders in the act,
> The skilfull shepherd pilled me certain wands,
> And in the doing of the deed of kind,
> He stuck them up before the fulsome ewes,
> Who then conceiving, did in eaning time
> Fall parti-coloured lambs, and those were Jacob's.
>
> (1.3.69–80)

In attempting to make sense of *The Merchant of Venice*'s discourse of usury, readers have largely overlooked this prolix parable, and focused their attention on Antonio's Christian-inflected denunciation of Shylock's money-lending practices. By contrast, I will argue here that Shylock's parable of Jacob and his "parti-coloured" lambs drives to the heart of an anxiety that loomed large in the emergent mercantilist discourse of transnational commerce.

In his essay on usury, Bacon recommends that "these licensed lenders [should] be in number indefinite, but restrained to certaine principall cities and townes of merchandizing; for then they will be hardly able *to colour* other men's moneyes in the country" (italics mine). Bacon's choice of verb here is fascinating. "To colour" is synonymous in this context with "to dye" or "to stain" and hence, in a more metaphorically pathological sense, "to corrupt" or "to infect." The *Oxford English Dictionary* lists Bacon's use of "to colour" under the now obsolete sense of "to lend one's name to; represent or deal with as one's own." I would argue that this meaning of "colour" also sheds light on Shylock's otherwise enigmatic vision of usury. Although they are the offspring of Laban's sheep, the eanlings become Jacob's by virtue of his ability to (parti-) "colour" them, and hence "represent or deal with" them as his "own." Shylock instructively aligns Jacob's profit with the usurer's interest, therefore, by means of an image of staining; like Bacon's "coloured" money, the "parti-coloured" fleeces embody the lambs' categorical hybridity as goods that have become alienated from Laban to Jacob, or Israel, father of the Jewish nation. For both Bacon and Shakespeare, then, "colour" is the mark of a national boundary transgression intrinsic to usury.

In the process, the "colouring" usurer generates a potential crisis of uncertain identity, goods, and coin. Paraphrasing Portia, one might ask: which is the merchant's, and which the lender's "moneys"? For the mercantilists, this question was of pressing importance when the lender was a stranger, and English bullion stood to be alienated across national borders. Thomas Milles, for example, argues that "many merchants do collour the conueying of ready Money out of the Realme of England."[10] The transnational undecidability generated by the foreign usurer's "colouring" also informs the early modern phrase "to colour strangers' goods," which the *OED* glosses as "to enter a foreign merchant's goods at the custom-house under a freeman's name, for the purpose of evading additional duties" (*colour,* v., 4). Gerard Malynes uses this very phrase in his treatise *Lex Mercatoria* (1622): "a Factor or Merchant, doe colour the goods of Merchant Strangers in paying but English Customes."[11] For Malynes, such "colouring" is tantamount to usury, inasmuch as it involves a crafty profiting from transnational dealership less in goods than in money. In both Bacon's and Malynes's texts, then, the "colouring" effects of usury are made to figure a two-fold indeterminacy that is the product of transnational commerce. First, the usurer "colours" goods and money in such fashion as to obscure knowledge of who owns them, and whether they are domestic or foreign (or both). Second, the usurer confuses national borders, both by merging with his host nation, and by obtaining money from—or sending it to—uncertain destinations in which he has family, factors, or trading connections. The "colouring" usurer thus *both* embodies *and* transmits national indeterminacy.

The transnational dimension of the "colouring" usurer is particularly evident in Gerard Malynes's *Saint George for England Allegorically Described.* This text, which takes the form of a brief allegorical fable about England's economic ills, may be seen as a boiled down *Faerie Queene* set on London's Lombard Street. Malynes recounts a dream he has had, in which he visits a city ("Diospolus," or London) on a "most fruitfull Iland" ("Niobla," an anagram of Albion).[12] The country, however, is suffering. A beautiful princess, whom Malynes equates with the nation's treasure, is tormented by a rampaging dragon, which he identifies with usury. The dragon is named "*Poenus politicum* [hardship of the polity]"; one of his wings is called "*Vsuria palliata* [disguised usury]," the other "*Vsuria explicata* [explicit usury]"; the dragon's tail is called "inconstant *Cambium* [exchange rates]" (sig. A8). As this allegorical blazon suggests, Malynes imagines usury quite differently from Aristotle, Aquinas, and the medieval scholastics. By identifying usury with fluctuating exchange rates, Malynes understands it as a problem arising from the systematic practice of commerce across national borders.

Throughout his allegory, Malynes employs a resolutely pathological vocabulary to figure transnational commerce. In his dedication, he compares statesmen to the "Phisitions of commonweales" whose job is to heal "the biles, botches, cankers and sores thereof"; chief amongst these is the "venimous sore" of usury (sig. A7v). And in the fable proper, Malynes describes the dragon of usury as "this contagion, wherewith we are infected" (13). This pathological metaphor is, I would argue, crucial to Malynes's vision of usury. The term "infection" had not yet decisively acquired its modern sense, i.e., the communication of a determinate, exogenous illness. Although it was increasingly associated with foreign bodies as a result of new explanations of epidemic diseases such as syphilis, the dominant meaning of "infection" was contamination or pathological mixing. The term derives from Latin "inficere," to stain or taint; for Galenic physicians, it came to mean corruption, including the miasmic putrefaction of water or of air. But in the late sixteenth century, "infect" still retained vestiges of its residual meaning, "to dye, tinge, colour."

Malynes's infected dragon is thus "coloured" and "colouring" in both pathological and economic senses. As Malynes says, the dragon has a "compounded body" (56); he is "half a man & halfe a beast" (73). This pathological mixing figures the hybridity of the usurer's capital, which "hath transported our treasure into forraine parts" (71). The usurer thus "colours" —i.e. alienates—the nation's bullion. As this might suggest, the dragon's infected state entails the fusion and confusion of discrete national identities. "His tridented toung," Malynes tells us, is "like vnto a Turkish dart"; but his body is "like an Elephant." Indeed, Malynes repeatedly associates the dragon with Islamic nations: the dragon's tail, he informs us, "is marked with the new Moon of the Turkes, like vnto the letter C" (57).

Yet even as Malynes exoticizes the dragon, he also brands it as a recognizably domestic villain. Its "compounded body" may have an orientalized tail, but its head is marked with "an F, like a fellon" (57). Malynes's remark

seems calculated to exploit "fellon"'s linked early modern legal and pathological associations. The term derives from the Latin *fel,* gall, and was used
in early modern medical writing as a synonym for a carbuncle or boil. In
law, however, a "felon" was originally anyone who breached the feudal
bond of trust between man and lord; he or she was thus understood as a
domestic disease, disrupting the internal balance of the body politic. Interestingly, the *OED* tells us that a "taint" was a mark applied to anyone con-
victed of a felony.[13] Hence Malynes's "fellon"-marked dragon is "tainted"
in both pathological and legal senses. The beast is a conflation of exotic
and domestic ills, and thus embodies Frances E. Dolan's model of the early
modern "proximate other," a suppositious social threat that was perceived
to be simultaneously foreign and domestic.[14]

In focusing explicit attention on the dragon's "compounded body," however, Malynes diverts attention from the extent to which the England of his
fable is itself already hybrid. Niobla's beautiful princess is by no means
nationally pure; rather, she sports a transnational, oriental motley. She
wears clothes that are "odiferous as the smell of Lebanon" (52); her cheeks
are like "a bed of spices" (52); she is "this *Indian Phenix*" (55). Yet it is the
dragon of usury that is made to bear the burden of transnational mixing,
and the "coloured" indeterminacy that underwrites it. In the most eerie passage of the fable, Malynes describes the literal impossibility of pinning
down the dragon's precise location: "albeit he seemeth with the *index* of
the dyall not to moue, when he is continually moouing, and stirred in such
sort, that when men begin to perceiue his motion, and pretend to runne from
him: he doth so allure them, that the more they runne, the more he seemeth
to follow them, as the moone doth to the little children, whereby his motion is the lesse regarded" (57–8). The dragon is always in motion, but his
most dangerous skill lies in his ability to create the illusion that he occupies
a fixed location. This passage captures particularly well the distinctive
qualities of the usurer as he is rhetorically produced in mercantilist discourse: for all his seeming fixity, he is a fluid shapeshifter, "continually
moouing" across categorical and national boundaries.

In mercantilist writing, the oscillation between fixity and fluidity is most
at work in the seemingly firm attribution of usury to the figure of the Jew.
Thomas Milles, for example, follows Malynes in imagining usury as a
practice that alienates bullion across national borders, thereby transforming
"our Christian *Exchange* into Iewish *Vsury.*"[15] The same strategy is evident at a crucial moment in Bacon's essay on usury. In his list of "witty
invectives" against usury, he reports the view that "usurers should have
orange-tawney bonnets, because they doe judaize" (133). "Judaize" serves
here as both a metaphor for usury's undecidability, and a cure for it. Bacon's
use of the verb "Judaize" lends a reassuring local name, if not habitation,
to a practice that involves a transnational blurring of discrete categories:

usurers should wear the orange hats mandated of Jews in the Papal States not because they are Jewish, but because their transnational alienations of money "colour" them as Jews. "The Jew" thus both figures transnational fluidity and lends it a provisionally stable identity.

Something similar happens in *Saint George for England Allegorically Described*. Malynes makes reference to Jews only once; but this reference is rhetorically crucial to his demonization of the transnational Turkish/ English dragon. Admonishing the supporters of usury, he asks: "Will not the daunger that the leaguors of this Dragon do runne into, give them warning, when as at one time fiue hundreth Iewes were transported with *Carons* boate the ferrie man of hell, which were slaine by the Cittizens of *Troynouant* for feeding him?" (65). It is difficult to know at which historical incident Malynes glances here; it may well be an attack against the London Jewry in 1264, when a large number of the community—thirteenth-century estimates vary between 400 and 700—were killed by a rampaging mob.[16] In any case, Malynes, like Bacon, makes "the Jew" the certain material in which to clothe usury's transnational uncertainty.

TAINTED WETHERS

This uncertainty might seem to problematize "the Jew," making his or her identity far more refractory than critical responses to *The Merchant of Venice* have usually supposed. Yet I would argue that the play partially recuperates such undecidability as the condition of the Jewish usurer, and in ways that resonate with the mercantilist rather than the traditional Christian discourse of usury. This is particularly the case with Shylock's parable about Laban and Jacob's sheep. Critics have had enormous difficulty with this speech, puzzling over its relevance to usury. In an otherwise insightful essay, for example, Elizabeth Spiller argues that "Shylock's use of the Jacob and Laban story becomes important not so much as an argument about usury but as a narrative about imaginative miscegenation."[17] Rightly noting that early modern readers repeatedly used the Jacob and Laban story to interject their concerns about not usury but racial impurity and intermixture, Spiller nevertheless neglects the extent to which such concerns were themselves integral to the mercantilist problematic of usury. As Malynes's "Judaized" dragon indicates, usury was repeatedly regarded as a colored and coloring practice whose very condition was national and monetary indeterminacy.

In Shylock's allegorical reading of the Jacob and Laban story, there are two crucial levels of hybridity. The first is evident in Shylock's figuration of Jacob's eanlings as Jews. The text of the passage in the first folio contains a telling lexical indeterminacy: according to Shylock, the "parti-coloured" eanlings "were *Iacobs*"—thereby confusing the genitive and the plural noun forms of "Jacob" (or "Israel"). And indeed, the very phrase "parti-coloured" may have conjured up for the play's original audiences an image of Jews. Although Shakespeare could have found the phrase in Bishop Miles Coverdale's 1535 translation of the Bible, it was also used to refer to the colored clothes that Italian Jews were notoriously forced to wear. In Henry Glapthorne's play *The Hollander,* for example, "the Jewes at Rome" are described as wearing "party coloured garments to be knowne from Christians."[18]

There is a second level at which "parti-coloured" hybridity is crucial to Shylock's parable. If Shylock equates the spotty eanlings with Jacob and *Jews,* he identifies the animals equally with the usurer's *profit.* As I have already argued, the "parti-coloured" fleeces of the sheep entail a specifically mercantilist pun: Jacob has "coloured" the sheep both physically and legally, in the sense of alienating them from Laban. Once again we see how the Jewish usurer not only embodies hybridity; he also transmits it, "colouring" money or goods to generate profit—which in Jacob's case, takes the form of hybrid fleeces that are no less valuable than the "golden fleece" with which the play's romantic venturers associate Portia, Nerissa, and the wealth of Belmont (1.1.169, 3.2.240).

The language of disease does not figure explicitly in Shylock's parable of usurious interest, even though—as we have seen—the mercantilist term "coloured" participates within a string of similar words with pathological associations. But a later scene casts a retrospective, pathological light on Shylock's interpretation of Jacob's "parti-coloured" sheep. When Antonio famously refers to himself as a "tainted wether of the flock" (4.1.114), the text does far more than style him as a Christlike martyr, the lamb of God. Just as importantly, I would argue, he has here become a type of Jacob's "pied and streaked" sheep. Crucial to Antonio's self-representation is a language of pathological contamination and coloring that is highly redolent of the mercantilist discourse of usury.

"Taint" was itself a hybrid term. The *OED* tells us that it derives from two words of distinct origin which "appear to have run together in the formation of later senses" (*OED, taint,* sb.). The first word was the aphetic form of "attaint"—the past participle of "attain"—in the sense of "reach," "touch," or "strike." This produced the various meanings of a "hit" in tilting, a criminal conviction and, significantly, a disease in horses (a pathology whose etymology recalls that of plague, which derives from *plaga,* the Greek term for "strike"). The second form of "taint" was derived from the Latin *tinctus,* meaning "tint" or "colour." The interplay between "taint" as a blow or animal disease and "taint" as color produced a variety of hybrid senses in Shakespeare's England, all of them with pathological connotations of varying degrees. First, "taint" possessed the still familiar sense of a stain, blemish, or spot; this was used almost invariably in a metaphorical sense, as in Viola's remark that she hates "ingratitude more in a man / Than . . . any taint of vice" (*Twelfth Night,* 3.4.390). Second, "taint" assumed the pathological sense of contamination or infection, as in *Henry VIII,* where Gardiner speaks of "a general taint of the state" (5.3.28). And finally, "taint" became a more specialized medical term referring to a trace of disease in a latent state. This last meaning seems implicit in Antonio's description of himself as "tainted." Indeed, the *OED* lists two pathological meanings for the adjective "tainted"—"contaminated, infected, or corrupted"; and "having a taint of disease; infected with latent disease," for which it offers Antonio's remark in *The Merchant of Venice* as the first recorded example.

Yet the *OED* decisively fixes the meaning of the line in a way that is at odds with the play's fascination with the indeterminacy of "coloured" identities. I would argue that the "tainted" Antonio is physically *stained* as much as he is pathologically *infected,* and in a way that harks back to Shylock's justification of usury. If the usurer's skill lies in the production and expropriation of hybrid goods, the "tainted wether" Antonio has here become Shylock's "parti-coloured" sheep. The implication of Antonio's pathological self-representation, then, is that his very flesh has become Shylock's usurious interest. This interpretation is at odds with readings of the play inflected by the traditional Christian interpretations of usury. W. H. Auden, for example, insisted that insofar as it does not involve the taking of monetary interest, Shylock's bond is more typical of Christian jurisprudence and nonusurious conventions of lending.[19] But my suggestion that Antonio is Shylock's "parti-coloured" sheep is highly compatible with the mercantilist discourse of usury that I have sketched throughout this chapter. Like Malynes's dragon of usury, Shylock is a "proximate other" who is, as James Shapiro has argued, indeterminately Venetian and Jew, citizen and alien.[20] Moreover, Shylock not only embodies but also transmits his hybridity. The "tainted wether" Antonio has become property alienated to Shylock, legally comparable to the lambs that Jacob usuriously expropriated from Laban. Hence Antonio's body is "tainted" or "coloured" in both economic and pathological senses of the terms. Even though Auden called his collection of critical essays *The Dyer's Hand,* his analysis of *The Merchant of Venice* is oddly color-blind to the images of dyeing/coloring/staining/tainting that are integral to the play and its reproduction of the mercantilist discourse of transnational usury.

The play seems to suggest that the threat of transnational hybridity originates in and ends with the Jewish usurer. Just as the stranger Jacob stains Laban's seemingly pure property, so does Shylock the Jewish usurer hybridize the Christian Venetians to whom he lays claim, in the process pathologically tainting them. But this reading ignores another possibility raised by the play. When decoding the hybridity of the Jewish usurer, it is useful to recall the hybridity of postcolonial identity as theorized by Homi Bhabha: that is, an imitation that displaces the supposedly pure origin by mimicking its very impurity.[21] As Shylock famously remarks to Salario, "the villainy you teach me, I will execute, and it shall go hard but I will better the instruction" (3.1.56–57). Shylock learns his villainy from the Christians, so that his hard "Jewish heart" (4.1.80) is arguably "coloured" Christian nastiness. But even as Shylock reflects the *moral* taints within Venetian culture, he also reflects the more systematic *transnational* taints that comprise Venetian "identity." As Antonio remarks, "the trade and profit of the city / Consisteth of all nations" (3.3.30–31). Venice is hybrid, both physically and rhetorically; it cannot help but blur the boundaries between itself and "all nations."

This suggests how even as the "parti-coloured" hybridity of the Jew ostensibly functions as a foil to the economic and cultural purity of the Gentile, it can equally work to disclose the latter's own originary hybridity. As Mathew Martin notes in his essay in this volume, "the Jews were not only the rejected other of [European] identity but also its mirror image."[22] In the courtroom scene, Antonio (who has adopted Shylock's script of "patient" suffering [4.1.11–12]), Graziano (who thanks Shylock for teaching him the word "Daniel" [4.1.337]), and Portia (who uses Shylock's literal interpretation of "justice" against him [4.1.317–18]) all seem to have "coloured" or expropriated the language of the Jew. At the end of the play, in a Belmont supposedly purified of the taint of Shylock, the Christian Lorenzo similarly identifies with the starving Jews in the desert, feasting on "manna" (5.1.294–95). Old Gobbo tells Bassanio that the protean Launcelot—who during the play not only trades his Jewish master for a Christian, but shapeshifts from morality play Everyman, to born-again Jacob, to "Hagar's" offspring (2.5.42)—has "a great infection, sir, as one would say, to serve" (2.2.103). Thus does the old man's compulsive habit of malapropism comically degrade his son's "affection" or desire. It is a revealing slip nonetheless. Given the play's fascination with "tainting" and "colouring," "infect" here cannot help but assume its residual sense of "dye, tinge, colour, stain." Launcelot, like his fellow Venetians, is thus an infected hybrid, possessed of no determinate national identity.

It is not only the Venetians who have "a great infection" in this latter sense. Perhaps the most notable instance is that of the English would-be suitor, whom Portia imperiously dismisses in act 1, scene 2 along with her German, Neapolitan, French, Scottish, and Polish gentleman callers. In a satirical tableau of national stereotypes, Shakespeare represents the Englishman as wearing garments that derive from everywhere but England: "How oddly he is suited! I think he bought his doublet in Italy, his round hose in France, his bonnet in Germany, and his behaviour everywhere" (1.2.60–62). Portia lends voice here to a common theme. Mathew Martin notes how

English travelers were often represented as taking on the characteristics of the foreign nations they visited; but as Sara Warneke and Lloyd Edward Kermode among others have argued, this metamorphosis was seen to be equally the product of England's participation in global trade.[23] In 1616, John Deacon characterized the effects of England's mercantile adventures as follows: "So many of our English-mens minds are thus terribly Turkished with Mahometan trumperies . . . thus fantastically Flanderized with flaring networks to catch English fooles; thus huffingly Hollandized with ruffian-like loome-workes, and other laded fooleries; thus greedily Germanized with a most gluttonous manner of gormandizing; thus desperately Danished with a swine-swilling and quaffing; thus skulkingly Scotized with Machiavellian projects; thus inconstantly Englished with every fantastical foolerie."[24] This transnational motley, so redolent of the globally diverse garb of "English" treasure in Malynes's *Saint George for England Allegorically Described,* offers a subtle reminder of what *The Merchant of Venice* and mercantilist discourse try so hard to disavow by locating the origin of hybridity within the figure of the contagious Jew: in the universe of global trade, *everyone* is colored by the traces of transnationality.

NOTES

1. All references to Shakespeare cited parenthetically in the text are from Stephen Greenblatt et al. (eds.), *The Norton Shakespeare* (New York: W. W. Norton, Co., 1997).

2. James Shapiro, *Shakespeare and the Jews* (New York: Columbia University Press, 1996).

3. Owsei Temkin, *Galenism: Rise and Decline of a Medical Philosophy* (Ithaca, NY: Cornell University Press, 1973).

4. Andrew Boorde, *The Breuiary of Helthe, for All Maner of Syckenesses and Diseases the Whiche May Be in Man, or Woman* (London, 1547).

5. Jonathan Gil Harris, *Foreign Bodies and the Body Politic: Discourses of Social Pathology in Early Modern England* (Cambridge: Cambridge University Press, 1998), chap. 2, esp. 22–30.

6. Margaret Cavendish, *A Discovery of the New World Called the Blazing World,* in *The Blazing World and Other Writings,* ed. Kate Lilley, 158–59. (Harmondsworth, UK: Penguin, 1994).

7. Claude Quétel, *History of Syphilis,* trans. Judith Braddock and Brian Pike, 16. (Baltimore: Johns Hopkins University Press, 1992).

8. Gerard Malynes, *A Treatise of the Canker of England's Commonwealth* (London, 1601), passim; Edward Misselden, *Free Trade or, The Meanes To Make Trade Florish: Wherein, The Causes of the Decay of Trade in this Kingdome, are Discovered* (London, 1622), sig. B5v; Thomas Mun, *Englands Treasure by Forraign Trade; Or, The Ballance of our Forraign Trade is The Rule of our Treasure* (London, 1669), passim.

9. Francis Bacon, "On Usurie," in *The Essayes or Counsels Civill & Morall of Francis Bacon, Baron Verulam Viscount Saint Alban* (Norwalk, CT: Easton Press, 1980), 133. All further references will be cited parenthetically in the text.

10. Thomas Milles, *The Customers Replie, Or Second Apologie* (London, 1614), C4.

11. Gerard Malynes, *Consuetudo, Vel, Lex Mercatoria: Or, the Ancient Law-Merchant* (London, 1622), 114.

12. Gerard Malynes, *Saint George for England Allegorically Described* (London, 1601), 2. All further references will be cited parenthetically in the text.

13. Frederick Pollock and Frederic William Maitland, *The History of English Law Before the Time of Edward I*, 2nd ed. (Cambridge: Cambridge University Press, 1968), 2:464–70.

14. Frances E. Dolan, *Whores of Babylon: Catholicism, Gender, and Seventeenth-Century Print Culture* (Ithaca, NY: Cornell University Press, 1999), passim.

15. Thomas Milles, *The Custumers Alphabet and Primer: Conteining, Their Creede or Beliefe in the True Doctrine of Christian Religion* (London, 1608), G2v.

16. See Joe Hillaby, "London: The 13th-century Jewry Revisited," *Jewish Historical Studies: Transactions of the Jewish Historical Society of England* 32 (1990–92): 89–158, esp. 135–36.

17. Elizabeth A. Spiller, "From Imagination to Miscegenation: Race and Romance in Shakespeare's *The Merchant of Venice*," *Renaissance Drama* n.s. 29 (2000 for 1998): 137–64, esp. 138.

18. Henry Glapthorne, *The Hollander* (London, 1640), E3.

19. W. H. Auden, *The Dyer's Hand and Other Essays* (New York: Random House, 1948), 227–28.

20. Shapiro, *Shakespeare and the Jews,* 189.

21. Homi K. Bhabha, "Signs Taken for Wonders: Questions of Ambivalence and Authority under a Tree outside Delhi, May 1817," in *Race, Writing and Difference,* ed. Henry Louis Gates, 163–84. (Chicago: University of Chicago Press, 1986).

22. Mathew Martin, "Jack Wilton and the Jews: The Ambivalence of Anti-Semitism in Nashe's *The Unfortunate Traveller,*" 89.

23. Sara Warneke, "A Taste for New-fangledness: The Destructive Potential of Novelty in Early Modern England," *Sixteenth Century Journal* 26 (1995): 881–96; Lloyd Edward Kermode, "The Playwright's Prophecy: Robert Wilson's *The Three Ladies of London* and the 'Alienation' of the English," *Medieval and Renaissance Drama in England* 11 (1999): 60–87.

24. John Deacon, *Tobacco Tortured, Or The Filthie Fume of Tobacco Refined* (London, 1616), 69.

BIBLIOGRAPHY

Auden, W. H. *The Dyer's Hand and Other Essays.* New York: Random House, 1948.

Bacon, Francis. *The Essayes or Counsels Civill & Morall of Francis Bacon, Baron Verulam Viscount Saint Alban.* Norwalk, CT: Easton Press, 1980.

Bhabha, Homi K. "Signs Taken for Wonders: Questions of Ambivalence and Authority under a Tree outside Delhi, May 1817." In *Race, Writing and Difference.* Edited by Henry Louis Gates, 163–84. Chicago: University of Chicago Press, 1986.

Boorde, Andrew. *The Breuiary of Helthe, for All Maner of Syckenesses and Diseases the Whiche May Be in Man, or Woman.* London, 1547.

Cavendish, Margaret. *A Discovery of the New World Called the Blazing World.* In *The Blazing World and Other Writings.* Edited by Kate Lilley. Harmondsworth, UK: Penguin, 1994.

Deacon, John. *Tobacco Tortured, Or The Filthie Fume of Tobacco Refined.* London, 1616.

Dolan, Frances E. *Whores of Babylon: Catholicism, Gender, and Seventeenth-Century Print Culture.* Ithaca, NY: Cornell University Press, 1999.

Glapthorne, Henry. *The Hollander.* London, 1640.

Harris, Jonathan Gil. *Foreign Bodies and the Body Politic: Discourses of Social Pathology in Early Modern England.* Cambridge: Cambridge University Press, 1998.

Hillaby, Joe. "London: The 13th-century Jewry Revisited." *Jewish Historical Studies: Transactions of the Jewish Historical Society of England* 32 (1990–92): 89–158.

Kermode, Lloyd Edward. "The Playwright's Prophecy: Robert Wilson's *The Three Ladies of London* and the 'Alienation' of the English." *Medieval and Renaissance Drama in England* 11 (1999): 60–87.

Malynes, Gerard. *Consuetudo, Vel, Lex Mercatoria: Or, the Ancient Law-Merchant.* London, 1622.

———. *Saint George for England Allegorically Described.* London, 1601.

———. *A Treatise of the Canker of England's Commonwealth.* London, 1601.

Milles, Thomas. *The Customers Replie, Or Second Apologie.* London, 1614.

———. *The Custumers Alphabet and Primer: Conteining, Their Creede or Beliefe in the True Doctrine of Christian Religion.* London, 1608.

Misselden, Edward. *Free Trade or, The Meanes To Make Trade Florish: Wherein, The Causes of the Decay of Trade in this Kingdome, are Discovered.* London, 1622.

Mun, Thomas. *Englands Treasure by Forraign Trade; Or, The Ballance of our Forraign Trade is The Rule of our Treasure.* London, 1669.

Pollock, Frederick, and Frederic William Maitland. *The History of English Law Before the Time of Edward I.* 2 vols. 2nd edition. Cambridge: Cambridge University Press, 1968.

Quétel, Claude. *History of Syphilis.* Translated by Judith Braddock and Brian Pike. Baltimore: Johns Hopkins University Press, 1992.

Shakespeare, William. *The Norton Shakespeare.* Edited by Stephen Greenblatt et al. New York: W. W. Norton, 1997.

Shapiro, James. *Shakespeare and the Jews.* New York: Columbia University Press, 1996.

Spiller, Elizabeth A. "From Imagination to Miscegenation: Race and Romance in Shakespeare's *The Merchant of Venice.*" *Renaissance Drama* n.s. 29 (2000 for 1998): 137–64.

Temkin, Owsei. *Galenism: Rise and Decline of a Medical Philosophy.* Ithaca, NY: Cornell University Press, 1973.

Warneke, Sara. "A Taste for New-fangledness: The Destructive Potential of Novelty in Early Modern England." *Sixteenth Century Journal* 26 (1995): 881–96.

Speaking the Language, Knowing the Trade: Foreign Speech and Commercial Opportunity in *The Shoemaker's Holiday*

Marianne Montgomery

HISTORICALLY MINDED CRITICS OF *THE SHOEMAKER'S HOLIDAY* (1599) have long complicated early readings of the play as entirely festive, ahistorical, and celebratory by acknowledging the economic and social tensions raised by Thomas Dekker's representation of the commercial life of London. Peter Mortenson, for example, sees a fundamental conflict between the play's mercantile transactions and its festive holiday, concluding that "Dekker creates a grim world and encourages us to pretend that it is a green one," but he does not explain why the play clothes its urban economic realities in a pastoral guise. David Scott Kastan begins to offer an answer by usefully introducing the idea of wish fulfillment: "The play cannot be understood as a realistic portrait of Elizabethan middle-class life. It is a realistic portrait only of Elizabethan middle-class dreams—a fantasy of class fulfillment that would erase the tensions and contradictions created by the nascent capitalism of the late sixteenth century." Kastan goes on to claim that the play resolves these tensions generically: "The comic form offers itself as an ideological resolution to the social problems the play engages." In a more recent essay, Marta Straznicky goes further, arguing that the comic form does not resolve the play's tensions but rather "conserves a state of discord" even in its festive ending; the holiday is, after all, a holiday for workers, and at the feast the king grants Eyre a commercial patent.[1]

As this brief sampling of the play's recent critical reception shows, readings of *The Shoemaker's Holiday* suggest that comedy can dissolve commercial tensions or at least have tended to locate comic festivity in opposition to commerce. I want to build on Straznicky's contention that the play preserves an "end of discord" by showing how Dekker, even before the play's conclusion, causally *links* the comic and the commercial by representing the economic opportunities made possible by comic foreign speech. In Simon Eyre's shop, commerce depends on comedy. As profligate aristocrat Lacy speaks stage Dutch in his disguise as a shoemaker, Dekker represents in theatrically perceivable terms the foreign commercial pressures bearing upon the play's economy.[2] Steven Mullaney describes such representations of the alien and marginal on the early modern stage as a "rehearsal of cultures," a form of temporary license for an English culture in the process of redefining its limits.[3] In these terms, *The Shoemaker's Holiday* rehearses Dutch commercial culture while rehearsing its language. With its strange speaker, *The Shoemaker's Holiday* acknowledges and even celebrates England's openness to linguistic and commercial influences from abroad. Social harmony at the play's close is achieved not despite potentially discordant Dutch speech, but because of it. Since the audience always knows that the Dutch shoemaker is really an English gentleman, this harmony is all the more striking. It suggests that Lacy can be *both* Dutch and English, with two languages and two identities that allow him to negotiate in London's polyglot markets of artisans and merchants.

What cultural assumptions particular to late sixteenth-century England shaped audience responses to Lacy's Dutch speech? Elizabethan intellectuals aiming to define a specifically English poetics generally shared an underlying anxiety about the poetic and rhetorical capacities of English and about its potentially troubling porousness to the words and grammatical constructions of foreign languages. George Puttenham, in *The Arte of English Poesie* (1589), defends "our vulgar language," insisting that English can be adapted to classical meter: "one may easily and commodiously lead all those feet of the ancients into our vulgar language." Richard Carew adopts a similarly defensive posture in "The Excellency of the English Tongue" (1596), claiming English "matchable, if not preferrable before any other [language] in use at this day." Concerned that English, unlike other vernaculars, had not received adequate praise, Carew defends at some length its significance, easiness, copiousness, and sweetness.[4]

English's attributes were worth debating at all because, in the Elizabethan formulation, language cannot be separated from national character. William Camden, who printed Carew's essay on English in his *Remains Concerning Britain* (1605), makes the history of English coterminous with the history of England. Both emerge from the same excellent source: "This English tongue is extracted, as the nation, from the Germans the most glorious of all now extant in Europe for their morall, and martiall vertues."[5] Camden constructs a history for English that corresponds to his desire to assign Germanic virtues to the English character. Carew defends Saxon monosyllables on similar grounds: "As every *Individuum* is but one, so in our native English-Saxon language, we find many of them suitably expressed by words of one syllable."[6] Single syllables make perfect sense, in Carew's view, because they correspond to a principle of English liberty and individualism. In admiring English monosyllables, Carew is in effect advancing an argument for the strength of England's national character, suggesting that England's character, like its language, is direct, simple, and forceful. In his essay "Barbarous Tongues," Richard Helgerson traces this shift from defending English as classically apt to celebrating its "Gothic" barbarism. Although a rough language that could only awkwardly be forced into classical forms was a source of cultural shame earlier in the sixteenth century, it came by the end of Elizabeth's reign to seem a mark of English custom and a source of English pride.[7]

If the English language was imagined to show the qualities of the English people, similar correspondences were drawn between foreign languages and foreign nationals. Carew points out the weaknesses of other vernaculars: "The Italian is pleasant but without sinewes as a still fleeting water. The French, delicate, but over nice as a woman, scarce daring to open her lippes for feare of marring her countenance. The Spanish, majesticall, but fulsome, running too much on the O, and terrible like the divell in a play. The Dutch manlike but withall very harsh, as one readie at every word to pick a quarrel."[8] These criticisms seem as much to impugn national characters as languages. Interestingly, Carew associates Spanish with plays, indicating both his own playgoing and the extent to which the experience of hearing foreign vernaculars, or at least foreign accents, was tied to the experience of the theater. Carew identifies the sounds if not the words of Spanish with stage devils like *Dr. Faustus's* Mephistophilis, suggesting that he hears foreign speech in the theater as a signal to distrust its speaker. To an extent, this reaction supports Janette Dillon's claim that staged foreign language produces "a shiver of recognition in the audience, a recognition of foreignness."[9] But Carew's comment suggests that the shiver also works in reverse, that the terrible sounds of stage devils might lead one to recoil at the similar-sounding Spanish language. By extension, the harsh sounds of stage Dutch might lead the audience into a quarrel with a Dutchman, although, as Peter McCluskey has shown, Dekker's play neatly skirts official prohibitions against anti-alien satire by aiming its satire at a disguised Englishman.[10] The way language is staged in the theater and the way foreign language is heard and interpreted more generally, Carew implies, are inseparable.

Foreign languages are also inseparable from English itself. Carew relates the historical influences of "divers languages" on English and notes the fears of some: "It may be objected that such patching makes *Littletons* hotchpot of our tongue, and in effect brings the same to a Babellish confusion."[11] Carew's reference to "Littleton's hotchpot" has a double sense. In Sir Thomas Littleton's influential 1481 treatise on property law, "hotchpot" denotes unequal parcels of land collected together to be redistributed. He draws this definition from hotchpot's culinary sense: "And it seemeth that this word (Hotchpot), is in English a pudding, for in this pudding is not put one thing alone, but one thing with other things together."[12] Yet Littleton's text itself is also an example of a linguistic hotchpot. In the late sixteenth century, legal texts like Littleton's, written in highly specialized law—French mixed with English and Latin legalisms—were considered particularly potent and available sources of terms that might corrupt English. Puttenham feared "the corruption of our speech" by the incorporation into English of unaltered Greek, Latin, and vulgar French words by "clerks and scholars or secretaries . . . not content with the usual Norman or Saxon word."[13] Carew further emphasizes the threat of linguistic hotchpot by invoking the biblical Babel, site of the fall of language from its single, perfect original. He positions English as the new single language, national if not universal, and suggests that it is potentially poised for a second fall into a new "Babellish confusion."[14] The openness of English to influence from other languages and hence to "Babellish confusion" is clearly a source of anxiety. Camden speaks admiringly of ancient Britons who cut out the tongues of their French wives "lest their children should corrupt their language with their mothers tongues."[15] This violent image testifies to a deep concern that the porousness of English to foreign influences would do irreparable damage to England's mother tongue, and, by association, to the English character.

In response to this anxiety, Carew claims that English can resist corruption because it absorbs only the best features of other languages, remedying the weaknesses of foreign vernaculars and preserving their strengths: "Now we in borrowing from them, give the strength of consonants to the Italian, the full sound of words to the French, the varietie of terminations to the Spanish, and the mollifying of more vowels to the Dutch, and so (like Bees) gather the honey of their good properties and leave the dregges to themselves." Suggesting that English, rather than declining into "Babellish confusion," can selectively incorporate only the best qualities of foreign tongues reconciles the reality of linguistic influence with a protonationalistic impulse to affirm England's strength and singularity even in the realm of language. What emerges is an idealization of what Camden calls "plaine English" and Carew calls "right English"—its ability to absorb "good" foreign influences the sign of its English virtue.[16]

While the intellectual positioning of "plain English" and "right English" as both flexible and stable generally points to anxiousness about the influence of other vernaculars on English, foreign vernaculars were regularly heard on London's stages. A range of languages appears in Shakespeare's plays, from the untranscribed Welsh song in *1 Henry IV* (1597) to French in *Henry V* (1599) to the French-accented Latin of *The Merry Wives of Windsor* (1597). This kind of linguistic variety works as an audible version of spectacle, and the pleasure it brings is part of what makes a play worth paying for. Foreign languages could also reinforce the audience's confidence in its Englishness. Invited to laugh at Frenchmen and at the French princess Kate's English lessons in *Henry V*, the audience hears France's defeat in part through the play's repeated mockery of its language. Helen Ostovich has called attention to the reductive "sexualized political propaganda" that the play deploys as it represents the French as "effeminate clowns" and their princess as a body that becomes a series of dirty words as she is possessed by conquering Henry.[17] Such a portrayal of the French, though crude, reinforced the English audience's sense of its own superiority to those mincing Frenchmen. *Henry V* also represents the English coalition as a collection of accents, one that binds together Scotch, Welsh, and English into a potentially fractious but ultimately cohesive alliance. In this sense, too, the pleasure of hearing language reinforces the London audience's confidence in its superiority to the Welsh and Scotch provincials and celebrates the English king's ultimate rule over foreign sounds.[18]

The way that foreign language works in Dekker's comedy is of course not identical to the way that French is used to construct Englishness in Shakespeare's history, but *Henry V* offers a cogent and familiar example of the various charges that foreign speech carried for Elizabethans. As potentially invasive stores of words that might corrupt the mother tongue, sources of theatrical excitement, and negative examples that defined Englishness, foreign vernaculars dwelt in an uneasy relation to English. Incorporating foreign speech, Dekker recognizes and even applauds England's openness to foreign influences and thereby reaffirms its productive appropriation of those influences. In *The Shoemaker's Holiday,* this appropriation takes place in the commercial sphere. The somewhat anxious interest in linguistic influence registered by Carew, Camden, and Puttenham is reflected in the commercial power that Dekker grants to foreign speech spoken by a disguised Englishman.

In *The Shoemaker's Holiday,* Lacy, a gentleman, deserts the army and returns to London to woo Rose, a citizen's daughter. To escape the class objections to the match raised by his uncle Lincoln and Rose's father Oatley and the treasonous implications of his desertion, Lacy disguises himself as a Dutch shoemaker. As Hans, a "brother of the Gentle Craft," Lacy gains employment in Simon Eyre's shoemaking shop with the support of Eyre's other shoemakers, Hodge and Firk.[19] With Hans's help, Eyre buys the contents of a Dutch ship at a steep discount and rapidly rises to become sheriff of London and ultimately Lord Mayor. In the play's festive conclusion, Lacy and Rose secretly marry, another pair of lovers is reunited after being separated by the war in France, and Eyre celebrates his new social and political status by holding a feast attended by both the city's apprentices and the king. The king forgives Lacy's desertion, lectures Lincoln and Oatley that "love . . . cares not for difference of birth or state," and grants a patent for Eyre's new market at Leadenhall (21.105–6). *The Shoemaker's Holiday* welcomes foreign speech for the mirth it offers and the economic possibilities it delivers; it ultimately absorbs Dutch influence into London's craft community as easily as Dutch-speaking Hans is absorbed into the fellowship of shoemakers in Eyre's shop. Work, this play suggests, can be a more meaningful basis of community than national-linguistic allegiance, so that the king's arrival at the end of the play is oddly beside the point. The king attempts to ratify and claim as English what the play has already shown to be a transnational culture of work.

Several Dutch transactions enable this festive conclusion. Two characters in the play speak Dutch: an alien worker (or, more precisely, an Englishman impersonating an alien worker) and a foreign trader.[20] With these two characters, their otherness easily audible, Dekker's play links two questions of its historical moment: Could English absorb foreign words? Could England absorb foreign labor and goods? Both foreign labor and foreign trade were actively at issue in the late sixteenth century. The century's closing decade alone saw anti-immigrant riots fueled by increasing housing costs and growing foreign membership in trade guilds as Protestant refugees entered London. Generally, though, London's companies acted as a stabilizing force, in part because their officers benefited from immigration even if the yeomen did not. One notable letter from the Weavers' company referred to French Huguenots as "foreign brothers," a title that shows at least some commitment, albeit probably self-serving, to elevating the bond of shared trade and religion above suspicion and anti-alien feeling.[21]

While companies struggled to absorb foreign labor, economists and merchants worried about foreign goods and England's unfavorable balance of trade, made more severe by the import of luxury items like those on the Dutch ship that Simon Eyre buys.[22] In buying the ship's goods, Eyre operates as a merchant—a middleman—rather than a producer. Eyre's profit, as Kastan notes, therefore comes not from the artisanal work of his shop but from "capitalist enterprise which permits enormous profit and negligible risk."[23] Traffic in goods by English and foreign merchants was accompanied by traffic in languages. Each trading area had its own lingua franca, and merchants of necessity often spoke the languages of their suppliers and customers.[24] The English traveler Fynes Moryson was particularly struck by the linguistic skills of Dutch merchants: "It stands with reason, that they who are very industrious in traffic, and having little of their own to export, (except linen) do trade most with the commodities of other nations, should themselves learn many languages."[25] For Moryson, Dutch merchants' tongues match the commodities that they trade.

The Shoemaker's Holiday represents both foreign labor and trade and makes both dependent on Dutch speech, so that stage Dutch becomes a kind of dramatic shorthand for Dutch influence on both the artisanal and mercantile economies of London. Dekker's changes to his main source, Thomas Deloney's *The Gentle Craft,* introduce a systematic link between language and commerce not present in the source. Dekker consolidates the multiple languages and nationalities of *The Gentle Craft* into Dutch in *The Shoemaker's Holiday*. In Deloney's version of the Lacy plot, the noblemen disguise themselves as shoemakers but not as *foreign* shoemakers. In Deloney's Eyre plot, Eyre hires a Frenchman as well as a Dutchman, and Eyre's successful bargain is made because a Greek skipper happens to understand French.[26] The Greek skipper and French shoemaker make a fortunate linguistic connection, but not one based on shared national language. Further, neither French nor Greek carried the powerful commercial associations of Dutch for the Elizabethan audience.

By substituting Dutch for the "Babellish confusion" of foreign speech in his source, Dekker explicitly connects foreign speech and economic opportunities. When Lincoln recognizes Lacy in disguise as Hans, he explains to Oatley, "My cousin speaks the language, knows the trade" (16.130). The play wishes for a world in which an Englishman can learn the trade by learning the language, in which the English can absorb economic lessons from the Dutch as easily as Lacy can absorb and make use of their language for his disguise. Within the space of the comedy, such a world can be realized. Before Lacy even appears onstage, we learn from Lincoln that he has taken the tour of a profligate, with a twist: rather than traveling to France and Italy, he ran out of money in Germany and "became a shoemaker in Wittenberg" (1.29). Wittenberg had no particular connection with shoemaking and Dekker may even have thought it was a Dutch town.[27] Moreover, because the geographical identity of the Netherlands was in flux during the wars with Spain and because the distinction between early modern German and Dutch would not be easy for Dekker's audience to hear, the line between German and Dutch in Dekker's characterization of Lacy is not stable.[28] As the site of Martin Luther's university and a cradle of the Reformation, Wittenberg is invoked here less as a specific place on the map than as a Protestant site of citizen work as opposed to aristocratic play. Although an English gentleman might acquire fine clothes and Continental pretensions in Venice or Lyons, in Wittenberg, he learns to make sturdy shoes. Since Lacy's uncle Lincoln finds his humble occupation unfit for a gentleman, Lacy's new work ethic works for him. It allows him to stay near Rose and to evade his foreign service, entering Eyre's shop not as a fugitive aristocrat but as a merry and hardworking Dutchman. He soliloquizes on his disguise: "Mean I a while to work. I know the trade . . . Do Fortune what she can, / The Gentle Craft is living for a man!" (3.20, 23–24). While Fortune may be necessary for long-term success, in the short term Lacy will work for his living.

Although a stage direction at the beginning of scene three, "*Enter* LACY, *like a Dutch shoemaker*," implies that Lacy wears a Dutch costume for the soliloquy, Lacy's entrance singing in the next scene suggests that he can be heard before he can be seen by the other characters on stage; his disguise puts sound before costume (4.42). Lacy comes onstage singing a drinking song and greets Simon Eyre's shoemakers in his stage Dutch, which mixes recognizable English-sounding words with Dutch words and a Dutch accent: "Goeden dach, meester, and yo fro, auch . . . Yaw, yaw; ik ben den skomawker" (4.77, 81). While an English-speaking audience would easily understand the gist of this speech, such an audience would probably not understand each individual word. To an extent, the shoemakers onstage act as surrogates for the audience; they clearly see Hans as a foreigner, albeit a familiar foreign type. For example, in a Dutch stereotype common in sixteenth-century London, Hans is frequently called "butter-box." Firk finds Hans's speech amusing: "'Yaw, yaw'—he speaks yawing like a jackdaw, that gapes to be fed with cheese curds. O, he'll give a villainous pull at a can of double beer" (4.98–102). Even though Firk describes Hans as a stereotypical Dutchman, his observation is welcoming insofar as it is admiring; in Eyre's shop, being a good drinker seems to be a prerequisite, in Firk's mind at least, for membership. Eyre affirms Hans's place among the shoemakers: "Give me thy hand, thou'rt welcome. Hodge, entertain him. Firk, bid him welcome" (4.105–6). Because Eyre, Firk, and Hodge welcome Hans, the audience welcomes him too. My goal in emphasizing this welcome is not to minimize Firk's anti-Dutch stereotyping but to show how the play elides it both by bidding Hans welcome, and, more importantly, by suggesting a link, within Eyre's shop, between foreign speech and economic productivity.

Hans's Dutch speech, amusing as it might be for Eyre's journeymen, is central to Hans's identity as a working shoemaker. Upon hearing his Dutch drinking song, Firk exclaims, "Yonder's a brother of the Gentle Craft!" While Firk may seem to be identifying Lacy merely as a fellow drinker, he immediately follows this exclamation by identifying him to Eyre as a fellow *worker:* "If he bear not St. Hugh's bones, I'll forfeit my bones" (4.49–50). Rhetorically willing to risk his own body on Hans's body of knowledge, Firk connects Hans's Dutch to the language of the trade, with its invocations of Saint Hugh, the shoemakers' patron. The shoemakers advance Hans's interests as synonymous with their own; as part of their advocacy for Hans, Firk and Hodge even threaten to quit the shop (4.63–71). Firk explicitly connects Hans's foreign speech not only to the trade of shoemaking but to the work of Eyre's particular shop: "He's some uplandish workman. Hire him, good master, that I may learn some gibble-gabble. 'Twill make us work the faster" (4.50–52). He argues further, "Good master, hire him. He'll make me laugh so that I shall work more in mirth than I can in earnest" (4.90–91). Dekker's characters never face the hard choices that a mercantile economy would seem to demand; they can have, for example, both integrity in love and the money that might have tempted them away from that love.[29] Here, Firk can both laugh at the Dutchman and work with the Dutchman. Mirth facilitates work; Firk's mockery of Hans's Dutch as "gibble-gabble" also suggests that the mirth it raises will increase productivity by making the shoemakers "work the faster." That we rarely see the shoemakers actually working and that the precise means whereby mirth at Hans's speech will lead to faster or better work are never explained do not diminish the rhetorical appeal of Firk's formulation. The fantasy that English artisans can laugh at Dutch and thereby work better is a potent one. They gain the economic opportunities associated with Dutch without relinquishing their English privilege of laughter.

While the shoemakers can laugh at Hans's strange speech, they share with him the particular lexicon of shoemaking. When Hans confirms upon his arrival that he is indeed a shoemaker, Firk responds with a list of tools that seems to test Hans' knowledge of their craft by testing his knowledge of its jargon: "'Den skomawker', quoth 'a; and hark you, skomawker, have you all your tools—a good rubbing-pin, a good stopper, a good dresser, your four sorts of awls, and your two balls of wax, your paring-knife, your hand- and thumb-leathers, and good Saint Hugh's bones to smooth up your work?" (4.82–87) By answering, Hans confirms that he understands the language of their trade: "Yaw, yaw, be niet vorveard. Ik hab all de dingen voour mack skoes groot end klene" (4.88–89). Firk's use of terms of the shoemaker's art also calls attention to the audience's lack of comprehension, although in a different way than stage Dutch does. The list of tools demonstrates that the shoemakers share a commercial world and social fellowship that is partially obscure but impressive to those who do not understand its cant. Although we may not be able to tell a rubbing-pin from an awl, we can tell by their shared language that Hans and Firk are brothers in the craft. While of course Hans is Lacy and thus understands English perfectly, the way that this scene sets up a dialogue between Firk's shoemaker's lexicon and Hans's Dutch suggests that specialized languages belonging to crafts and trades offer a way of communicating across national language barriers. Firk speaks English and Hans speaks Dutch, but both understand shoemaking. They also both understand drinking. Hans picks up Firk's hint: "O, ik verstaw you. Ik moet een halve dossen cans betaelen. Here, boy, nempt dis skilling, tap eens freelick" (4.115–16). To the shop's fraternity, Hans contributes both tools and beer.

In addition to introducing Lacy's knowledge of the trade and offering the possibility of a more productive shop in which mirth facilitates work, Hans's Dutch opens a significant commercial opportunity for Eyre. Speaking Dutch, Lacy as Hans is able to buy at a bargain the contents of a Dutch ship. Hodge reports the transaction: "this skipper . . . for the love he bears to Hans, offers my master Eyre a bargain in the commodities" (7.18–20).

"The love he bears to Hans" must be based on their common Dutch speech in a city full of English speakers, since it is unlikely, given Lacy's real aristocratic identity, that they could have a prior relationship.

Various critics have pointed out the shady elements of Eyre's transaction: the skipper is drunk, Eyre disguises himself as an alderman to meet the skipper, and the owner of the ship "dares not show his head" due to unexplained troubles (7.18). These problems represent fissures in the play's sympathetic treatment of Eyre and celebration of London's commercial life. For Kastan, they are the contradictions that Dekker's fantasy "apparently would repress." Mortenson notes the differences between Deloney's treatment of Eyre's rise and Dekker's. In *The Gentle Craft,* Eyre's good fortune is the result of a storm, and his rise a credible and somewhat ordinary "model success story" of a smart businessman. In Dekker's play, by contrast, Eyre gains the ship because of another's troubles and profits to an incredible degree, a change that, Mortenson argues, underscores that "one man's gain is another man's loss."[30] Dekker deflects attention away from the moral problems of this episode, however, by first showing the Dutch exchange between Hans and the skipper. This conversation establishes, at least initially, a legitimate basis for the transaction. Because he can speak the skipper's language, Hans is in an advantageous position to represent Eyre. In addition to providing linguistic help, Hans provides venture capital, lending Eyre twenty portagues as a down payment (7.25).

Hans's new position poses a problem for Firk: his fellow shoemaker has become Eyre's patron. Firk recognizes that Dutch determines the skipper's relation to Hans and therefore emphasizes the skipper's foreign speech rather than abstracting it as "the love he bears to Hans." It should be noted that, throughout the play, Firk seems more interested than any other character in Hans's Dutch. Firk's repeated mockery of Dutch is in part accounted for by his conventional role as the fool. Peter McCluskey thinks Firk's anti-Dutch stereotyping becomes tiresome and banal and concludes that "Dekker invites audience members to laugh at, rather than with, Firk."[31] While this may be true, and does work to raise the audience's sympathies for Hans, Firk's interest in Hans need not be fully explained away as a stage convention. Firk's interest in Hans as a Dutch speaker and Hans as a worker can be traced in part to his own identity as a London journeyman. Hans is a foreign competitor, and his economic aid to Eyre—strange aid for a shoemaker to offer—further emphasizes the destabilizing potential that this linguistically flexible foreigner holds for the longer-term inhabitants of Eyre's shop. In the play, these concerns are drowned out by the comic laughter of the shop and the audience's laughter at Firk's repetitive mockery of Dutch. They are also muted by the play's fantasy of easy social mobility.[32] Eyre's profit from the purchase makes possible his social and political gains later in the play as he rises to the position of Lord Mayor. In the market-driven world of Dekker's London comedy, foreign speech facilitates economic negotiation, economic success, and finally social success.

At the play's end, all share in Eyre's economic and social success. The shoemakers are summoned to their holiday by the pancake bell, the king grants Eyre's patent, and Lacy's identity is revealed. Yet this revelation is less a triumph of English identity over Dutch disguise than a productive combination of the two. The Dutch influence in the play is always positive; Hans's Dutch signals his disguise as a worker, makes the shop more industrious, and helps Eyre to a financial windfall, but it never requires Lacy to lose his Englishness or his identity as an aristocrat. At the same time, Eyre continues to refer to Lacy as Hans, so Lacy in effect gets to remain a Dutch shoemaker even when he reemerges as an English gentleman. He appropriates Dutch commercialism without losing his English or his Englishness, becoming flexible enough both to marry as an aristocrat and to capitalize on commercial opportunity as a shoemaker. Lacy at the end of the play is a kind of hybrid, a character who speaks multiple languages, knows multiple livings, and thus can be both English and Dutch. Dekker's play, with its links between language and commerce, mirth and work, suggests a wishfully productive if decidedly impractical way for Londoners to deal with foreign influences: laugh and learn. In this play, England is not deprived but enriched by foreign words and the Dutchman who speaks them. Dekker's vision of holiday camaraderie, commercial celebration, and royal authority is self-consciously both fantastical and outdated; it belongs not to history but to the imagined origins of London craft culture. That a Dutchman plays such a crucial role in this myth of origins suggests the expansiveness of Dekker's idealization of foreign influences on English commerce. Audiences, by laughing at Dutch, complete the process of transforming mirth into work that began with the first notes of Hans's merry Dutch song.

NOTES

1. Peter Mortenson, "The Economics of Joy in *The Shoemaker's Holiday*," *SEL* 16 (1976): 252; David Scott Kastan, "Workshop and/as Playhouse: Comedy and Commerce in *The Shoemaker's Holiday*," *Studies in Philology* 84 (1987): 325; Marta Straznicky, "The End(s) of Discord in *The Shoemaker's Holiday*," *SEL* 36 (1996): 358.

2. Because Lacy the English gentleman almost fully becomes Hans the Dutch shoemaker, naming this character poses a problem. I use "Lacy" to refer to the character's English identity and "Hans" to refer to the identity performed by his shoemaker's guise.

3. Steven Mullaney, *The Place of the Stage: License, Play, and Power in Renaissance England* (Chicago: University of Chicago Press, 1988), 82.

4. George Puttenham, *The Arte of English Poesie* (1589; reprint, Menston, UK: Scolar Press, 1968), 86; Richard Carew, "The Excellency of the English Tongue," in *Remains Concerning Britain*, ed. R. D. Dunn, 37 (Toronto: University of Toronto Press, 1984).

5. William Camden, *Remains Concerning Britain*, ed. R. D. Dunn, 23 (Toronto: University of Toronto Press, 1984).

6. Carew, "Excellency," 38.

7. Richard Helgerson, "Barbarous Tongues: The Ideology of Poetic Form in Renaissance England," in *The Historical Renaissance: New Essays on Tudor and Stuart Literature and Culture,* ed. Heather Dubrow and Richard Strier, 288–89 (Chicago: University of Chicago Press, 1988).

8. Carew, "Excellency," 43.

9. Janette Dillon, *"The Spanish Tragedy* and Staging Languages in Renaissance Drama," *Research Opportunities in Renaissance Drama* 34 (1995): 32.

10. Peter McCluskey, "'Shall I Betray My Brother': Anti-Alien Satire and Its Subversion in *The Shoemaker's Holiday," Tennessee Philological Bulletin* 37 (2000): 43–54.

11. Carew, "Excellency," 41.

12. Thomas Littleton and Edward Coke, *The First Part of the Institutes of the Laws of England, or A Commentary Upon Littleton,* 6th ed. (London: 1664), Sec. 267. I quote Coke's translation of Littleton's law-French.

13. Puttenham, *Arte of English Poesie,* 89.

14. For a detailed discussion of the Babel topos, see Janette Dillon, *Language and Stage in Medieval and Renaissance England* (Cambridge: Cambridge University Press, 1998), 2–4.

15. Camden, *Remains Concerning Britain,* 32.

16. Carew, "Excellency," 43, 42; Camden, *Remains Concerning Britain,* 36.

17. Helen Ostovich, "'Teach you our princess English?' Equivocal Translation of the French in *Henry V,"* in *Gender Rhetorics: Postures of Dominance and Submission in History,* ed. Richard C. Trexler, 146, 154–55 (Binghamton, NY: Center for Medieval and Early Renaissance Studies, 1994). See also Corinne S. Abate, "'Once More Unto the Breach': Katharine's Victory in *Henry V," Early Theatre* 4 (2001): 75; Jean Howard and Phyllis Rackin, *Engendering a Nation: A Feminist Account of Shakespeare's English Histories* (London: Routledge, 1997), 210; Karen Newman, *Fashioning Femininity and English Renaissance Drama* (Chicago: University of Chicago Press, 1991), 101.

18. On this linguistically articulated alliance, see Stephen Greenblatt, *Shakespearean Negotiations: The Circulation of Social Energy in Renaissance England* (Berkeley and Los Angeles: University of California Press, 1988), 56–57; Christopher Highley, *Shakespeare, Spenser, and the Crisis in Ireland* (Cambridge: Cambridge University Press, 1997), 146; Alan Powers, "'Gallia and Gaul, French and Welsh': Comic Ethnic Slander in the Gallia Wars," in *Acting Funny: Comic Theory and Practice in Shakespeare's Plays,* ed. Frances Teague, 110 (Rutherford, NJ: Farleigh Dickinson University Press, 1994); Alan Sinfield and Jonathan Dollimore, "History and Ideology: The Instance of *Henry V,"* in *Alternative Shakespeares,* ed. John Drakakis, 225 (London: Methuen, 1985). On the limits and fissures in the construction of a unified Britain in *Henry V,* see Paula Blank, *Broken English: Dialects and the Politics of Language in Renaissance England* (New York: Routledge, 1996), 138–39; Claire McEachern, *The Poetics of English Nationhood, 1590–1612* (Cambridge: Cambridge University Press, 1996), 107, 20–22.

19. Thomas Dekker, *The Shoemaker's Holiday,* ed. Robert Leo Smallwood and Stanley W. Wells, *Revels Plays* ed., 4.48–49 (Manchester, UK: Manchester University Press, 1979). The Revels edition is numbered only by scene. All further references to *The Shoemaker's Holiday* are cited parenthetically by scene and line number.

20. On Dekker's unusually positive treatment of foreigners, see A. J. Hoenselaars, *Images of Englishmen and Foreigners in the Drama of Shakespeare and His Contemporaries: A Study of Stage Characters and National Identity in English Renaissance Drama, 1558–1642* (Rutherford, NJ: Farleigh Dickinson University Press, 1992), 60–64.

21. Steve Lee Rappaport, *Worlds within Worlds: Structures of Life in Sixteenth-Century London* (Cambridge: Cambridge University Press, 1989), 57; Joseph P. Ward, *Metropolitan Communities: Trade Guilds, Identity, and Change in Early Modern London* (Stanford, CA: Stanford University Press, 1997), 126–31.

22. Kastan, "Workshop," 325–28.

23. Ibid., 327.

24. Richard Grassby, *The Business Community of Seventeenth Century England* (Cambridge: Cambridge University Press, 1995), 181.

25. Fynes Moryson, *Shakespeare's Europe: A Survey of the Condition of Europe at the End of the 16th Century, Being Unpublished Chapters of Fynes Moryson's Itinerary (1617),* ed. Charles Hughes, (New York: Benjamin Blom, 1967), 378.

26. Smallwood and Wells, in Dekker's *The Shoemaker's Holiday,* Appendix A, 204.

27. Ibid., 1.29 n.

28. On the changing geographical and linguistic identity of the United Provinces in the sixteenth and seventeenth centuries, see Simon Schama, *The Embarrassment of Riches: An Interpretation of Dutch Culture in the Golden Age* (New York: Knopf, 1987), 55–58. On the problem of drawing firm distinctions between early modern languages, which were not yet easily connected to nation-states, see Peter Burke, *Languages and Communities in Early Modern Europe* (Cambridge: Cambridge University Press, 2004), 7–8, 63.

29. Kastan, "Workshop," 330.

30. Ibid., 327; Mortenson, "Economics of Joy," 244, 47.

31. McCluskey, "'Shall I Betray My Brother,'" 50.

32. Some social mobility, both upward and downward, was possible among London citizens. Gentlemen preferred wholesale and middlemen positions to retailing and crafts, which makes Lacy's choice of shoemaker's work all the more striking. While some masters did rise to positions of authority in their companies, significant wealth was required to hold city office, wealth held by only a few percent of the free population (Grassby, *Buisness Community,* 119, 61).

Bibliography

Abate, Corinne S. "'Once More Unto the Breach': Katharine's Victory in *Henry V.*" *Early Theatre* 4 (2001): 73–85.

Blank, Paula. *Broken English: Dialects and the Politics of Language in Renaissance England.* New York: Routledge, 1996.

Burke, Peter. *Languages and Communities in Early Modern Europe.* Cambridge: Cambridge University Press, 2004.

Camden, William. *Remains Concerning Britain.* Edited by R. D. Dunn. Toronto: University of Toronto Press, 1984.

Carew, Richard, "The Excellency of the English Tongue." In *Remains Concerning Britain.* Edited by R. D. Dunn, 37–44. Toronto: University of Toronto Press, 1984.

Dekker, Thomas. *The Shoemaker's Holiday.* Edited by Robert Leo Smallwood and Stanley W. Wells. *Revels Plays* edition. Manchester, UK: Manchester University Press, 1979.

Dillon, Janette. *Language and Stage in Medieval and Renaissance England.* Cambridge: Cambridge University Press, 1998.

———. "*The Spanish Tragedy* and Staging Languages in Renaissance Drama." *Research Opportunities in Renaissance Drama* 34 (1995): 32.

Grassby, Richard. *The Business Community of Seventeenth Century England.* Cambridge: Cambridge University Press, 1995.

Greenblatt, Stephen. *Shakespearean Negotiations: The Circulation of Social Energy in Renaissance England.* Berkeley and Los Angeles: University of California Press, 1988.

Helgerson, Richard. "Barbarous Tongues: The Ideology of Poetic Form in Renaissance England." In *The Historical Renaissance: New Essays on Tudor and Stuart Literature and Culture.* Edited by Heather Dubrow and Richard Strier, 273–92. Chicago: University of Chicago Press, 1988.

Highley, Christopher. *Shakespeare, Spenser, and the Crisis in Ireland.* Cambridge: Cambridge University Press, 1997.

Hoenselaars, A. J. *Images of Englishmen and Foreigners in the Drama of Shakespeare and His Contemporaries: A Study of Stage Characters and National Identity in English Renaissance Drama, 1558–1642.* Rutherford, NJ: Farleigh Dickinson University Press, 1992.

Howard, Jean, and Phyllis Rackin. *Engendering a Nation: A Feminist Account of Shakespeare's English Histories.* London: Routledge, 1997.

Kastan, David Scott. "Workshop and/as Playhouse: Comedy and Commerce in *The Shoemaker's Holiday.*" *Studies in Philology* 84 (1987): 324–37.

Littleton, Thomas, and Edward Coke. *The First Part of the Institutes of the Laws of England, or A Commentary Upon Littleton.* 6th edition. London, 1664.

McCluskey, Peter. "'Shall I Betray My Brother': Anti-Alien Satire and Its Subversion in *The Shoemaker's Holiday.*" *Tennessee Philological Bulletin* 37 (2000): 43–54.

McEachern, Claire Elizabeth. *The Poetics of English Nationhood, 1590–1612, Cambridge Studies in Renaissance Literature and Culture.* Cambridge: Cambridge University Press, 1996.

Mortenson, Peter. "The Economics of Joy in *The Shoemaker's Holiday.*" *SEL* 16 (1976): 241–52.

Moryson, Fynes. *Shakespeare's Europe: A Survey of the Condition of Europe at the End of the 16th Century, Being Unpublished Chapters of Fynes Moryson's Itinerary (1617).* Edited by Charles Hughes. New York: Benjamin Blom, 1967.

Mullaney, Steven. *The Place of the Stage: License, Play, and Power in Renaissance England.* Chicago: University of Chicago Press, 1988.

Newman, Karen. *Fashioning Femininity and English Renaissance Drama.* Chicago: University of Chicago Press, 1991.

Ostovich, Helen. "'Teach you our princess English?' Equivocal Translation of the French in *Henry V.*" In *Gender Rhetorics: Postures of Dominance and Submission in History.* Edited by Richard C. Trexler, 147–61. Binghamton, NY: Center for Medieval and Early Renaissance Studies, 1994.

Powers, Alan, "'Gallia and Gaul, French and Welsh': Comic Ethnic Slander in the Gallia Wars." In *Acting Funny: Comic Theory and Practice in Shakespeare's Plays.* Edited by Frances Teague, 109–22. Rutherford, NJ: Farleigh Dickinson University Press, 1994.

Puttenham, George. *The Arte of English Poesie.* 1589. Reprint, Menston, UK: Scolar Press, 1968.

Rappaport, Steve Lee. *Worlds within Worlds: Structures of Life in Sixteenth-Century London, Cambridge Studies in Population, Economy, and Society in Past Time.* Cambridge: Cambridge University Press, 1989.

Schama, Simon. *The Embarrassment of Riches: An Interpretation of Dutch Culture in the Golden Age.* New York: Knopf, 1987.

Sinfield, Alan, and Jonathan Dollimore. "History and Ideology: The Instance of *Henry V.*" In *Alternative Shakespeares.* Edited by John Drakakis, 206–27. London: Methuen, 1985.

Straznicky, Marta. "The End(s) of Discord in *The Shoemaker's Holiday.*" *SEL Studies in English Literature* 36 (1996): 357–72.

Ward, Joseph P. *Metropolitan Communities: Trade Guilds, Identity, and Change in Early Modern London.* Stanford, CA: Stanford University Press, 1997.

The Subject of Smoke:
Tobacco and Early Modern England

Sandra Bell

IN THE LATE 1590s AND EARLY 1600s, TOBACCO WAS PRAISED AS A BOTH A medicinal drug of wondrous potential and as a social lubricant which (at the height of its powers) could make smokers more mentally adept. Many opponents laughed off tobacco as a passing fad, similar to vogues for foreign clothing. Others treated it more seriously, as a threat to national customs and sovereignty; critics declared that tobacco imperiled the health of the individual smoker, and further suggested that it endangered the very fabric of the commonwealth. England's increasing taste for tobacco was threatening enough that King James felt it necessary to admonish his new subjects in *A Counterblaste to Tobacco* (1604), stating, "Our Peace hath bred wealth: And Peace and wealth hath brought foorth a generall sluggishnesse, which makes vs wallow in all sorts of idle delights, and soft delicacies, the first seedes of the subversion of all great Monarchies."[1] In its insatiable desire for foreign commodities, England embraced tobacco, and tobacco's ability to change the very nature of the smokers' bodies jeopardized the existence of England itself, its customs, its civility, and its government.

From its introduction in the mid-sixteenth century, tobacco became increasingly popular. To satisfy the demand, importation of tobacco rose from approximately 25,000 pounds in 1603 to approximately 38 million pounds by 1700; these numbers reflect only official importation, and do not include the vast quantities smuggled into the country.[2] In 1614, Barnaby Rich claimed that "in London & neare about London . . . there are found to be vpward of 7000, houses, that doth liue" by selling tobacco. This apparently refers only to houses selling tobacco exclusively, and not "euery Tauerne, Inne, and Alehouse . . . Apothocaries Shops, Grosers Shops, Chaundlers Shops" and so on that also sold tobacco.[3] The Venetian ambassador Horatio Busino remarked in 1618 that "[s]o much money is expended daily in this nastiness that at the present moment the trade in tobacco amounts to half a million in gold, and the duty on it alone yields the king 40,000 golden crowns yearly."[4] The rapid and unprecedented increase in the use of tobacco only heightened the sense of panic among the many anti-tobacco writers.

From James I, King of England. *Two broadsides against tobacco the first given by King James of famous memory, his Counterblast to tobacco: the second transcribed out of that learned physician Dr. Everard Maynwaringe, his treatise of the scurvy. . . .* London: Printed for John Hancock, 1672, p. 63. By permission of the Syndics of Cambridge University Library.

This was no passing fad, and unlike the changing vogues for foreign clothing, this import did not simply transform a person's appearance superficially; tobacco could change one from the inside out, and the change threatened to be irreversible. As Philaretes states in his early anti-tobacco tract *Work for Chimny-Sweepers: or A warning for Tabacconists* (1602), "Custom changeth nature, & at length turneth into nature itself; for it is another nature."[5] Tobacco use could thus change and subvert the very nature of the English character.

"Divine Tobacco"

The introduction of tobacco, and the increase in tobacco use, were dependent upon the support which came initially and principally from the medical community. While this might seem surprising, given today's heightened awareness of tobacco as addictive and life-threatening, the early medical community readily accepted tobacco as a new "simple," like many other medicinal herbs already in use.[6] The methods of using tobacco were also similar to methods already in practice: the leaf could be applied directly to the body; its juice could be taken internally or applied externally; often it was mixed with other "corrective" herbs; and, like other herbal medicines, the smoke was either applied externally—wafted over the body—or inhaled, either through a pipe or in the form of a cigar. As medical doctor William Barclay states, "Suffumigation or receiving of smoke is not a new invented remedy; it is an old and well approved form of medicine in many diseases."[7] Tobacco was also easily incorporated into the Galenic theory of the four humors or complexions, its hot and dry properties the perfect counterbalances to the cold and wet diseases rife in England; it was especially popular as a cure for the rheum—similar to a feverish flu—a common English complaint. The medical community's advocacy of tobacco, and the many anecdotes of miraculous cures, bolstered tobacco's reputation as the new panacea. Some of the medical applications of tobacco are outlined in Nicolas Monardes's *Segunda parte del libro* (Seville, 1571), translated into English by John Frampton in 1577 as *Joyful Newes out of the New World*. This popular book records at length the various medical uses—or "diuine effects"—of tobacco; it could treat ailments as diverse as "paines of the head," "griefes of the Brest," "griefes of the windes," "euill of the Mother," "tothache" and "rotten and cankered woundes (43v)."[8] This list of cures is repeated and extended in later texts; it soon became common to state that tobacco could cure "almost all diseases."[9] Even some mental illnesses, such as melancholy, could be treated with tobacco.

As tobacco's reputation as a panacea for physical ailments grew, the language describing it became increasingly metaphysical. Frampton's reference to the "diuine effects" of tobacco is echoed in many other texts. The earliest reference to tobacco in fictional literature in England is in Edmund Spenser's *The Faerie Queene,* where it is hailed as "divine";[10] Sir John Beaumont (brother to Francis), in his poem *The Metamorphosis of Tabacco* (1602) (the first lengthy fictional work devoted to the subject), praises the "sacred fume" of this "glorious simple . . . Belou'd of heau'nly Gods, and earthly Kings"; Roger Marbecke, a physician, claims it came from God, "who is the author of all good gifts"; Barclay, a Scottish physician, also professes "diuine Tobacco" was a "precious plant."[11] By referring to its God-like or at least God-given virtues, supporters attempted to provide tobacco with an irrefutable authority.

Tobacco's medicinal and increasingly mystical properties facilitated its acceptance; it was given further authority by its fashionable association with the upper classes and courtiers. Marbecke claims that "men of great learning and iudgement, men of right good bringing up, men of fine, and deinty diet, men of good worth, and worship, yea men, of right honourable estate, and calling; do like the smell of Tobacco well enough."[12] A number of very prominent courtiers smoked tobacco pipes, and the equipment associated with smoking—and the art of smoking itself—became increasingly complex and ostentatious: along with carved pipes decorated with silver, smoking kits included a decorated box for the tobacco, tongs to carry the embers to the pipe, a pick to clean the pipe, a knife to cut the tobacco, and even silver porringers to spit in.[13] Pipe smoking became an essential part of sophisticated socializing: as Barclay states, tobacco "is the only medicament in the world ordained by nature to entertaine good companie: insomuch that it worketh neuer so well, as when it is giuen from man to man, as a pledge of friendshippe and amitie."[14]

In addition to strengthening the physical body and enhancing social customs, tobacco was seen to increase mental abilities; Marbecke declares that tobacco can be used "to clear the brains and make the mind more able to come to her self, and the better to exercise her heavenly gifts and virtues."[15] For Beaumont, the importation of tobacco brings with it some of the heat of the New World, correcting the fear that England's climate cooled one's mental abilities.[16] In his long poem *The Metamorphosis of Tabacco,* tobacco both mimics and surpasses traditional poetic muses:

> Infume my braine, make my soules powers subtile,
> Giue nimble cadence to my harsher stile:
> Inspire me with thy flame, which doth excell
> The purest streames of the Castalian well,
> That I on thy ascensiue wings may flie
> By thine ethereall vapours borne on high,
> And with thy feathers added to my quill
> May pitch thy tents on the Parnassian hill.[17]

A number of the introductory poems to Beaumont's text echo this sense of tobacco both as the subject of and the inspiration for poetry.[18] Advocates for tobacco emphasized the positive effects of tobacco on the English consumer: tobacco cured diseases to which the English were especially susceptible; it heightened positive social bonds, especially amongst the upper classes; and it produced a sharp and agile, even poetic wit.

AN UNSAVOURY ANTIDOTE

Despite the broad medical support and the conviction of tobacco devotees, the majority of texts referring to tobacco question its medical and divine claims, and emphasize instead the destructive effect of tobacco smoking on both the individual body and the body politic. The texts denouncing tobacco range from serious attacks in medical and political tracts, to comic ridicule in a variety of poems, plays, and satirical pamphlets.

As early as 1598 Jonson caricatured the fashionable tobacconist in his portrait of the braggart Captain Bobadill in *Every Man In His Humour.*[19] Enjoying a pipe of tobacco,[20] Bobadill voices a number of the claims popularly made about tobacco's powers:

> I have been in the Indies, where this herb grows, where neither myself, nor a dozen gentlemen before, of my knowledge, have received the taste of any other nutriment in the world, for the space of one and twenty weeks, but the fume of this simple only.[21] Therefore, it cannot be, but 'tis most divine! Further, take it in the nature, in the true kind so, it makes an *antidote,* that, had you taken the most deadly poisonous plant in all *Italy,* it should expel it, and clarify you, with as much ease, as I speak. And, for your green wound, your *Balsamum,* and your St. John's wort are all mere gulleries, and trash to it, especially your *Trinidado:* your *Nicotian* is good too. I could say what I know of the virtue of it, for the expulsion of rheums, raw humours, crudities, obstructions, with a thousand of this kind; but I profess myself no *quacksalver.* Only, thus much, by HERCVLES, I do hold it, and will affirm it, before any prince in *Europe,* to be the most sovereign, and precious weed, that ever the earth tendered to the use of man.[22]
>
> (3.5.77–95)

The mockery in Jonson's very popular plays might have provided some of the material for the later anti-tobacconists, though the methods of attack were various. Jonson mentions tobacco's original country here; in other texts, tobacco's roots in the Americas and its use by the native population there became proof of its barbarity and led to a questioning of its divinity; its claim to superiority over traditional English customs, such as Balsamum and St. John's wort, became an example of tobacco's reverse colonization. Its pretension to sovereignty would be countered by the king himself.

One of the first English texts to question seriously the medical efficacy of tobacco appeared in 1602, the pseudonymous pamphlet by "Philaretes" entitled *Work for Chimny-sweepers: Or A warning for Tabacconists*.[23] Philaretes begins his argument by questioning the authority of the "many excellent Physitions and men of singuler learning and practise, together with many gentlemen and some of great accompt," who "by their daily use and custom in drinking Tobacco, give great credit and authority to the same" (A3). He recognizes he stands on shaky ground in arguing against such an influential group, and apologizes that "to the wiser sort this treatise will seeme at the first a fruitlesse labour, of an idle braine." However, the authority for his position, he claims, will be "reason and experience." Many of Philaretes's comments on the medical properties of tobacco point to the paradoxical claims of physicians and patients: "What thing can be more absurd and phantasticall, then to minister one & the self same remedy to contrary & repugnant affects, hot & cold, dry and moist, emptie and repleat, acute and cronicall" (B3v). The very mysterious, healing nature of tobacco praised by others is here questioned because of its apparent irrationality. To counter the usual list of miraculous cures, Philaretes provides a lengthy list of "symtomes and accidents which doo immediately follow and ensue the large drinking[24] thereof. That are, violent vomits, many and infinite stooles, great gnawings and torments in the guts and inward parts. Coldnesse in the outward and externall members, Crampes, Convultions, cold sweats, ill colour, and wannesse of skinne, defect of feeling, sense, & understanding, losse of sight, giddiness of the head and braine, profound and deep sleep, faintnesse, soundings [swoonings], and to some hastie and vntimely death" (E4v). Tobacco's hot and dry properties, which physicians claimed helped to cure the inevitably wet and cold diseases of England, are the very reason to avoid taking it. Rather than improving the health of the English subject, tobacco unbalances the natural humors of a healthy body, and is too violent to cure a weakened one.[25]

The most vehement and authoritative anti-tobacconist, however, was King James I. *A Counterblaste to Tobacco* appeared in 1604, the first piece of writing (outside of speeches) the king composed specifically for his English subjects.[26] Despite his obviously authoritative position, even James feels the need to apologize for writing about tobacco, such a "trifle," and states, in language echoing Philaretes, "If any thinke it a light Argument, so is it but a toy that is bestowed vpon it. And since the Subiect is but of Smoke, I think the fume of an idle braine, may serue for a sufficient battery against so fumous and feeble an enemy."[27] Looking past the king's rather surprising claim of "an idle braine," such apologies point to the paradoxical nature of tobacco: like smoke, it is ephemeral, light, "feeble," and thus, as James states, it is "too low for the Law to looke on, and too meane for a King to interpone his authoritie, or bend his eye vpon (85)." Smoke has enough weight, however, that James does bend his eye upon it, and he questions the medical efficacy of tobacco in a highly satiric section in which he shows his thorough grounding in both contemporary medicine and the rhetoric prevalent in the many arguments about tobacco: "such is the miraculous omnipotencie of our strong tasted *Tobacco,* as it cures all sorts of diseases (which neuer any drugge could do before) in all persons, and at all times.... It cures the Gowt in the feet, and (which is miraculous) in that very instant when the smoke thereof, as light, flies vp into the head, the vertue thereof, as heauie, runs downe to the little toe.... It refreshes a weary man, and yet makes a man hungry. Being taken when they goe to bed, it makes one sleep soundly, and yet being taken when a man is sleepie and drowsie, it will, as they say, awake his braine, and quicken his vnderstanding.... O omnipotent power of Tobacco!" (94–95) Although James does briefly allow that tobacco may be "healthfull for some sorts of diseases" (95), he thoroughly undermines the idea that the drug is a new panacea. He mocks the use of terms such as "miraculous omnipotencie" as excessive, almost blasphemous. Representations of tobacco's paradoxical nature are ridiculed, perhaps because they become, in fact, uncomfortably similar to the ways in which monarchs used the rhetoric of paradox to represent themselves; they are familiar and yet mysterious, known and unknown; they are associated with both the physical world and the divine.[28] And, as James points out in his "Letter to the Reader," "it is the Kings part (as the proper Phisician of his Politicke-body) to purge it of all those diseases, by Medicines meet for the same: as by a certaine milde, and yet iust forme of gouernment, to maintaine the Publicke quietnesse, and preuent all occasions of Commotion" (85). James here ousts the usurping tobacco from its role as sovereign cure; the king, not tobacco, is the one to physic the country.

Jonson, Philaretes, and James all use concerns about tobacco's medical claims as a means to address larger issues of the decay of English customs and the safety of the nation. One means of representing the moral decay of tobacconists was to emphasize the barbarity of its source and original users. In his *Counterblaste,* James denigrates tobacco by debasing the original consumers, the "beastly Indians, slaues to the Spaniards, refuse to the world, and as yet aliens from the holy Couenant of God": "Why doe we not as well imitate them in walking naked as they doe? in preferring glasses, feathers, and such toyes, to golde and precious stones, as they do? yea why do we not denie God and adore the Deuil as they doe?" (88). In Philaretes's introductory poem, he claims that he will

> Trinididos smokie face vnmaske,
> Who being but a swartie Indian,
> Hath plaid the painted English Curtesan....
> But hence thou Pagan Idol: tawnie weede,
> Come not with-in our Fairie Costs to feede.
> (*Work for Chimny-sweepers,* A4v–B)[29]

Philaretes, like James, repeats the common colonial belief that the Native Americans are uncivilized savages and heathens—the "swartie Indian[s]" and "Pagan Idol[s]"—to discredit tobacco. The "swarthie" or "tawnie" colour of both Indians and tobacco is connected in a traditional symbolic association to a moral or religious darkness; Philaretes mentions that "Indian Priests (who no doubt were instruments of the diuell whom they serue)" (Bv) used tobacco to induce demonic visions. The blackness is not only associated with moral degradation; it also refers to the blackness the *inside* of the body turns to through tobacco smoking. James is one of a number to comment on the blackened internal organs of the smoker: tobacco "makes a kitchin also oftentimes in the inward parts of men, soiling and infecting them, with an vnctuous and oily kinde of Soote, as hath bene found in some great *Tobacco* takers, that after their death were opened (*Counterblaste,* 97–98)."[30] The English subject is changed from the inside out, and the barbarous and heathen nature generally associated with the dark body is subsumed by the white body, collapsing the traditional differences between the Old and the New World.[31]

The connection between native Americans, tobacco, and the pox further complicated the representation of tobacco. Some physicians stated that tobacco cured sexual diseases; others insisted that it made the smoker sterile.[32] Anti-tobacconists did not deny that tobacco might be a cure for some sexual diseases; in fact James insisted that tobacco was a cure for the pox, and tied both to the original consumers: "[tobacco] was first found out by some of the barbarous Indians, to be a Preseruatiue, or Antidot against the Pockes, a filthy disease, whereunto these barbarous people are (as all men know) very much subject . . . so that as from them was first brought into Christendome, that most detestable disease, so from them likewise was brought this vse of Tobacco, as a stinking and vnsavourie Antidot" (87–88). Indeed, James implies that smokers are simply broadcasting that they are suffering from the pox, that they have "taken so farre the imputation of that disease vpon them" (89). The shifting associations between the source, the disease, and the cure only deepened suspicions regarding tobacco. Philaretes extends the association from the pox to prostitution; he pictures tobacco as the temptress, playing "the painted English Curtesan." Many authors connected tobacco with disease, brothels, and taverns in an attempt to lower its credibility.[33]

To counter this corruption, Philaretes writes not simply as an anti-tobacconist, but as a protector of England's "fairy coasts" against an attack by a foreign import; as he says, his "[d]utie and due allegiaunce" is to "Englands soile, and my deere Countrymen" (*Work for Chimny-sweepers,* A4V).[34] An argument based in medicine becomes one that evokes the invasion of the Old world by the New, and thus an argument of national and religious import. Citing the lack of method or order in the use of tobacco, Philaretes claims that "where no method or order is vsed . . . [there results] naught else but dissolations and confusion, a thing, as in the Common weal it is pernicious, so in the preseruation of mans health it hath been alwaies adiudged most dangerous" (B2). The association of the individual physical body to the larger body politic heightens the threat of tobacco—or "this Indian stranger" (B2)—to the nation itself.[35] As Richard Braithwait states in *The Smoaking Age, or the Life and Death of Tobacco* (1617), England is falling under "a late Negro's introduced fashion, / Who brought his Drugs here to corrupt our Nation."[36]

At a time when expansion into the Americas promised to carry English customs and values to the New World, the New World import appeared to be undermining that very Englishness within England itself.[37] The custom of taking tobacco was changing the nature of the English body, and for many this extended into a potentially destructive change in the body politic. England's imperialist drive into the Americas, which was motivated at least partially by tobacco, was threatening to undermine rather than expand England's power.

Tobacco's threat to England—to its sovereignty, to its monarch—is repeated by many writers, and the source of the danger is perceived to be both foreign and internal. James associated tobacco's introduction to England with Sir Walter Ralegh, "a father so generally hated" (*Counterblaste*, 89), who, in 1604, was a condemned traitor in the Tower of London. Ralegh is supposed to have cured his own tobacco while in the Tower, and to have smoked just before his execution to "settle his spirits."[38] A number of writers describe the threat of tobacco through its association with traitors. In 1605, "T.W." notes that the imprisoned Gunpowder Plotters "'rather feasted with their sins, than fasted with sorrow for them; were richly appareled, fared deliciously, and took Tobacco out of measure, with a seeming carelessness of their crime'."[39] In *Tobacco Battered and the Pipes Shattered* (1633), Joshua Sylvester connects tobacco smoke to the "*smoak* of *Powder-Treson, Pistols, Knives,* / To blow-up Kingdoms, and blow-out Kings lives."[40] In 1616, John Deacon wrote a lengthy tract condemning tobacco and associating it with recent riots about enclosures. He details the slippery slope from tobacco smoking to treason:

those men (for the most part) they were formerly held for professed *Tobacconists:* namely, for disordered and riotous persons. Who falling first from Tobacco to tippling; from tippling to whoring; from whoring, to a Court-like brauing; from a Court-like brauing, to a superfluous building; from a superfluous building, to a prodigall dispending of their ancient patrimonies, & other their alloted preferments; from a prodigall spending, to an excessive want. . . . For their intolerable wants became so heauie a burden vnto their vnbended backes, as . . .they rather most damnably resolued among themselues to massacre our most Christian King, our gracious Queene; our peerlesse young Prince, the whole royall of-spring, the honorable Councell; the Nobles, the Gentrie, the Cleargie, the Communaltie, and the happie estate of this our whole countrey.[41]

Tobacco was not simply an idle threat; the corruption of the physical body was affiliated with and even instigated social barbarity and degeneration— a complete upheaval of accepted hierarchies and traditions—and subsequently endangered the nation and monarchy itself. Even in Sir John Beaumont's praise of tobacco, *The Metamorphosis of Tabacco,* he hints that tobacco can inspire "the braue spirit, and ambitious mind" to "leape at Crownes, and reach aboue their birth."[42] As English customs changed and English bodies were transfigured, the English body politic was threatening to fall apart.[43] In his *Counterblaste,* James states that smokers "harm [them]selves both in persons and goods" (99) and that this in turn weakened their ability to uphold English customs and defend England. Neither weakened persons nor diminished purses could support the crown against internal threat or foreign invasion.

The king's vociferous public condemnation of tobacco gave authority to all later anti-tobacconists, who would no longer need to apologize for speaking out against "men of great learning and iudgement, men of right good bringing up" (Marbecke, *Defence,* 24). Many of the later criticisms, however, did not display the same fear of imminent threat; indeed, many authors criticizing tobacco began to mock the excessive and self-righteous tone of anti-tobacconists themselves. Jonson's *Every Man In His Humour* (1598) satirizes tobacconists along with anti-tobacconists. In 1605 it was presented to the court; presumably the publication of James's *Counterblaste* prompted the performance. The play ridicules the social acceptance of tobacco in the figure of the self-important, excessive tobacconist Bobadill, but the character of Cob, a lowly waterbearer, argues more directly against "filthy, roguish tobacco": "I'd have it present whipping, man, or woman, that should but deal with a tobacco-pipe; why, it will stifle them all in the end, as many as use it; it's little better than ratsbane, or rosaker."[44] The court audience then watched the bizarre spectacle of Cob being imprisoned for voicing complaints similar to those made by the king; Cob is imprisoned by Justice Clement, who praises tobacco as "an herb, so generally received in the courts of princes, the chambers of nobles, the bowers of sweet ladies, the cabins of soldiers!"[45] If these sections of the play were performed in 1605 as written, it appears to be an odd way to celebrate the king's presence and his newly published tract.[46] Jonson mocks those who support tobacco, but he does not withhold his satire from those who— like the king—proclaim against it. Tobacco becomes one folly in the long list which provided fodder for satirists; if these texts pictured a barbarous and demonized England, they also recognized and reveled in the excess of their own representations.

John Taylor, the "water poet," wrote a pamphlet dedicated to King James entitled *The Nipping or Snipping of Abvses* (1614), which included the devil's own "Proclamation or approbation, from the King of execration, to euery Nation, for Tobacoes propagation."[47] Having already conquered "these blacke Nations that adore my name" (D), the devil desires that "throughout all Christian lands, / Tobacco be disperst, that they may be / As Moores and Pagans are, all like to me. / That from the Palace to the paltry nooke, / Like hell in Imitation all may looke" (Dv).[48] Taylor points directly to tobacco's colonization of England, and the subsequent corruption of England's religion and social hierarchy. Taylor also addresses the issue of tobacco as an inspiration for poetry; included at the end of Pluto's proclamation are "Certaine verses written in the Barbarian tongue, dropt out of a Negroes pocket, which I thought good to insert, because they tend to the honour of Tobaco" (D3):

> Vaprosh fogh stinkquash slavorumques fie fominoshte
> Spitterspawlimon, loathersohem halkish spewriboshte
> Mistrum fog smoakrash, choakerumquesolifa trish trash
> Dam durticum belchum, contagioshte vomitroshe:
> Whifferum, puffegulpum, allisnuffhuff fleaminon odish,
> Rewmito contaminosh diabollish dungish odorish: [*sic*]

> (D3)

The poem seems a combination of corrupted English and Latin, with a heavy emphasis on bodily excretions. It both satirizes the intellectual and artistic abilities of the "barbarian negro," and undermines the notion that tobacco inspires (good) poetry.[49] Like other satirists, Taylor is highly critical of tobacco, recognizing its destructive potential regarding the minds and bodies of English smokers and the body politic itself. However, his comic approach to his subject tends to diminish the sense of an imminent threat; tobacco can be laughed at rather than feared.

Tobacco thus had a complicated reception in early modern England. Tobacco use was spurred on by the herb's novelty, by the medical claims and social graces associated with it, and by the potential for English imperialism. Tobacco was, however, the focus of critics who feared that the wholeness of the English body, the civility of English customs, and the sovereignty of the English body politic, were being threatened by the expansion of England into the New World—and the New World into England. Samuel Daniel, in *The Queenes Arcadia,* wondered at his fellow citizens' devotion to tobacco, and contemplated a distant, wiser, tobacco-less future that, four hundred years later, has yet to arrive:

> But sure the time's to come, when they [who] looke backe
> On this, will wonder with themselves to thinke

> That men of sense could ever be so mad,
> To suck so grosse a vapour that consumes
> Their spirits, spends nature, dries up memorie,
> Corrupts the blood, and is a vanitie.[50]

The counter-arguments of doctors who warned of health hazards, of satirists who ridiculed human folly, and of the king and others who raised the specter of a complete undermining of English customs, religion, and sovereignty could not stem the tide of tobacco use. The tensions surrounding the nature and effects of tobacco are an analogue of a larger uncertainty about the meaning of Englishness in the diversifying, metamorphosing world of the early modern period.

NOTES

1. James VI/I, *A Counterblaste to Tobacco, 1604,* in *Minor Prose Works of Kings James VI and I,* ed. James Craigie, 84 (Edinburgh: Scottish Text Society, 1982). All further page references will be cited parenthetically in the text.

2. See S. Gray and V. J. Wyckoff, "The international tobacco trade in the seventeenth century," *Southern Economic Journal* 7.1 (July 1940): 1–26. Similar numbers are also found in Jeffrey Knapp, *An Empire Nowhere: England, America, and Literature from the* Utopia *to* The Tempest (Berkeley and Los Angeles: University of California Press, 1992), 134; and John Goodman, *Tobacco in History: The Cultures of Dependence* (London: Routledge, 1993), 59. This information on tobacco importation is repeated in my article "'Precious Stinke': James I's *A Counterblaste to Tobacco,*" in *Royal Subjects: Essays on the Writings of James VI and I,* ed. Daniel Fischlin and Mark Fortier, 323–43 (Detroit, MI: Wayne State University Press, 2002), 323–43. Jerome E. Brooks's study is an excellent source for tobacco literature: *Tobacco: Its History Illustrated by the Books, Manuscripts and Engravings in the Library of George Arents, Jr.* (New York: Rosenbach, 1937–52). See also Sarah Dickson's *Panacea or Precious Bane: Tobacco in Sixteenth Century Literature* (New York: New York Public Library, 1954), which extends the discussion of Arents's collection. Jeffrey Knapp's article "Elizabethan Tobacco," *Representations* 21 (Winter, 1988): 26–66, is an excellent analysis of tobacco's role in English imperialism, and provides an analysis of tobacco as inspiration for English literature.

3. Barnaby Rich, *The Honestie of this Age* (London, 1614), 26, 25.

4. *Calendar of State Papers, Venice,* vol. 15 (London, 1617–1619), 101. January 10, 1618. (London: HMSO, 1909).

5. Philaretes, *Work for Chimny-Sweepers: or A warning for Tabacconists* (London, 1602), F2v. All subsequent references will be cited parenthetically in the text. For a discussion of the connection between habit or custom and identity, see Paul A. Cefalu, "'Damnéd Custom . . . Habits Devil': Shakespeare's *Hamlet,* Anti-Dualism, and the Early Modern Philosophy of Mind," *English Literary History* 67, no. 2 (2000): 399–431. Cefalu argues that "In the *Confessions,* Augustine describes the force of habit as a permanent chain or addiction" (410): "For the older Augustine, habitual sin, ultimately ineradicable, stubbornly insinuated itself into the inner life of the sinner until it became second nature" (409).

6. A "simple" is a herb or drug which can be used in isolation, unlike a "compound," which is combined with other herbs or drugs.

7. See William Barclay, *Nepenthes, or the Vertues of Tabacco* (Edinburgh, 1614), [A8].

8. These medical cures are mentioned in a series of marginalia in Monardes's text, qtd. in Brooks, *Tobacco: Its History.*

9. Barclay, *Nepenthes* [A5v].

10. Spenser, *The Faerie Queene*, ed. A. C. Hamilton (New York: Longman, 1977), 3.5.32.6. In *The Faerie Queene*, Belphoebe cures Timias's wound: "She pownded small, and did in peeces bruze, / And then atweene her lilly handes twaine, / Into his wound the iuyce thereof did scruze" (3.5.33.2–4). A. C. Hamilton notes that Spenser is "guilty of being the first English poet to praise Tobacco" (stanza 32 n 6–7).

11. Sir John Beaumont, *The Metamorphosis of Tabacco*, 1602 (New York: Da Capo, 1971), B4v, F1v, B1v, Roger Marbecke, *A Defence of Tabacco: With a Friendly Answer to Worke for Chimny-Sweepers*, 1602 (New York: Da Capo, 1968), 57; Barclay, *Nepenthes* [A6v], [A2v].

12. Marbecke, *A Defence of Tabacco*, 24; he personifies tobacco itself as a "poor gentleman, and a stranger . . . of some good account in his country" (8–9). Marbecke also hesitates to divulge all of tobacco's medicinal powers, fearing the diverse readership of these tracts: "I think it not meet to acquaint the vulgar sort with any such secrets" (67). Although Marbecke may be protecting his position as a physician, he also associates knowledge of tobacco with the "better sort."

James I, in a letter to the High Treasurer, Thomas Earl of Dorset, compares the "use which Persons of good Callinge and Qualitye make thereof" to the practice of a "number of ryotous and disordered Persons of meane and base Condition, whoe . . . doe spend most of there time in that idle Vanitie [tobacco smoking], to the evil example and corrupting of others, and also do consume that Wages whiche manye of them gett by theire Labour, and wherewith there Families should be relieved" (quoted in Brooks, *Tobacco: Its History*, 1:406–7). The association of moderation and proper usage with the upper classes, and reckless abandonment with the lower classes, is not unusual, but it is made more difficult to believe if one considers the not inconsequential cost of buying tobacco.

13. See Brooks, *Tobacco: Its History*, 1:53–54.

14. *Nepenthes*, A4. Busino comments on the English social rituals of using tobacco in terms which sound similar to the passing of a peace pipe: "Amongst themselves they are in the habit of circulating toasts, passing the pipe from one to the other with much grace" (101). James complained of the pervasiveness of social smoking: "is it not a great vanitie, that a man cannot heartily welcome his friend now, but straight they must bee in hand with *Tobacco?* No it is become in place of a cure, a point of good fellowship, and he that will refuse to take a pipe of *Tobacco* among his fellowes, (though by his owne election he would rather feele the sauour of a Sinke) is accounted peeuish and no good company" (*Counterblaste*, 98).

15. Marbecke, *A Defence of Tabacco*, 59.

16. Beaumont also comments on tobacco's reforming temperament: "Blest age, wherein the *Indian* Sunne had shin'd, / Whereby all Arts, all tongues haue been refin'd: / Learning long buried in the darke abysme / Of dunsticall, and monkish barbarisme" (*Metamorphosis*, E3). The reformation in arts and religion is instigated by, rather than threatened by, tobacco.

17. Ibid., Bv.

18. The ten dedicatory poems are all signed by initials only. "W.B." writes, "There didst thou gather on Parnassus clift / This pretious herbe, Tabacco most diuine, / Than which nere Greece, nere Italy did lift/ A flower more fragrant to the Muses shrine;" "H.H" agrees that "Castile nere did such a pipe afford."

19. Nine of Jonson's comedies include a satire about tobacco.

20. Smoking on stage—by both actors and spectators—seems to have been a regular occurrence.

21. Beaumont makes a similar claim in his poem *The Metamorphosis of Tabacco,* though his appears to parody Jesus's forty days in the desert: "Here could I tell you, how vpon the seas / Some men haue fasted with it fortie daies" (F).

22. Jonson, *Every Man In His Humour,* in *Ben Jonson,* ed. C. H. Herford and Percy and Evelyn Simpson, vol. 3 (Oxford: Clarendon Press, 1925–52), 3.5.77–95.

23. The pamphlet is signed with the initials "I" or "J. H." "Tobacconist" refers to the smoker, not the seller of tobacco.

24. The term "drinking" rather than "smoking" was used to describe the inhalation of tobacco smoke.

25. While early modern writers note that sickness results from tobacco smoking, they rarely see the smoking itself as a sickness. The term "addiction" was understood more as a voluntarily devotion to tobacco, but the sense of involuntary drug addiction does not appear until the late eighteenth century (*OED*). Very similar arguments are made by a number of later authors, perhaps influenced by Philaretes.

26. For a detailed analysis of this tract, see my "'Precious Stinke.'" Some arguments about the king's tract mentioned here are discussed at length in that chapter.

27. Roger Marbecke, responding to Philaretes's tract, also calls tobacco a "trifling argument" (*A Defence of Tabacco,* 70). James, like Philaretes, also states that he argues from reason and experience; the similarities between the two tracts may be the result of both authors drawing on generally acknowledged terms of reference, but the frequency of them suggests that James had Philaretes's tract in mind when he wrote.

28. See, for example, Jonathan Goldberg, who notes that such paradoxical representations are "essential to the discourse of power." *James I and the Politics of Literature* (Baltimore: Johns Hopkins University Press, 1983), 11. I also make this argument in "'Precious Stinke'."

29. Later in the poem, Philaretes envisions his revenge on tobacco in rather enthusiastic terms: "In England it [tobacco] should little rest ytake, / O I would whip the queane with rods of steele, / That euer after she my ierks should feele" (B).

30. Philaretes makes a clear connection between Native Americans and the devil. In his argument proper, Philaretes divides his evidence into eight sections; seven of these examine medical properties of tobacco, and one condemns it for its association with the devil. The association with the devil is based on Monardes's text: "That the diuell was the first author hereof, Monardus in his Treatise of Tabacco dooth sufficiently witnesse" (*Work for Chimny-sweepers,* F4v). Because the devil knows the virtue of herbs, and because the "Indian Priests . . . were no doubt instruments of the diuell whom they serue" (F4), tobacco should be eschewed by Christians.

31. Kim F. Hall discusses sunburn in terms equally applicable to tobacco: "With the exploration of the Americas, literary, scientific, and popular discussions of sunburn become the conduit through which existing and comfortable oppositions—typically expressed through traditional black/white images—become questioned and altered as Europeans discovered a world of threatening difference," in *Things of Darkness: Economies of Race and Gender in Early Modern England* (Ithaca, NY: Cornell University Press, 1995), 93.

32. Philaretes states that "the continuation & propagation of mankinde (consisting principally in his perfect & vncorrupt seed) is in these men [smokers] much abridged. . . . *Tabacco* dryeth vp the sperme & seed of man" (*Work for Chimny-sweepers,* E2). In 1669, Bendetto Stella considered the benefits of tobacco to priests and monks: "The natural cause of lust is heat and humidity. When this is dried out through the use of tobacco, these libidinous surges are not felt so powerfully" (qtd. in Goodman, *Tobacco,* 78).

33. James states that other tobacco is now necessary to the continuation of other vices: "yet can you neither be merry at an Ordinarie, nor lasciuous in the Stewes, if you lacke Tobacco to prouoke your appetite" (*Counterblaste,* 96).

34. Philaretes' construction of a sexualized foreign invasion is similar to the earlier image constructed by Queen Elizabeth in her "Speech to the troops at Tilbury," where she envisions the Spanish Armada invading the realm of England as the forced impregnation of her own virginal body: "[I] take foul scorn that Parma or any prince of Europe should dare to invade the borders of my realm. To which rather than any dishonor shall grow by me," in *Elizabeth I: Collected Works,* ed. Leah S. Marcus, Janel Mueller, and Mary Beth Rose, 326 (Chicago: University of Chicago Press, 2000). Of course, Philaretes constructs the sexual threat as feminine.

35. In his dedicatory letter to King James, John Deacon connects the "natural body" to the "Oeconomicall body," the "Politicall bodie" and the "Ecclesiasticall bodie." Deacon closely follows many of James's arguments against tobacco, but emphasizes the monarch's responsibility in upholding the health of the political stomach—"I mean the poor husbandsmans state," in *Tobacco Tortured,* 1616, (New York: Da Capo, 1968).

36. Braithwait, *The Smoking Age, or the Life and Death of Tobacco* (London, 1617), O3.

37. Jeffrey Knapp argues that what should have strengthened England's sovereignty by freeing it from its desire for Spanish tobacco actually further bound England to its old enemy, and to its new American "conquest": "most of the tobacco Englishmen 'drank' before that time [i.e. the time of Virginia's growth] was indeed the enemy's—Spain's—so rather than alleviate England's trade woes, tobacco actually only exacerbated them" ("Elizabethan Tobacco," 34).

38. Aubrey qtd. in Brooks, *Tobacco: Its History,* 1:342. The information on Ralegh curing tobacco is found in Dickson, *Panacea or Precious Bane,* 3:99.

39. Qtd. in Knapp, *An Empire Nowhere,* 305 n 34.

40. Sylvester's list of likely tobacconists extends beyond traitors to include every form of criminal: "Theeves, Unthrifts, Ruffians, Robbers, Roarers, Drabbers, / Bibbers, Blasphemers, Shifters, Sharkers, Stabbers, / This is the Rendez-vous, These are the Lists, / Where doe encounter most TOBACCONISTS," in *Tobacco Battered and the Pipes Shattered* (London, 1672) 53.

41. Deacon, *Tobacco Tortured,* 82.

42. Beaumont, *Metamorphosis,* E4–E4v.

43. In "'Precious Stinke,'" I also claim that tobacco provided James with a vehicle to show his support for English customs at a time when the English feared James would change English customs and laws, and to deflect suspicion of himself as Scottish import.

44. Jonson, *Every Man,* 1.3.79–80, 3.2.305–08.

45. Ibid., 3.3.112–14.

46. James does not appear to have been personally insulted by Jonson's mockery of antitobacconists along with tobacconists; Jonson became James's main masque writer.

47. Taylor, *The Nipping or Snipping of Abvses* (London, 1614), [Dv]. All subsequent references shall be cited parenthetically in the text.

48. Taylor, like the king, envisions smoking as a type of hell on earth.

49. In *A Sixe-Folde Politician* (1609), Sir John Melton also rejects the idea that tobacco inspires good writing: "the writing of ordinarye Play-bookes, Pamphlets, & such like, may be tearmed the mushrum cōceptions of idle braines, moste of them are begotte ouer night in Tobacco smoake and muld-sacke" (qtd. in Dickson, *Panacea or Precious Bane,* 1:472). In *The Smoaking Age,* Braithwait includes a poem about "Chaucers incensed Ghost" that also complains that modern writers relied on tobacco for inspiration: "As if no Poets Genius could be ripe / Without the influence of Pot and Pipe" (02v).

50. *The Queenes Arcadia* was performed during a royal visit to Oxford. These lines are spoken by Alçon, a quack doctor. In *Three Renaissance Pastorals: Tasso, Guarini, Daniel,* ed. Elizabeth Story Donno, 3:198–203, 208–213 (New York: Medieval and Renaissance Texts and Studies, 1993).

BIBLIOGRAPHY

Barclay, William. *Nepenthes, or the Vertues of Tabacco.* Edinburgh, 1614.

Beaumont, Sir John. *The Metamorphosis of Tabacco.* 1602. New York: Da Capo, 1971.

Bell, Sandra. "'Precious Stinke': James I's *A Counterblaste to Tobacco.*" In *Royal Subjects: Essays on the Writings of James VI and I.* Edited by Daniel Fischlin and Mark Fortier. Detroit, MI: Wayne State University Press, 2002.

Braithwait, Richard. *The Smoaking Age, or the Life and Death of Tobacco.* 1617.

Brooks, Jerome E. *Tobacco: Its History Illustrated by the Books, Manuscripts and Engravings in the Library of George Arents, Jr.* 4 Vols. New York: Rosenbach, 1937–52.

Busino, Horatio. *Calendar of State Papers, Venice.* Vol. 15. 1617–1619. Edited by A. B. Hinds. London: HMSO, 1909.

Cefalu, Paul A. "'Damnéd Custom . . . Habits Devil': Shakespeare's *Hamlet,* Anti-Dualism, and the Early Modern Philosophy of Mind." *English Literary History* 67, no. 2 (2000): 399–431.

Daniel, Samuel. *The Queenes Arcadia.* In *Three Renaissance Pastorals: Tasso, Guarini, Daniel.* Edited by Elizabeth Story Donno. New York: Medieval and Renaissance Texts and Studies, 1993.

Deacon, John. *Tobacco Tortured.* 1616. New York: Da Capo, 1968.

Dickson, Sarah. *Panacea or Precious Bane: Tobacco in Sixteenth Century Literature.* New York: New York Public Library, 1954.

Elizabeth I. "Speech to the troops at Tilbury." In *Elizabeth I: Collected Works.* Edited by Leah S. Marcus, Janel Mueller, and Mary Beth Rose. Chicago: University of Chicago Press, 2000.

Goldberg, Jonathan. *James I and the Politics of Literature.* Baltimore: Johns Hopkins University Press, 1983.

Goodman, John. *Tobacco in History: The Cultures of Dependence.* London: Routledge, 1993.

Gray, S., and V. J. Wyckoff, "The international tobacco trade in the seventeenth century." *Southern Economic Journal* 7, no. 1 (July 1940): 1–26.

Hall, Kim. *Things of Darkness: Economies of Race and Gender in Early Modern England.* Ithaca, NY: Cornell University Press, 1995.

James VI/I. *A Counterblaste to Tobacco.* 1604. In *Minor Prose Works of King James VI and I.* Edited by James Craigie. Edinburgh: Scottish Text Society, 1982.

Jonson, Ben. *Every Man In His Humour.* In *Ben Jonson.* Edited by C. H. Herford, and Percy and Evelyn Simpson. Vol. 3. Oxford: Clarendon Press, 1925–52.

Knapp, Jeffrey. "Elizabethan Tobacco." *Representations* 21 (Winter 1988): 22–66.

————. *An Empire Nowhere: England, America and Literature from the* Utopia *to* The Tempest. Berkeley and Los Angeles: University of California Press, 1992.

Marbecke, Roger. *A Defence of Tabacco: With a Friendly Answer to Worke for Chimny-Sweepers.* 1602. New York: Da Capo, 1968.

Middleton, Thomas. *The Black Book.* London, 1604.

Philaretes. *Work for Chimny-sweepers: Or A warning for Tabacconists.* London, 1602.

Rich, Barnaby. *The Honestie of this Age.* London, 1614.

Spenser, Edmund. *The Faerie Queene.* Edited by A. C. Hamilton. New York: Longman, 1977.

Strong, Roy. *Gloriana: The Portraits of Queen Elizabeth.* New York: Thames and Hudson, 1987.

Sylvester, Joshua. *Tobacco Battered and the Pipes Shattered. In Two Broad-Sides Against Tobacco: The First Given by King James of Famous Memory.* London, 1672.

Taylor, John. *The Nipping or Snipping of Abvses.* London, 1614.

Sassafras

Graham Roebuck

Sᴵʀ Wᴀʟᴛᴇʀ Rᴀʟᴇɢʜ, ᴄᴇʟᴇʙʀᴀᴛᴇᴅ ɪɴ ᴘᴏᴘᴜʟᴀʀ ᴄᴜʟᴛᴜʀᴇ ᴀɴᴅ ᴇᴍʙᴇʟ-lished by myth for introducing tobacco from the Americas to Europe, especially to the British Isles, wrote to Sir Robert Cecil on August 21, 1602, to complain that his monopoly in "sarsephraze woode" had been breached and to remind Cecil: "I have a patent that all shipps and goods are confescate that shall trade ther without my leve."[1] He was writing to an old friend, the immensely powerful Secretary Cecil, son of Burghley, who became, after his father's death, effectively the supremo of Queen Elizabeth's regime. Because of his small stature and delicate health, the Queen called him her "little elf," and, subsequently, King James I, inheritor of Cecil's services, renamed him "pigmy." Several years earlier, in 1598, Ralegh had been a member of Cecil's mission to France charged with preventing a threatening Spanish-French alliance that certainly would have curtailed English maritime adventures and commercial prospects in the New World.[2] Although they had been old friends, Ralegh's postscript to this letter reveals his anxiety about their inequality of station and influence, even as he invokes the great bond of friendship: "Butt what yow thinck unfitt to be dun for mee shall never be a quarrell either internal or externall. I thanck yow evermore for the good and what cannot be effected farewell hit" (*Documentary History,* 3:347).

Although Cecil still seemed to Ralegh to be a trusted friend and business partner, in reality Cecil was arranging for Ralegh's imprisonment. He was duly committed on December 16, 1603. Ralegh seems to have been unaware of the full measure of Cecil's animosity. Trevelyan remarks that Ralegh did not comprehend that Cecil "had absolutely no intention of ever letting him out of the Tower."[3]

Ralegh's monopoly, about which he also wrote to the Lord Admiral, the Earl of Nottingham, entitled him to confiscate the sassafras that had been gathered in Virginia, landed at Weymouth, then distributed, for the most part, to London. On this consignment he hoped that the Lord Admiral would "make seasure," for if "a stay be not made it wilbe spent and sold into many hands" (*Documentary History,* 3:347). Ralegh's claims had obvious limits: the source of sassafras was either under de facto Spanish control, or within the reach of Spanish naval power. Only when it was landed for market in England had he any realistic hope of enforcing his monopoly. Furthermore, those poachers, or rather, those who financed their expedition, were men of more potent influence, who also had Cecil's ear. "Captayne" Bartholomew Gilbert, as Ralegh at first took him to be when he apprehended him at Weymouth attempting to sell the cargo, was actually a London merchant on a voyage led by Bartholomew Gosnold, financed by powerful investors intending to cash in on the newest, wildest European thirst for exotic botanical panaceas. Understandably hostile to competition for this lucrative commodity, Ralegh shrewdly links his position on the sassafras trade to the prospects for English colonial expansion in America, arguing that, if the control of the sassafras trade were to fail, the colonization process would likewise founder: "And it were a pitty to overthrow the enterprize for I shall yet leve to see it an Inglishe nation." Thus Ralegh, who never set foot in Virginia, links the sassafras tree to the destiny of the nation and its nascent empire. More pragmatically, he adds that the "2200 waight" of sassafras brought by the Gosnold voyage on which Bartholomew Gilbert sailed, would "distroy the trade which otherwize would yield 8 or 10 for one in certenty and a return in xx weekes" (3:347).

It is unclear how long before this incident the sassafras trade had been flourishing in England. The national significance that Ralegh imputes to it, however, is latent in Thomas Harriot's *A Briefe and True Report of the New Found Land of Virginia,* published in 1588 (the year of the Armada), a report subsequently taken up by Richard Hakluyt in *Principal Navigations.* Harriot, the celebrated empirical and theoretical scientist, a polymath, in Ralegh's employ, probably made his first voyage to Virginia in 1584, where he learned the Algonkian language and made remarkably detailed notes about the lives and habits of the natives, as well as describing the botanical curiosities. He took to tobacco enthusiastically, strongly endorsing its therapeutic qualities. He also listed sassafras among the bountiful commodities of the New World that should entice Englishmen and women to migrate to the new colony, judging it to be far more valuable and useful than guaiacum, or "lignum vitae"—the "wood of life," from the New World—with which supposed curative sassafras was to be frequently compared. Perhaps not coincidentally, Harriot died of cancer of the nose.[4]

What follows here is an account of the part played by an exotic New World import in molding the attitudes and actions of English adventurers in America, and of its surprising influence on colonial expansion in the late Tudor and early Stuart periods.

One can set against Harriot's botanical optimism a contemporary account. Ralph Lane, in charge of the colony of Virginia from August 1585 to June 1586, wrote a report for Ralegh. It is a hair-raising account of his antagonistic, do-or-die relationship with the Indians during his up-country explorations in search of the source of copper mines, from which the natives made jewelry. Quinn suggests it is also confusing, perhaps because of censorship designed to prevent detailed information reaching Spain (*Documentary History,* 3:295). The report features sassafras in a life-saving role. Lane tells of an exploration party that had exhausted its food rations. The party had with it two mastiffs, "upon the pottage of which with sassafras leaves (if the worst fell out) the companie would make shift to live two dayes" (3:298). Later, as prospects grew increasingly dire for the explorers, they "lodged upon an Islande, where wee had nothing in the worlde to eate but pottage of sassafras leaves, the like whereof for a meate was never used before as I thinke" (3:299). Despite this apparent endorsement of the life-saving properties of sassafras, Lane concludes that "the discovery of a good mine, by the goodnesse of God, or a passage to the Southsea, or someway to it, and nothing els can bring this country in request to be inhabited by our nation." Only when that condition is fulfilled, he writes, "will Sassafras, and many other rootes & gummes there found make good Marchandise and lading for shipping, which otherwise of themselves will not be worth the fetching" (3:300). This would not be good news for Ralegh, of course. The sought-after mine is copper, not gold. Lane thinks of sassafras as a food supplement, or seasoning for mastiff stew, evidently giving no credit to its therapeutic reputation. Indeed, the scarcity of food and threat of starvation without the good will of the Indians, or even of violent death at their hands, is uppermost in his narrative. Fortunately for the English adventurers and merchants, as guaiacum grew worthless, sassafras found a more exalted role.

Ships returning from Ralegh's colony in 1585 "probably brought back some sassafras; those that returned in 1586 certainly did."[5] According to Charles Carroll, the 1602 Gosnold and Gilbert expedition that challenged Ralegh's monopoly over Virginia and New England trade was backed by the Earl of Southampton (Shakespeare's patron, and a particular enemy of Ralegh),[6] and other greatly influential men. Carroll underscores the reasons for Ralegh's alarm about destruction of the trade: Ralegh had been enjoying profits of a thousand percent when the "fantastically high price of sassafras" plunged on the return of the Gosnold expedition, and fell even further on the arrival of another ton (43). "Sarsephraze," Ralegh complained, "was worth 10s 12s and 20s a pound before Gilbert returned his cloying of the markett will overthrow all myne and his owne also" (*Documentary History,* 3:347). Did he send a free sample to Cecil to alleviate his frail health, along with his letter?

The voyage from April 10, to October 2, 1603, under Martin Pring, set its sights on sassafras above other possible commodities, presumably on the assumption that the market glut was temporary. The account of this voyage bears witness to attentive and alert observation of the Indians and their customs. Also of prudence: "we carried with us from Bristoll two excellent

Mastives, of whom the Indians were more afraid, then of twentie of our men" (3:361). The use of sassafras is here unusually clearly stated: "a plant of sovereigne vertue for the French Poxe, and as some of late have learnedly written good against the Plague and many other Maladies" (3:361). Gathering sassafras does not go uncontested. The narrative tells of sassafras cutters taking a noontide nap in the woods, guarded by their mastifs, Foole and Gallant. Shots from the palisaded encampment, warning of a stealthy Indian attack, summon back the sassafras cutters with their dogs. The sight of Foole and Gallant is enough to make the Indians dissemble their intentions, and turn their presence at the palisades "all to a jest and sport." Pring observes that the Indians are "given to treacherie." But the Indians soon drive out the intruders by setting fire to the woods (3:361–62). Carroll calls this expedition "the last recorded English voyage undertaken exclusively to procure sassafras" (44).

Although the first bubble had burst, sassafras remained an alluring commodity, as we shall see, and, as Carroll adds, the publicity served Richard Hakluyt's project of drawing adventurers and colonists to North America (43). It was not Ralegh's fate to see it become an English nation founded on the miracle drug. Nor was it Bartholomew Gilbert's fate to make his fortune: in 1603, serving now with Ralegh's final Virginia expedition, he was killed by Chesapeake Indians. The leader of the party, Samuel Mace, returned in September 1603, but Ralegh was already in the Tower, beginning his long incarceration, a prelude to his final, and tragic, expedition to the New World's "El Dorado" of Guiana. The chimera of gold, which had always obsessed him, as it had many others, beckoned him for the last time. Expectation of finding gold is, of course, an ever-present item in Tudor-Stuart promotional tracts for America, but it may be that the relatively short-lived sassafras craze buttered more parsnips.

Why were Ralegh and Harriot, both tobacco men, so interested in sassafras? The likely answer lies in the popularity of a work by the Spanish physician Nicolas Monardes, translated into English by John Frampton and published in 1577, with the title *Ioyfvll Newes out of the newe founde worlde.* Its subtitle advertises a treatise on botanical discoveries relevant to physic and surgery. Monardes, a pioneer of tropical medicine, published his work in two parts (1569 and 1571), in Seville, where he practiced. There were subsequent editions at Seville and Amsterdam before the English version. Some idea of the popularity of the work may be gauged by the frequency of editions in the early modern period: in England there were two in 1580 and another in 1596; in Italy at least four (1576, 1582, 1605, and 1616); and several in France. It was a seminal influence. Subsequent writers widely borrowed from it. Among them was Guido Panciroli, Professor of Civil Law at the University of Padua, whose Latin work *Rerum memorabilium jam olim depærditarum,* first published in 1599, attempts to penetrate the meaning of the losses of valuable commodities in the Old World and gains of new, valuable commodities in the New World.[7]

First, a consideration of *Ioyfvll Newes*. John Frampton, a retired merchant who worked in Iberia, familiar with Romance languages (he also translated a Portuguese treatise on navigation as well as Marco Polo's *Travels*), was well connected in court circles, judging by his dedication of *Ioyfvll Newes* to Sir Edward Dyer, the poet, courtier, and intimate friend of Sir Philip Sidney. Although Dyer had spent a period out of favor, Gabriel Harvey, in a letter to Spenser, described Sidney and Dyer as "two very diamandes of her maiesties court for many speciall and rare qualities." Sometime after this dedication Dyer did Burghley some service.[8] Dyer was also an advisor to Sir Christopher Hatton, characterized by Knapp as the greatest proponent of imperialism in the Queen's circle.[9] But there was more to it than that. Frampton had been in the hands of the Spanish Inquisition, which experience fired him with resolve against the Spanish.[10] Such prominent English connections, receptive to expansionist ideas, ensured a ready and well-heeled readership for *Ioyfvll Newes*. Even without such local conditions, however, Monardes's work would still have excited widespread interest, for accounts of the biological uniqueness of America engaged and challenged the European mind at every level, as did the questions raised by the nature of the native inhabitants of America. Europe's finest minds grappled with the implications of America on every subject from the most abstruse aspects of theology to the practicalities of navigation, trade, and cures for every common ague and the pox.

Yet Monardes was certainly not the first to address the subject of American botany and its potentials. He is in the forefront of the second wave that took advantage of a disillusionment with earlier, seemingly miraculous, cures, especially those initially promised by guaiacum, and other simples. As his text suggests, Monardes is hopeful, rather than cynically opportunistic. Many of his readers, we may well believe, were eager to hear the gospel of healing. The quasi-religious title Frampton chooses indicates his readiness to play also to that air of expectation. Monardes's title is straightforward and sober: *Dos libros, el uno que trata de todas las cosas que se traen de nuestras Indias Occidentales, que sirven al uso de la medicina* [etc.] (Two books, one which deals with all the things brought from our West Indies that serve the ends of medicine.) The second part, Seville (1571), adds "Do se trata del Tabaco, y de la Sassafras."[11]

Frampton's Epistle Dedicatory to Dyer brings two urgent concerns to the reader's attention. As Frampton well knew by his professional experience, the new "medicines mentioned in the same worke of Doctour Monardes, are now by Marchauntes and others, brought out of the West Indies into Spaine, and from Spain hether into Englande, by suche as dooeth daiely trafficke thether."[12] This meant, of course, the loss of potential profit to English merchants as well as the loss of gold needed to pay for exotic imports to the foremost enemy power—a matter of growing concern as mercantilist economic theory about the nature of trade and the good of the commonwealth was gaining hold in economic thought. The second concern reflects anxiety at being left behind the advances of the modern age: "thei haue fledde verie muche from the olde order and maner of Physicke, which was used before, that this was knowen, as thynges not so healthfull as these are, and by greate experience thereof in Spaine, and other Countries, throughly and effectuously proued" (*Ioyfvll Newes,* sig. * [iii]). There is a corollary to the flight from the old, and rush to the new, almost certainly apparent to Frampton, but unexpressed for diplomatic and commercial reasons, in Monardes' chapter, "*Of the Balsamo.*" The new physic, however "effectuously proued," may be as vulnerable to turbulent market forces as the old. Monardes is alert to this, as is Ralegh: they brought such quantities that "it is nowe of small valewe, this doeth the aboundaunce of thyngs"; what fetched one hundred ducats the ounce now brings "so vile a price" (fol. 8r). Worse, the medicine fails to work as its price declines! "When it was verye deere all menne did profite of the vertue of it"; now, although it is the same product that once cost a hundred ducats the ounce, "it is not so muche esteemed" (fol. 8r). Monardes strikes a rueful and a pious note reflecting on this state of affairs: God has provided a new source of balsam from New Spain to repair the loss of it from Egypt where the vine that provided it failed, and the new is every bit as good as the old (fol. 8v). Like Panciroli-Salmuth, Monardes is moved by the redemptive symmetry of God's providence. In this example, there is the biblical flavor of redemption out of Egypt, but Monardes strongly implies that it is wrong of man to cheapen "marueilous workes" (fol. 8r).

In many respects the dilemma of the mountebank is like that of the physician: how to dispose of increasingly familiar, and thus increasingly denigrated, "cures" for high prices, in a cynical world. *Volpone* provides a vivid dramatization. Disguised as "Scoto Mantuano"—a sixteenth-century Italian actor, whose name had become synonymous with deceit—Volpone sets out his stall to peddle his "Oglio del Scoto," assisted by Mosca and Nano, who sing a commercial for it:

> Had old Hippocrates or Galen,
> (That to their books put med'cines all in)
> But known this secret, they had never
> (Of which they will be guilty ever)
> Been murderers of so much paper,
> Or wasted many a hurtless taper.
> No Indian drug had eer been famed,
> Tobacco, sassafras not named;
> Ne yet of guacum one small stick, sir,

> Nor Raymond Lully's great elixir.
> Ne had been known the Danish Gonswart,
> Or Paracelsus, with his long sword.[13]

Scoto's oil makes the labors of the ancients and the Old World redundant, along with those of the Renaissance alchemists, and, of particular interest here, the three most prized New World drugs: tobacco, guaiacum, and sassafras. But the mountebank's pageant has been framed, even as it is being set up, by Peregrine's cool appraisal: their medicines, he says,

> they will utter upon monstrous oaths,
> Selling that drug for twopence ere they part,
> Which they have valued at twelve crowns before.
>
> (2.2.13–15)

A case in point was guaiacum, which had become almost worthless. The "holy wood," used to make a cure-all decoction, once thought to be especially efficacious against the great scourge of early modern Europe, syphilis, had been denounced by none other than Paracelsus himself. As Alfred W. Crosby, Jr. explains, the price of guaiacum had risen to such heights, that "like a poor man's soup bone, the sawdust of guaiacum was boiled up again and again for those not lucky enough or wealthy enough to buy the first decoction. Counterfeit guaiacum flooded the market and pieces of the wood were hung in churches to be prayed to by the most impecunious syphilitics."[14] Mercury, originally an Arabic treatment for scabies, returned as the treatment of choice for syphilis, but its effects were usually so terrible, especially in the first decades of the epidemic (soon to become a pandemic) that there was a general longing for another miraculous cure. Crosby speculates that there was a "general abatement of the malignancy of the disease" from 1526 onward, which may have made it possible to be persuaded that taking guaiacum was, however gradually or intermittently benefits were perceived, curative. Even after it lost its kudos, the need for a treatment less dire than mercury persisted strongly, raising market consciousness for sassafras.

In his section on guaiacum, Monardes comforts the reader with the widely held belief that God has arranged a cure for the disease from the source of the disease (*Iofyvll Newes,* fol. 10v). As with Panciroli, writing some time later, the need for a deeply structured symmetry in human affairs informs the discourse. This view holds equally well, if not better, for sassafras—an as yet undiscredited cure. This section is the longest in Monardes's book, and comes with an illustration of "the Tree," but Monardes is careful to locate his account of how the pox arrived in Europe alongside the guaiacum discussion. It does not spill over into the section on sassafras. He is far into the catalog of illnesses that sassafras can cure, interspersed with appropriate anecdotes and recipes, before—between toothache and gout—he remarks that sassafras has similar effects to those of "the holie woodd, the *China* [-root], and the *Sarcarparillia*" (fol. 53r), in treatment of the pox, and that it must be taken for extended periods, having better effects on those who are without appetite. Quietly, Monardes has relinquished the spectacular claims for sassafras as a cure for syphilis—now it is a palliative—thereby aiming to preserve its commercial prospects from the effects of disenchantment.

"In the yere of our Lorde God 1493 . in the warres that the Catholike kyng had in Naples, with kyng Charles of Fraunce . . . sir Christopher Colon, came from the discouerie that he had made in the Indias." (fol. 11) Here Monardes dates the first occurrence of syphilis in Europe. Columbus brought to Naples Indian men and women from Santa Domingo, who, at the conclusion of peace between the Spanish and the French, transmitted to these now fraternizing armies, comprised of men of all nations, "the fruite of their countrie whiche was the Poxe." "The one and the other were infected of this euill seede: and from thence it hath spred abrode into all the worlde" (fol. 11).

The account of syphilis in Panciroli-Salmuth, *Nova Reperta,* following an extended discussion of guaiacum that compares the relative merits of that from the island of St. John with that from San Domingo, and questions whether the ancients knew it as "ebeno," follows the same lines as Monardes. There is an added trope: For their efforts, the Neapolitan soldiers were loaded not with gold, but death ("milites illi non tam auro, quam morbo onusti") (87), and thus they spread this terrible infection throughout the world (88). Prompted by the commonplace that "whence the disease, thence the cure," china root and sarsaparilla are described and the section ends on sassafras (112 ff.).[15]

Crosby's succinct review of the syphilis debate, concurring with orthodox Renaissance accounts, includes the testimony of Ulrich von Hutten, the celebrated humanist, correspondent of Erasmus, and sufferer. His *Of the Wood called Guaiacum* supports the 1493 date, and the American origin theory. The origin of syphilis has been called, however, as Crosby notes, "the most controversial subject in all medical historiography."[16] Furthermore, he notes that there is no known mention of syphilis (a name derived from a 1530 poem by Girolamo Fracastoro, about a shepherd so named, with the pox) until guaiacum was popularized as a cure (127). His persuasive epidemiological analysis explains why, within a decade, the scourge had spread from the Caribbean to China (151).

Guaiacum and sassafras are derived from trees, and as such take their place in the attractions, for Europeans, of the vast North American forest, as adventurers found it in the late sixteenth century—the habitat of "salvages"—

who understood and used the mysterious properties of their sylvan home. An almost obligatory feature of accounts of North America and of all the promotional tracts of the period is the catalog of trees to be found in the region described. In the Elizabethan-Jacobean economy, as a result of the deforestation begun in the high Middle Ages, the scarcity of good timber amounted to a national crisis. Demand made by the building boom of the 1580s, and by urgently needed new shipping, as well as by burgeoning industrial needs such as smelting and timber supports for deep coal mining, are all well documented by Charles F. Carroll.[17] Reforestation was no sufficient answer. As Carroll notes, the first official attempt with thirteen acres was made in 1560 by Burghley, and the second, when those oaks were mature, on eleven thousand acres of trees planted by order of Parliament in 1668. The oaks of this planting "would not be of use to the Royal Navy until the time of the American Revolution" (*Timber Economy,* 14). Extended consequences of deforestation and the feebleness of scrub that replaced timber trees, the declining yields from unmanured arable land, the reduction of game, and the late sixteenth-century population boom, were widespread weakened health in a broad band of the population of England and a succession of epidemics. A similar condition marked the late fourteenth century (5–6). Thus deforestation led to ill health, which led to the search for cures in the forests of the New World.

An instance of the heat generated by the question of timber supply and the importation of exotic drugs, spices, and dyes, is supplied by Dudley Digges in *The Defence of Trade* (London, 1615). Digges defends the East India Company's need for timber to build ships to ply its trade against the accusations that a "parricide of Woods should be committed by building of Shippes," and that these vessels would not be available to the navy in time of emergency and, a point stressed in mercantilist thought, that valuable currency is expended on luxuries.[18] Digges's rebuttal includes defending "health-full drugges" (41), and a suggestion that should other sources of timber, including Ireland, not suffice, they may try "a conclusion in *Virginia*" (30).[19]

The attraction of American trees, therefore, was double: mature timber for ships and furniture, and drugs to alleviate ubiquitous sickness. As if to dramatize the point, accounts of the Indians stress their fine physique and robust health in comparison with English settlers. Also attractive was the prospect of being able to transport these commodities across an ocean not controlled by other powers (notwithstanding the Spanish threat). To the East, whence timber was imported from the Baltic states, Sweden, and Norway, political interruption of the timber trade was likely at any time. The obvious disadvantages of Western traffic, however, were the distance and the danger of ocean crossing in small ships unable to carry sufficiently large loads of large timber to turn a profit. In the decades before English migrants

were able to construct their own ships in America, the payoff from sassafras
subsidized a timber trade that without it would have foundered. The 1603
expedition may well have been the last exclusively given to procuring sassafras, but it continued to be a cash crop. Thus, as well as for therapeutic
values, sassafras continues to appear in the advertisements for North American trees.[20]

✿

The longest and most important section in *Ioyfvll Newes* is that on sassafras. It comes from Florida, we read, around the twenty-five degrees
latitude, the mainland of the Spanish Indies (fol. 46r). However, as a geographical designation this is not identical with the current state of that
name. In his authoritative *Microcosmvs* of 1621, Peter Heylyn designates
Florida as stretching to Virginia. Both regions, in his view, are English
discoveries: Virginia is a flourishing colony since being founded by Ralegh
in 1584 (although some settlers, not liking it, have returned home), but
Florida, on the other hand, has a history of violence: "It was discouered by
the *English* vnder the guiding of *Sebastian Cabot,* Anno 1497. Afterward
possessed by *Iohn Ponce* a *Spaniard* 1527, who called it *Florida,* because
he came first to it on Easter day, which the posterity of *Tubal* call *Pascha
Florida.* It fell next into the possession of *Iohn Ribaulte* & the *French* Anno
1562. but the *Spaniards* vnwilling to let the *French* be eie witnesses of their
rich bootie, waged warre with them so long, that there was not a man left
on either side to maintaine the quarrell: and *Florida* was againe abaudoned
[sic] Anno 1567."[21]

Monardes explains how knowledge of "the Tree"—sassafras—came to
him from Spaniards who heard from Frenchmen in Florida whose sicknesses
were healed by Indians showing them "the Tree." He writes, without elabo-
rating causes, "After that the Frenche menne were destroied" (*Ioyfvll Newes,*
fol. 46), it becomes Spanish property. Monardes's implication, however,
is that sickness wasted the French and then the Spanish, rather than that
there was struggle to the death. That the Spanish zealously guarded this
property—their "rich bootie" in Heylyn's phrase—and that they were in
sufficient numbers (either surviving or resupplied from Spain) to do so,
is illustrated by the fate of the *Castor and Pollux,* an Anglo-French vessel,
sent to trade from the Bay of Fundy to the West Indies, and captured by the
Spanish off Florida in 1605.[22] On board was a learned French herbalist, Dr.
Bonnesemaine (or "Bona Semana" or "Goodwick"), interrogated by Spanish authorities to discover not only the intentions of the expedition, but also
whether there were heretical books on board. The doctor seems to have
sidestepped the question by answering that he spoke no English. The intended trade, he tells the interrogators, is for aloes, sassafras, China root,
and tobacco. It seems that the Spanish of Florida regarded sassafras as a

secret commodity since Dr. Bonnesemaine was asked what he thought its purpose was. Part of his reply was that sassafras sold for eight reales a pound in St. Malo, and China root at two ducats a pound—evidently a good price. Two ducats was close to two thirds of a pound sterling, according to Peter Heylyn (sig. ¶¶ 4v.), nearly 15 shillings; and sassafras was more expensive. These were the market prices that Ralegh coveted.

The record of Dr. Bonnesemaine's interrogation shows that he acknowledged that sassafras and China root were good for making medicines, and could be obtained from the Indians by barter for beads and cauldrons. This expedition, in addition to trade, was also intended both to take note of all valuable commodities and mines, noting their locations, and to seek out the supposed lost English colonists, a declared aim of Ralegh-sponsored voyages to Virginia. On the capture of the *Castor and Pollux,* Spanish proceedings caused diplomatic repercussions in London and Paris, since peace had been concluded with Spain in 1604. What happened to the crew is not fully clear. Quinn suggests that they were not killed at once, but perhaps were enslaved (*Documentary History,* 5:108–9).

No such report of violence invades Monardes's measured, professional account of sassafras. He describes how to make concoctions, and how to take the temperature and complexion of patients; he recounts case histories and relentlessly builds a catalog of the virtues of the drug, warning from time to time that it should not be taken without consulting the physician. His tone of practicality is subtly blended with an almost sacramental reverence for "the Tree" whose water, best drunk in place of wine, and whose wood, carried in the pockets of men who come to see him saying "Maister, doe you see here the woodde, that euery one of us doth bryng for to heale us with all," effects "meruelous workes" (*Ioyfvll Newes,* fol. 47r). It clears all blockages, cures quotidian agues, restores appetite, relieves headache, can cure indigestion, wind, stinking breath, toothache, gout, regulate menstruation, and restore fertility. In this list the cure of syphilis is present, but unstressed, as if Monardes is tacitly recognizing its near-futility: "In the euill of the Poxe, it doeth the same effectes that the reste of the water of the holie woodd, the *China,* and the *Sarcaparillia* dooeth: takyng it as these waters bee taken with sweates" (fol. 53). Although acclaimed as a "universall remedy" (fol. 49v), it can pose problems which Monardes is careful to document. A woman suffering from "the Mother," for example, disobeying doctor's orders and taking too much, "put her life in aduenture, and did infamie to the remedie" (fol. 49r). It is not ordinarily to be taken for the stone, although a priest in Florida, drinking sassafras passed many small stones. But when the stone is large, only the surgeon's razor, if used in time, might give a sixty-year-old man another twenty years of life (fol. 52r).

It is probable that Monardes's account, restrained by the standards of the day, thus preserving him from suspicion of quackery, made it "the most frequently issued book of overseas interest in the Elizabethan period," according to John Parker,[23] and thus ensured a continuance of the sassafras trade, despite periodic oversupply and failure as a cure for the pox. Sassafras might otherwise have vanished. Parker's observation on Frampton's translation of Monardes that the "popularity must be ascribed to the value the book had for physicians rather than any imperial urge it inspired," applies just to that decade, for, as he notes, it appealed to expansionists such as Hakluyt, Ralegh, and Harriot. To this might be added that what appealed to physicians might also appeal to a section of the literate public in thrall to panaceas, the philosopher's stone, and the elixir of life—a frequent theme of the popular stage and literature.

Sassafras's appeal continued for decades to come, appearing, for instance, in the catalog of trees in *A briefe Relation of the Discovery and Plantation of New England,* published in 1622, the year of the Virginia massacre, for the President and Council of New England.[24] On March 22, 347 colonists were killed by the Indians. The New England *briefe Relation,* however, is preoccupied with its own problems: "disasters, calamities, misfortunes, oppositions, and hindrances" (sig. Dr). It also acknowledges its bad relations with the natives, "that so much abhorred our Nation, for the wrongs done them by others" (sig. C3r). Notwithstanding these discouragements, the commodities of New England beckon to prospective colonists: "[There are] islands, fit for Plantation; replenished with Plants and Wood of all sorts; as Oake, Cedars, Spruce, Firre, Pyne, Walnut, Chestnut, Elme, Sassafras, Plum-trees, and Calamus Aromaticus, &c." (sig. D[2v]). The use of "replenished" and "oak" as the first-named tree, which is usually the case in promotional literature, suggests an awareness of the timber crisis at home. If the reader did not know the uses of sassafras, it might well be assumed that it was valuable as timber, rather than as a drug. In the light of these cataloged riches, the pamphlet now represents the natives as "tractable (if they be not abused) to commerce and Trade," and, in an apparent acknowledgment of anxiety about foreign trade depleting the national store of wealth—gold and silver coinage to pay for commodities—that characterizes mercantilist thinking, the reader is assured that there is no commodity from France or Germany that cannot be obtained in New England. The natives are not paid in coin, but in goods manufactured in Britain. As a colony—the Epistle Dedicatory to Prince Charles suggests as much—it is an extension of the realm. More desirable mercantilist conditions would be hard to devise.

We may suppose that sassafras, highly profitable in small quantities to the merchant adventurer, underwrote the cost of carrying bulky, but essential, timber. A letter of February 1629 from Governor Cradock to Captain Endicott asks for commodities to be ready for lading ships returning from New England, including sassafras, dye stuffs, and good cured sturgeon. His comment that wood could also be included, for there has not been a better sale price "these two seven years," reminds us of the close economic relationship established between sassafras and timber. The sassafras, in this instance, is simply for general use in physic, not specifically a nostrum against pox.[25]

Sassafras is not only mentioned, but "sung" in William Wood's influential and unjustly neglected work, *New Englands Prospect* (1634). In this, the best, most literary and intellectually agile of the promotional tracts from early modern America, Wood celebrates the bounty of the land not so much with an eye to its market prospects in Old England, but for its potential in the nascent New England settlement. With the cadence of a hymn, Wood's ten rhymed couplets (starting with oak) come to "sweet Saxafage, / Whose spurnes in beere allayes hot fevers rage."[26] Now, sassafras has become not so much an exotic drug as a domesticated ingredient in homemade beer.

John Josselyn, an accomplished scientist, made two trips to New England, first in 1638–39, and again from 1663 to 1671. Antagonistic to the suffocating Puritanism of the Massachusetts Bay settlement, he attached himself to the Maine colony of Sir Ferdinando Gorges—a Royalist venture. Josselyn became deeply familiar with the landscape, the fauna and the flora, and sympathetic to the native inhabitants of the New England coastal region. He is in debt to Wood's account, but notices many new things himself, including the devastation of the carrier pigeon population by the firepower of the few Europeans there. It is a bad omen. But his descriptions of trees are more detailed than any before him. Of sassafras, he writes of its color in the rind, and in the inner parts, of its "excellent smell like Fennel," of its taste and of its therapeutic properties, "a decoction of the Roots and bark thereof sweetned with Sugar, and drunk in the morning fasting will open the body and procure a stool or two."[27]

꙰

Today sassafras has a modest place in the world. It is used as a condiment in Cajun cuisine, in filé, and in certain natural herbal supplements, such as "LaKota." Its fragrant oil is used in perfumes and soaps. Its shredded bark and root is used to make an infusion. One would hardly guess at its former, brief glory, nor at its influence on the development of North America. Without the "Tree" of Monardes, and the explorers and colonists, the world would have been very different. To sample its seductive powers why not follow Monardes's own recipe? "Halfe an Ounce of the woodde, little more or lesse . . . and seeth it in three Pottels of water. . . . And of this water you may drinke continually . . . it doth and hath doen marueilous effectes. . . . It doth profit in large and colde deseases, and where there is windines, and other euilles" (fols. 56r, v).[28]

NOTES

1. Transcribed from the Cecil Papers in David B. Quinn, ed. and commentary, *A Documentary History of North America to 1612* (New York: Arno Press, 1979), 3:347; hereafter all volume and page numbers will be cited parenthetically in the text.

2. *Dictionary of National Biography*, s.v. "Cecil, Sir Robert."

3. Raleigh Trevelyan, *Sir Walter Raleigh* (London: Penguin, 2002), 356.

4. Andrew Hadfield, ed., *Amazons, Savages & Machiavels: Travel & Colonial Writing in English, 1550–1630* (Oxford: Oxford University Press, 2001), 266–67.

5. Charles F. Carroll, *The Timber Economy of Puritan New England* (Providence, RI: Brown University Press, 1973), 42; hereafter all page numbers will be cited parenthetically in the text. Carroll's succinct two-page discussion, "The Great Sassafras Hunts" (42–44), summarizes a range of original English accounts and modern scholarship.

6. Trevelyan, *Raleigh*, 365.

7. Guido Panciroli (Pancirollus), *Rerum memorabilium jam olim depoerditarum* [etc.] (Ambergæ [Amberg, Bavaria], 1599), is the first book, the whole being completed with Heinrich Salmuth's (Henrico Salmuth) copious commentary in *Nova Reperta Sive Rerum Memorabilium Recens Inventarum & Veteribus Incognitarum Guidonis Pancirolli. . . . & Commentariis illustratus Ab Henrico Salmuth* (Ambergæ, [Amberg, Bavaria] MDCVIII [1608]). This is "editio secunda," from which I quote (British Library 1137.b.2,3), principally from Salmuth's commentary on New World phenomena. Hereafter page numbers will be cited parenthetically in the text. Salmuth heard Panciroli lecture at Padua with much pleasure and profit. There were numerous Latin editions of this work. It was well known in England, although it has been almost entirely overlooked by literary scholarship. John Donne borrows several recondite references from Panciroli, including one to "Tullia's tombe," in the Somerset Epithalamium. See Helen Gardner, *John Donne: The Elegies and the Songs and Sonnets* (Oxford: Clarendon Press, 1965), 180. The first English translation of *Rerum memorabilium*, in 1715, curtails Salmuth's commentary and substitutes comments from an up-to-date perspective on the Americas and the Old World.

8. *Dictionary of National Biography*, s.v. "Frampton, John," "Dyer, Sir Edward."

9. Jeffrey Knapp, *An Empire Nowhere: England, America, and Literature from Utopia to The Tempest* (Berkeley and Los Angeles: University of California Press, 1992), 5–6. Knapp is endorsing the view of John Parker, *Books to Build an Empire* (Amsterdam: N. Israel, 1965), 94. That Ralegh introduced tobacco to England Knapp regards as a "demonstrably false legend" (*An Empire Nowhere*, 140).

10. Parker, *Books to Build an Empire*, 76.

11. Frampton perhaps aims at two different readerships: *Ioyfvll Newes* (see note 12 below) is the Black Letter edition. In the same year he issued his translation soberly entitled, *The Three Bookes written in the Spanish tonge, by the famous Phisition D. Monardes*.

12. Nicolas Monardes, *Ioyfvll Newes ovt of the newe founde worlde, wherein is declared the rare and singular vertues of diuerse and sundrie Hearbes, Trees, Oyles, Plantes and Stones, with their aplications, aswell for Phisicke as Chirurgerie*. trans. John Frampton, 1577 (Amsterdam: Da Capo, 1970), sig. *11v. Further quotations are from this facsimile edition, with page numbers hereafter cited parenthetically in the text.

13. Ben Jonson, *Volpone*, in *Jonson: Four Comedies*, ed. Helen Ostovich (London: Longman, 1997), 2.2.111–22. All further references will be cited parenthetically in the text.

14. Alfred W. Crosby, Jr., *The Columbian Exchange: Biological and Cultural Consequences of 1492* (Westport, CT: Greenwood, 1972), 155, where Crosby also notes that guaiacum was not removed from the British Pharmacopoeia until 1932, even though its

reputation "as *the cure* had evaporated." The following citation in this paragraph in the text is to p. 152.

15. The anonymous editor of the 1715 English edition of Panciroli (see note 7 above), evidently in reaction to Panciroli's stress on what from the ancient world has been irretrievably lost, and also in reaction to Salmuth's now-antique wonder at the botanical marvels of the Americas, adds a passage, "Things newly found out." Under the heading "Geography," we read, "the whole Continent of *America,* with the appendant Isles, from whence yearly are fetched such vast Quantities of Gold, Silver, Silks, Spices, and many other rich Commodities, were unknown altogether to the Ancients: but are now so well known to our Age, that in them we have established factories, and a continual Traffick to their ports, as if they were our own native Countries, continually importing into them what they need, out of our Plenty; and again, bringing from them what our native Soil does not at all, or at least not so plentifully produce" (*The History of Many Memorable Things In Use Among the Ancients, but now Lost.* (trans. of *Rerum* and *Nova Reperta,* 428).

16. Crosby, *The Columbian Exchange,* 123.

17. See "The Timber Shortage in England," in Carroll, *Timber Economy,* 3–18.

18. Dudley Digges, *The Defence of Trade,* 1615 (Amsterdam: Da Capo, 1968), 7–9; hereafter all page numbers will be cited parenthetically in the text.

19. Adventurers in the Americas argued that colonial products complemented English needs and industry and created a market for English industrial products without loss of bullion.

20. For example, Francis Higginson, *Nevv-Englands Plantation. Or, a Short and Trve Description of the Commodities and Discommodities of that Country* (London, 1630). In his list of timber he includes "saxatras" (a variant unrecorded in *OED*) along with "sumacke" for dying and tanning leather and for perfumes (sig. B3v). Higginson is attempting to attract settlers, assuring them that they will find sufficient employment as native commodities have a place in the economy of the homeland. He is also anxious to exclude undesirables from a colony that he envisages as self-sustaining.

21. Peter Heylyn, *Microcosmvs, or a Little Description of the Great World: A Treatise Historicall, Geographicall, Politicall, Theologicall,* Oxford, 1621, (Amsterdam: Da Capo, 1975), 407–8; hereafter all page numbers will be cited parenthetically in the text. Heylyn's rather complacent account of Virginia comes a year before the great massacre. Soon after, the Virginia Company was dissolved. North of "fruitfull" Virginia lie Norumbega and Nova Francia, discovered by Jacques Cartier of France in 1534. Compared with Virginia they are "barren, the people barbarous" (408).

22. The following account is largely derived from Quinn, *Documentary History,* 5:108–23.

23. Parker, *Books to Build an Empire,* 76.

24. Anon., *A briefe Relation of the Discovery and Plantation of New England: and of Svndry Accidents therein ocvrring, from the yeere of our Lord M.DC.VII to the present M.DC.XXII,* 1622 (Amsterdam: Theatrum Orbis Terrarum, 1975), Sig. D[2 v]; hereafter all page numbers will be cited parenthetically in the text.

25. Alexander Young, *Chronicles of the First Planters of the Colony of Massachusetts Bay from 1623 to 1636. Now First Collected from the Original Records and Contemporaneous Manuscripts and Illustrated with Notes* (Boston: C. Little and James Brown, 1846), 132–33.

26. William Wood, *New Englands Prospect: A true, and lively, and experimental description of that part of America, commonly called New England,* 1634 (Amsterdam: Da Capo, 1968), 16. "Spurnes" are outward growing roots or rootlets (*OED*). For a fuller account of Wood's promotional pamphlet—its purpose, methods, and arguments—see my "'This innocent worke'; Adam and Eve, John Smith, William Wood and the North American Plantations," *Early Modern Literary Studies* 1, no. 1 (1995): 4.1–38. http://www.purl .oclc/emls/01-1/roebsmit.html

27. Paul J. Lindholdt, ed. and intro., *John Josselyn, Colonial Traveler: A Critical Edition of Two Voyages to New-England* (Hanover, NH: University Press of New England, 1988), 49. Lindholt adds that "in the colonial period sassafras was a very important New World export." Josselyn notes that the pox is endemic among the natives, perhaps, he suggests, because of their cannibalism. He notices the native custom of using sweat houses for treating plague and smallpox, but does not mention their using concoctions of sassafras in conjunction (94).

28. I am grateful to Mr. George Condon, former editor of the venerable magazine, *Canadian Grocer,* in its 120th year, for supplying samples of the finest powdered albidium sassafras leaf, from Live Oak, Florida, root bark of albidium, from the same source, and "Sassafras biologique Bois coupé" from Quebec.

BIBLIOGRAPHY

Anonymous. *A briefe Relation of the Discovery and Plantation of New England: and of Svndry Accidents therein ocvrring, from the yeere of our Lord M.DC.VII to the present M.DC.XXII.* 1622. Amsterdam: Theatrum Orbis Terrarum, 1975.

Carroll, Charles F. *The Timber Economy of Puritan New England.* Providence, RI: Brown University Press, 1973.

Crosby, Alfred W., Jr. *The Columbian Exchange: Biological and Cultural Consequences of 1492.* Westport, CT: Greenwood, 1972.

Digges, Dudley. *The Defence of Trade.* London, 1615. Reprint, Amsterdam: Da Capo, 1968.

Gardner, Helen. *John Donne: The Elegies and the Songs and Sonnets.* Oxford, Clarendon Press, 1965.

Hadfield, Andrew, ed. *Amazons, Savages & Machiavels: Travel & Colonial Writing in English, 1550–1630.* Oxford: Oxford University Press, 2001.

Heylyn, Peter. *Microcosmvs, or a Little Description of the Great World: A Treatise Historicall, Geographicall, Politicall, Theologicall.* Oxford, 1621. Amsterdam: Da Capo, 1975.

Higginson, Francis. *Nevv-Englands Plantation. Or, a Short and Trve Description of the Commodities and Discommodities of that Country.* British Library C.33.c.6. London, 1630.

Jonson, Ben. *Volpone.* In *Jonson: Four Comedies.* Edited by Helen Ostovich. London: Longman, 1997.

Knapp, Jeffrey. *An Empire Nowhere: England, America, and Literature from* Utopia *to* The Tempest. Berkeley and Los Angeles: University of California Press, 1992.

Lindholdt, Paul J., ed. and intro. *John Josselyn, Colonial Traveler: A Critical Edition of Two Voyages to New-England.* Hanover, NH: University Press of New England, 1988.

Monardes, Nicolas. *Ioyfvll Newes ovt of the newe founde worlde, wherein is declared the rare and singular vertues of diuerse and sundrie Hearbes, Trees, Oyles, Plantes and Stones, with their aplications, aswell for Phisicke as Chirurgerie.* Translated by John Frampton. 1577. Amsterdam: Da Capo, 1970.

Panciroli, Guido (Pancirollus). *Rerum memorabilium jam olim depœrditarum* [etc.] Ambergæ [Amberg, Bavaria], 1599.

———. Nova Reperta sive Rerum Memorabilium . . . . & Commentariis illustratus Ab Henrico Salmuth. Ambergæ [Amberg, Bavaria], 1608.

Parker, John. *Books to Build an Empire.* Amsterdam: N. Israel, 1965.

Quinn, David B., ed. and comm. *A Documentary History of North America to 1612.* 5 vols. New York: Arno Press, 1979.

Roebuck, Graham. "'This innocent worke'; Adam and Eve, John Smith, William Wood and the North American Plantations." *Early Modern Literary Studies* 1, no. 1 (1995): 4.1–38.

Salmuth, Heinrich (Henrico). *Nova Reperta Sive Rerum Memorabilium Recens Inventorum & Veteribus Incognitarum Guidonis Pancirolli. . . . & Commentariis illustratus Ab Henrico Salmuth.* Ambergæ [Amberg, Bavaria], MDCVIII [1608].

Trevelyan, Raleigh. *Sir Walter Raleigh.* London: Penguin, 2002.

Wood, William. *New Englands Prospect: A true, and lively, and experimental description of that part of America, commonly called New England.* 1634. Amsterdam: Da Capo, 1968.

Young, Alexander. *Chronicles of the First Planters of the Colony of Massachusetts Bay from 1623 to 1636. Now First Collected from Original Records and Contemporaneous Manuscripts and Illustrated with Notes.* Boston: C. Little and James Brown, 1846.

Othello the Liar

Philip D. Collington

But whom shall we beleeve, speaking of himselfe, in this corrupted age? since there are few or none, whom we may beleeve speaking of others, where there is lesse interest to lie. . . . Men frame and fashion themselves unto it, as to an exercise of honour; for, dissimulation is one of the notablest qualities of this age.

—Michel de Montaigne

MUCH HAS BEEN MADE OF THE ISSUE OF "HONESTY" IN *OTHELLO,* A TERM which encompasses both the contested sexual fidelity of Desdemona and the questionable veracity of "honest Iago." She is honest; he is not. The tragic events are seen to stem from the protagonist's inverted perception of this reality. Othello trusts his adviser ("This fellow's of exceeding honesty"), but comes to suspect his wife ("Heaven truly knows that thou art false as hell").[1] What has received less critical attention is the honesty of the general himself.[2] That Othello places great stock in this quality is suggested by his repetition of such adages as "thou shouldst be honest" (3.3.384), "men should be what they seem" (3.3.131). Yet a close examination of Othello's own words and deeds reveals a startling discrepancy between what he expects of others, and what he performs himself.

This paper shall treat Iago's comment that Desdemona "first loved the Moor, but for bragging and telling her fantastical lies" (2.1.220–21), not as a jibe to be dismissed, but as a hypothesis to be tested. A careful sifting of Othello's statements using Francis Bacon's heuristic categories of *secrecy, dissimulation,* and *simulation* reveals dozens of verbal untruths ranging from the seemingly innocuous to the deadly serious.[3] Taken together, their profusion underscores a myth-making process by which Othello overstates his foreignness to gain acceptance among his European admirers. I will argue that Iago is not the only character who "lies to th' heart" (i.e., is a compulsive or habitual liar [5.2.152]); that much of what Othello says is fabricated or exaggerated for personal gain. I will also argue that critical controversies regarding contradictory accounts of his mother's/father's handkerchief, or the base Indian/Judean who discarded a pearl, may not stem from slips of Shakespeare's pen or from typesetters' errors. Instead, the instability of these stories may have been designed to alert playgoers that Othello simply makes things up (such as the provenance of his hidden sword), then mis-remembers the details (was it forged in Toledo, or in Innsbruck?). All this despite his shrill insistence, in the case of the magical handkerchief, that the stories are "true" and "most veritable" (3.4.71, 78). Othello illustrates the cynical relativism of Montaigne's observation, "Nowadaies, that is not the truth which is true, but that which is perswaded to others" (II.xviii.603). Past victories and adventures notwithstanding, Othello manages his current military position and social status using a tissue of lies that remains unexamined in criticism that lionizes the general and demonizes his ancient.[4]

For centuries, readers and playgoers have wondered at Othello's irresistible fusion of poetry and bravery, as exemplified by his autobiographical speech to the Venetian Senate in which he describes recounting "moving accidents," "hair-breadth scapes," and encounters with exotic "others" such as "the Cannibals that each other eat, / The Anthropophagi, and men whose heads / Do grow beneath their shoulders" (1.3.135–45). Such lines prompted A. C. Bradley to marvel that Othello is "by far the most romantic figure among Shakespeare's heroes; and he is so partly from the strange life of war and adventure which he has lived from childhood. He does not belong to our world, and he seems to enter it . . . almost as if from wonderland."[5] Like Desdemona, who would "seriously incline" to hear these stories (1.3.146–47), countless critics have echoed Bradley and seemingly accept that Othello actually saw the marvels he relates.[6] Yet as T. W. Baldwin and Kenneth Muir have since demonstrated, such marvels may have been received (and rejected) by playgoers as obvious borrowings from Pliny the Elder's popular *History of the World* (1601).[7] The most extravagant passages are found in Book 7 which describes such improbable wonders as Ethiopians who have no noses; Cinamolgi who have snouts like dogs; and Anthropophagi who live at "the North pole," adorn themselves with scalps, and drink out of human skulls.[8] Erasmus recommended authors incorporate such wonders as "Scythians, cannibals, Indians, troglodytes, and so on" as rhetorical embellishments.[9] By the late sixteenth century, Pliny was being ransacked by armchair travelers and storytellers alike as a "stock source of literary decoration,"[10] prompting Montaigne to scoff: "If any credit may be given unto Plinie . . . [s]ome Countries there are, where men are borne headlesse, with eyes and mouthes in their breasts; where all are Hermaphrodites; where they creep on all foure" (II.xii.470).

Montaigne's prefatory "if" suggests that, after having been cited uncritically for over a thousand years, Pliny's marvels were no longer being taken literally—especially since a new wave of empirically-minded explorers were returning home to Renaissance Europe with more sober eyewitness descriptions of the world.[11] By 1604, two versions of Africa—one legendary, the other revisionary—co-existed in the popular imagination.[12] Discerning readers became less inclined to give "any credit" to Pliny, such that Robert Burton devotes a chapter of his *Anatomy of Melancholy* (1621–52) to questioning reports of monsters and marvels, stating categorically: "I would censure all [of] Pliny's . . . lies."[13] Playgoers, too, increasingly saw onstage travelers being mocked for telling stories, such as the idiotic Babulo in Thomas Dekker's *Patient Grissil* (1603), who claims to have seen, among other wonders, people "without heads, hauing their eyes nose and mouths in their breasts."[14] Scoffing at Pliny's marvels had become a sign of education and sophistication, such that in *The Tempest* (1609) Gonzalo remarks that even "boys" had become skeptical of the existence of "men / Whose heads [stand] in their breasts."[15] This skepticism has been noted by numerous scholars, yet few have considered the implications of Othello's asserting the veracity of, or Desdemona's seriously inclining to hear, such "yarns."[16]

If Othello's incorporation of tall tales into his life story would undermine his credibility, why would Shakespeare have his African general present discredited legends as facts, and perpetuate monstrous lies about his homeland? To Mark Burnett, "an audience is encouraged to recognize in Othello's storytelling . . . an outmoded 'monstrous' exoticism"—not simply exaggerations, but obvious "fairground" clichés.[17] Andrew Hadfield proposes that Othello deliberately forgets his firsthand knowledge of Africa in order to join the ranks of those with none: "by identifying with European travellers against the bizarre races of his native Africa [and by] writing his own traveller's tale[,] he gives the Venetians exactly what they want to hear." In other words, the self Othello fashions is "elaborately constructed to suit the role of a European adventurer, and his [limited] access to knowledge."[18] According to this logic, Othello's tales are forged in order to transform an "erring" (i.e., wandering) Barbarian (1.3.356) into an *erring* (i.e., mistaking) European.

I propose that early playgoers who kept abreast of developments in exploration and anthropology may have recoiled less from Othello's race than from his pseudo-exoticism.[19] In fact, the play uses verbal inconsistencies and Pliny-esque excesses to signal to playgoers that the storied general may actually be a braggart, a liar, a traveler telling tales. Erasmus may have recommended the embellishment of tales, but Elizabethans were increasingly troubled by the way ambitious raconteurs "of base descent and lineage" could use such stories to achieve unwarranted social prominence: "[They] haue thereby not only bin commended to the Honourable; but also their owne experience and triall of occurents in trauelling, doth procure thus much more than ordinary vnto them."[20] Marlowe's *Edward II* evokes this process when Gaveston invites a traveler to audition for his coterie of favorites, "To wait at my trencher and tell me lies at dinnertime, / And as I like your discoursing, I'll have you."[21] Othello, too, tells tales at dinnertime, and Desdemona "wished / That heaven had made her such a man" (1.3.163–64). Upon learning that Othello parlayed exotic stories into the "mangled matter" of a secret marriage, the Duke comments, "I think this tale would win my daughter too," not so much confirming the veracity of his stories as their self-aggrandizing impact (1.3.172–73).

In arguing that Othello lies, that he wants his on-stage auditors to believe his lies, and that Shakespeare prompts playgoers to recognize these lies, my argument departs from Hadfield's theory of rhetorical integration, as well as from Walter S. H. Lim's similar proposal that Othello seeks to "obliterate his African self" and become a "tabula rasa" onto which he would "inscribe all the values of Venetian culture."[22] Venice does not need another Venetian. It needs an exotic "other" to entertain dinner guests and defend its borders, and Othello exaggerates his differences for their amusement and his own advancement. By 1580 it was proverbial that "Africa is always producing something new (monsters, serpents)," an adage contemporaries directed toward "inconstant and wauerynge persons" and "men of small trust, or confidence."[23] In short, to be an African, or merely to speak of Africa, was to invite skepticism or mistrust.

To assist his contemporaries with discerning forms of verbal untruth, Francis Bacon composed a provocative short essay "Of Simulation and Dissimulation" (1625), a kind of how-to guide for politicians and other would-be discerners and deceivers.[24] As Montaigne does so cynically in my epigraph, Bacon acknowledges the prevalence of lying; yet rather than condemn the practice outright, he merely warns that excessive reliance on deception could be interpreted by others as an indicator of weakness: "DISSIMULATION is but a faint kind of policy or wisdom . . . it is the weaker sort of politics that are the great dissemblers" (VI.18). If Othello is one such "great dissembler," it would therefore indicate a signal weakness in his character, one overshadowed by more familiar problems (e.g., his advancing age, his irrational jealousy, his racial insecurity, his periodic bouts of falling sickness). This core weakness is obscured by customary polarizations in which Iago "lards his discourse" with lies, whereas Othello "draws on an inward certainty about himself, a radiant clarity about his own well-founded moral position."[25] If Othello's assertions prove to be embellished or untrue, then this would necessitate a revision of our understanding of his conception by Shakespeare and reception by early audiences.

Bacon's first category of deception is secrecy, defined as "when a man leaveth himself without observation, or without hold to be taken, what he is" (VI.19). Synonymous with closeness or reservation, secrecy conceals a politician's innermost thoughts, feelings, and motives from opponents; to paraphrase Iago, it entails "[to] think, and ne'er disclose [one's] mind" (2.1.156). Othello practices secrecy in both his personal and professional life. For example, he concealed his love for Desdemona during their protracted courtship, such that when Brabantio warns Othello, "She has deceived her father, and may thee" (1.3.293), it bears repeating that Othello also deceived her father. When Iago begins to instill suspicions in the temptation scene, Othello conceals his growing discomfiture, insisting that he is "not a jot" moved (3.3.219) and that he "will not" become suspicious (line 225). Othello later conceals his murderous intentions by inviting Desdemona to dismiss her lady so that they can be alone in her chamber; "He looks gentler," remarks Emilia (4.3.9), this after playgoers see him contemplate strangling, poisoning, and chopping his bride into messes. Othello conceals his suicidal intentions (and dagger) in the final scene, prompting Cassio to remark after the general stabs himself, "This did I fear, but thought he had no weapon" (5.2.358).

With respect to professional secrecy, when pressed by "mediators" for Iago's request for military promotion, Othello "[e]vades them, with a bombast circumstance" and then admits that, unbeknownst even to his own entourage, he has "already" chosen his officer (1.1.11–16). When Othello demotes Cassio following the drunken street brawl, Emilia reassures the latter that "[Othello] protests he loves you" (3.1.48–49); that he outwardly punishes, but secretly supports, his disgraced officer. Indeed Desdemona later confirms that Othello is maintaining but "a politic distance" from Cassio (3.3.13). Now it might be objected that Bacon's secrecy is for worldly politicians, and that Othello is an uncorrupted military commander: "little of this great world can I speak / More than pertains to feats of broil and battle" (1.3.87–88). The claim is frequently echoed in criticism, such as when Marion Trousdale argues that Othello is "brought down by one who is above all a superb rhetorician. Lacking knowledge of the skill, Othello lacks any defense against it."[26] Yet Othello exhibits rhetorical sophistication, such as in the temptation scene when he implicitly recognizes what George Puttenham terms *aposiopesis,* "the figure of silence" (when a speaker begins a sentence and then breaks off in the middle),[27] in Iago's maddening use of verbal "stops": "such things in a false disloyal knave / Are tricks of custom" (3.3.123–25). An unsophisticated soldier may have overlooked these verbal gaps, but Othello himself harbors secrets, and fears that others may do the same. Therefore when he complains, "O hardness to dissemble!" (3.4.34), he is not troubled by unfamiliarity with the procedure, but by the strain of employing secrecy to conceal his burgeoning jealousy.

Bacon's next category of deception is dissimulation, defined as "when a man lets fall signs and arguments, that he is not that he is" (VI.19). This category encompasses the sense of what we commonly term "lying" as defined in St. Augustine's influential treatise, *De Mendacio* (*On Lying* [c. 395]): "a false statement made with the intention to deceive."[28] The essence of dissimulation is the outward expression of something that contradicts what the speaker knows inwardly to be true, such as when Desdemona dissimulates her anxiety on shore in Cyprus: "I am not merry, but I do beguile / The thing I am by seeming otherwise" (2.1.122–23). Dissimulation is so widespread in *Othello* that I have broken it down into four subcategories: *false modesty, false pretenses, self-serving lies,* and *self-contradiction.*

The first subcategory of Othello's dissimulation is false modesty. For all his propensity to brag, Othello occasionally downplays his qualities and abilities. When Brabantio issues a warrant for his arrest, Othello proclaims, "when I know that boasting is an honour, / I shall promulgate" (1.2.20–22), even though at Brabantio's house he would "oft" relate his life story (1.3.129, 133). Othello also downplays his rhetorical abilities, such as when he prefaces his Senate narrative by saying, "Rude am I in my speech / And little blest with the soft phrase of peace," even though his stories have made him the toast of the town (1.3.82–83).[29] Later he wonders aloud that because he is "black" he does not have "those soft parts of conversation / That chamberers have" (3.3.264–65), even though he correctly interpreted Desdemona's subtle invitation, that "if I had a friend that loved her, / I should but teach him how to tell my story / And that would woo her. Upon this hint I spake" (1.3.165–67).

Othello's alternation between plain speaking and rhetorical sophistication contradicts contemporary accounts about the intellectual abilities of Moors. One influential eyewitness, Leo Africanus, writes of the Moors living in Barbary: "Most honest people they are, and destitute of all fraud and guile . . . imbracing all simplicitie and truth." Yet these same Moors are "rusticall" and "void of good manners. . . . Their wits are but meane, and they are so credulous, that they will beleeue matters impossible, which are told them."[30] Iago perpetuates such a view in his observation that "The Moor is of a free and open nature / That thinks men honest that but seem to be so, / And will as tenderly be led by th' nose / As asses are" (1.3.398–401). Such tendencies resemble what Anthony Barthelemy identifies as traits of "Moors of the nonvillainous type" on the English stage: innocence, foolishness, credulity, passivity, humility. Barthelemy then traces the method by which Iago "ensnares" Othello in malicious stereotypes, transforming a sympathetic hero into a stock "black fiend" or "villainous Moor."[31] In his chapter on "black villains on the mimetic stage," Barthelemy traces their genealogy back to the "blackface" vice figure Shakespeare inherited from the Medieval and Tudor stage. Among the vice's signal traits were tendencies to brag, dissemble, and conceal his identity: "the vice operates under a cloak of secrecy, hiding his true nature from his dupe. . . . [and taking] great pride in his ability to deceive and seduce the innocent and the righteous."[32] These are traits commonly attributed to Iago; rarely are they applied to the general. Yet if one recognizes Othello's own propensity to "seduce" and "deceive" auditors with his words—"This only is the witchcraft

I have used" (1.3.170)—then this should undermine the persistent allegorical polarization of the two men (as summarized by G. K. Hunter); namely, that "Iago is the white man with the black soul while Othello is the black man with the white soul."[33] The understandable urge to distance the general from his malevolent nemesis has obscured the extent to which their overlapping characteristics may have generated ambivalence in early playgoers acculturated to discern forms of secrecy, dissimulation, and simulation, and to associate these with stage villainy.

The second subcategory of dissimulation is adapted from Bacon's citation of a Spanish proverb, "Tell a lie and find a truth" (VI.21). Othello employs such false pretenses several times. Following Iago's initial imputations in the temptation scene, Othello pretends to have "a pain upon [his] forehead" (3.3.288) to see how Desdemona will react to the insinuation that she is the cause of budding cuckold's horns. Later, in order to determine whether she possesses the handkerchief, Othello feigns a cold and demands it so he can blow "a salt and sorry rheum" into the storied token of their love (3.4.51). Before smothering Desdemona, he employs a timeworn interrogation tactic, trying to elicit an admission of guilt by claiming that her co-accused "hath confessed" (5.2.68)—even though Cassio makes no such admission.

Following her murder, Othello's claim becomes even more outrageous—"she with Cassio hath the act of shame / A thousand times committed. Cassio confessed it" (5.2.209–10)—though this statement may also be placed in the third subcategory, the self-serving lie. Indeed, in the last scene Othello utters a cluster of such untruths. When Emilia bursts into the chamber with news that "foul murders [are] done" outside, Othello responds with another far-fetched explanation reminiscent of Pliny's *Natural History:* "It is the very error of the moon, / She comes more nearer earth than she was wont / And makes men mad" (5.2.105, 108–10; cf. Pliny, 2:30–31). This is merely to divert attention from the true cause of the street violence, Iago's errand to slay Cassio. When Emilia discovers Desdemona's body, Othello initially implies he too found her dead ("how should she be murdered?" [5.2.124]). Then he denies killing her ("it was not I" [line 125]). When Othello finally does confess the murder—"She's a liar gone to burning hell: / 'Twas I that killed her" (lines 127–28)—he protests too much that someone else is a liar, not him. These self-serving lies contribute to a pattern of misrepresenting events that playgoers know (or have seen) to be otherwise. For instance, Othello earlier boasts, "I had been happy if the general camp, / Pioneers and all, had tasted her sweet body, / So I had nothing known" (3.3.348–50), a grotesque statement which proves to be patently false, but which intensifies his pathos. Likewise, when he is disarmed by Montano in the final scene, Othello complains, that "every puny whipster gets my sword" (5.2.241–42), demeaning an opponent hitherto praised as "valiant" and "of most allowed sufficiency" (1.3.41, 225), to heighten the pathos of his own defeat.

Othello's sudden expertise in lunar orbits, despite an earlier vow not to "follow still the changes of the moon" (3.3.181), brings us to the fourth subcategory of dissimulation: self-contradiction. There are numerous instances of this. Othello convinces the Senate to allow Desdemona to travel to Cyprus by claiming that he "beg[s] it not / To please the palate of [his] appetite" (1.3.262–63), yet upon their safe arrival, he seems anxious to part company with the men and enjoy the "fruits" of his bride's company (2.3.8–9).[34] When he quells the drunken brawl in Cyprus, Othello describes the island as "a town of war, / Yet wild, the people's hearts brimful of fear" (2.3.209–10), contradicting his proclamation that, in light of the destruction of the Turkish fleet, the townspeople and soldiers could revel, sport, dance, feast, and light bonfires (2.2.3). Othello tries to stop Desdemona's persistent advocacy for Cassio by promising to "deny [her] nothing" and to "come to [her] straight" if she would leave him alone (3.3.84–87); she exits, yet he does neither. In spite of his boast to the Senate that if domestic concerns distract him from official duties in Cypress, "Let housewives make a skillet of my helm" (1.3.273), Desdemona's apparent infidelity causes him to forget to attend a dinner to which he has invited "the generous islanders" (3.3.285). In spite of his demand to see "ocular proof" of Desdemona's infidelity (3.3.362), Othello vows to "tear her all to pieces" merely on hearing Iago's report of Cassio's erotic dream. Shakespeare underscores this last contradiction by having Iago admonish Othello, "Nay, yet be wise, yet we see nothing done, / She may be honest yet" (lines 434–36).

Perhaps no self-contradiction is more apparent (or melodramatic) than the following exchange through the locked door of Desdemona's bedchamber in the final scene:

> OTHELLO. Look in upon me then, and speak with me,
>   Or, naked as I am, I will assault thee.
>   [*Enter* Gratiano]
> GRATIANO. What is the matter?
> OTHELLO.   Behold, I have a weapon
>
>   (5.2.255–57)

Gratiano is thus duped into believing that Othello is "naked" (i.e., unarmed), and nearly facilitates the murderer's escape. Othello earlier vows to kill Desdemona straight—"I'll not expostulate with her" (4.1.201–2)—but in the final scene he interrogates her before her murder. Othello earlier vows to spot her bed with "lust's blood" (5.1.36), but he subsequently refrains from staining her sheets by "stop[ping]" her breath instead (5.2.200). Othello earlier invokes "black vengeance, from the hollow hell" to assist his "tyrannous hate" (3.3.450–52)—yet following the murder he claims "nought I did in hate, but all in honour" (5.2.292). Othello promises not to "kill her unprepared spirit," but when she attempts to "say one prayer" he cuts her off: "it is too late" (5.2.31, 82). Othello denies being easily jealous, yet he is. Othello says he does not cry easily, yet he does.[35] In sum, this pattern of self-contradictions belies a man of empty boasts and hollow promises, one who breaks his word more often than he keeps it.

Bacon's final category is simulation, defined as "when a man industriously and expressly feigns and pretends to be that he is not" (VI.19). Simulation is a kind of affirmative untruth in which perpetrators invent false materials, embellish their achievements, or exaggerate their talents in order to achieve self-promotional goals. Perez Zagorin highlights differences between the two terms: "in a strict sense dissimulation is pretending not to be what one actually is, whereas simulation is pretending to be what one actually is not."[36] Othello's first simulation is his Senate narrative (discussed above), the implausibilities of which alert playgoers and readers to the suspicious nature of subsequent marvelous truth-claims in the play. To be sure, some simulations are innocuous or not made in earnest. Upon arrival in Cyprus Othello affectionately greets his wife as "my fair warrior" (2.1.180), when she is less a soldier than a senator's daughter on her inaugural foreign adventure. Othello also praises her musical talents—"she will sing the savageness out of a bear" (4.1.186)—though this charming exaggeration becomes ominous when the Willow Song fails to protect her from death.[37] When Desdemona cries after being slapped by Othello, he garbles the proverbial expression about crocodile tears and intimates that "each drop she falls" could sprout a live crocodile (4.1.244–45). Thus Othello assigns marvelous attributes even to mundane events, such as his wife's traveling, singing, and crying.

No simulations are more deadly serious, however, than those surrounding that most mundane object of all, her handkerchief. Many inquiries have uncovered important contexts for this love token, ranging from the allegorical to the narratological to the anthropological.[38] Many commentators seem prepared to take Othello at his word; that it was designed especially for his mother, composed of silk spun by hallowed worms, dyed with mummy "[c]onserved of maiden's hearts," decorated with strawberries sewn by a Sibyl, and given by an "Egyptian charmer" to Othello's mother to "subdue [his] father / Entirely to her love" (3.4.58–77). After all, Othello insists that the story is "[m]ost veritable" (line 78). Yet the devil is in the details. He claims that the Sibyl was two hundred years old: how is this possible? He claims that the dye was made of mummy, without specifying whether it was applied to the cloth (which should be white), or to the strawberries (which should be red). The ambiguity is compounded by the fact that the *Oxford English Dictionary* says "mummy" is brown, and others suggest it may actually have been black.[39] Black strawberries? Furthermore, Othello later claims in a second story of the handkerchief that it was "an antique token / My father gave my mother" (5.2.214–15). Can his mother's made-to-order handkerchief also be his father's "antique" family heirloom? Can the sibyl of version one and the father of version two give the same gift? Eldred Jones wonders, "Are we to believe at all that this story of the hand-kerchief is true?"[40]

Both stories cannot be "most veritable," but attempting to determine which one is true (and some critics prefer version two[41]) merely implicates investigators as beguiled auditors of Othello's simulated tales. The hand-kerchief recalls those curios, talismans, and oddities assembled in the early modern wonder cabinet. According to Steven Mullaney, such objects fas-cinated Shakespeare's contemporaries who didn't much care whether, say, an Indian monkey-tooth charm actually worked; its functions were less to cure illness or further scientific knowledge than to entertain and satisfy the Elizabethan "cultivation of wonder."[42] It therefore seems harmless enough that Desdemona should cherish her handkerchief: "she reserves it evermore about her," notes Emilia, "To kiss and talk to" (3.3.297–300). But when Othello makes high-stakes truth-claims about its actual abiding properties, he violates the spirit of marvelous collectibles.[43] By protesting too much, he transforms a harmless lie into a much more damaging one; as Bacon observes in his essay "Of Truth," "it is not the lie that passeth through the mind, but the lie that sinketh in and settleth in it, that doth the hurt" (I.6).

When changes in Othello's exotic details go un-noticed by other char-acters, that does not necessarily mean that early playgoers did the same. Thomas Rymer may not have been the first to object to Othello's fustian circumstances and Desdemona's credulity: "Nothing is more odious in Nature than an improbable lye; And certainly never was any Play fraught like this of *Othello* with improbabilities."[44] Shakespeare peppers Othello's assertions with contradictions in order to underscore their simulative nature. During the period, it was proverbial that "a liar should have a good mem-ory," for the garbling of details exposes an untruth.[45] Yet modern editions of *Othello* counter this phenomenon. Editorial emendations that "rectify" inconsistencies create the erroneous impression that they stem from au-thorial lapses or print-shop errors; in the process, Othello's "corrected" tales gain unwarranted credibility. For example, when in his final moments Oth-ello reaches for a hidden weapon, "a sword of Spain, the ice-brook's tem-per" (5.2.251), three prominent editors (Ridley, Sanders, and Honigmann) emend the Quarto's spelling of "Isebrookes" (i.e., Innsbruck's) to "ice-brook's" and heap up circumstantial details (including citations from classical authorities) about how Toledo blades were forged and then cooled in mountain streams fed by melting snow.[46] Yet here, typically, Othello does some narrative forging of his own, borrowing associations from two weapons centers whose precise geographic locations are a little fuzzy in his mind, in order to invent a marvelous provenance for his Ibero-Tyrolian sword.

In his essay "Of Travel," Bacon admonishes the novice traveler not to spice up his tales upon returning home: "in his discourse let him be rather advised in his answers, than forwards to tell stories" (XVIII.58). Yet from the "antres vast" of Africa to his bridal chamber in Cyprus, Othello ignores such advice as he parlays a pseudo-exotic past into a marriage and generalship that are undone by the lies of another, more adept at dissimulation, Iago. Indeed, the ancient gains Othello's trust precisely by mirroring his penchant for telling strange tales. Whereas Othello specializes in African exoticism, Iago trains his proto-anthropological sights on the strange customs of Europe, such as in his warning of a veritable pandemic of cuckoldry: "There's millions now alive / That nightly lie in . . . unproper beds" (4.1.67–68). No evidence is provided other than the credibility of the observer who claims to "know [his] country disposition well" (3.3.204). Iago's opening warning to Brabantio, that "you'll have your daughter covered with a Barbary horse; you'll have nephews neigh to you, you'll have coursers for cousins and jennets for germans" (1.1.109–15), enlists the same racist prurience and excess that had begun to discredit Pliny among Shakespeare's contemporaries. Pliny reports that "Indians engender with beasts, of which generation are bred certain monstrous mongrels, half beasts and half men," and cites as an example "men with heads like dogs, clad all over with the skins of wild beasts, who in lieu of speech used to bark" (VII.79, 76–77). As with Iago's millions of European cuckolds, Pliny claims that the population of Indian dog-men is "known" to be "above 120,000 in number" (77). It seems inconsistent, even hypocritical, to celebrate Othello's tales of headless Africans, but recoil from Iago's and Pliny's tales of bestial children. Playgoers may not have made such distinctions.

The telling of such lies prevents Othello from securing a place in Venetian society—not because of his race, but because as Castiglione's Sir Frederick might say, "in his communicatyon . . . [he is not] alwayes heedefull not to goe out of the lykelyhoode of truth . . . as manye doe, that never speake but of wonders, and will be of suche authoriteye, that everye uncredyble matter must be beleaved at their mouth." Sir Frederick goes on to specify that a truly honorable courtier "shall be no babbler, not geven to lyghtenesse, no lyar, no boaster, nor fonde flatterer, but sober, and keapinge hym alwayes within his boundes."[47] Yet Othello frequently lapses into boundless rhetorical flights, such as in his transformation of one wife's adultery into a cosmic event: "Heaven stops the nose at it, and the moon winks" (4.2.78). In his final moments, Othello tries to keep within bounds

("No more of that . . . Speak of me as I am" [5.2.340]), but he cannot resist translating mediocrity into marvels, humiliating defeat into an act of
civic heroism:

> say besides that in Aleppo once,
> Where a malignant and a turbanned Turk
> Beat a Venetian and traduced the state,
> I took by th' throat the circumcised dog
> And smote him—thus!   *[He stabs himself]*
>
>   (5.2.350–54)

His introductory phrase "say besides" makes the account sound more like
a present supposition ("Let us *say* [suppose] a Turk attacked a Venetian,
here is how I would respond . . .") than a command to relate an event from
his past.[48] No matter how malignant the threat may have been (and typically we have no eyewitness to corroborate Othello's story), because of the
unexpected storm at sea his present response to the Turkish menace can
only be hypothetical. Once again, editorial attempts to determine whether
this final speech refers to a "base Indian" throwing away a pearl (a common sixteenth-century traveler's tale, according to Sanders) or a "base
Judean" (a multivalent allusion to Judas and Christ, or Herod and Mariam)
seem to miss the point.[49] The garbling of Shakespeare's text mirrors the
garbling of Othello's stories; neither emendation can be "true" because
the tale's inconsistency identifies it as a simulation.

Lies may be indispensable for Bacon's politician and the stock in trade
of the story-telling traveler, but they must not be uttered by a military man
of honor. Othello is all three; but he was a soldier first, and he cannot live
with the contradictions. When interrogating Iago about the street brawl in
Cyprus, Montano reminds the assembled garrison, "[If thou] dost deliver
more or less than truth, / Thou art no soldier" (2.3.215–16). Bacon confirms the sentiment in "Of Truth," where he writes, "There is no vice that
doth so cover a man with shame as to be found false and perfidious" (1:7)—
though typically he qualifies the observation. Lying is at times necessary,
but only when done with discretion and restraint; the key is, one must not
be found false. Othello's heavy reliance on secrecy (less than truth), simulation (more than truth), and dissimulation (outright lies) prevents him
from attaining a solid foundation for his identity as soldier, husband, or
governor. Othello commits suicide as much to end his life, as to put an end
to the stories of his life. Yet this, too, is doomed to fail. Earlier Lodovico had
wondered at Othello's striking of Desdemona, "this would not be believed
in Venice / Though I should swear I saw't" (4.1.241–42). Now he, Cassio,
Montano, and Gratiano can relate Othello's "monstrous act" (5.2.186) to
the listeners back home; another traveler's tale, to be sure, but with a cru-

cial difference: this time there are bodies, bloodstains, and witnesses to corroborate their incredible story.

In his important early lecture on *Othello,* Hunter questions the critical tradition that "paints the Moor as a savage at heart, one whose veneer of Christianity and civilization cracks as the play proceeds, to reveal and liberate his basic savagery." Hunter counters that Othello is led to believe crude Venetian stereotypes about duped husbands and lascivious wives—that he is a cuckold, and that Desdemona "lies elsewhere and everywhere."[50] I have argued that the play strips away Othello's pseudo-exotic veneer to reveal a Moor who, like Iago, "lies to th' heart" in a manner all too familiar to observers like Bacon, Castiglione, and Montaigne. Hunter concludes, rather wistfully, that "we admire him [Othello]—I fear that one has to be trained as a literary critic to find him unadmirable—but we are aware of the difficulty of sustaining that vision of the golden world of poetry" (163). One may continue to indulge Othello his magnificent speeches—after all, it was also proverbial that "Poets and trauellours may lie by authority"[51]—but we owe it to Shakespeare's craft to recognize that dozens of verbal untruths constitute an unsettling foundation for his most glamorous tragic protagonist.

In *Timber* (1640–41), Ben Jonson alluded to lines from *Othello* when he observed of his late rival playwright, "He was, indeed, honest, and of an open and free nature; had an excellent fantasy, brave notions, and gentle expressions; wherein he flowed with that facility that sometime it was necessary he should be stopped."[52] S. Schoenbaum interprets this implicit comparison of Shakespeare to Othello as the highest possible "praise," evidence of Jonson's admiration for his late rival.[53] But this seems more like a barb than a tribute. Jonson conjures up Othello's "honesty," a notion I believe we have dispensed with at this point. Jonson also recalls his gullibility—"The Moor is of a free and open nature" (1.3.398)—as well as his "brave" notions and overflowing flights of "fantasy." In light of the foregoing analysis of *Othello,* Jonson seems rather to be satirizing the playwright who produced such marvels as Caliban, a sea coast in Bohemia, and that "mouldy tale" *Pericles,* without ever blotting a line. Jonson refuses to be taken in by Shakespeare's tall tales, though the persistent romanticization of Othello's exotic past and the inexplicable mitigation of his present crimes attest to their enduring appeal—even among the most discerning playgoers and readers.

NOTES

Montaigne, "Of Giving the Lie," in *The Essayes of Montaigne,* trans. John Florio, 1603; ed. J. I. M. Stewart (New York: Bennett A. Cerf, 1933), II.xviii.603, italics omitted; hereafter cited parenthetically.

1. *Othello,* ed. E. A. J. Honigmann, Arden 3 Shakespeare (Walton-on Thames, UK: Thomas Nelson, 1996), 3.3.262, 4.2.40; hereafter cited parenthetically. One exception to this polarization—Desdemona's single explosive lie at 3.4.85–87—is explored by Paula McQuade in "Love and Lies: Marital Truth-Telling, Catholic Casuistry, and *Othello,*" in *Shakespeare and the Culture of Christianity in Early Modern England,* ed. Dennis Taylor and David Beauregard, 415–38 (New York: Fordham University Press, 2003). On the use of the term "honesty" in the play, see William Empson's essay "Honest in *Othello,*" in *The Structure of Complex Words* (1951; repr., London: Chatto and Windus, 1977), 218–49.

2. In "Modes of Story-Telling in *Othello,*" Derek Cohen examines Othello's "compulsive" and "involuntary" fictionalization of his past, but overlooks many of the general's significant fabrications in the present; see *Shakespearean Motives* (London: Macmillan, 1988), 88–103.

3. Bacon, "Of Simulation and Dissimulation," in *The Essays of Francis Bacon,* ed. Clark Sutherland Northup (Boston: Houghton Mifflin, 1936), VI.18–21; hereafter cited parenthetically.

4. E.g., see Stanley Cavell's polarization, "[Iago] is everything, we know, Othello is not. Critical and witty, for example, where Othello is commanding and eloquent; retentive where the other is lavish; concealed where the other is open; cynical where the other is romantic; conventional where the other is original; imagines flesh where the other imagines spirit," in *Disowning Knowledge in Six Plays of Shakespeare* (New York: Cambridge University Press, 1987), 136.

5. A. C. Bradley, *Shakespearean Tragedy: Lectures on* Hamlet, Othello, King Lear, Macbeth (1904; repr. London: Macmillan, 1964), 152.

6. See Bradley's own encomium beginning, "He has watched with a poet's eye the Arabian trees dropping their med'cinable gum, and the Indian throwing away his chance-found pearl" in *Shakespearean Tragedy,* 153.

7. T. W. Baldwin, "A Note upon William Shakespeare's Use of Pliny," in *Essays in Dramatic Literature: The Parrott Presentation Volume,* ed. Hardin Craig, 157–82 (1935; repr., New York: Russell and Russell, 1967); Kenneth Muir, *The Sources of Shakespeare's Plays* (London: Methuen, 1977), 186–90.

8. References are taken from *Selections from The History of the World Commonly Called The Natural History of G. Plinius Secundus,* trans. Philemon Holland, ed. Paul Turner (Carbondale, IL: Southern Illinois University Press, 1962), 7:73; hereafter cited parenthetically. Geographical consistency was never Pliny's strong point, and elsewhere his Anthropophagi are grouped with Ethiopian tribes such as the Blemmyi whose faces grow in their breasts— clearly Othello's men whose heads grow beneath their shoulders (5:52, 6:67).

9. Erasmus, *De Copia,* trans. Betty I. Knott, in *Collected Works of Erasmus: Literary and Educational Writings 2,* ed. Craig R. Thompson (Toronto: University of Toronto Press, 1978), 581. I am grateful to Patricia Parker for this reference.

10. Henry Burrowes Lathrop, *Translations from the Classics into English from Caxton to Chapman 1477–1620* (1933; repr., New York: Octagon, 1967), 219–20.

11. Margaret T. Hodgen, *Early Anthropology in the Sixteenth and Seventeenth Centuries* (Philadelphia: University of Pennsylvania Press, 1964), chaps. 5, 6; Eldred D. Jones, *Othello's Countrymen: The African in English Renaissance Drama* (London: Oxford University Press, 1965), 1–26, and *The Elizabethan Image of Africa* (Charlottesville: University Press of Virginia, 1971), 1–15.

12. See Jones, *Elizabethan Image of Africa,* 7, 14–31.

13. Burton, *The Anatomy of Melancholy,* ed. Holbrook Jackson (1932; repr., London: J. M. Dent, 1948), 2:34–69, quotation on p. 40.

14. Thomas Dekker, *Patient Grissil,* in *The Dramatic Works of Thomas Dekker,* ed. Fredson Bowers (Cambridge: Cambridge University Press, 1970), 2:278 (5.1.18–50).

15. Shakespeare, *The Tempest,* ed. Frank Kermode, Arden 2 (1954; repr., London: Routledge, 1994), 3.3.44–49. Montaigne likewise scoffs at Pliny, "Yet is there no scholler so meanely learned, but will convince him of lying" (I.xxvi.142–43); in the original French, the phrase is *"si petit escolier"; Essais,* ed. Maurice Rat (Paris: Garnier, 1962), I.xxvii (1:196).

16. Alden T. Vaughan and Virginia Mason Vaughan, "Before *Othello:* Elizabethan Representations of Sub-Saharan Africans," *William and Mary Quarterly* 54 (1997): 19–44, quotation on p. 19. The Vaughans conclude that Othello attains "his unusual heroic stature" by transcending racist caricatures found in travelers' tales (44). Yet as early as 1710, the Earl of Shaftesbury noted that the telling of tales itself undermined Othello's heroic stature: "What passionate reader of *Travels,* or Student in the prodigious Sciences, can refuse to pity that fair Lady, who fell in Love with the *miraculous* Moor? especially considering with what sutable grace such a Lover cou'd relate the most monstrous Adventures"; cited in *Othello,* ed. Horace Howard Furness, 57 (italics in original), New Variorum (1886; repr., Philadelphia: Lippincott, 1914).

17. Mark Thornton Burnett, *Constructing "Monsters" in Shakespearean Drama and Early Modern Culture* (New York: Palgrave-Macmillan, 2002), 102–3.

18. Hadfield, *Literature, Travel, and Colonial Writing in the English Renaissance 1545–1625* (1998; repr., Oxford: Clarendon Press, 2001), 217–42, quotations on 233–34.

19. On early modern interest in revisionary accounts of Africa, see Hodgen, *Early Anthropology;* Jones, *Othello's Countrymen;* Virginia Mason Vaughan, Othello*: A Contextual History* (1994; repr., Cambridge: Cambridge University Press, 1996), 51–70.

20. John Stell, dedication to *The Nauigations, Peregrinations and Voyages Made into Turkie by Nicholas Nicholay Daulphinois,* 1585; cited in Louis B. Wright, *Middle-Class Culture in Elizabethan England* (1935; repr., Ithaca, NY: Cornell University Press, 1958), 509.

21. Marlowe, *Edward II,* in *The Complete Plays,* ed. J. B. Steane (1969; repr., London: Penguin, 1986), 1.1.29–32.

22. Lim, *The Arts of Empire: The Poetics of Colonialism from Ralegh to Milton* (Newark: University of Delaware Press, 1998), 104–41, quotations on p. 112.

23. Morris Palmer Tilley, *A Dictionary of the Proverbs in England in the Sixteenth and Seventeenth Centuries* (Ann Arbor: University of Michigan Press, 1950), 4 (item A56), and sources cited there.

24. See Perez Zagorin, *Ways of Lying: Dissimulation, Persecution, and Conformity in Early Modern Europe* (Cambridge, MA: Harvard University Press, 1990), 256–57.

25. G. K. Hunter, "Othello and Colour Prejudice," *Proceedings of the British Academy* 53 (1967): 139–63, 150.

26. Marion Trousdale, "Rhetoric," in *A Companion to English Renaissance Literature and Culture,* ed. Michael Hattaway, 623–33 (London: Blackwell, 2000), 629.

27. Puttenham, *The Arte of English Poesie,* 1589; excerpted in *English Renaissance Literary Criticism,* ed. Brian Vickers, 190–296 (Oxford: Clarendon Press, 1999), 238–39.

28. Cited in Zagorin, *Ways of Lying,* 20–21.

29. Thomas Rymer quotes Othello's false modesty (i.e., 1.3.77–95) before scoffing, "All this is but *Preamble* to tell the Court that He wants words"; *A Short View of Tragedy,* 1691, in *Critical Essays of the Seventeenth Century,* ed. J. E. Spingarn (1908; repr., London: Oxford University Press, 1957), 2:208–55, 228–29 (italics in original).

30. Johannes Leo (Leo Africanus), *A Geographical Historie of Africa,* trans. John Pory, 1600, facsimile (Amsterdam: Theatrum Orbis Terrarum / New York: Da Capo, 1969), 40–41.

31. Anthony Gerard Barthelemy, *Black Face, Maligned Race: The Representation of Blacks in English Drama from Shakespeare to Southerne* (Baton Rouge: Louisiana State University Press, 1987), 147–81, especially 151–61.

32. Iibd., 72–146, quotation on p. 73.

33. Hunter, "Othello and Colour Prejudice," 151.

34. Jones cites other intimate passages (e.g., "her sweet body" [3.3.349], her "balmy breath" [5.2.16]) to illustrate Othello's "enthusiasm for Desdemona's body" which he "deliberately concealed from the senate"; *Othello's Countrymen,* 97.

35. Honigmann notes that throughout he "weeps copiously" (Arden 3 edition, 20); F. R. Leavis notes two contradictions (Othello not being jealous, and allowing Desdemona to confess her sins) in *The Common Pursuit* (1952; repr., London: Chatto and Windus, 1965), 138–39, 150; Rymer notes the "absurd" contradiction about the town at war in *A Short View of Tragedy,* 237.

36. Zagorin, *Ways of Lying,* 3.

37. This enthusiasm also contradicts the Clown's earlier observation: "But, as they say, to hear music the general does not greatly care" (3.1.16–17).

38. See, respectively, John A. Hodgson, "Desdemona's Handkerchief as an Emblem of Her Reputation," *Texas Studies in Language and Literature* 19 (1977), 313–22; Harry Berger, Jr., "Impertinent Trifling: Desdemona's Handkerchief," *Shakespeare Quarterly* 47 (1996), 235–50; and Lynda E. Boose, "Othello's Handkerchief: 'The Recognizance and Pledge of Love,'" *English Literary Renaissance* 5 (1975): 360–74.

39. Vaughan cites its blackness in *Othello: A Contextual History,* 33 and note 61; *The Oxford English Dictionary,* compact ed. (Oxford: Oxford University Press, 1987), sb. 2d.

40. In *Othello's Countrymen,* Jones answers "no" to his own question, proposing that the story is fabricated to conceal Othello's "disproportionate passion over such a trifle" (102).

41. Hodgson seems skeptical of the first version, stating that it is a "wild story"; "Desdemona's Handkerchief," 315. Honigmann proposes that the first story may have been invented to frighten Desdemona, but that contradictions in version two may also stem from an "oversight" (Othello's? Shakespeare's?); Arden 3 edition, note to 5.2.215 (321). Cf. the comments supporting version two in the New Variorum edition of *Othello,* note to 5.2.269 (317).

42. Mullaney, "Strange Things, Gross Terms, Curious Customs: The Rehearsal of Cultures in the Late Renaissance," *Representations* 3 (Summer 1983), 40–67, 40–43; cf. Hodgen, *Early Anthropology,* chap. 4 and pp. 162–63.

43. Louise Noble has recently taken Othello's claims at face value, placing the handkerchief in contexts of cannibalistic "corpse medicines"; "The *Fille Vièrge* as Pharmakon: The Therapeutic Value of Desdemona's Corpse," in *Disease, Diagnosis, and Cure on the Early Modern Stage,* ed. Stephanie Moss and Kaara L. Peterson, 135–50 (Aldershot, UK: Ashgate, 2004).

44. Rymer, *A Short View of Tragedy,* 223.

45. See Tilley, *Dictionary of Proverbs,* 377 (item L219).

46. See *Othello,* ed. M. R. Ridley, Arden 2 Shakespeare (1958; repr., London: Methuen, 1984), 5.2.254 note; *Othello,* ed. Norman Sanders, New Cambridge Shakespeare (1984; repr., Cambridge: Cambridge University Press, 1989), 5.2.251 note; and Honigmann, *Othello,* Arden 3 edition, 5.2.251 longer note (p. 341).

47. Count Baldassare Castiglione, *The Book of the Courtier,* trans. Thomas Hoby, 1561; ed. Virginia Cox (London: J. M. Dent, 1994), II.xli (149) and II.xviii (121).

48. On Shakespeare's use of "say" to introduce a supposition or hypothesis, see *The OED* (sense B.10 and sources cited there).

49. *Othello,* ed., Sanders, New Cambridge edition, supplementary note to 5.2.343 (pp. 191–92). Honigmann notes that the "Indian" version may originate in Pliny's *History* (34:17), reason enough to take it with a grain of salt; Arden 3 *Othello,* long note to 5.2.345 (pp. 342–43).

50. Hunter, "Othello and Colour Prejudice," 159.

51. Tilley, *Dictionary of Proverbs,* 520 (item P28) and sources cited there.

52. Jonson, *Timber: or Discoveries Made Upon Men and Matter,* excerpted in *English Renaissance Literary Criticism,* ed. Brian Vickers, 558–89, qtd. on p. 561 (Oxford: Clarendon Press, 1999).

53. S. Schoenbaum, *William Shakespeare: A Compact Documentary Life,* rev. ed. (New York: Oxford University Press, 1987), 258–59.

BIBLIOGRAPHY

Bacon, Francis. *The Essays of Francis Bacon.* Edited by Clark Sutherland Northup. Boston: Houghton Mifflin, 1936.

Baldwin, T. W. "A Note upon William Shakespeare's Use of Pliny." *Essays in Dramatic Literature: The Parrott Presentation Volume.* Edited by Hardin Craig, 157–82. 1935. Reprint, New York: Russell and Russell, 1967.

Barthelemy, Anthony Gerard. *Black Face, Maligned Race: The Representation of Blacks in English Drama from Shakespeare to Southerne.* Baton Rouge: Louisiana State University Press, 1987.

Berger, Harry, Jr. "Impertinent Trifling: Desdemona's Handkerchief." *Shakespeare Quarterly* 47 (1996): 235–50.

Boose, Lynda E. "Othello's Handkerchief: 'The Recognizance and Pledge of Love.'" *English Literary Renaissance* 5 (1975): 360–74.

Bradley, A. C. *Shakespearean Tragedy: Lectures on Hamlet, Othello, King Lear, Macbeth.* 1904. Reprint, London: Macmillan, 1964.

Burnett, Mark Thornton. *Constructing "Monsters" in Shakespearean Drama and Early Modern Culture.* New York: Palgrave-Macmillan, 2002.

Burton, Robert. *The Anatomy of Melancholy.* Edited by Holbrook Jackson. 3 vols. 1932. Reprint, London: J. M. Dent, 1948.

Castiglione, Count Baldassare. *The Book of the Courtier.* Translated by Thomas Hoby. Ed. Virginia Cox. London: J. M. Dent, 1994.

Cavell, Stanley. *Disowning Knowledge in Six Plays of Shakespeare.* New York: Cambridge University Press, 1987.

Cohen, Derek. *Shakespearean Motives.* London: Macmillan, 1988.

Dekker, Thomas *Patient Grissil.* In *The Dramatic Works of Thomas Dekker.* Edited by Fredson Bowers. Vol. 2 of 4. Cambridge: Cambridge University Press, 1970.

Empson, William. *The Structure of Complex Words.* 1951. Reprint, London: Chatto and Windus, 1977.

Erasmus, Desiderius. *De Copia.* Translated by Betty I. Knott. In *Collected Works of Erasmus: Literary and Educational Writings 2.* Edited by Craig R. Thompson. Toronto: University of Toronto Press, 1978.

Hadfield, Andrew. *Literature, Travel, and Colonial Writing in the English Renaissance 1545–1625.* 1998. Reprint, Oxford: Clarendon Press, 2001.

Hodgen, Margaret T. *Early Anthropology in the Sixteenth and Seventeenth Centuries.* Philadelphia: University of Pennsylvania Press, 1964.

Hodgson, John A. "Desdemona's Handkerchief as an Emblem of Her Reputation." *Texas Studies in Language and Literature* 19 (1977): 313–22.

Hunter, G. K. "Othello and Colour Prejudice." *Proceedings of the British Academy* 53 (1967): 139–63.

Jones, Eldred D. *The Elizabethan Image of Africa.* Charlottesville: University Press of Virginia, 1971.

———. *Othello's Countrymen: The African in English Renaissance Drama.* London: Oxford University Press, 1965.

Jonson, Ben. *Timber: or Discoveries Made Upon Men and Matter.* In *English Renaissance Literary Criticism.* Edited by Brian Vickers, 558–89. Oxford: Clarendon Press, 1999.

Lathrop, Henry Burrowes. *Translations from the Classics into English from Caxton to Chapman 1477–1620.* Madison: University of Wisconsin Press, 1933. Reprint, New York: Octagon, 1967.

Leavis, F. R. *The Common Pursuit.* 1952. Reprint, London: Chatto and Windus, 1965.

Leo, Johannes (Leo Africanus). *A Geographical Historie of Africa.* Translated by John Pory. 1600. Facsimile. Amsterdam: Theatrum Orbis Terrarum / New York: Da Capo, 1969.

Lim, Walter S. H. *The Arts of Empire: The Poetics of Colonialism from Ralegh to Milton.* Newark: University of Delaware Press, 1998.

Marlowe, Christopher. *Edward II.* In *The Complete Plays.* Edited by J. B. Steane. 1969. Reprint, London: Penguin, 1986.

McQuade, Paula. "Love and Lies: Marital Truth-Telling, Catholic Casuistry, and *Othello.*" In *Shakespeare and the Culture of Christianity in Early Modern England.* Edited by Dennis Taylor and David Beauregard, 415–38. New York: Fordham University Press, 2003.

Montaigne, Michel de. *Essais.* Edited by Maurice Rat. 2 vols. Paris: Garnier, 1962.

———. *The Essayes of Montaigne.* Translated by John Florio. 1603, Edited by J. I. M. Stewart. New York: Bennett A. Cerf, 1933.

Muir, Kenneth. *The Sources of Shakespeare's Plays.* London: Methuen, 1977.

Mullaney, Steven. "Strange Things, Gross Terms, Curious Customs: The Rehearsal of Cultures in the Late Renaissance." *Representations* 3 (Summer 1983): 40–67.

Noble, Louise. "The *Fille Vièrge* as Pharmakon: The Therapeutic Value of Desdemona's Corpse." *Disease, Diagnosis, and Cure on the Early Modern Stage.* Edited by Stephanie Moss and Kaara L. Peterson, 135–50. Aldershot, UK: Ashgate, 2004.

The Oxford English Dictionary. Compact edition. 3 vols. Oxford: Oxford University Press, 1987.

Pliny (Gaius Plinius Secundus). *Selections from The History of the World Commonly Called The Natural History of C. Plinius Secundus.* Translated by Philemon Holland. Edited by Paul Turner. Carbondale: Southern Illinois University Press, 1962.

Puttenham, George. *The Arte of English Poesie.* 1589. In *English Renaissance Literary Criticism.* Edited by Brian Vickers, 190–296. Oxford: Clarendon Press, 1999.

Rymer, Thomas. *A Short View of Tragedy.* In *Critical Essays of the Seventeenth Century.* Edited by J. E. Spingarn. 3 vols., 2:208–55. 1908. Reprint, London: Oxford University Press, 1957.

Schoenbaum, S. *William Shakespeare: A Compact Documentary Life.* Revised edition. New York: Oxford University Press, 1987.

Shakespeare, William. *Othello.* Edited by Horace Howard Furness. New Variorum Edition. 1886. Reprint, Philadelphia: Lippincott, 1914.

———. *Othello.* Edited by M. R. Ridley. Arden Shakespeare (2nd Series). 1958. Reprint, London: Methuen, 1984.

———. *Othello.* Edited by Norman Sanders. New Cambridge Shakespeare. 1984. Reprint, Cambridge: Cambridge University Press, 1989.

———. *Othello.* Edited by E. A. J. Honigmann. Arden Shakespeare (3rd Series). Walton-on Thames, UK: Thomas Nelson, 1996.

———. *The Tempest.* Edited by Frank Kermode. Arden Shakespeare (2nd Series). 1954. Reprint, London: Routledge, 1994.

Tilley, Morris Palmer. *A Dictionary of the Proverbs in England in the Sixteenth and Seventeenth Centuries.* Ann Arbor: University of Michigan Press, 1950.

Trousdale, Marion. "Rhetoric." In *A Companion to English Renaissance Literature and Culture.* Edited by Michael Hattaway, 623–33. London: Blackwell, 2000.

Vaughan, Alden T., and Virginia Mason Vaughan. "Before *Othello:* Elizabethan Representations of Sub-Saharan Africans." *William and Mary Quarterly* 54 (1997): 19–44.

Vaughan, Virginia Mason. *Othello: A Contextual History.* 1994. Reprint, Cambridge: Cambridge University Press, 1996.

Wright, Louis B. *Middle-Class Culture in Elizabethan England.* 1935. Reprint, Ithaca, NY: Cornell University Press, 1958.

Zagorin, Perez. *Ways of Lying: Dissimulation, Persecution, and Conformity in Early Modern Europe.* Cambridge, MA: Harvard University Press, 1990.

Schelte Adams Bolswert, Dutch, c. 1581–1659. Detail from *Bird Trappers*. nd. From the *Large Landscapes* after Rubens. Gift of Herman Levy, Esq., O.B.E. McMaster University Collection, Hamilton, Canada. © McMaster Museum of Art, McMaster University, 2006. 1984.007.0103. Photo credit: Jennifer Pettiplace.

III
The Domestication of the Mysterious and Foreign

Was Illyria as Mysterious and Foreign as We Think?

Patricia Parker

Amurath invaded Illyricum (otherwise called now Sclavonia) conteining in it Dalmatia, Croatia, Istria, and Liburnia. . . .
—Foxe, *Actes and Monuments* (1583)

BOSNA (in time past called ILLYRIA). . . .
—Knolles, *Generall Historie of the Turke* (1603)

EDITORS AND CRITICS DO NOT USUALLY ASSUME WITH SOME REVIEWERS
of *Twelfth Night* that "Illyria" was an imaginary name or an invented realm.
But it has still been traditional to assume that (as the Norton edition puts
it) the name was "probably not suggesting a real country to Shakespeare's
audience."[1] Shakespeare famously domesticates foreign settings—and transforms Illyria at least in part into the England evoked by the names of Andrew Aguecheek and Toby Belch. The present contribution to the discussion does not seek to deny that any Shakespearean setting is a palimpsest
or heterotopia—in this case interlayering multiple potential spaces with the
delirium (or ill-lyre) its name suggests. Rather it is to record how much was
published or known about Illyria in England prior to the play and (given
the play's own striking eastern allusions) especially about its relation to the
Turk.[2]

First, even in Shakespeare, Illyria figures in multiple references beyond
Twelfth Night—in "Bargulus the strong Illyrian pirate" in *2 Henry VI*
(4.1.108), evoking the association of Illyria with piracy from classical writing to the Uskoks and others on the Illyrian coast in the years before the
play; in the naming of the pirate Ragozine in *Measure for Measure* (4.3.71)
from Ragusa (or present-day Dubrovnik), Illyria's most famous city, whose
name also yielded English "argosy" for its celebrated ships; in the "Epidaurus" and "Epidamium" of *The Comedy of Errors* (1.1.41, 93), the former the ancient name of Ragusa itself and the latter the city Lucan called
"Illyrian Epidamnos," the location of Plautus's original play of twins;
and in the "Dalmatians" of *Cymbeline* (3.1.73), the region that Cooper's
Thesaurus (1578) tells us was "part of the great countrey called Illeria or

Sclavonia" (and one of the lands in which Musco in Jonson's *Every Man in His Humour* claims he had more recently served). For any schoolboy or reader familiar with the texts that provided the sources for Shakespeare's Roman histories and other plays before *Twelfth Night,* Illyria was at the same time familiar as the territory given to Julius Caesar along with Gaul; as the site (on the Illyrian shore or what Lucan called the "Illyrian waters") of Caesar's struggles with Pompey; as the province transferred to Brutus after Caesar's assassination (reflected in the "Illirian bands" commanded by Brutus in *Caesar's Revenge*); as the dividing point between East and West in the division between Octavius and Antony prior to Actium and the place conquered by the new Augustus Caesar after the Actium victory; and as the territory associated with Tiberius Caesar, whose subjugation of its inhabitants (in 10 B.C.) is reflected in "He tamed the foxes of Illiria" in *Tiberius* (1607). It also appears in references to "Illyricum or Slavonia" in Holinshed, who elsewhere provides the account of the "Pannonians and Dalmatians" used in *Cymbeline* as well as details on its early history. And it yielded several famous figures. Sixteenth-century writers repeatedly refer to the origin of St. Jerome in "Dalmatia, now called Sclauonia" (as Peter Martyr's *History of Trauayle* put it in 1577); while Marc'Antonio de Dominis, who would later be immortalized as the "Fat Bishop" of Middleton's *Game at Chess,* was already in the 1590s the Bishop of Senj (another Illyrian coastal city), who defended its Uskok pirates (up to a point) because of their attacks on the Turks.[3]

Illyria simultaneously conjured up associations with romance and retirement from the world. Multiple sixteenth-century writers cite the familiar instance of the emperor Diocletian (born in Dalmatia), who retired to "gardens in Illiria." Samuel Daniel, for example, has the imprisoned Richard II contrast his cares to this celebrated instance of Illyrian retirement ("O thou great Monarch, and more great therefore / For skorning that whereto vaine pride aspires, / Reckning thy gardens in *Illiria* more / Then all the Empire; took'st those sweet retires").[4] Although this connection has not been recognized by critics or editors of the play, Illyria similarly appears in multiple romances in the years before *Twelfth Night,* including in romances that underscore its proximity to Saracen or Turk. Barnabe Riche's *Adventures of Brusanus, Prince of Hungaria* (1592)—the first book of which has long been cited as a source for *Measure for Measure*—gives its second book entirely over to Illyria, in a plot that includes love, letters, and a triangle in which a love-sick suitor is rejected by the Princess of Illyria, who in turn woos another man who rejects her.[5] Munday's translation of *The Palladine of England* (1588)[6] includes "succour from Illiria" (58) in a plot that involves "Dukes of Sclauonia and Liburnia" (61) and describes Dalmatia (a source of "expert warriors," 61) as "vnder the Turkes gouernement" (55). *Blanchardine & Eglantine Queene of Tormaday* (1595) pictures

Tormaday as the "principall place and Citie" in Dalmatia and its Queen as besieged by a "Panim King."[7] Ford's popular *Parismus* (1598)—already considered a possible source for *Twelfth Night* because of its Olivia and disguised Violetta—refers like Greene's *Pandosto* before it to "the coast of Bohemia," in a passage in which it can only be the Illyrian coast.[8] Even after *Twelfth Night,* Wroth's *Urania* features a princess of Slavonia, the well-known other name for Illyria itself.[9]

Illyria was likewise familiar from the New Testament travels of Paul and Titus, whose travel to Dalmatia (2 Tim. 4) may even be echoed in the choice of Titus as the name for Orsino's nephew at sea (5.1.63). The description in Romans of Paul spreading the Gospel from Jerusalem to Illyricum was part of the idiom of his famous "peregrinations," appearing in text after text in the period as well as in the maps of his travels in Ortelius and the Geneva Bible.[10] Because Acts 27 describes Paul's "shipwracke" in the Adriatic in the midst of a storm at sea, the conflation of these texts produced the tradition of Paul's shipwreck off the coast of Illyria itself, the coast on which Shakespeare's twins are shipwrecked in *Twelfth Night.*[11] Still other writers conflated Titus's travel to Dalmatia with Paul's own Illyrian peregrinations, giving Illyria even more prominence in relation to this biblical mapping.[12] In a period when such palimpsests of ancient and early modern were common, texts such as Ralph Carr's *Mahumetane or Turkish Historie* (1600) could at the same time refer, in recounting more recent struggles with the Turk, to the island off the Illyrian shore where "some affirme that Saint Paul after shipwracke there did land," citing the passage in Acts where "Saint Paule in the sea Adriatico otherwise called the gulfe of Venice, was tossed too and fro with cruell tempests of weather."[13]

Illyria in the period of *Twelfth Night* was also famous for its language. John Jewel insists against Harding that the same St. Jerome who "translated the Scriptures into the Sclauon tongue, procured also that the Common Service there should be saide in the Sclauon tongue"; while those on the side of Rome—including Robert Parsons—argued that there is no "example out of all antiquitie or histories that any one Catholyke country from Christ downewards to Luther vsed publike seruice in a vulgar tongue," except "only some perticular dispensation for some short tyme and vpon especial causes," as when priests were "permitted by the Pope to say masse in their Slauonian vulgar tongue vntil they might be instructed in the Latyn."[14] Edward Topsell includes in *Of Foure-Footed Beasts* (1607) an Index devoted to their names in "Illirian" and refers in his text to what "Illirians" and "the Illirian tongue" call its various animals, while his *Historie of Serpents* (1608) lists "Illyrica" as one of the languages it repeatedly cites, referring in the text to what the "Lizard" is called in "Illiria" and what the "Illirians" call its other creatures.[15] Other texts of the period comment on how widely it is spread, and even provide English-Sclavonian language lessons. Ortelius's *Theatre* stresses that the "Slauonian tongue" (by some "now called Windish") was "thought to be that, which the Latines called *Lingua Illyrica,* the Illyrian tongue" and "at this day is very farre spread" into European countries and Russia, as well as "much vsed amongst the Turkes."[16] Knolles's *Generall Historie of the Turkes* (1603) features "The bloudie and tirranicall precepts left by Selymus to his son Solyman" printed in Greek, Turkish, and "the Sclavonian tongue."[17] Peter Martyr's *History of Trauayle* observes not only that "the commentaries and homelies of saint Ambrose, Augustine, Ierome, & Gregorie" have been "translated into the Illyrian or Slauon tongue" along with "a great number of bookes of holy scripture" but that the Moscovites use "both the Slauon tongue and letters, as doe also the Sclauons, Dalmates, Bohemes, Pollones, and Lithuanes."[18] Commenting that "The Slauon tongue [is] spred further then any other at this day," it records that "Illyrian" is "familiar at Constantinople, in the court of the Emperours of the Turks, and was of late hearde in Egypte among the Mamalukes" (298). Long before both of these texts, Giovio's *Shorte Treatise vpon the Turkes chronicles* (1546) already prominently mentions Sclavonian or Illyrian as one of the principal languages of the court of the Great Turk himself; Cambini's *Two very notable commentaries* (1562) notes that Scanderbeg understood Sclavonian as well as Turkish; and Goughe's translation of Georgijević's *Ofspring of the house of Ottomanno* (1569) provides a dialogue with English and Sclavonian interleaved and information on the widespread use of this tongue: "Understand therfore that it is lawfull for all men, skilefull in that tounge, safelye to passe into Croatia Dalmatia, Russia Walachia, Seruia, Boeme, & Poole" (or Poland) and that "The Turkes conuersant in their kings courte, and confines of Sclauony do use the same language."[19]

But perhaps most important in relation to *Twelfth Night*—with its references to a "eunuch" and "mute," to the "Sophy," and to the transformed Malvolio as a "renegado"—is the extent of contemporary writing on the relation of Illyria to the Turk. Bruce Smith's recent edition of *Twelfth Night* cites the map and description of Dalmatia from George Sandys's travels in 1610, including its tribute to the Turk.[20] And Knolles's *Generall Historie* includes multiple references to the embattled Illyrian territory and shore. But Illyria already appears as part of the territory of the Turk in *Tamburlaine,*[21] and references to Illyria and Illyrian territories in relation to the Turk appear in texts published in England long before Shakespeare's play, together with reminders that it was a source of renegades as well as youths who turned Turk and submitted (or were submitted) to circumcision or castration (suggesting another dimension to the C-U-T of the Letter Scene). Illyria was famous not only for the many nameless renegades or forcibly circumcized tribute children from its borderlands but for the upward mobility of Illyrians who rose to become Grand Viziers of the Ottoman empire itself. Such figures included the renegade "Cherseogles Bassa (whom the Turks cal also Achmet Hertezec-ogli)" described by Knolles as the "sonne of one Chersechius a small prince of Illyria" (484), who fled to Constantinople and turned Turk as an adult, becoming not only the son-in-law of Sultan Baiazet II but a Grand Vizier who served under three successive sultans. Another was the Grand Vizier Mehmet Sokollu, made famous more recently by the Nobel-prize winning *Bridge on the Drina,* who was "born a Christian Bosnian" and was "an obscure youth living near Ragusa when he was carried off at the age of eighteen by the sultan's recruiting officers," but rose to become Grand Vizier under Suleiman I, Selim II, and Murad III, a figure known in England for promoting its own favorable trade relations with the Turk.[22]

Ortelius provides a comprehensive description of Illyria (including of its shifting borders and uncertain extent) in *Theatrum Orbis Terrarum,* whose map of the Empire of the Turk shows how close the borders of Ottoman power came to Ragusa, whose tribute to the Turk it describes.[23] But already in the early sixteenth century, texts by English writers or translated into English stressed the in-between or borderland position of Illyria and its coastline. In 1511, the record of the travels of Richard Guylforde, Henry VII's comptroller, on his pilgrimage to Jerusalem by the route that had already taken medieval pilgrims along the Illyrian coast, describes the coastal cities of Pula, Senj, and Zadar and provides a detailed description of Ragusa as a tributary to the Turk close to the borders of Ottoman power, together with its Christian "relics."[24] Thomas Becon's *Pollecye of Warre* (1542) chronicles the Ottoman expansion through "Asia, Grece, Illiria and Thracia, with diuers other Regions."[25] Antoine Geuffroy's *Order of the greate Turckes courte,* translated by Richard Grafton in 1542, describes Baiazet I as spoiling "Bosue" (or Bosnia), "Croace, and Sclauonie, whiche are Dalmacia and Liburnia," all part of the original Illyria, Amurath II as coming within a few miles of "Ragusa, which was called Epidaurus," and Mehmet the Conqueror as entering Bosnia, cutting off the head of its "lorde or deputye named Stephyn Hierchec" and forcing his son to "bee circumcized" and "surnamed Achmath."[26] Bosnia itself—as a part of Illyria early conquered by the Turk—is prominently mentioned both in such sixteenth-century descriptions and in later texts such as Knolles's *Historie of the Turkes,* which refers to it as "BOSNA (in time past called ILLYRIA")," Fougasses' *Historie of the magnificent state of Venice* (1612) which refers to "that part of Illiria, which at this day is called Bossina," and D'Avity's *Estates, Empires, & Principalities of the World,* which notes that "Bossina, or Bosne is a countrie of Illyrie" and that the "Turk made himselfe maister of this realme in the year 1464."[27]

Geuffroy's history repeatedly makes clear how much of Illyria was already conquered or threatened by the Turk. He reports that Mehmet the

Conqueror "sent to Marbeye, Samgiac of Bosue, whyche was the sonne of a Genevoye, to spoyle the countrye of Istrie, called Liburnie," yet another part of Illyria along its coast, and of "Stirie, whiche they call Steirmarch, & in ye old tyme called Valeria, whiche all are comprysed within Illirium" (fol. cxx–cxxi) in the same passage as he notes that "Mehemet sent Achmath Bacha surnamed Ghendich . . . the sonne of Stephyn late deputee of Bosne" to the other side of the Adriatic, where he took Otranto (fol. cxxi). Illyria and the Illyrian coast figure repeatedly as Geuffroy proceeds with his history of the Ottoman advance, in an account that stresses elsewhere the eunuchs or "gelded men" of Ottoman courts (xxxviii) and the Christian captives circumcised and forced to turn Turk. In a passage headed "How Pazait returned into Sclavony," he describes how Baiazet II took "the toune of Duraz, of olde tyme called Dyrrachium and Epidamnus" (fol. xxix), the location of Plautus's original plot of twins, and in 1498 sent "a greate armye by sea unto Iara or Iadera, beynge upon the goulfe of Venyce, called Mare Adriaticum, on the coaste of Sclauonye" (fol. cxxx) or the city of Zara (present-day Croatian Zadar) on that same Illyrian coast.

Four years later, Giovio's *Shorte Treatise vpon the Turkes chronicles* (1546), a subsequent source for the Turk play *Selimus,* described Amurath II—"the first whiche did ordayne and appoint that kynd of fotemen which they call Janizars," or janissaries, chosen "oute of suche christiens, which before had forsaken Christe" (fol. xvii)—as overrunning "Bosyne" or Bosnia and other territories (fol. xvii). He further cites the famous example of Scanderbeg, from Albanian territory bordering on Illyria, who was taken by the Turk, circumcised, and raised by the Sultan but returned to his homeland to make "warre uppon ye turkes" (Epistle Dedicatorie); and the famous Illyrian renegade who did not return—the figure he calls "Cherseolus Bassa" (fol. xxxviii), the son-in-law of Baiazet II featured as a character in *Selimus* itself.[28]

Like Geuffroy, Giovio chronicles the multiple Ottoman incursions along the Illyrian coast, including Baiazet II's marching into the city that Lucan called "Illyrian Epidamnum" (fol. xliiii). In ways that underscore the proximity of this city to Illyria's still-unconquered parts, he describes the "Sclavoniens" opposed to the Turk (fol. xlv) and the powerful "Halys Bassan an eunuch . . . borne in Albanye" now under Turkish control who came "with the Turkes nauye into Iadra" or Zara and "utterly wasted al the prouince" of Dalmatia "with sword and fyre" (fol. xlvi). Stressing the importance of Sclavonians or Illyrians among those who were circumcised and turned Turk, he describes the janissaries used to expand Ottoman power (fol. cxxiiii) as youths or young "boyes whiche be eyther payed to the Turke for trybute, or else that his souldiers get with theyr forragynges in warre" (fol. cxxiii). And he prominently mentions the Sclavonian or Illyrian tongue, both as one of the principal languages of the court of the Great Turk and as the language of the areas from which so many janissaries were taken (fol. cxxxiii).

In the decades after Giovio's text appeared in London, Lanquet's expanded *Epitome of chronicles* (1559) not only detailed Illyria's classical history, including its relation to the Caesars, but recorded that in the late fourteenth century "the Turkes wasted and burnt Bossina, Croatia, and the farther partes of Illyria," making clear how much of Illyria had already been invaded by the Turk long before Shakespeare's Illyrian play.[29] Cambini's *Two Very Notable Commentaries* (1562) likewise reminded English readers that "Illiria, whiche at thys daye is called Schiavonia, in the which there is contained Dalmatya, Croacya, and Istria, with the people called Iburni" or Liburnians (7r) had long been menaced by the Turk, recounting how Baiazet I "made a great course through Bossina and Seruia" (2v), taking captives in his wake; how "Amorathe taketh Schyauonia" with "exceding great spoile and destruction" (7r); how "Machomethe the second" not only "toke the Citie and Empire of Constantinople" but soon after "the whole kingedome of Seruia" and "the kingdome of Bossina" (Ffiii); and how by the end of the fifteenth century, tributary forces from Dalmatia and Bosnia were under Ottoman control (50v). In a narrative that stresses that Scanderbeg himself had been forcibly "circumcised" as a boy ("this tiran Amorathe caused him in his chyldhod to be circumcised") and brought to the Sultan, who "seeing him beautifull and to have a maiestie in his countenance . . . determyned neuer to suffer him to retorne home againe, but to kepe him in his courte" (Siiir)—a description that hints at the homoerotic or sodomitical identified repeatedly in the period with the Turk—Cambini makes reference to the Illyrians or "Schiauoneses" among the forces he subsequently united to fight the Ottoman power (30r). Only a few years later, in 1569, Goughe's translation of *The ofspring of the house of Ottomanno* by Bartolomej Georgijević—himself a Croatian—warned of the progressive obliteration of the memory of Christianity in the Balkans, that "the like will happen in Croatia, Hungarie, & Sclauonie, which are late additions and augmentinges of the Turkish empire" (Hiiiir), and included both a lament for Christian children taken from these and other borderlands, subjected to the cut of circumcision (Fi) and turned Turk, and a warning that the expansion of the Ottoman empire posed a threat to England as well (Jiir).

Multiple other texts in the decades prior to *Twelfth Night* put the increasingly fragmented Illyrian territories at the forefront of the conflict between East and West, both before and after the rise of the Ottoman Turk. Curio's *Notable historie of the Saracens* (1575), like Giovio a source for the Turk play *Selimus,* records that "the Saracenes . . . hauyng wasted Illyrium and Dalmatia . . . coasted alonge the Adrian [or Adriatic] Sea," that "the Affricane Saracens" besieged "Ragusium (whiche is a Citie standinge in the borders and coasts of Illyria)," and that in 969 Ragusa was "rescued and deliuered from the Siege by the Greekish camp"—yet another sign of the constant shifting of power in the conflict for these Illyrian lands.[30] The celebrated seacoast of Illyria figures similarly in his account of the exploits of Baldwin and Godfrey of Bulloigne, including an incident where "Saracens" are described as having "wasted the coast of Illyricum" (91) en route back to the East, engaging in sea fights with Christians in the Adriatic.

In his account of the rise of the Ottoman Turk, Curio cites the advances of Baiazet I, who "spoyled Bosna, Croacia, Illyria, Albania and Wallachia, kyllyng many thousands of Christians, being partly slaine and partly caryed into captiuitie" (128v); the conquests of Mehmet I, who "subdued Seruia, Walachia, and a great part of Slauonie" (129v); the in-between position of the Illyrian coast in 1498 when "The Turke warred against the Venetians, spoylinge with fire and sword the Countrye Dalmatia" (134v) and in 1500, when the "Venetians lost Naupactum and Dryrrachium," or ancient Epidamnum (135r). This borderland position also figures in his account of the truce between Venice and the Turk in 1573—after the battle of Lepanto and the assault on Cyprus that figures in *Othello*—when it was agreed that the Venetians "for Dalmatia and certeyne other peeces about Zara," along the Illyrian coast, should pay a "certaine tribute" to the "Turke" (143v).

Nicolas de Nicolay's *Nauigations, peregrinations and voyages, made into Turkie*—translated into English in 1585—similarly opens with the return voyage of the French ambassador to Constantinople from Ragusa to Venice along the Illyrian coast, and describes "Dirrachium, by the auncients called Epidamne," whose ill-omened name was changed by the Romans because "Damnum" signifed "damage" (152v), together with the lands stretching to the northern boundaries of "Illiricque" (152v).[31] He devotes several entire chapters to the subject of "Ragusa in times past called Epidauia" (or Epidaurus), the "citie in Dalmatia most rich and famous, cituated vpon the Sea Adriatique" (1), describing its combination of "broken Italian" with "Sclavonian speeche," its "daughters" kept "so close shut in, as they are not to be seen" (136), its famous merchants and letter carriers (137–38), and its payment of tribute to the Turk: "They are tributaries vnto the great Turke of twelue thousand ducats, which they are bound to send vnto him euerie yere with two Oratours to Constantinople" (136v). He further provides an extraordinary description of what he calls the "true Illyrians" from "the parties of Bossine, & Seruia" whose inhabitants are now called "Seruians or Crouats, whiche are the true Illyrians, whom Herodian in the life of Seuerus, describeth to bee men most valiaunt, of greate stature, well shapen, and bigge sette, their colour beyng yealowishe, but of nature most malitious, and of custome more then barbarous, of grosse vnderstanding, and easie to be deceiued," though they were "in great estimation with Alexander the great" (126r). And he goes on to describe an Illyrian renegade who "for his religion notwithstanding that hee dissembled to liue with the Turks according to their law, yet was he from his birth of heart & wil, a christian," who recited to him the Lord's prayer and other evidences of his "heart & wil" in "the Esclauon tongue" (126v), providing yet another instance of the position of such "true Illyrians" between Christian and Turk.

In the decades leading up to *Twelfth Night,* texts that invoke the expanding empire of Saracen and Turk repeatedly refer to the historical Illyria's strategic location. Lodowick Lloyd's *Consent of Time* (1590) ranges not only over the classical history of Illyria but over its Ottoman history, noting that Baiazet I "inuaded Bossina, Croatia, and other parts of Illyria" and that Baiazet II subdued "Dyrrhachium" or the ancient Epidamnum. Louis Leroy's *Of the interchangeable course or variety of things in the whole world* (translated into English in 1594) records sea fights between Saracens and Venetians in the "Adriatick Sea" along the Illyrian coast.[32] In reference to more current events, Gabriel Harvey in 1593 celebrates the defeat of the Turk at "the late Turkish assiege of Sysseck in Croatia, the old Liburnia famous for seruiceable Shippes,"[33] as a victory that should be heralded together with "the renowned Lepanto," since "Croatia" had been so "prest" by the Turk—adding "Christ blesse his standard-bearers with many Lepantos, and Syssecks" (A3v) and arguing that this Croatian victory over the Ottoman power should be as "brauely extolled: as Orpheus glorified Iason; Homer, Achilles; Virgill, AEneas; Ariosto, Charlemaine; Tasso, Godfry of Bollen; and so forth" (A4r).

In 1596, the English translation of the *Historie of George Castriot, surnamed Scanderbeg,* expanded from Marin Barleti—a text that has been argued as an important influence on subsequent writers as well as on Shakespeare himself—recounted not only the history of Scanderbeg at length for English readers but also the gathering of his forces at Ragusa, in a description rich with detail about this principal city on the Illyrian coast.[34] Illyria figures prominently in its account of the truce between Scanderbeg and the Turks, when "the Infidel (after he had once assured himselfe not to be troubled by the armes of the Albanois) . . . went against the Thracians and the Illirians" (436) and in the oration of the Archbishop of Durazzo, who in urging Scanderbeg to renew his war against the Ottoman forces, notes that the Turk has already dominated the "Illirians or Sclavonians" (437). At the same time, it cites the letter from Mehmet the Conqueror taunting Scanderbeg with the litany of territories already crushed: "Doest not thou see the Greekes how they are all destroyed and consumed away to nothing. . . . the Illyrians broken and wasted, and all the realmes of Asia, with many other Princes tamed and subdued?" (443).[35] Illyria continues to figure strategically in Scanderbeg's subsequent urging of his "next neighbours" to rise up against the "tyrant Mahomet" who has subdued the "Sclavonians" along with other neighboring peoples (477) and in his oration in

Rome, which includes the reminder that "Sclavonie is subdued by his forces" (479), as well as through the assembling of forces from the still-unconquered parts of "Sclavony and Dalmatia" as part of his resistance (478). The long history of struggles along the Illyrian coast is explicitly foregrounded in his description of the Turkish siege of Croy and of Durazzo or Epidamnum itself, the location of the defeat of Pompey by "Iulius Caesar" (483), in the well-known account in Lucan that prominently included the "Illyrian waters" where Caesar's forces were trapped and Caesar himself beaten back by shipwreck onto the Illyrian shore. In a narrative where the example of Caesar is held before Scanderbeg as a classical incentive to victory, Barleti even quotes from Lucan's description of the former Epidamnum or Roman Dyrrachium (487), strengthening the link between the Caesarian history and this more contemporary struggle. But the entire narrative has something ultimately tragic or elegiac about it, since after Scanderbeg's death the resistance collapsed, and Lucan's "Illyrian Epidamnum" itself was conquered by the Turk, an event that by 1596 was already long part of the history of such collapses.

No account of the potential familiarity of Illyria—including its relation to the Turk—would be complete for the period leading up to *Twelfth Night* without reference to Hakluyt, who makes multiple references to "Sclauonia" as well as the Dalmatian-Sclavonian coast in both the 1589 and the 1599–1600 editions of *Principal Navigations*. The latter includes the "little Mapp or Carde of the world" prepared by the Englishman Robert Thorne in 1527, citing the situation of "Sclauonia" south of "the citie of Venice" on the "Mare Adriaticum."[36] It informs its readers (in a journal for the year 1253) that "the Sclauonians speake all one language with the Vandals" and that "those prouinces beyond Constantinople, which are now called Bulgaria, Valachia, & Sclauonia, were of old time prouinces belonging to the Greekes."[37] It also includes another account dated 1243 that treats of the "prince of Dalmatia" as having apprehended a fugitive known to be "an English man, who was perpetually banished out of the Realme of England, in regard of certaine notorious crimes by him committed."[38] In accounts that underscore the importance of this region even in that earlier period, including in relation to England, both the 1589 and the later edition include in both Latin and English "The trauailes of a certaine English man, whom master Bale remembretch in his 2. Centurie," called Robert Ketenensis, who "florished in the yeere 1143" and "trauayled through France, Italie, Dalmatia, and Greece," studying "Astrologie" under "Hermannus a Dalmatian, who had accompanied him in his long voyage."[39] Even more prominently, the importance of the Illyrian coast is foregrounded in relation to the travels of Richard the Lion-Heart, England's absent king, who because of a tempest or "distresse of weather" on his way back from Palestine, was forced onto the shores of "Histria" (or Istria) and sold to the Em-

peror, affirming once against the association of that coast with both tempests and shipwreck.[40]

With regard to England's more recent relations with this Illyrian territory as well as the Turk, Hakluyt includes much more information. In a report on "Turkie" intended for the "great profite" of England itself, written
"for a principall English Factor at Constantinople" in 1582, Hakluyt observes that the "Souldiers continually attending vpon the Beglerbegs the
gouernours of Prouinces and Saniacks, and their petie Captaines main-
teined of these Prouinces" include "fifteene thousand" from "Sclauonia."[41]
And two prominent travel narratives from the decades leading up to *Twelfth
Night* affirm the strategic position of the Illyrian coast between Venice
and the Turk. The "Voyage of M. John Locke to Jerusalem, Anno 1553"
contains "a wealth of place names" from the Illyrian or Sclavonian coast,[42]
as it proceeds from Venice down "the coast of Istria," past "the hilles of
Dalmatia, or else of Sclauonia both at one time," and the islands belonging to Ragusa, and records (once again) a storm at sea near Ragusa itself
("we were within 7 or 8 miles of Ragusa, that we might see the white walls,
but because it was night, we cast about to the sea, minding at the second
watch, to beare in againe to Ragusa, for to know the newes of the Turkes
armie, but the winde blew so hard and contrary, that we could not"). It notes
that "This citie of Ragusa paieth tribute to the Turke . . . besides other
presents which they giue to the Turkes Bassas when they come thither" and
after describing "a rocke or cragge within a mile of the said towne" where
there is "a Monasterie called Sant Ieronimo" for St. Jerome, it comments
on its proximity to the empire of the Turk ("The maine of the Turkes countrie is bordering on it within one mile, for the which cause they are in great
subiection"). The Turk continues to dominate the narrative as the voyagers
pass Ragusa, recounting their meeting with Venetian ships en route from
Cyprus ("we were desirous to talke with them, to knowe the newes of the
Turkes armie"), their sighting of "Castel nouo" which "a fewe yeeres past
the Turke tooke from the Emperor," and the proximity in the hills of "Sclauonia" of warring towns possessed by "the Venetians" and "the Turkes." On
his return voyage from Jerusalem to Venice, Locke similarly passes in the
reverse direction, once again describing islands and other sights along this
coast.[43]

The Turk likewise figures in "The Voyage of M. Henry Austell by Venice
to Ragusa and then over-land to Constantinople . . . anno 1586," an account
by "a member of the English embassy in Constantinople" who may have
been "sent to Constantinople from London with a message for the ambassador."[44] Austell's account records his journey from Venice, passing through
"Zara in Dalmatia, a strong towne of the Venetians," "Sebenico, which
standeth in a marueilous goodly hauen, with a strong castle at the entrie
thereof," and other cities on the way to Ragusa, where he and his company

"stayed three daies," finding not only "many friendly gentlemen" but also a "Ianizarie," before traveling overland with him "from Ragusa in the company of halfe a dosen Marchants of that towne" to Constantinople, through "Sophia . . . our Ianizaries home" where they "lay in a Marchants house of Ragusa."[45]

Around the time of *Twelfth Night* itself, such travels and accounts continued. Samuel Chew reports in *The Crescent and the Rose* that Anthony Sherley "crossed the Adriatic to Ragusa" from Italy in 1601, though he was not able to "sail for the Levant or ever see Persia again," a "change of plans [that] was perhaps due to fear of the Turks,"[46] while Captain John Smith records in his autobiography that he spent time in Ragusa and Dalmatia in 1601.[47] At the same time, Carr's *Mahumetane or Turkish historie* (1600) provides a detailed description of Illyria and its strategic position between Christian and Muslim, from the ninth century when "Sarrazins" overran the "coast of Sclauonie" (7v) to the rise of the Ottoman power. It describes Baiazet I (the sultan by now famous from Marlowe's *Tamburlaine*) as spoiling "the territories of Bosna . . . Croacia and Sclauonie (that are named anciently Dalmatia and Liburnia)," Mehmet I as having "subdued the countrie of Bosnia" (31–33), and Amurath II as advancing to within "fiue and twentie maile from the towne of Ragusa (in ancient time named Epidaurus)." Echoing earlier accounts, Carr details how Mehmet the Conqueror "sent Omarbey, the Sangiac of Bosnia" to "ouerrune the countrie of Istria (called Liburnia) as likewise to spoile the territorie of Carinthia (commonly called Crayn) & so to furrow the land of Stiria (anciently called Valeria, now at this day named Stiermark) all which countries are comprehended vnder the name of Illirium" (38v); and how this "same Mahumet did send Achmath Bacha (surnamed Ghendich . . . sonne of Stephen sometime Despot of Bosnia)" to take Otranto (38v). He mentions the powerful Illyrian renegade Cherseogles in his account of the Mamalukes in Egypt who "overthrew the Turkes armie, and tooke prisoner the Generall of the same, called Cherseogli sonne in law of Bazait whom they brought to the Soldain then being at his great Citie of Cair" (40). And he repeats the oft-cited taking by Baiazet of "the town of Durazo (aunciently called Dirrachium) and Epidamnus" (41) and his sending of "eight thousand horsemen" to "ouer runne the Countries lying between Hungarie and Sclauonie" (with the defeat of the "Nobility of Hungary, Croace and Sclauony" united against him) as well as his sending of "Haly Basha" the "Eunuch" to "the towne of Iara" (or Zara) situated on the "coast of Sclauony" (41).

Illyria and another convert from the Illyrian borderlands figure prominently as well in Carr's account of the more recent tensions between Venice and the Turk after the Turkish invasion of Cyprus in 1570, recording that the "Turkish nauie on purpose to with-hould the Venetians from attempting aught for the regayning of the said Isle, entred the Gulfe of Venice, persecuting all such Cities on the coast of Dalmatia, both by sea and land, as were vnder the obedience of the sayd Venetians" (104), wreaking havoc on the Illyrian coast to distract Venice from Cyprus. In ways that simultaneously underscore the position of Ragusa between Christian and Turk, Carr further records the role of a Ragusan go-between in the negotiations prior to the Turkish conquest of Cyprus: "They likewise laboured to compounde a Peace with the Turks, for which cause they sent to Constantinople, Iacobus Ragazonus, to deale with Mahomet Bassa, whom they well hoped to haue found fauorable and better inclining thervnto, then the rest" (107)—the powerful renegade Vizier otherwise known as Sokollu, already well known in England for his central role in promoting English trade relations with the Sultan.

Such multiple references to Illyria—including Carr's own earlier-cited reminder of the Illyrian travels of Paul in his account of the Turk in the Adriatic—were not, however, restricted to texts exclusively devoted to the Turk. *Batman vppon Bartholome* (1582), in treating, among many other subjects, the "increase of the Turkish Empire, and howe by litle and litle, it hath growen to this greatnesse, wherein at this day it seemeth to threaten vs," observes that these conquests include "the most part of Sclauonia" and that Baiazet II took "Dirrahium" or Epidamnum and "spoiled all Dalmatia," the territory whose "Sea theeues" it had earlier described.[48] John Foxe refers in *A Sermon of Christ Crucified* (1570) to the growing empire of the Turk as including "Constantinople, Greece, Illyria, with almost all Hungary and much of Austria,"[49] while Illyrian territories appear repeatedly in his influential *Actes and Monuments,* which describes Ragusa (or ancient "Epidaurus") as "a citie in Illiria" now shadowed by the Turk and reminds its readers of the apostle Titus's travels by putting "2 Tim. 4" beside "Dalmatia"—in "A table of certaine Cities and countries wonne from the Christians" in his "history of the Turkes," which includes within the former "Illyria, or Illyricum" not only the regions of Croatia, Carinthia, and Istria but also cities such as Ragusa, Sebenica, Zara, Segna or Senj, and "Stridone, where S. Hierome was borne."[50] Of "Bosna" or Bosnia, Foxe notes that "Stephanus kyng of Bosna, & afterward of Rascia and Mysia, was by subtil trayne allured to come and speake with Mahumet the Turk, who being come, was taken and his skinne flayne off," subsuming the region within the larger history of the Ottoman advance.

Foxe not only inscribes Illyria within the history of the Church—including the Illyrian origin of St. Jerome—but by assigning specific New Testament passages to places now "subdued and subiect to the Turke" (761) makes clear how many of the lands visited by Titus, Paul, and other apostles have come within the Ottoman sphere, including much of Illyria itself. *Actes and Monuments* at the same time underscores the crucial position between Christian and Saracen occupied by Illyria in its earlier history, detailing Richard the Lion-Heart's involvement with Illyria or "Sclauonia" in the context of letters from England to the absent king while Richard was not only "busie in repulsing the Saladine, and prepared to lay siege against Hierusalem," but had already "got Sclauonia, with diuers other towns from the Saracens." Writing that as Richard was "preparing to lay his siege against Ierusalem, the Saladine glad to fall into some composition wt the king, sent vnto him, that if he would restore to him againe Sclauonia, in as good state as it was when he tooke it, he would graunt to him, and to all Christians in the lande of Ierusalem truce for 3. yere," Foxe adds that Richard, having learned of the attempt of "Iohn hys brother to possesse his kingdome," tooke "the truce offred of the Saracens, & so began to draw homeward" (248). Even in as early a period of English history as the struggle that led to the accession of King John—under whom a transplanted Ragusan became Bishop of Carlisle—Illyria or "Sclauonia" was thus a crucial pawn in England's own relations with the Muslim world.[51]

Foxe's influential text makes even more specific reference to the territories within "Illyria, or Illyricum" in relation to the rise of the Ottoman Turk. Under "The Prophecies of Methodius, Hildegardis and other, concerning the reyne and ruyne of the Turkes," he repeats the prophecy that the "seede of Ismaell" shall "obtein the whole world," including "Rome and Illyricum" (768). He begins his account of Baiazet I—under whom "the power of the Turkes began to encrease in Europe"—with his overthrowing of "all the nobility of the Seruians and Bulgarians" and his putting "all those partys vnder his suiection vnto the fines and borders of the Illyrians" (738). His account of Amurath II records that he "inuaded Illyricum (otherwise called Sclauonia) conteining in it Dalmatia, Croacia, Istria, and Liburnia," which along with "Bosna" were "spoyled and wasted by the turke" (740). Of Mehmet II, he registers the presence of Illyrians on the side of this Turkish conquerer at the taking of Constantinople itself, noting that "Mahometes brought an army of 400. thousand, collected out of the countryes and places adioyning nere about, as out of Grecia, Illirico" and other places that "had the name yet of Christians," commenting, "Thus one neighbour for lucre sake, helped to destoy an other" (708). He recounts Mehmet's taking of "Scodra" (744), the ancient capital of Illyria under Queen Teuta,[52] and his "passing forward towards Europe," subduing "all Illiria, slaieng Stephanus the King of Bosna, about the yeare of our Lord 1463" (744). He also makes clear that Illyria, like other borderlands, passed repeatedly between Christian and Turk, chronicling the struggle to regain such territories under "Mathias Coruinus [who] recouered againe the said kingdome of Bosna, with many other Cities neare vnto Croacia and Dalmatia" (744) as well "Sirmium, and the confines of Illyrica, from the hands of the Turks" (723). Recounting Mehmet's sending "into Dalmatia . . . two Captaines of the Turke, who fighting against the prouinces of the Venetians, made great spoyle and waste about the regions of Stiria & Carinthia," and glossing Carinthia in his Table as originally part of "Illyria, or Illyricum," he reports that a "truce was taken between the Turke & the Venetians, upon this condition," that Scodra and other territories should be "yeelded unto" the Turk and "pay to him yearely 8. thousand duckets for the free passage of their Merchants" (744).

Illyria continues to figure prominently in Foxe's account of Baiazet II, who—unsuccessful in Egypt—"directed his army into Europe, where he got Dyracchium" or Epidamnum and "had a great victory ouer the Christian armye in the countrye of Croatia, where the Illyrians, Pannonians and Croatians ioyning their power together, encountered with the Turke and lost the field, about the yeare of our Lord, 1493" (745). "About the yere of our Lord 1498," he records, as part of "diuers and doubtfull conflicts" with Venice in which "the Turke was sometimes put to the woorse, and sometimes again preuailing," Ottoman forces invaded Zara or "Iadra and diuers other cities about Dalmatia," carrying away "great multitudes of Christians into captiuitie" (745). He even describes in detail the Illyrians fighting on the side of the Turk in the siege of Vienna in 1529, in a passage that notes that Solyman I "vsed the helpe of the Illyrians, of whome he had a great number in his camp" to undermine the walls of the city. Reporting that "These Illyrians beginning to breake the earth at the gate Carinthia and coming neare to the foundations of the Tower" were "perceiuved by certayne men aboue," who filled the trenches with gunpowder, Foxe records that the Tower exploded, smothering some "8000" Illyrian and other "Turke" pioneers, whose "deade mens skuls" are still "found in the ground" at Vienna's walls (749).

Though the siege of Vienna was unsuccessful, Foxe's narrative continues to chronicle Turkish successes in Illyria itself, observing that with "Nouum Castellum in Dalmatia," ouerthrowen by the turke," the Ottoman power "had great aduauntage ouer all those quarters of Dalmatia, Stiria, Carinthia and Hungaria" (752) and including "Dalmatia, "Bosna," and other formerly Illyrian territories in his "recitall of Christen townes & forts wonne of the turke in Europe" (755). Of the Ottoman conquest of Venetian Modon, he writes that the command that the captives be "cut and deuided in sonder" (755) included one body "cut in two" that some affirmed to be "an Illyrian" (755) and describes there the in-between position of the prominent Illyrian renegade Cherseogles, observing that many thousand captives were "cruelly slaine, except certain Nobles whom Cherseugles, sonne in lawe to Baiazetes, got to be pardoned" (745).

Foxe's influential text includes Illyria in multiple other contexts—in its mention of the Lenten observances of "the Illyrians and the west churches" (56), of the papal requirement that "all Church seruice should be in Latine" but allowing the "Sclauonians" to retain their "vulgar language" (137), of the importance in the debates over John Hus of the Ragusan cleric known as "Ragusinus" (692), and of the opinions of "Illyricus" the prominent Lutheran theologian he repeatedly cites (202, 419, and elsewhere). But as the above passages suggest, "Illyria, or Illyrica" figures even in Foxe most prominently in relation to the Turk, in an account overlaid with multiple reminders of the losses in the lands familiar from the travels of Titus and Paul.

These repeated descriptions of Illyria, its cities, and its peoples in work published in England before *Twelfth Night*—together with the long history of contacts between England and the Illyrian coast, and between London and the Ragusan merchants who were by the sixteenth century its most prominent and wealthy foreign inhabitants—suggest that Illyria (both as a more ancient name and as a name still used in contemporary accounts by Carr, Knolles, and others) was much more familiar in England by the time of the play than critics or editors have realized.[53] This in no way negates the possibility that Shakespeare's "Illyria" un-realizes or renders less familiar or current the place described in so many available sixteenth-century texts, including in Foxe, Hakluyt, or in Gabriel Harvey's reference to current events in 1593. Such a defamiliarization or transformation would be consistent with the way that *Twelfth Night* occludes its sources' mercenary transactions, or transfers its location from the Constantinople of the story it inherits from Barnabe Riche.[54] But it does suggest—in a period in which Hakluyt himself could remark that he would not stop to describe Aleppo (the apparently mysterious and foreign place readers of *Othello* encounter in Othello's final speech) because it was already familiar to English readers —that it might be more unfamiliar and foreign to us than to the England of the period we study.

NOTES

1. See *The Norton Shakespeare*, ed. Stephen Greenblatt et al. (New York: W.W. Norton, 1997), 1768; and David Bevington's note on Illyria—"Nominally on the east coast of the Adriatic Sea, but with a suggestion also of 'illusion' and 'delirium'"—reprinted in Bruce R. Smith's Texts and Contexts edition of *Twelfth Night* (Boston: Bedford / St. Martin's, 2001), 30. The edition used for all references to Shakespeare here is *The Riverside Shakespeare*, ed. G. Blakemore Evans et al. (Boston: Houghton Mifflin, 1974).

2. Some of this work has already begun, including in scholarship published in English in Zagreb and Belgrade several decades ago, though it has not been largely known to critics and editors elsewhere. See, for example, *Dubrovnik's Relations with England: A Symposium, April 1976,* ed. R. Filipović and M. Partridge (Zagreb, Croatia: University of Zagreb, 1977). Though he does not cite this particular volume, Goran Stanivukovic has foregrounded some of this work in his "Illyria Revisited: Shakespeare and the Eastern Adriatic," in *Shakespeare and the Mediterranean: The Selected Proceedings of the International Shakespeare Association World Congress, Valencia, 2001,* ed. Tom Clayton, Susan Brock,

and Vicente Forés, 400–415 (Newark: University of Delaware Press, 2004). Also not widely available is the issue of *Litteraria Pragensia* devoted to "Shakespeare's Illyrias: Heterotopias, Identities, (Counter) Histories," edited by Martin Procházka, vol. 12, no. 23 (2002), which contains many interesting essays (including a version of Stanivukovic's essay), though it does not include Foxe, the Turk texts, or other texts foregrounded here. The present essay is intended as a supplement and complement to this already-initiated work.

    3. See Plautus, *Menaecmi,* trans. William Warner (London, 1595); the Loeb edition of Lucan, *The Civil War (Pharsalia),* trans. J. D. Duff (London: Heinemann, 1969) for "Illyrian Epidamnos" (Book II.624, pp. 102–3) and the repeated references to the Illyrian waters and Illyrian shore as sites in Caesar's civil war with Pompey, in Book IV.433 *(Illyricae . . . undae),* pp. 206–7, where Caesar's men are trapped in Illyrian waters (IV.402–581), and reference to this event in Book V.38–39 *(undis . . . Illyricis),* pp. 240–41, with the narrative where Caesar is also shipwrecked in the Adriatic and cast back onto the shore (V.564–699, pp. 280–91); Ben Jonson, *Euery man in his humor* (London, 1601), 2.1; Anon., *The Tragedy of Caesar's Revenge* (1607), in Malone Society Reprints (London: Oxford University Press, 1911), 3.5; *The statelie tragedie of Claudius Tiberius Nero* (London, 1607), in Malone Society Reprints (London: Oxford University Press, 1914), C3ir; Raphael Holinshed, *The First and Second Volumes of Chronicles* ([London], 1587), 72; Pietro Martire d'Anghiera, *The history of trauayle in the West and East Indies . . . done into Englysshe by Richarde Eden. Newly set in order, augmented, and finished by Richard Willes* (London, 1577), 299. On the Uskoks and De Dominis, see Catherine Wendy Bracewell, *The Uskoks of Senj* (Ithaca, NY: Cornell University Press, 1992), 189, 242–43. The Brutus and Tiberius references are provided in Edward H. Sugden, *A Topographical Dictionary to the Works of Shakespeare and his Fellow Dramatists* (Manchester, UK: Manchester University Press, 1925), 263. For Thomas Cooper, *Thesaurus Linguae Romanae et Britannicae* (London, 1578), see under "D" for "Dalmatia" in the unpaginated *Dictionarium Historicum & Poeticum* at the end of this text. Of classical texts well known to Shakespeare, Plutarch's *Lives of the Noble Grecians and Romans,* trans. Thomas North (London, 1579) cites the division between Antony and Octavius ("Octavius Caesars dominions all that was in our HEMISPHAERE, or halfe part of the world, from ILLYRIA, vnto the Occean sea vpon the west") in a passage from "The Life of Marcus Antonius" (p. 999) later echoed in *Antony and Cleopatra* (3.7.34–36), while Suetonius's *Historie of the twelve Caesars emperours of Rome,* trans. Philemon Holland (London, 1606), used by Shakespeare in Latin for *Julius Caesar* prior to *Twelfth Night,* cites Tiberius's "hard warfare in Illyricum" (p. 96), treats of "Gaule and Illyria appointed vnto Caesar" (p. 702), and Augustus Caesar in Illyria after Actium (pp. 46ff.). Norman Nathan, in "Cesario, Sebastian, Olivia, Viola and Illyria in 'Twelfth Night,'" *Names* 37, no. 3 (September 1989), cites also the fact that "Augustus was a student . . . in Illyricum" (282) but misses most of the connections between the Caesars and Illyria, though he argues that the connection to Augustus Caesar is important for the naming of "Cesario" as well as other characters in the play.

    4. Samuel Daniel, *The Poeticall Essayes* (London, 1599), 56. See Sugden, *Dictionary,* 144: "The Emperor Diocletian was born in Dalmatia, and on his resignation of the purple he retired to his native country, where he spent the last nine years of his life in retirement at Salona. There he died in A.D. 314." Diocletian's Dalmatian origin—and his retirement there—were well known before *Twelfth Night.* In addition to the reference in Daniel, Lodowick Lloyd's *The Consent of Time* (London, 1590) observes that "Dioclesianus [was] borne at Dalmatia, a Scriueners sonne, as Eutropius saith, but others affirme he was a bondman to Amulinus the Senator" (576–77), commenting that he "resigned vp the imperial state, and liued a priuat life" in "the citie of Solona" in Dalmatia. Thomas Lodge's *The Life and Death of William Long Beard* (London, 1593), in a passage entitled "Of many famous men whoe leauing the gouernement of the Commonweale gaue themselues ouer to a priuate

life," cites this same example: "Dioclesian, after he had gouerned Rome and the emperie for the space of eighteene yeares, vtterlie refusing all the Empire, departed Rome, and repaired to Salona in Dalmatia where he was borne" (H4r).

5. See Barnabe Riche, *The Aduentures of Brusanus, Prince of Hungaria* (London, 1592), Book 2, which spells Illyria as "Illeria."

6. Claude Colet, *The famous, pleasant, and variable historie, of Palladine of England . . . Translated out of French by A.M.* (London, 1588).

7. William Caxton, *The moste pleasaunt historye of Blanchardine, sonne to the King of Friz; & the faire lady Eglantine Queene of Tormaday, (surnamed) the proud ladye in loue* (London, 1595), H2r. See also Diego Ortúñez de Calahorra, *The second part of the first booke of the Myrrour of knighthood . . . Now newly translated out of Spanish into our vulgar tongue by R.P.* (London, 1599) which features princes and a princess of Dalmatia.

8. See Emanuel Ford, *Parismus, the renoumed prince of Bohemia* (London, 1598), chap. xviii, R3v.

9. On Wroth's princess of Slavonia, see Sheila T. Cavanagh, *Cherished Torment: The Emotional Geography of Lady Mary Wroth's Urania* (Pittsburgh, PA: Duquesne University Press, 2001), 36, 235.

10. For the repeated citation of Rom. 15:19 on Paul's travels to Illyricum, see, for example, the works of John Jewel: *An exposition vpon the two epistles of the apostle S. Paul to the Thessalonians* (London, 1584), 1 ("from Ierusalem, rounde about to Illyricum"); 299 ("he trauailed . . . from Ierusalem to Illyricum: from Illyricum to Rome"); *A replie vnto M. Hardinges answeare* (London, 1565), 167 ("S. Paule saith, that he him selfe had filled al places with the Gospel of Christe, euen as farre as Illyricum"); *A Viewe of a seditious bul sent into Englande, from Pius Quintus Bishop of Rome, anno. 1569* (London, 1582), 21 ("Rom. 15 from Ierusalem, and rounde aboute to Illyricum"); William Fulke, *A retentiue, to stay good Christians* (London, 1580), 73 ("Apostle Paule, who from Hierusalem to Illyricum filled all the contryes with the doctrine of the Gospell"). John Speed's *The History of Great Britaine* (London, 1611) also records that "Paul came to Illyricum, Gallia, and Spaine." In the Geneva Bible (1560), "Illyria, or Sclauonia" is not only included on the map (where it covers a broad area extending down the entire coast) but is included in the list of place names on the map as "Countreis and Places Mencioned in the Actes of the Apostles," even though Paul's mention of his travels "vnto Illyricum" is in Romans rather than Acts. See *The Bible and the Holy Scriptures conteyned in the Olde and Newe Testament* (Geneva, 1560), between pp. 69 and 70 in the New Testament. On this map and the *Peregrinationis Divi Pauli* map in the 1595 Latin edition of Abraham Ortelius, *Theatrum Orbis Terrarum,* see Sara Hanna, "From Illyria to Elysium: Geographical Fantasy in *Twelfth Night,*" *Litteraria Pragensia* 12, no. 23 (2002), 32. For the maps appearing in different editions of Ortelius from the original 1570 Latin edition forward, see Marcel P. R. Van den Broecke, *Ortelius Atlas Maps: An Illustrated Guide* (Utrecht: HES Publishers, 1996).

11. See, for example, Rudolf Gwalther, *An hundred, threescore and fiftene homelyes or sermons, vppon the Actes of the Apostles, written by Saint Luke* (London, 1572), 403.

12. Thomas Hall, *A Practical and Polemical commentary, or, Exposition upon the Third and Fourth Chapters of the Latter Epistle of Saint Paul to Timothy* (London, 1658), 411, comments of Titus's travels that "Dalmatia was a Region of Illyricum, where Paul is said to spread the Gospel, Romans 15.19." William Patten's *Calender of Scripture* (London, 1575), 56v, also combines the two by referring to "Illyrici" in the midst of a reference to Titus's travels from 2 Tim. 4.

13. Ralph Carr, *The Mahumetane or Turkish Historie* (London, 1600), 58v.

14. Jewel, *A replie,* 158; Robert Parsons, *The Warn-word to Sir Francis Hastinges Wast-Word* (Antwerp, 1602), 91.

15. See Edward Topsell, *The historie of foure-footed beastes* (London, 1607), Index; and *The historie of serpents, Or, The second booke of liuing creatures* (London, 1608), 203.

16. I am quoting here from the English translation of Abraham Ortelius, *The Theatre of the Whole World* (London, 1606), 92.

17. Richard Knolles, *The Generall Historie of the Turkes* (London, 1603), 563.

18. Martire d'Anghiera, *History of Trauayle,* 298. In Veselin Kostić, *Cultural Relations between Yugoslavia and England before 1700* (Belgrade, 1972), 502. Kostić writes: "The first book in English in which a few Serbo-Croat words are quoted is R. Eden's *Decades of the New World*" and "Among the papers of the English Embassy at Constantinople which are preserved in the Public Record Office there is a 'Sclavonian'-English vocabulary. This word list dates from 1595 or 1596 but it is not known who compiled it."

19. See Paulo Giovio, *A Shorte Treatise vpon the Turkes chronicles* (London, 1546), fol. cxxxiii; Andrea Cambini, *Two very notable commentaries the one of the originall of the Turcks and Empire of the house of Ottomanno, written by Andrewe Cambine, and thother of the warres of the Turcke against George Scanderbeg, prince of Epiro,* trans. John Shute (London, 1562), 3v; Bartolomej Georgijević, *The ofspring of the house of Ottomanno and officers pertaining to the greate Turkes court . . . Englished by Hugh Goughe* (London, 1569), Jii–Jiiii.

20. See *Twelfth Night,* ed. Bruce R. Smith, 126–28.

21. Christopher Marlowe, *Tamburlaine the Great,* ed. J. W. Harper (London: Ernest Benn, 1971; repr., London: A & C Black, 1992), *The Second Part* 3.1.1–6 (p. 122). Part 2 also includes Sclavonians in Sigismond's forces.

22. For the quotations concerning Sokollu's origin, see Daniel Goffman, *The Ottoman Empire and Early Modern Europe* (Cambridge: Cambridge University Press, 2002), 55; and Fernand Braudel, *The Mediterranean and the Mediterranean World in the Age of Philip II,* trans. Sian Reynolds (New York: Harper & Row, 1973), 2:690, together with the more general description of the taking of tribute children in Goffman, 67, and Braudel, 2:681, 779, 685. For Sokollu's central role in promoting English trade relations and acting as a go-between for Elizabeth and the Sultan, see also S. A. Skilliter, *William Harborne and the Trade with Turkey 1578–1582: A Documentary Study of the First Anglo-Ottoman Relations* (London: Oxford University Press, 1977), 78–80. Skilliter, 67, also quotes contemporary reference to Sokollu's "ironic comment on the proposed match" between Elizabeth and Alençon.

23. This map appears in all Latin editions of *Theatrum Orbis Terrarum* from 1570 to 1601. See Hanna, "From Illyria to Elysium," 45. For English translations of Ortelius on Ragusa's tribute to the Turk, see Ortelius, *Theatre of the Whole World,* fol. 92r, which includes this map between folios 110 and 111; and *An Epitome of Ortelivs His Theatre of the World* (London, 1601), fol. 89v.

24. *This is the begynnynge, and contynuaunce of the pylgrymage of Sir Richarde Guylforde Knyght [and] controuler vnto our late soueraygne lorde kynge Henry the. vij. And howe he went with his seruauntz and company towardes Iherusalem* (London, 1511). The reference to "reliques" in *Twelfth Night* (3.3.19) is one of the details used by Josip Torbarina, in "The Setting of Shakespeare's Plays (with special reference to Illyria in *Twelfth Night*)," in *Studia Romanica et Anglica Zagrabiensia* 17–18 (July–December 1964), pp. 35–36, to argue for Ragusa, Illyria's principal city, as its setting. Both of these are also cited in Stanivukovic, "Illyria Revisited," 404, 414 n. 27.

25. Thomas Becon, *The new pollecye of warre wherin is declared not only how [ye] mooste cruell tyraunt the great Turke may be ouercome but also all other enemies of the Christen publique weale, lately deuised by Theodore Basille* (London, 1542), sig. Ciiiir.

26. Antoine Geuffroy, *The Order of the greate Turckes courte . . . and of all hys conquestes,* trans. Richard Grafton (London, 1542), fol. lxxxi; Cv.

27. See Knolles, *Generall Historie of the Turkes,* 197; Thomas de Fougasses, *The generall historie of the magnificent state of Venice . . . Englished by W. Shute* (London, 1612), 416; Pierre d'Avity, *The estates, empires, & principallities of the world,* trans. Edward Grimestone (London, 1615), 1007.

28. This Illyrian renegade is mentioned multiple times in Giovio's text, at fol. xxxviii, as well as later in relation to the crucial role played by "Cherseolus Bassa Bayazet his owne sonne in law" (fol. lvii). For *Selimus*, attributed to Robert Greene, see *Three Turk Plays from Early Modern England*, ed. Daniel J. Vitkus (New York: Columbia University Press, 2000), 16–23, 61–148.

29. Thomas Lanquet, *Epitome of chronicles conteyninge the whole discourse of the histories as well as of this realme of England, as al other countries* (1559), 247.

30. Augustine Curio, *A notable historie of the Saracens*, trans. Thomas Newton (London, 1575), 122r, 79r, 80r.

31. *The nauigations, peregrinations and voyages, made into Turkie by Nicholas Nicholay Daulphinois*, trans. T. Washington the younger (London, 1585), 1.

32. See Lloyd, *The consent of time*, 308; Louis Leroy, *Of the interchangeable course, or variety of things in the whole world . . . translated into English by R.A.* (London, 1594), 99.

33. Gabriel Harvey, *A nevv letter of notable contents With a straunge sonet, intituled Gorgon, or the wonderfull yeare* (London, 1593), A2.

34. See Jaques de Lavardin, *The historie of George Castriot, surnamed Scanderbeg, King of Albanie*, trans. Z[achery] I[ones] (London, 1596), 407–8, the English translation of Lavardin's French translation and expansion of the Latin text of Barleti (or Barlezio). For Shakespeare in relation to Scanderbeg and this text, see Richard Hillman, "'Not an Amurath an Amurath Succeeds': Playing Doubles in Shakespeare's Henriad," *English Literary Rennaissance* 21, no. 2 (Spring 1991): 161–89.

35. Parts of Barleti's text had already been made available in English in Thomas Norton's *Orations* (1560), which cites the Turk's conquest of "Sclavonia" (Giii) and includes the oration of the Archbishop of Durazzo, who asks, "Where are the kynges of Sclauonie" (Hiiii) and refers to the Turk's besieging of Scodra, among other references to the former Illyrian territories. For these *Orations*, see Hillman, "Playing Doubles," 166 n. 8. I am grateful to Elizabeth Pentland for this reference.

36. Richard Hakluyt, *The principal nauigations, voyages, traffiques and discoueries of the English nation* (London, 1599–1600), 1:215–16.

37. Ibid., 1:112.

38. Ibid., 1:20.

39. See Richard Hakluyt, *The principall nauigations, voiages and discoueries of the English nation* (London, 1589), 6.

40. Ibid., 12.

41. Hakluyt, *Principal nauigations* (1599–1600), 2:293.

42. I am quoting here from p. 67 of Rudolf Filipović, "Dubrovnik in Early English Travel Literature," in *Dubrovnik's Relations with England*. Filipović cites Ketenensis and Richard I as well as the later voyages of Locke and Austell, though he does not focus on the references to the Turk in the later narratives.

43. All of the above is cited from Hakluyt, *Principal nauigations* (1599–1600), 2:101–2, 111.

44. Filipović, "Dubrovnik," 68.

45. Hakluyt, *Principal nauigations* (1599–1600), 2:195–96.

46. Samuel C. Chew, *The Crescent and the Rose: Islam and England during the Renaissance* (New York: Oxford University Press, 1937), 279.

47. See John Smith, *The True Travels, Adventures, and Observations of Captaine Iohn Smith, in Europe, Asia, Affrica, and America, from anno Domini 1593. to 1629* (London, 1630), 6.

48. See Bartholomaeus Anglicus, *Batman vppon Bartholome his booke De proprietatibus rerum, newly corrected, enlarged and amended* (London, 1582), 252r, 222v.

49. See Chew, *Crescent and the Rose*, 132, citing John Foxe, *A Sermon of Christ Crucified* (London, 1570).

50. John Foxe, *Actes and Monuments* ([London], 1583), 762. All subsequent parenthetical references to Foxe are to this text.

51. On the Archbishop of Ragusa (Dubrovnik) who left for England at the end of the twelfth century, and "probably became the Bishop of Carlisle some time after 1203," see Kostić, *Cultural Relations,* 494; with Josip Lucić, "The Earliest Contacts Between Dubrovnik and England," in *Dubrovnik's Relations with England,* ed. Filipović and Partridge, 21–23. There is also a tradition in Dubrovnik (which Lucić discusses) that Richard the Lion-Heart, en route back from the Crusades, encountered a storm and landed on Lokrum Island opposite Ragusa, whose cathedral he endowed; but it has not been proven. See Francis W. Carter, *Dubrovnik (Ragusa) A Classic City-state* (London: Seminar Press, 1972), 458; and Robin A. Harris, *Dubrovnik: A History* (London: SAQI, 2003), 221–22.

52. On the Illyrian Queen Teuta, as a frequently cited figure of female rule in early modern England, see Elizabeth Pentland, "Beyond the 'Lyric' in Illyricum: Some Early Modern Backgrounds to *Twelfth Night,*" forthcoming in *Twelfth Night: New Critical Essays,* ed. James Schiffer (New York: Routledge, 2007).

53. Veselin Kostić has published studies on Ragusans in London, some available in English, including "The Ragusan Colony in London in Shakespeare's Day," in *Dubrovnik's Relations with England,* ed. Filipović and Partridge, where he discusses Ragusan merchants living in London in the sixteenth century. Included are Nikola Naljesković (or Niccolo de Nale) whose family "was engaged in Anglo-Ragusan trade for generations" and who himself "managed the English branch of the family firm" (261) in a network involving London, Ragusa, and Venice, became an English denizen under Queen Mary (262), and knew Thomas Gresham and others; his brother Augustin, who was among the "wealthiest foreigners in London" (264), and who was sued for debt by one of Elizabeth's courtiers (in a case in which the Privy Council became involved); and Nikola Gucetić (also known as Niccolo de Gozzi), member of "a rich patrician family of Ragusa" whose father had become, from 1516, "one of the largest importers of English cloths in Ragusa" (265), who after joining other Ragusan merchants in London established "a commercial network which covered almost the whole of Europe" (265), became "the richest alien in England in the last quarter of the sixteenth century" (267), and at his death left a huge inheritance that became the subject of an action "instituted in the Court of the Exchequer" (268) and an internationally famous lawsuit in England. Goran Stanivukovic has subsequently described this suit in "Illyria Revisited," 408–9. See also Kostić's *Ragusa and England 1300–1650* (Belgrade: Serbian Academy of Sciences and Arts, 1975), which chronicles long-standing trade and other contacts; and G. D. Ramsay, "The City of London and the Republic of St. Blaise in the Later Sixteenth Century," in *Dubrovnik's Relations with England,* ed. Filipović and Partridge, 31–42. I am grateful to Ivan Lupić for providing these and other difficult-to-obtain materials.

54. See Valerie Forman, "Material Dispossessions and Counterfeit Investments: The Economies of *Twelfth Night,*" in *Money and the Age of Shakespeare: Essays in New Economic Criticism,* ed. Linda Woodbridge (New York: Palgrave Macmillan, 2003), 113–27; and Constance Relihan, "Erasing the East from *Twelfth Night,*" in *Race, Ethnicity, and Power in the Renaissance,* ed. Joyce Green MacDonald (Madison, NJ: Fairleigh Dickinson University Press, 1997), 80–94 (with whose more general argument I would, however, take issue given the clear relationship of Illyria with the East, and Turk, as well as its logic as a location because of the Illyrian location of Paul's shipwreck and Plautus's plot of twins).

BIBLIOGRAPHY

Avity, Pierre d'. *The estates, empires, & principallities of the world.* Translated by Edward Grimestone. London, 1615.

Bartholomaeus Anglicus. *Batman vppon Bartholome his booke De proprietatibus rerum, newly corrected, enlarged and amended.* London, 1582.

Becon, Thomas. *The new pollecye of warre wherin is declared not only how [ye] mooste cruell tyraunt the great Turke may be ouercome but also all other enemies of the Christen publique weale, lately deuised by Theodore Basille.* London, 1542.

The Bible and the Holy Scriptures conteyned in the Olde and Newe Testament. Geneva, 1560.

Bracewell, Catherine Wendy. *The Uskoks of Senj.* Ithaca, NY: Cornell University Press, 1992.

Braudel, Fernand. *The Mediterranean and the Mediterranean World in the Age of Philip II.* Translated by Sian Reynolds. 2 vols. New York: Harper & Row, 1973.

Broecke, Marcel P. R. Van den. *Ortelius Atlas Maps: An Illustrated Guide.* Utrecht: HES Publishers, 1996.

Calahorra, Diego Ortúñez de. *The second part of the first booke of the Myrrour of knighthood . . . Now newly translated out of Spanish into our vulgar tongue by R.P.* London, 1599.

Cambini, Andrea. *Two very notable commentaries the one of the originall of the Turcks and Empire of the house of Ottomanno, written by Andrewe Cambine, and thother of the warres of the Turcke against George Scanderbeg, prince of Epiro.* Translated by John Shute. London, 1562.

Carr, Ralph. *The Mahumetane or Turkish Historie.* London, 1600.

Carter, Francis W. *Dubrovnik (Ragusa) A Classic City-state.* London: Seminar Press, 1972.

Cavanagh, Sheila T. *Cherished Torment: The Emotional Geography of Lady Mary Wroth's Urania.* Pittsburgh, PA: Duquesne University Press, 2001.

Caxton, William. *The moste pleasaunt historye of Blanchardine, sonne to the King of Friz; & the faire lady Eglantine Queene of Tormaday, (surnamed) the proud ladye in loue.* London, 1595.

Chew, Samuel C. *The Crescent and the Rose: Islam and England during the Renaissance.* New York: Oxford University Press, 1937.

Colet, Claude. *The famous, pleasant, and variable historie, of Palladine of England . . . Translated out of French by A.M.* London, 1588.

Cooper, Thomas. *Thesaurus Linguae Romanae et Britannicae.* London, 1578.

Curio, Augustine. *A notable historie of the Saracens.* Translated by Thomas Newton. London, 1575.

Daniel, Samuel. *The Poeticall Essayes.* London, 1599.

Filipović, Rudolf. "Dubrovnik in Early English Travel Literature." In *Dubrovnik's Relations with England: A Symposium, April 1976,* Edited by R. Filipović and M. Partridge, 63–78. Zagreb, Croatia: University of Zagreb, 1977.

Filipović, Rudolf, and M. Partridge, eds. *Dubrovnik's Relations with England: A Symposium, April 1976.* Zagreb, Croatia: University of Zagreb, 1977.

Ford, Emanuel. *Parismus, the renoumed prince of Bohemia.* London, 1598.

Forman, Valerie. "Material Dispossessions and Counterfeit Investments: The Economies of *Twelfth Night.*" In *Money and the Age of Shakespeare: Essays in New Economic Criticism,* edited by Linda Woodbridge, 113–27. New York: Palgrave Macmillan, 2003.

Fougasses, Thomas de. *The generall historie of the magnificent state of Venice . . . Englished by W. Shute.* London, 1612.

Foxe, John. *Actes and Monuments.* [London], 1583.

———. *A Sermon of Christ Crucified.* London, 1570.

Fulke, William. *A retentiue, to stay good Christians.* London, 1580.

Georgijević, Bartolomej. *The ofspring of the house of Ottomanno and officers pertaining to the greate Turkes court . . . Englished by Hugh Goughe.* London, 1569.

Geuffroy, Antoine. *The Order of the great Turckes courte . . . and of all hys conquestes.* Translated by Richard Grafton. London, 1542.

Giovio, Paulo. *A Shorte Treatise vpon the Turkes chronicles.* London, 1546.

Goffman, Daniel. *The Ottoman Empire and Early Modern Europe.* Cambridge: Cambridge University Press, 2002.

Guylforde, Sir Richard. *This is the begynnynge, and contynuaunce of the pylgrymage of Sir Richarde Guylforde Knyght [and] controuler vnto our late soueraygne lorde kynge Henry the. vij. And howe he went with his seruauntz and company towardes Iherusalem.* London, 1511.

Gwalther, Rudolf. *An hundred, threescore and fiftene homelyes or sermons, vppon the Actes of the Apostles, written by Saint Luke.* London, 1572.

Hakluyt, Richard. *The principall nauigations, voiages and discoueries of the English nation.* London, 1589.

———. *The principal nauigations, voyages, traffiques and discoueries of the English nation.* London, 1599–1600.

Hall, Thomas. *A Practical and Polemical commentary, or, Exposition upon the Third and Fourth Chapters of the Latter Epistle of Saint Paul to Timothy.* London, 1658.

Hanna, Sara. "From Illyria to Elysium: Geographical Fantasy in *Twelfth Night.*" *Litteraria Pragensia* 12, no. 23 (2002): 21–45.

Harris, Robin A. *Dubrovnik: A History.* London: SAQI, 2003.

Harvey, Gabriel. *A nevv letter of notable contents With a straunge sonet, intituled Gorgon, or the wonderfull yeare.* London, 1593.

Hillman, Richard. "'Not an Amurath an Amurath Succeeds': Playing Doubles in Shakespeare's Henriad." *English Literary Renaissance* 21, no. 2 (Spring 1991): 161–89.

Holinshed, Raphael. *The First and Second Volumes of Chronicles.* [London], 1587.

Jewel, John. *An exposition vpon the two epistles of the apostle S. Paul to the Thessalonians.* London, 1584.

———. *A replie vnto M. Hardinges answeare.* London, 1565.

———. *A Viewe of a seditious bul sent into Englande, from Pius Quintus Bishop of Rome, anno. 1569.* London, 1582.

Jonson, Ben. *Every man in his Humor.* London, 1601.

Knolles, Richard. *The Generall Historie of the Turkes.* London, 1603.

Kostić, Veselin. *Cultural Relations between Yugoslavia and England before 1700.* Belgrade: Serbian Academy of Sciences and Arts Monographs, 1972.

———. *Ragusa and England 1300–1650.* Belgrade: Serbian Academy of Sciences and Arts, 1975.

———. "The Ragusan Colony in London in Shakespeare's Day." In *Dubrovnik's Relations with England: A Symposium, April 1976,* edited by R. Filipović and M. Partridge, 261–73. Zagreb, Croatia: University of Zagreb, 1977.

Lanquet, Thomas. *Epitome of chronicles conteyninge the whole discourse of the histories as well as of this realme of England, as al other countries.* London, 1559.

Lavardin, Jaques de. *The historie of George Castriot, surnamed Scanderbeg, King of Albanie, trans. Z[achery] I[ones].* London, 1596.

Leroy, Louis. *Of the interchangeable course, or variety of things in the whole world . . . translated into English by R.A.* London, 1594.

Lloyd, Lodowick. *The Consent of Time.* London, 1590.

Lodge, Thomas. *The Life and Death of William Long Beard.* London, 1593.

Lucan. *The Civil War (Pharsalia).* Translated by J. D. Duff. London: Heinemann, 1969.

Lucić, Josip. "The Earliest Contacts Between Dubrovnik and England." In *Dubrovnik's Relations with England: A Symposium, April 1976,* edited by R. Filipović and M. Partridge, Zagreb, Croatia: University of Zagreb, 1977.

Marlowe, Christopher. *Tamburlaine the Great.* Edited by J. W. Harper. London: Ernest Benn, 1971. Reprint, London: A & C Black, 1992.

Martire d'Anghiera, Pietro. *The history of trauayle in the West and East Indies . . . done into Englysshe by Richarde Eden. Newly set in order, augmented, and finished by Richard Willes.* London, 1577.

Nathan, Norman. "Cesario, Sebastian, Olivia, Viola and Illyria in 'Twelfth Night.'" *Names* 37, no. 3 (September 1989), 281–84.

Nicolay, Nicolas de. *The nauigations, peregrinations and voyages, made into Turkie by Nicholas Nicholay Daulphinois.* Translated by T. Washington the younger. London, 1585.

Norton, Thomas. *Orations of Arsanes agaynst Philip the trecherous kyng of Macedone.* London, [1560?].

Ortelius, Abraham. *An Epitome of Ortelivs His Theatre of the World.* London, 1601.

———. *The Theatre of the Whole World.* London 1606.

Parsons, Robert. *The Warn-word to Sir Francis Hastinges Wast-Word.* Antwerp, 1602.

Patten, William. *Calender of Scripture.* London, 1575.

Pentland, Elizabeth. "Beyond the 'Lyric' in Illyricum: Some Early Modern Backgrounds to *Twelfth Night.*" In *Twelfth Night: New Critical Essays,* edited by James Schiffer, New York: Routledge, 2007.

Plautus. *Menaecmi.* Translated by William Warner. London, 1595.

Plutarch. *Lives of the Noble Grecians and Romans.* Translated by Thomas North. London, 1579.

Procházka, Martin, ed. "Shakespeare's Illyrias: Heterotopias, Identities, (Counter) Histories." Special issue, *Litteraria Pragensia* 12, no. 23 (2002).

Ramsay, G. D. "The City of London and the Republic of St. Blaise in the Later Sixteenth Century." In *Dubrovnik's Relations with England: A Symposium, April 1976,* edited by R. Filipović and M. Partridge, 31–45. Zagreb, Croatia: University of Zagreb, 1977.

Relihan, Constance. "Erasing the East from *Twelfth Night.*" in *Race, Ethnicity, and Power in the Renaissance,* edited by Joyce Green MacDonald, 80–94. Madison, NJ: Fairleigh Dickinson University Press, 1997.

Riche, Barnabe. *The Aduentures of Brusanus, Prince of Hungaria.* London, 1592.

Shakespeare, William. *The Norton Shakespeare.* Edited by Stephen Greenblatt et al. New York: W. W. Norton, 1997.

———. *The Riverside Shakespeare.* Edited by G. Blakemore Evans et al. Boston: Houghton Mifflin, 1974.

———. *Twelfth Night.* Edited by Bruce R. Smith. Boston: Bedford / St. Martin's, 2001.

Skilliter, S. A. *William Harborne and the Trade with Turkey 1578–1582: A Documentary Study of the First Anglo-Ottoman Relations.* London: Oxford University Press, 1977.

Smith, John. *The True Travels, Adventures, and Observations of Captaine Iohn Smith, in Europe, Asia, Affrica, and America, from anno Domini 1593. to 1629.* London, 1630.

Speed, John. *The History of Great Britaine.* London, 1611.

Stanivukovic, Goran. "Illyria Revisited: Shakespeare and the Eastern Adriatic." In *Shakespeare and the Mediterranean: The Selected Proceedings of the International Shakespeare Association World Congress, Valencia, 2001,* Edited by Tom Clayton, Susan Brock, and Vicente Forés, 400–415. Newark: University of Delaware Press, 2004.

The statelie tragedie of Claudius Tiberius Nero [London, 1607]. Malone Society Reprint. London: Oxford University Press, 1914.

Suetonius. *Historie of the twelve Caesars emperours of Rome.* Translated by Philemon Holland. London, 1606.

Sugden, Edward H. *A Topographical Dictionary to the Works of Shakespeare and his Fellow Dramatists.* Manchester, UK: Manchester University Press, 1925.

Topsell, Edward. *The historie of foure-footed beastes.* London, 1607.

———. *The historie of serpents, Or, The second booke of liuing creatures.* London, 1608.

Torbarina, Josip. "The Setting of Shakespeare's Plays (with special reference to Illyria in *Twelfth Night*)." *Studia Romanica et Anglica Zagrabiensia* 17–18 (July–December 1964), 21–59.

The Tragedy of Caesar's Revenge [1607]. Malone Society Reprint. London: Oxford University Press, 1911.

Vitkus, Daniel J., ed. *Three Turk Plays from Early Modern England.* New York: Columbia University Press, 2000.

"We are yet strangers in our own country": Foreign and Mysterious Elements in the Elizabethan Settlement of Religion

Stephen Buick

IN 1559, JOHN JEWEL RETURNED TO ENGLAND. HE HAD FLED TO THE CON-tinent to escape persecution during the reign of Mary Tudor, but with the accession of Elizabeth I, Protestants were free to return home. Like many returning exiles, however, Jewel discovered that home was quite different from how he had left it. In a letter to his Continental host, he expressed his sense of alienation, "for we are all of us hitherto as strangers at home."[1] To Jewel and his colleagues, the Marian recatholicization of England had transformed the nation into a foreign and mysterious place. He bemoans that it is "hardly credible what a harvest, or rather what a wilderness of superstition had sprung up in the darkness of the Marian times." Harvest or wilderness? It's all a matter of perception. Because the English reformations were like an intergenerational pendulum swinging backwards and forwards between the familiar and the untried, each reformation precipitated innumerable changes to the religion and politics of the nation. Succeeding regimes sent many exiles of conscience abroad, both traditionalist and reformed; subsequently, some of them were welcomed back, but like John Jewel, many suffered a profound sense of alienation once they were back at "home." For religious leaders, the personal struggle was subsumed within the plight of directing the nation's future religious policy.

In what ways did concepts of the "mysterious" and the "foreign" affect the course of the reformations? When we consider representations of foreignness in early modern England, we typically think of English encounters with the *other* in mercantile exchanges in exotic locales, or in colonizing ventures in worlds new to European adventurers; we typically overlook the fact that the process of England's sixteenth-century religious reformations involved innumerable encounters with the foreign and the mysterious, often in unusual and compelling ways. I would like to focus on one precise moment of the English reformations, the Elizabethan Settlement, and consider ways in which the process of exile and alienation affected the religious leaders who were responsible for implementing the Settlement at the local level. Their encounter with the "mysterious" and the "foreign" during their Continental exile contributed to their zeal to create a nation where "pure religion" free of "superstition" would flourish, but their transformation of England's religious life, in turn, created a mysterious and foreign church for the majority of Elizabethan subjects.

EXILE, RETURN, AND ALIENATION

The English reformations sent many exiles of conscience abroad, both traditionalist and reformed; as legislation changed, individuals, whose consciences could not accept the changes or whose opinions would have made them targets for persecution, often sought refuge on the Continent. When times changed and proved to be more favorable, they usually returned home. With the accession of Mary, however, we see a noticeable difference. Instead of a trickle of malcontents leaving England, there was a mass exodus. In his *Acts and Monuments,* John Foxe said that eight hundred Protestants left England for refuge in Protestant cities on the Continent, like Geneva, Basle, and Strasbourg.[2] An unusual feature of the exodus was the collaboration of the Marian authorities who recognized that the nation's return to Roman Catholicism would be accomplished much more smoothly without the presence of Protestant agitators. It appears that Stephen Gardiner collaborated with William Cecil in permitting the hundreds of refugees to leave England. English merchants who remained at home heavily banked the operation.[3] Nearly every county and social class in England had representatives among the exiles: 166 of the exiles were gentry, including the Duchess of Suffolk whose retinue of eight included a joiner, a brewer, a "Greek rider of horses," and a fool; 67 were clergymen and 119 were theological students. Some of these young men must have been earmarked as potential future leaders should a Protestant regime return to England. Sir Nicholas Throckmorton, for instance, gave John Jewel the money to pay for his trip to the Continent.

Once settled on the Continent, troubles ensued. For many, there was a language barrier as English was unknown on the Continent. Edmund Grindal, the future Archbishop of Canterbury, was one of the few exiles who seriously applied himself to learning German. The academics fared better, of course, with Latin. Barriers of social class also proved problematic as living conditions were crowded, and gentleman, merchant, and artisan often shared a roof since as many as five families might live in the same house. Local guilds prevented merchants and artisans from pursuing their normal employment, while the gentlemanly class had no estates on the Continent to occupy them. Many of the exiles labored at menial tasks; for example, many educated men, including John Foxe, were involved in the printing trade, typically as proofreaders. Although living in reduced circumstances, the exiles were also afforded the unusual opportunity of learning from the esteemed leaders of Continental Protestantism, especially John Calvin, Peter Martyr, and Heinrich Bullinger. The peculiar brand of xenophobic English Protestantism nurtured in the Henrician and Edwardine eras was bound to be challenged and altered by interaction with the Continental leaders. At Frankfort, the exiles moved toward ecclesiastical democracy so that artisans and servants discovered their worth as individuals when voting on controversial matters in the congregation. Unsurprisingly, within two years the Frankfort church declared itself a self-governing body politic with the congregation as the source of law. With no bishop and no king, the air of exile could be heady indeed; it would be another ninety years before Englishmen of these social classes would be offered a say in such matters again.

As time passed, many of the exiles became impoverished, and the Marian authorities were less sanguine about their absence, and attempted to disturb the exiles by depriving them of their income from their property in England. In December 1555, the Crown introduced a bill in Parliament which would have required the exiles to immediately return to England or face having their property confiscated. Significantly, the bill was defeated.[4] Aside from homesickness, and a sense of idling in wait for better times, the exiles were the recipients of disturbing news from home once the Marian regime revived the old heresy laws in December 1554, and began a crackdown on Protestantism. In the next forty-six months, the Marian regime burned more than 280 people for heresy.[5] For those in exile, they learned of the martyrdoms through letters, and remember that the victims were not statistics to them as they are to us, but oftentimes relations, friends, and beloved pastors and teachers. We can imagine the emotional response of the exiles as punishment or death for heresy was precisely what had motived their mass exodus in the first place. John Foxe was still in exile when he began collecting and writing the narratives of the martyrdoms, which would eventually become the mammoth and influential *Acts and Monuments.*

On December 19, 1558, reliable confirmation of the news of Mary's death was received at Strasbourg. The exile may have been of only five years' duration, but for many of them, it must have been long enough. The very next day, Sir Anthony Cooke with a large party left for England.[6] A music hall song, popular at the time American troops were returning home from Europe after fighting in the Great War, asks, "How 'ya gonna keep 'em down on the farm (after they've seen Paree)?"[7] The Marian exiles present us with a similar challenge. After five years of living amongst "the best reformed churches," how would these spiritual refugees react to the Elizabethan Settlement? The exiles found themselves returning to a mysterious

and strange place: the England fashioned by Mary Tudor. Like many returning exiles, John Jewel discovered that home was quite different from
how he had left it. Indeed, Jewel's culture shock was such that he claimed
to feel homesick for his place of exile. He wrote, "O Zurich! Zurich! How
much oftener do I now think of thee than ever I thought of England when
I was at Zurich!" and then the complaint that "we are yet strangers in our
own country."[8] In addition to the dislocation typical of estrangement from
one's native habitation, there were the additional problems of finances, and
the exiles' fear that they were being sidelined from important decisions being made by the Elizabethan regime. John Strype tells us that the returned
exiles "were much discouraged, having little notice or regard taken of them,
nor any orders given for the restoration of them to their former preferments
and benefices."[9] Many of the exiles expected an instantaneous restoration
of Protestantism, whereas Elizabeth I was determined to do things by the
book, and awaited her first Parliament to legislate a new religious settlement. Jewel found that the news he had heard of England while traveling
back was "far more pleasant in the hearing, than I afterwards found it to be
in reality on my return home" for the Protestant transformation of England
that he had anticipated had yet to occur.[10] John Jewel could tell Peter Martyr that "*we*"—meaning the exiles—"are not consulted," and Edwin Sandys
summed up the exiles' difficulties in a letter he wrote at the end of April:
"They [meaning the Elizabethan regime] never ask us in what state we
stand, neither consider that we want; and yet in the time of our exile were
we not so bare as we are now brought."[11] John Jewel had to lodge for three
months with Nicholas Culverwell of St. Martin Vintry, a member of the
Haberdashers' Company. When Jewel subsequently accepted the bishopric
of Salisbury, he had to borrow £307, the entire amount required to discharge the initial installment of first fruits, from Culverwell's friend, "Mr
Heton." John Foxe wrote more than one letter seeking money from the
Duke of Norfolk whom he had tutored years before.[12] If the exiles had
rushed home to restore a Protestant state and church, they found that instead of being at the center of the changes, they were in a state of suspension
on the sidelines. There were some token gestures of the regime's public
affirmation of the exiles, such as the sermon at Westminster Abbey that preceded the convening of Parliament. The preacher, Richard Cox, had just
returned from exile in Frankfort, and the suppression of idolatry was one of
the issues he pursued in his sermon which lasted for one and a half hours.[13]
In most cases, however, the exiles' expectations were obviously thwarted.
Sir Anthony Cooke thought that he would be made Lord Chancellor, and
although two of his sons-in-law, Sir William Cecil and Sir Nicholas Bacon,
were the principal advisors to the new queen, Cook was overlooked for the
position. It was a time of uneasy waiting until the parliamentary session

would complete the legislative reformation. Edwin Sandys wrote, "The parliament is like to end shortly, and then we shall understand how they mind to use us."[14]

The Religious Settlement and the
Reordering of the Nation's Parishes

By the end of April Parliament had enacted the legislation for the Settlement of Religion in its approval of the Acts of Supremacy and Uniformity. The Elizabethan Settlement has often been called the "via media," the "middle way," meaning a compromise midway between Rome on the one hand, and Geneva on the other; a comprehensive Settlement creating a church that is simultaneously Catholic and Reformed. It was just the sort of Settlement that Continental Reformers would disapprove of; Rudolph Gualter of Zurich had even written to the new queen warning her against the introduction of "a form of religion which is an unhappy compound of popery and the gospel, and from which there may at length be an easy passage to the ancient superstition."[15] Protestants who survived the Marian years in England had only done so because they discreetly compromised; this was true of the queen herself, and her principal advisors, Cecil and Bacon. It was also true of the first men they appointed to senior positions in the church: Matthew Parker, who became Archbishop of Canterbury, and George Carew who became Dean of the Chapel Royal. The moral dilemma of what those of the reformed faith should do in a recatholicized England had troubled many at home during Mary's reign, as well as the exiles in their Continental havens. Andrew Pettegree notes that the issue obsessed the exiles, particularly in their writings, where "perhaps as many as two-thirds of the original tracts addressed themselves to a more faithful witness and defending their own conduct in going abroad."[16] Fair-weather friends to the reformed cause were known as "Nicodemites," after Nicodemus, the Pharisee who discreetly visited Jesus by night in order to dissemble his interest in Jesus's teachings. Conformity to Roman Catholic worship during the Marian years was apostasy to the exiles, and it was undoubtedly difficult for them, as they had taken such a strong stand against conformity, to now join forces with the Nicodemites in establishing the Elizabethan church. Dissimilar experiences during the Marian years resulted in dissimilar outlooks on what the Elizabethan Church should be. Diarmaid MacCulloch writes: "[the] leaders of the newly conceived Elizabethan Church had been involved in the muddle and humiliation of compromise in order to survive under Mary. It was unlikely that they would feel the same fervour for religious revolution as those who had made a different sacrifice and kept their consciences clean from Marian taint by finding refuge abroad."[17] The establishment presented the compromise as "a golden mean," but the exiles were not fooled by the rhetorical nicety. Jewel wrote, "Others are seeking after a *golden,* or as it rather seems to me, a *leaden* mediocrity; and are crying out, that the half is better than the whole."[18] However disappointed the exiles felt, it was obvious that the regime required them if any sort of Protestant Church was to be established in England. Offers of preferment were made to the leading exiles; of the twenty-three new bishops appointed, fourteen were returned exiles. Some of the exiles had crises of conscience as to whether or not to assume positions of authority, and sought the opinions of the Protestant Continental leaders before they accepted.

Before assuming their new positions, however, the exiles were required to implement the Elizabethan Settlement at the local level by serving as commissioners for the royal visitation. The Privy Council had commissioned a new oath of Supremacy that was to be administered to the clergy, judges, and justices of the peace throughout the realm, and therefore required a royal visitation.[19] Their mandate was to obtain subscriptions to the Royal Supremacy, the *Book of Common Prayer,* and the Injunctions for Religion. The lists of commissioners included the Lord Lieutenants of each county, several clergymen who supported the Settlement of Religion (and usually preachers of reputation), two or three lawyers, and local gentry.[20] The clerics among the commissioners were dominated by returned Marian exiles, among whom were John Jewel, Edwin Sandys, and Alexander Nowell. Among the lay visitors were more exiles, some of whom were now privy counsellors, such as Francis Earl of Bedford (one of the queen's most trusted counsellors, and a correspondent of the Swiss reformers) and Sir Francis Knollys. If the exiles had felt undervalued while Parliament was in session, they now had the perfect opportunity to leave their mark, literally, on the Church. They did not waste the opportunity.

The first item of the queen's "Injunctions for Religion" was concerned with the royal supremacy; the second item with the material fabric of the Church by disallowing acts of traditional devotion.[21] Iconoclastic acts are officially endorsed as Item 23 orders "that they shall take away, utterly extinct, and destroy all shrines, covering of shrines, all tables, candlesticks, trindles, and rolls of wax, pictures, paintings, and all other monuments of feigned miracles, pilgrimages, idolatry, and superstition, so that there remain no memory of the same in walls, glasses, windows, or elsewhere within their churches and houses."[22] What constituted the "true ornaments" of the Church was a vexing question that had been endlessly debated in England since the 1530s. Its significance has often been underplayed by academics until the past decade, when the English Reformation was subjected to intense scrutiny as revisionist historians like Margaret Aston, Eamon Duffy, and Christopher Haigh have reappraised the "success" of Tudor Protantism. Where traditional historiography had concentrated on the

Reformation as an intellectual movement with an emphasis on the introduction of controversial doctrines, the research of the revisionist historians
indicates that the locus of debate was typically experienced in changes to
ritual, and devotional practices. Subtle distinctions in matters of doctrine
were less likely to trouble the populace than massive changes to the externals of traditional religious customs. The recent revisionist studies have
emphasized the significance of this enforced destruction in parish life, especially as it did not reflect the will of the people. The returned exiles
played prominent roles in the Visitation, for as authorities, armed with the
queen's injunctions, they systematically visited each parish and enforced
the Elizabethan Settlement by administering the oath, publicly reading the
injunctions, and defacing or destroying the utensils condemned by Protestants, but essential for the proper administration of Roman Catholic worship. The 1559 Visitation can be likened to a traveling road show where
each parish was a stop on the tour.

Only the *Northern Act Book* for the 1559 Visitation has survived.[23] We
know that the Visitation was resented, and in many cases obstructed by the
populace, and for many obvious reasons, one of which was economic as
the Visitation could be a costly affair. The existing records are sparse, so
there are many details that are not specified. Were the parish churches filled
with local villagers as the royally appointed preachers condemned idolatry
and the superstition of traditional devotion, or was it a small congregation
comprised of commissioners and those locals required to swear the new
oath? Did the people actually witness the destruction of their parish's furnishings, or did they observe, from a distance, the smoke from the bonfires
in the churchyard? One can only conjecture about the myriad possibilities
as to how the 1559 Visitation was experienced. The Marian exiles may have
felt that they had returned to a mysterious and strange place once they were
back in England, but as commissioners in the 1559 Visitation, the exiles
were responsible for creating, for the majority of Elizabethan worshippers,
mysterious and strange parishes throughout the realm. The populace was
resistant to the changes, and for the next twenty years, episcopal injunctions and admonitions are concerned with the minutiae of ecclesiastical
furnishings and rituals.

Before the Visitation began, John Jewel conjectured that he would travel
seven hundred miles over four months. By the time the Visitation had
ended, he was exhausted, as was Edwin Sandys who complained to Peter
Martyr that he had been occupied until the beginning of November "in a
constant discharge of the duties entrusted to me, and with excessive fatigue
both of body and mind."[24] If the exhausted reformers were pleased with their
work, the Supreme Governor of the Church was not. Although the queen
was in Kent and Surrey during the Ecclesiastical Visitation, it is highly
unlikely that she was unaware of the iconoclasm being conducted under

the auspices of her authority; nonetheless, with her return to London at the end of September, the issue of iconoclasm escalated into a direct confrontation between Elizabeth and her bishops-elect. Whether she was motivated by caprice or conviction, Elizabeth deliberately set up a silver crucifix with candles on the altar in her chapel, and proved to be obstinately inflexible in her refusal to remove them. The fear of the bishops-elect, and the exiles in particular, was that Elizabeth would reverse the Church's position on images, which they had painstakingly destroyed. Bishop de Quadra, that wonderful source of gossip, certainly understood her action that way, and duly reported, "The fact is that the crucifixes and vestments that were burnt a month ago are now set up again in the royal chapel, as they soon will be all over the kingdom."[25] Had the Ecclesiastical Visitors overstepped their mark and perversely interpreted the Injunctions contrary to the queen's intentions, or was the Supreme Governor of the Church deliberately asserting "the ancient jurisdictions, authorities, superiorities and pre-eminences" of her Royal Supremacy?[26] The disagreement precipitated a terrific controversy that raged for several years, and eventually blended with a debate about vestments that grew into a serious crisis in 1565. The issue was serious enough that some of the exiles who were bishops-elect considered resignation from office. Peace was eventually restored, but the issue of the queen's crucifix simmered for years.

The chief result of the conflict was that Elizabeth effectively divided her bench of bishops. One of the effects was that Parker, who had not been a Marian exile, became suspicious of the "Germanical natures" of some of his episcopal brethren who had spent Mary's reign abroad. Edwin Sandys discovered that the archbishop had been keeping a supervisory eye on his activities during the Ecclesiastical Visitation, and he had to defend himself to Parker, saying "first, I visited with your consent; I proceeded orderly, according to laws and injunctions; I innovated nothing; I was altogether led by laws; what sobriety I used let the adversary report."[27] The fear that the iconoclasts were behaving in an extreme manner had legislative repercussions as the Settlement's Injunctions were tempered by a royal proclamation on September 19, 1560, "against breakinge or defacing of monumentes of antiquitie, being set up in Churches or other publique places for memory, and not for superstition."[28] Although the exiles literally left their mark on the English Church in the 1559 visitation, they were ultimately not permitted to complete what they set out to do in fashioning the Elizabethan Church. For most of them, frustration and alienation typify their later experiences.[29] Their encounter with the "mysterious" and the "foreign" during their Continental exile contributed to their zeal to create a nation where "pure religion" would flourish, but their transformation of the nation's parishes, in turn, created a mysterious and foreign church for the majority of Elizabethan subjects.

The exiles present us with something of an historical puzzle. Our knowledge of them and their experiences has undoubtedly been dominated by Christina Garrett's unsympathetic account of them. In the 1950s, J. E. Neale's interpretation of Elizabeth's First Parliament and Settlement of Religion hinged upon the premise that the exiles "constituted, as it were, an unofficial Convocation attached to Parliament, the pressure group of a revolutionary party."[30] Norman Jones's thorough reassessment of the First Parliament, which has completely displaced Neale's interpretation, indicates that "there is no concrete proof that they were organized and politically conscious in the early stages of the reign."[31] When we look at the subsequent careers of the exiles, it is evident that their experiences on the Continent were crucial to the divisions that beset the Elizabethan Church on the matters of liturgy, ritual, and church government. It is too easy for us to read history backwards, and see the seeds of the English civil wars germinating on the Continent in the Marian exile, but to the exiles themselves, their experiences on the Continent obviously loomed largely in their psyches and informed their understanding of the issues that divided the Elizabethan Church. In the 1570s, during the Admonition Controversy, one of the exiles felt that the divide between "Anglican" and "Puritan," to temporarily borrow these anachronistic designations, originated in a scuffle at Frankfort on whether the exiles should worship according to the rites of the Edwardine *Book of Common Prayer,* or follow the nonliturgical Reformed worship common in Frankfort.[32] Even in exile, the spiritual refugees had not formed a cohesive faction, and when they returned to England, the divisions remained; in fact, their divisions have all the unflattering and unedifying features identified by Matthew Arnold in his indictment of the "dissidence of dissent." Looking at John Foxe's relations with the Elizabethan Church, Patrick Collinson calls our attention to the essential struggle that the exiles faced on their return home: they had to make a transition from being persecuted and insignificant refugees under Mary to assuming authority as Lords Spiritual in the Elizabethan body politic, so that they were supporters and enforcers of a Settlement of Religion that ultimately prohibited them from effecting the reformation they desired. It is a "contradiction between the Church as a persecuted little flock, validated in its sufferings, and the Church as established, hierarchical, and royal, validated by the Constantinian figure of Elizabeth."[33] Sir Robert Naunton claimed that when Mary's councillors came to Hatfield Park to inform Elizabeth of her accession to the throne, she uttered words from Psalm 118, "A Deo factum est; et mirabile in occulis nostris" ("This is the Lord's doing and it is marvellous in our eyes.") As news of Elizabeth's accession reached the exiles, they too might have seen the Lord's work in action, but as the reign continued, the reality of the Elizabethan Church most likely made them look to another verse in Psalm 118 to affirm their experiences: "It is better to trust in the Lord than to put any confidence in princes."[34] Little wonder that the contradiction between a persecuted church and an established church should cause the exiles such unease, and little wonder that their unease should cause, in turn, such ripples in the Elizabethan Church and nation.

Two days after his return to England in 1559, John Jewel had written, "we are all of us hitherto as strangers at home." Long after they had returned to England, many of the exiles might have reiterated the sentiment. On the surface, it is not an unusual comment; even after a long trip, let alone years of exile, one is inclined to feel like a stranger upon returning home. Undergirding Jewel's statement, however, is a profounder truth, and that is of a mentalité of alienation. Protestantism began on the margins, and some, like Patrick Collinson, would argue that that is where it is logically most comfortable.[35] Protestantism's identification with biblical Israel, fortified by the direct experience of exile during Mary Tudor's reign, contributed to the English Protestant self-understanding of being persecuted, but also "a chosen generacion, a royal Priesthode, an holie nacion, a peculiar people."[36] God's people, the Marian exiles would argue, *ought* to find their worldly surroundings strange and mysterious in their temporal peregrinations. Pilgrimage is an important concept in many religious systems. It is significant in the Judeo-Christian tradition where pilgrimage is a motif that recurs throughout both testaments of scripture, but inherent to the concept of being a pilgrim is the less-lofty reality of being a stranger. The twin concepts are joined by the writer of the epistle to the Hebrews when he reviews the great figures of the Old Testament, and concludes: "All these dyed in faith, and receiued not the promises, but sawe them, and receiued them thankefully, and confessed that they were strangers and pilgremes on the earth.[37] I have quoted from the *Geneva Bible;* the work of Marian exiles. A marginal note explicates the verse: "Which was the enioying of the land of Canaan. With ye eyes of faith. And therefore put not their confidence in things of this worlde." The note was written by someone in exile with "ye eyes of faith," for when the note was written, the exiles did not know if they would ever go home. As it happens, they did. Their experiences, both in exile and as part of the Elizabethan regime, richly reveal how despite their bewildering experiences with the mysterious and the foreign, abroad and at home, the exiles remained, nonetheless, "strangers and pilgremes on the earth" who did not "put their confidence in things of this worlde."

NOTES

I would like to acknowledge my gratitude to my parents, Margaret Buick, and the late Samuel Buick, who endeavored to teach me to maintain an outlook with the "eyes of faith" even as a "stranger and a pilgrim." Our encounters with the mysterious and the foreign during our own perplexing experiences of exile precipitated my interest in how the mysterious and the foreign might have played a part in the Elizabethan Settlement. I am also grateful to my friends, formerly my colleagues, Valerie Kennedy, Leonard Knight, and Anthony Lake, for stimulating discussions from which I have benefited, and elements of which have filtered into this paper. I gratefully acknowledge the use I have made of the collections at the British Library, and Lambeth Palace Library, London, England; the Folger Shakespeare Library, Washington, D.C.; and in Canada, the libraries of the University of Guelph, the University of Toronto, and the University of Waterloo. I would also like to thank Helen Ostovich, Graham Roebuck, and Mary Silcox who organized the excellent conference at McMaster University on "The Mysterious and the Foreign in Early Modern England," and for their work in editing this collection of essays.

1. Letter IX, John Jewel to Peter Martyr (n.d.), *The Zurich Letters* (First Series), ed. Hastings Robinson (Cambridge: Cambridge University Press for the Parker Society, 1842), 23.

2. John Foxe, *Acts and Monuments,* ed. S. R. Cattley, rev. Josiah Pratt (London: Religious Tract Society, 1877), 6:430. Christina Hallowell Garrett wrote an unsympathetic history of the Marian Exiles, *The Marian Exiles: A Study in the Origins of Elizabethan Puritanism* (Cambridge: Cambridge University Press, 1938). See pp. 30–32 for Garrett's census of exiles. H.C. Porter identifies a further fourteen Cambridge exiles, and provides a list arranged by college as an appendix to his chapter on "The Cambridge Exiles" in *Reformation and Reaction in Tudor Cambridge* (Cambridge: Cambridge University Press, 1958), 91–98. See Andrew Pettegree, *Marian Protestantism: Six Studies* (Brookfield, VT: Ashgate, 1996), especially for the exiles at Emden, which have previously been overlooked. Dan G. Danner has devoted a study exclusively to the theology of the Genevan exiles in *Pilgrimage to Puritanism: History and Theology of the Marian Exiles at Geneva, 1555–1560* (New York: Peter Lang, 1999). Kenneth R. Bartlett has analyzed the English exiles in Venice, who were "essentially political rather than confessional in character," and their subsequent contribution to Elizabethan parliaments; see his "The English Exile Community in Italy and the Political Opposition to Queen Mary I," *Albion* 13 (1981): 223–41, and "The Role of the Marian Exiles," *The House of Commons 1558–1603,* ed. P. W. Hasler, Vol. 1, pp. 102–10 (London: HMSO for The History of Parliament Trust, 1981).

3. Garrett referred to a "committee of 'sustainers' of 1554" meaning the wealthy London godly who financed the Marian exile. Based on a comprehensive survey of the available evidence, Susan Brigden states that over sixty sustainers can be identified by name; see her *London and the Reformation* (Oxford: Oxford University Press, 1989), 604. Brett Usher believes "this number can certainly be doubled" when the evidence from the Exchequer Composition records is included; see his article, "Backing Protestantism: The London Godly, the Exchequer and the Foxe Circle," in *John Foxe: An Historical Perspective,* ed. David Loades, 105–34. (Brookfield, VT: Ashgate, 1999). I have quoted from p. 106.

4. See Bartlett, "Exile Community in Italy," 238–40, for Sir Anthony Kingston's role in defeating the bill, including his forcible closure of the doors to the Commons, and Pettegree, *Marian Protestantism,* 104–5, for Cecil's involvement.

5. Christopher Haigh, *English Reformations: Religion, Politics, and Society under the Tudors* (Oxford: Clarendon Press, 1993), 219–34.

6. Other exiles were slower about going home; those at Geneva stayed the longest in order to complete *The Geneva Bible,* which was published in 1560.

7. Sam M. Lewis and Joe Young. I have quoted the title of the song, written in 1919. See *The Oxford Dictionary of Quotations,* 4th ed., ed. Angela Partington (Oxford: Oxford University Press, 1992), 420.

8. *Zurich Letters* (First Series), 23. See note 1.

9. John Strype, *Annals of the Reformation and Establishment of Religion* (Oxford: Oxford University Press, 1824), Vol. 1, Pt. 1: 192.

10. Letter IV, John Jewel to Peter Martyr, March 20, 1559, *Zurich Letters* (First Series), 10. See note 1.

11. *Zurich Letters* (First Series), 23 (see note 1); Letter XLIX, Edmund Sandys to Matthew Parker, April 30, 1559, in *Correspondence of Matthew Parker*, ed. John Bruce (Cambridge: Cambridge University Press for the Parker Society, 1853), 65.

12. See Usher, "Backing Protestantism," 107, and Strype, *Annals*, Vol. 1, Pt. 1: 192–94; also Margaret Aston for Foxe's relationship with the Howards in *The King's Bedpost: Reformation and Iconography in a Tudor Group Portrait* (Cambridge: Cambridge University Press, 1993), 190–99.

13. *Calendar of State Papers and Manuscripts, Relating to English Affairs, Existing in the Archives and Collections of Venice, and in Other Libraries of Northern Italy*, eds. Rawdon Brown and G. Cavendish Bentinck (London: HMSO, 1890), 7:23.

14. Bruce, *Correspondence of Matthew Parker*, 66. Kenneth Bartlett's distinction between "political" and "confessional" exiles is particularly relevant in my discussion, and his research indicates the significant contribution that "political" exiles made in the Elizabethan parliaments.

15. Letter III, Rudolph Gualter to Queen Elizabeth, January 16, 1559, *Zurich Letters* (Second Series), 5. See note 1.

16. Pettegree, *Marian Protestantism*, 88. See also E. J. A. Baskerville, *A Chronological Bibliography of Propaganda and Polemic published in England between 1553 and 1558* (Philadelphia: American Philosophical Society, 1979).

17. Diarmaid MacCulloch, *Tudor Church Militant: Edward VI and the Protestant Reformation* (London: Allen Lane / Penguin Press, 1999), 189.

18. *Zurich Letters* (First Series), 23. See note 1.

19. The first royal visitation had taken place in September 1535 to enforce Henry VIII's newly defined supremacy of the Church. The Crown, in effect, assumed one of the Church's powers by suspending episcopal authority, and using the established procedure of metropolitan visitation to obtain subscription to the Oath of Supremacy. When Edward VI's regime created more radical injunctions, a second visitation was begun in August 1547 to ensure that they were implemented at the parish level. At that time the dioceses were arranged into six circuits which were subsequently used as a model for the Elizabethan visitation.

20. Henry Gee identifies the visitors in *The Elizabethan Clergy and the Settlement of Religion 1558–1564* (Oxford: Clarendon Press, 1898). The visitors are named on pp. 71–72, 94–95, 97, 98–99, 100–101, 130, 132.

21. "Announcing Injunctions for Religion," *Tudor Royal Proclamations: Volume II The Later Tudors (1553–1587)*, ed. Paul L. Hughes and James F. Larkin (New Haven, CT: Yale University Press, 1969), 117–18. They are also found in *Visitation Articles and Injunctions of the Period of the Reformation, Volume III 1559–1575*, ed. Walter Howard Frere (London: Longmans, Green, 1910), 8–29. The Injunctions with the Act of Supremacy, and the *Book of Common Prayer* form the three bases of the Elizabethan Settlement of Religion. In 1583, the Thirty-Nine Articles of Religion replaced the Injunctions in the subscription demanded of the clergy by Archbishop Whitgift, and in 1604 this change was adopted in the Canons.

22. Hughes and Larkin, *Tudor Royal Proclamations*, 2:123; Frere, *Visitation Articles and Injunctions*, 3:16.

23. *The Royal Visitation of 1559: Act Book for the Northern Province*, ed. C. J. Kitching, Surtees Society, Vol. 187. (Gateshead, UK: Northumberland Press Limited for the Surtees Society, 1975). No official report survives for the Province of Canterbury. C. G. Bayne, however, combed scattered references from a variety of sources and provided a coherent account of the Royal Visitation's activities in "The Visitation of the Province of Canterbury,

1559," *English Historical Review* 28 (1913): 636–77. Bayne supplements Henry Gee's information and analysis of the five circuits that occurred in the Province of Canterbury, and in "Appendix III" provides extracts from churchwardens' accounts which mirror the accounts recorded in the *Act Book for the Northern Province.*

24. *Zurich Letters* (First Series), 73 (see note 1). John Jewel also complained to Martyr of "a body worn out by a most fatiguing journey," 44.

25. *Calendar of Letters and State Papers Relating to English Affairs, Preserved Principally in the Archives of Simancas,* ed. Martin A. S. Hume (London: HMSO, 1892), 1:105.

26. I have quoted from I Eliz. c. 1. *The Statutes at Large,* 6:107.

27. Bruce, *Correspondence of Matthew Parker,* 126.

28. STC 7913 and No. 469 of *Tudor Royal Proclamations,* 2:146–48. See note 21.

29. This is particularly true of Edmund Grindal and his troubles, as Archbishop of Canterbury, with Elizabeth I. See Patrick Collinson's biography, *Archbishop Grindal 1519–1583: The Struggle for a Reformed Church* (London: Jonathan Cape, 1979). Entries for some of the other exiles in the new *Oxford Dictionary of National Biography* also indicate ways in which some of the subsequent careers of Marian exiles were thwarted.

30. J. E. Neale, *Elizabeth I and her Parliaments 1559–1581* (London: St. Martin's Press, 1958), 58.

31. Norman L. Jones, *Faith by Statute: Parliament and the Settlement of Religion, 1559* (London: Royal Historical Society, 1982), 4.

32. See William Whittingham, *A Brieff discours off the troubles begonne at Franckford in Germany Anno Domini 1554.* (Heidelberg: M. Schirat, 1574). STC 25442. See Patrick Collinson's "The authorship of *A Brieff Discours off the Troubles begonne at Franckford,*" in *Godly People: Essays in English Protestantism and Puritanism,* 191–212 (London: Hambledon Press, 1983). For an invaluable study on conformity to the Church of England after the Reformation and before the outbreak of the Civil War see Judith Maltby, *Prayer Book and People in Elizabethan and Early Stuart England* (Cambridge: Cambridge University Press, 1998).

33. Patrick Collinson, "John Foxe and National Consciousness," in *John Foxe and his World* (Aldershot, UK: Ashgate, 2002), 27. See also Richard Helgerson's chapter on "Apocalyptics and Apologetics" in his *Forms of Nationhood: The Elizabethan Writing of England* (Chicago: University of Chicago Press, 1992).

34. Psalm 118:9, 23. I have used Coverdale's translation as in the *Book of Common Prayer.*

35. See Collinson's comments in his essay on "England" in *The Reformation in National Context,* ed. Bob Scribner et al. (Cambridge: Cambridge University Press, 1994), 80–94. Collinson amplified these comments in discussions after his paper at an Oxford conference in September 1994 to honor the quincentenary of William Tyndale's birth. The published version found in Reformation 1 (1996): 72–97, however, does not include them.

36. 1 Pet. 2:9. I have quoted from *The Geneva Bible: A facsimile of the 1560 edition,* Introduction by Lloyd E. Berry (Madison: University of Wisconsin Press, 1969). I have normalized the long s.

37. Heb. 11:13, *The Geneva Bible* (1560); I have normalized the long s.

BIBLIOGRAPHY

Aston, Margaret. *The King's Bedpost: Reformation and Iconography in a Tudor Group Portrait.* Cambridge: Cambridge University Press, 1993.

Bartlett, Kenneth R. "The English Exile Community in Italy and the Political Opposition to Queen Mary I." *Albion* 13 (1981): 223–41.

————. "The Role of the Marian Exiles." In *The House of Commons 1558–1603*. Vol. 1. Edited by P. W. Hasler. 102–10. London: HMSO for The History of Parliament Trust, 1981.

Baskerville, E. J. A. *A Chronological Bibliography of Propaganda and Polemic published in England between 1553 and 1558*. Philadelphia: American Philosophical Society, 1979.

Bayne, C. G. "The Visitation of the Province of Canterbury, 1559." *English Historical Review* 28 (1913): 636–77.

The Bible and Holy Scriptures. Geneva, 1560.

Brigden, Susan. *London and the Reformation*. Oxford: Oxford University Press, 1989.

Brown, Rawdon, and G. Cavendish Bentinck, eds. *Calendar of State Papers and Manuscripts, Relating to English Affairs, Existing in the Archives and Collections of Venice, and in Other Libraries of Northern Italy*. London: HMSO, 1890.

Bruce, John, ed. *Correspondence of Matthew Parker*. Cambridge: Cambridge University Press for the Parker Society, 1853.

Collinson, Patrick. *Archbishop Grindal 1519–1583: The Struggle for a Reformed Church*. London: Jonathan Cape, 1979.

————. "The authorship of *A Brieff Discours off the Troubles begonne at Franckford*." In *Godly People: Essays in English Protestantism and Puritanism*, 191–212 London: Hambledon Press, 1983.

————. "John Foxe and National Consciousness." In *John Foxe and his World* 31–34. Aldershot, UK: Ashgate, 2002.

Danner, Dan G. *Pilgrimage to Puritanism: History and Theology of the Marian Exiles at Geneva, 1555–1560*. New York: Peter Lang, 1999.

Foxe, John. *Acts and Monuments*. Edited by S. R. Cattley. Revised by Josiah Pratt. London: Religious Tract Society, 1877.

Frere, Walter Howard, ed. *Visitation Articles and Injunctions of the Period of the Reformation, Volume III 1559–1575*. London: Longmans, Green, 1910.

Garrett, Christina Hallowell. *The Marian Exiles: A Study in the Origins of Elizabethan Puritanism*. Cambridge: Cambridge University Press, 1938.

Gee, Henry. *The Elizabethan Clergy and the Settlement of Religion 1558–1564*. Oxford: Clarendon Press, 1898.

Haigh, Christopher. *English Reformations: Religion, Politics, and Society under the Tudors*. Oxford: Clarendon Press, 1993.

Helgerson, Richard. *Forms of Nationhood: The Elizabethan Writing of England*. Chicago: University of Chicago Press, 1992.

Hughes, Paul L. and James F. Larkin, eds. *Tudor Royal Proclamations: Volume II The Later Tudors (1553–1587)*. New Haven, CT: Yale University Press, 1969.

Hume, Martin A. S., ed. *Calendar of Letters and State Papers Relating to English Affairs, Preserved Principally in the Archives of Simancas*. London: HMSO, 1892.

Jones, Norman L. *Faith by Statute: Parliament and the Settlement of Religion, 1559*. London: Royal Historical Society, 1982.

Kitching, C. J., ed. *The Royal Visitation of 1559: Act Book for the Northern Province*. Surtees Society, Vol. 187. Gateshead, UK: Northumberland Press Limited for the Surtees Society, 1975.

MacCulloch, Diarmaid. *Tudor Church Militant: Edward VI and the Protestant Reformation*. London: Allen Lane Penguin Press, 1999.

Maltby, Judith. *Prayer Book and People in Elizabethan and Early Stuart England*. Cambridge: Cambridge University Press, 1998.

Neale, J. E. *Elizabeth I and her Parliaments 1559–1581*. London: St. Martin's Press, 1958.

Partington, Angela, ed. *The Oxford Dictionary of Quotations,* 4th edition. Oxford: Oxford University Press, 1992.

Pettegree, Andrew. *Marian Protestantism: Six Studies*. Brookfield, VT: Ashgate, 1996.

Porter, H. C. *Reformation and Reaction in Tudor Cambridge*. Cambridge: Cambridge University Press, 1958.

Robinson, Hastings, ed. *The Zurich Letters*. Cambridge: Cambridge University Press for the Parker Society, 1842, 1845.

Strype, John. *Annals of the Reformation and Establishment of Religion*. Oxford: Oxford University Press, 1824.

Usher, Brett. "Backing Protestantism: The London Godly, the Exchequer and the Foxe Circle." In *John Foxe: An Historical Perspective,* edited by David Loades, 105–34. Brookfield, VT: Ashgate, 1999.

Whittingham, William. *A Brieff discours off the troubles begonne at Franckford in Germany Anno Domini 1554.* Heidelberg: M. Schirat, 1574. STC 25442.

Pirates, Merchants, and Kings: Oriental Motifs in English Court and Civic Entertainments, 1510–1659

Linda McJannet

From all parts of the *World,* thou hadst Supplie
Of what was wanting to thy *Luxurie:*

.   .   .   .

Barbary, Sugars: Zant, Oile: Tapestrie
T'adorne thy prowd *Walls, Brabant* made for *Thee:*
Nor were the *Indies* slowe to feed thy *Sence*
With *Cassia, Mirrhe* (farr-fetch'd with deere expence):
The *Sea,* her *Pearle:* and many a boystrous knock
Compelled the sparckling *Diomond,* from the *Rock,*
To deck thy *Daughters:* In a word th'adst All
That could in compasse of thy wishes fall.
But theis great *Guiftes* (abus'd) first bredd in *Thee*
A stupid *Sloth,* and dull *Securitie*
The *Parent* of *Destruction.* . . .
——Philip Massinger, "London's Lamentable Estate" 13–29

By THE 1620s EXOTIC GOODS WERE A COMMONPLACE FEATURE OF THE London scene. The merchant-adventurers of the Levant Company (founded 1581) and the East India Company (founded 1600) competed for Eastern luxury goods and brought them back for English consumption and their own profit. In "London's Lamentable Estate," Philip Massinger asserts that these luxuries were "abus'd" by Londoners; they "bredd . . . *Impieties*" that eventually called down God's *"Veng'ance"* in the form of the plague.[1] In the dramatic entertainments of court and city, however, exotic goods and the peoples and lands from which they were obtained were presented in a positive (albeit self-serving) light, as evidence of England's participation in global trade and of the dignity of her aristocrats and citizens alike.

Eastern characters constitute a third wave of iconography in such entertainments. In medieval times, festival imagery was generally homegrown or biblical: the English rose; virtues and vices; saints and devils; Old Testament kings and Christian heroes.[2] During the Renaissance, not surprisingly,

249

figures from Graeco-Roman mythology and history also became popular.[3] By the end of the sixteenth century, however, for some poets, classical mythology became stale. Writing in 1613, Thomas Campion observes that classical motifs have not utterly lost their use, "yet finde they so little credit, that our moderne writers have rather transfered their fictions to the persons of Enchaunters and Commaunders of Spirits, as that excellent poet Torquato Tasso hath done."[4] Thus, the revival of medieval romance with its crusaders and Saracens, as well as the growth of the Levant trade, turned writers' imaginations eastward. In practice, eclecticism was the order of the day: native, classical, and Eastern motifs were frequently combined. In 1594, King James VI celebrated his son's baptism in Edinburgh with a pageant featuring three Christians, three Turks, and three Amazons; three Moors were apparently planned but not included in the actual performance.[5] Similarly, in Dekker's *Magnificent Entertainment for James I* (1604), the triumphal arch depicting Britain as *Nova Fœlix Arabia* includes the figure of "Arabia Britannica" as well as classical emblems (the Fount of Arete and Fame with her trumpet) and morality characters (Detraction and Circumspection).[6]

In the decades following Edward Said's influential *Orientalism* (1978), critics of early modern literature stressed "demonization" of oriental figures and their association with exclusively negative qualities against which Britons sought to define their own (superior) national character.[7] More recently, however, critics have (rightly) argued that, in the sixteenth and seventeenth centuries, Eastern others are both "demonized and exalted, admired and condemned."[8] Paralleling Kim F. Hall's analysis of the images of black Africans in jewelry and portraiture designed to establish the superiority of white skin,[9] Richmond Barbour argues that Jonson's *Masque of Blackness* (1605) operated "in a triumphal mode" and sought to celebrate "Britain's difference from distant, 'darker' worlds."[10] Lord Mayors' Shows similarly "harnessed to domestic pomp" such "scary or magnificent" figures as a King of Moors, and thus "thrilled, without deeply threatening, London's spectators."[11] The appropriation of such exotic figures, several critics have argued, was in fact a compensatory fantasy: by basking in the reflected wealth and symbolic power of Eastern others, Londoners sought to downplay their relative marginality with respect to global politics and trade with the East.[12]

This essay surveys the use of oriental motifs and characters in civic and royal entertainments with two questions in mind. First, to what extent are oriental peoples distinguished from one another in these entertainments? As Barbour seems to suggest, do Turks, Persians, Moors, and "Indians" play one role in these events, or are their roles distinct? Second, are there significant differences in the way the court and the city employed exotic signifiers? The evidence suggests that both courtly and city poets and designers were attracted by the splendor of Eastern costumes and props and wished to "harness" it, as Barbour says, to aggrandize their patrons and fellows, but there were subtle differences in how each portrayed denizens of the East.[13]

OTTOMAN CHARACTERS

Turkish motifs appear very early in courtly revels. On Shrove Tuesday in 1510, Henry VIII and the Earl of Essex dressed "after Turkey fassion, in long robes of Bawdkin [rich embroidered cloth, shot with gold] . . . , hattes on their heddes of Crimosyn velvet, with great rolles of Gold, [and] girded with two swordes called *Cimeteries*."[14] At Greenwich in 1518, the French ambassador presented a tourney with fifteen Christian and fifteen Turkish knights to celebrate the betrothal of Princess Mary and the Dauphin and the signing of a treaty of "Universal Peace."[15] In 1552–53, the Christmas revels included musicians "apparelled like turkes," and a masque of "Turkish magistrates" was presented in 1555.[16] Although these early "Turks" were peaceful (alter egos of the sovereign and his earl, an honor guard, musicians, and magistrates), later they were presented in a more martial mode. The revels for 1571–72, which no doubt reflected the rare Christian victory over the Turks at Lepanto that year, included weapons ("Turky Bowe and iii arrowes") as well as turbans ("Bumbast to stuf Rowles for the Turkes heades").[17] According to Chew, these early examples of oriental motifs in court entertainments imitated eastward-looking Florentine revels and suggest "a persistent search after picturesque and exotic effects" rather than a genuine "interest in Mohammedan peoples, customs, and costumes, or . . . any particular interest in the Levant."[18] The two motives are not mutually exclusive, however. While Henry might have valued the picturesque effect of his Turkish dress, he was surely even more interested in the Great Turk as a symbol of power and imperial grandeur, qualities which Henry sought to appropriate for himself.

A century later, warlike Turks were prominent in mock naval battles performed on the Thames, but they were now always depicted as enemies rather than models of magnificence. The pirates are invariably identified as "Turks," but the term in context could refer to Muslims of any nationality and renegade Christians, since "turning Turk" signified conversion to Islam. The first of these extravaganzas was Anthony Munday's *London's Love to Prince Henry* (1610), which included classical and ancient British figures as well as oriental ones.[19] On the third day, the pageant presented "a Turkish pirate prowling on the seas, to maintain a Turkish castle." The "Turkishness" of the pirates was established by "their armes and streamers," presumably curved scimitars and banners with Turkish crescents. The description of the battle continues as follows (considerably abridged):

sculking abroade to finde a bootie, [the pirate] descried two merchant's shippes. . . . [He] sends a commanding shott, which the merchant answered. . . . When [the pirate] perceived his hope defeated and this bold resistance returned, he sent shot upon shot very fiercely. . . . [T]he fighte grewe on all sides to be fierce indeed, the castle assisting the pirate very hotly, and the other withstanding bravely and couragiously; divers men appearing on either side to be slayne and hurlled over into the sea. . . . In conclusion, the merchants and men of warre, after a long and well-fought skirmish, prooved too strong for the pirate, spoylde . . . him, and blewe up the castle, ending the whole batterie with verie rare and admirable fire-workes. . . .[20]

Although the aggressors, the pirates are presented as brave and determined (they are outnumbered two to one). The point of the battle is its spectacular fierceness and, of course, the victory of the stalwart Christian merchants, but there is little demonization of the pirates; like Falstaff, it would seem, they are laboring in their profession and providing an opportunity for the British seamen to prove their mettle.

Entertainments for the marriage of the Elector Frederick and Princess Elizabeth in 1613 expanded the scope of these imaginary encounters. One "represented a Christian Navie opposed against the Turkes."[21] The other showed an "English Navie" overcoming "seventeen Turkish gallies" after a brave fight "on both sides."[22] The setting was perceived as generic (a "Turkish or Barbarian Castle of Tunis, Algiers, or some other Mahometan fortification"[23]), but the admiral was specifically Turkish ("attired in a red jacket with blue sleeves, according to the Turkish fashion").[24] In this encounter, the English are outnumbered but still prevail. After a similar sea fight at Bristol in 1613, Queen Anne is reported to have reviewed the "captives," noting "laughingly" that the prisoners "were not only like Turks by their apparell but by their countenances."[25] Anne's complacency may seem more offensive to a modern reader than the even-handed heroics of the battles themselves. In royal entertainments, the Turks increasingly support the fantasy of English power relative to the Turks, as the conflicts escalate from pirate skirmishes to full-scale naval battles. In reality, however, England never mounted such a naval offensive. It had not joined the Catholic forces at Lepanto years before, and the English mercenaries who joined Portugal in the Battle of Alcazar in 1578 shared in their defeat.

By contrast, in the Lord Mayors' Shows of the early seventeenth century, Turks are less common and their warlike associations are muted or absent. This is not surprising, since the London Companies who sponsored the shows encountered the Turks in commercial rather than martial contexts. Their trade in the Levant was made possible by the "capitulations" granted by the sultan to English merchants in 1580 and renewed thereafter. A peaceable Turk joins a procession of well-wishers in Middleton's *Triumphs of Honour and Industry* (1617). Similarly, in Webster's *Monuments*

of Honour (1624), the "Turkes Metropolis" [Constantinople] takes its place
as one of "five eminent Cities" along with Rome, Venice, Antwerp, and
Paris to honor London. Webster also includes a Turk on a camel, "such as
use to Travaile with Caravans."[26] In *London's Tempe* (1629), Dekker presents an "Indian boy" on "an Estridge [ostrich]" escorted by "a Turke, and
a Persian," among others.[27] Unlike the pirates, the Turk in this show
protects—not threatens—a symbol of commerce, just as the capitulations
granted by the sultan obliged him to protect foreign merchants, and Turkish soldiers often protected caravans.[28] One pageant featured heroes known
for their exploits against the Ottomans; Webster's *Monuments of Honour*
represents two who resisted the Turks at Malta and Rhodes, respectively.[29]
One of them (Amade le Graunde) ends the day's events with a thirty-line
speech in praise of the late Prince Henry, but he does not mention conflict
with the Turks. Thus, the London guilds tend to cast the Turks as versions
of themselves, as intrepid fellow traders and as representatives of the great
cities with which they traded, rather than as enemies to be defeated.

Persian Characters

In contrast to the Turks, Persian characters in court masques were seen as
refined, elegant, and peaceable. As Anthony Parr has noted, for Western
writers Persia was "not a malign and unknowable neighbour but a fabulous
resource."[30] Since early modern Persians were seen as the heirs of the glorious empires of Xerxes, Darius, and Cyrus, they had a respectable place
in the early modern imaginative landscape.[31] In the early 1600s, as reflected in *The Travels of the Three English Brothers* (1607), the Sherley
brothers promoted an alliance with Persia, traditional enemy of the Turks.
A Persian Queen graces Jonson's *Masque of Queens* and Campion's masque
for the Earl of Somerset, and Persian youths are the heroes of *The Temple
of Love,* a 1634–35 collaboration between William D'Avenant and Inigo
Jones. The costumes of the youths were sumptuous, combining Turkish and
Persian elements:[32] "Asian coats of sea-green embroidered, that reached
down above their knees, with buttons and loops before, and cut up square
to their hips . . . ; on their heads they wore Persian turbans silver'd underneath, and wound about with white cypress."[33] With the exception of their
saucy page, the Persian characters are entirely noble, as the Argument
makes clear: "The fame of this Temple of Love . . . enflamed a company
of noble Persian youths, borderers on India, to travel in quest of it; who arriving, were by the illusions of the Magicians . . . almost seduced, as others
had been: but Divine Poesy . . . discovered unto them some part of the Temple unshadowed. . . . [and] these being spirits of the highest rank, forsaking
the false magicians and their allurements, were resolved to . . . contemplate

... this apparition, until the coming of the glorious Indian Queen."[34] These strangers undergo no religious conversion since they are already "spirits of the highest rank" devoted to Platonic love, the fashion in court at the time.[35] Thus, Persian characters in Jacobean and Caroline masques were imagined not as alien others, but as versions of an ideal self: noble, even royal (as in Jonson and Campion), peaceable, aesthetically sophisticated, and philosophically inclined.

The relative comfort with which the English viewed the Persians is indicated by the aristocracy's flirtation with Persian dress in the later 1600s. A portrait by Marcus Gheeraerts, "Lady attired as a Persian Virgin," depicts an Englishwoman in Persian fancy dress.[36] Even more striking is a portrait of Cecil Calvert, second baron of Baltimore, wearing a "Persian vest." As Kim Hall explains, the fashion was introduced by Charles II in 1666 to counteract imitation of the French.[37] That such a campaign was possible testifies to the positive English image of Persia, especially among the upper classes.[38]

Persian characters in the Lord Mayors' Shows are also benign, but they are rare. Trade with Persia was slower to develop than with Turkey; no English emissary was received in the Persian court until Sir Dodmore Cotton's arrival in 1626. A Persian figure joins the honor guard around the Indian boy in Dekker's *London's Tempe,* and a Persian appears in Tatham's *London's Triumph* (1659), but beyond that, Persians were not depicted in extant civic entertainments.

"MOORS" AND SUB-SAHARAN AFRICAN CHARACTERS

Moors and black Africans appear quite early in the records of court revels, and, in contrast to the Turks, skin color signals their identity. Generally, the term "Moor" designated a North or sub-Saharan African, but it might also refer to a Muslim (or other) resident of the Indian subcontinent. In 1510, when Henry and Essex entered dressed as "Turks," they were accompanied by torchbearers "lyke Moreskoes, their faces blacke." Two ladies also appeared as "Egipcians," their faces, necks, arms, and hands covered with fine black "pleasaunce," "so that [they] seemed to be nygros or blacke Mores."[39] For a masque of "Young Moors" in 1548, black leather gloves and "nether stocks of lether black" were purchased.[40] The "Masque of Moors" in 1560 also attempted to represent distinctive hair texture; the costume lists include "corled [curled] hed sculles" for Moors and their torchbearers.[41] All these figures seemed to have been fairly low status (youths, torchbearers, servants) with the possible exception of the Egyptian "ladies."

The most celebrated instance of black Africans in Stuart revels is Jonson's *Masque of Blackness* (1605), in which the River Niger and his twelve daughters (played by Queen Anne and her ladies) appear in full blackface and body paint.[42] Here both the actors (the ladies) and the characters are high ranking, though the daughters of a "River" probably don't merit royal status. Barbour argues that the masque's "hyperbolic praise of Albion works only if spectators find Niger's daughters, as their father does, *already* beautiful—an effect that Jones's costumes . . . were designed to secure."[43] Nonetheless, in the denouement, the daughters of Niger are persuaded to remain in England and, following the moon goddess's prescription, to bathe their skin into whiteness. Though their blackness is superficial and physical rather than morally symbolic, they view it as a defect to be removed.

One other masque presents Moors of noble rank: Campion's wedding masque presents the continent of Africa "like a Queene of the Moores, with a crown," but she does not speak.[44] These two aside, courtly works present Moors and sub-Saharan Africans as subalterns, even slaves. In Chapman's *Masque of the Middle Temple* (1613) each Virginian prince had "two Moors, attired like Indian slaves," and the torchbearers also "had every man his Moor attending his horse."[45] Whether minor Moorish characters also appeared in blackface cannot be asserted with confidence, but it seems likely.[46] Moors in court masques are neither threatening nor morally deficient. While gorgeously attired, the men especially are low in status, serving others.

In the Lord Mayors' Shows, "Moors" also have dark skin, but they are more likely to be royal than subaltern, and if royal, they are more likely to be male than female. In addition, the speaking characters challenge unthinking prejudice in the spectators. In Munday's *Chrysanaleia, or the Golden Fishing* (1616), co-sponsored by the Fishmongers and the Company of Goldsmiths, a King of Moors appears along with six "tributarie kings . . . gorgeously attired."[47] Tossing coins as they go, these figures are sumptuously dressed in clothes that seem more classical and European than "African" or Eastern (breastplates over short pleated tunics, garters, and shoes).[48] In the 1859 copy and in photographs of the original drawing, their faces are darkened but smiling and serene, their "darts" are ceremonial, and three carry ingots of silver rather than weapons (see figure). Thus they are associated with largesse and luxury, not servitude.

The King of the Moors who appears with his queen near the end of Middleton's *Triumphs of Truth* (1613) seems Indian rather than African, since he and his Queen arrive from the "five islands, artfully garnished with all manner of Indian . . . spiceries" that had been fashioned in the Thames. A speaking character, unlike Munday's Moors, the King challenges stereotypes related to his "complexion":

> I see amazement set upon the faces
> Of these white people, wonderings and strange gazes;
> Is it at me? does my complexion draw

"The King of Moors" from Anthony Munday, *Chrysanaleia* **(1616). From the copy by Henry Shaw in John Gough Nichols, ed.,** *The Fishmongers' Pageant* **(London, 1859).**

> So many Christian eyes, that never saw
> A King so black before?[49]

He goes on to challenge the "judgings of th'unwise," based only on appearances. He and his people have been converted to Christianity (from sun worship, not Islam) by the "religious conversation / Of English merchants" (who thus serve God as well as Mammon):

> However darkness dwells upon my face,
> Truth in my soul sets up the light of grace.[50]

Only the evil character Error is permitted to mock the Moors ("What, have my sweet-fac'd devils forsook me, too?").[51]

Whereas the Turks, Persians, and Indians in Lord Mayors' Shows are associated with domestic animals (camels and elephants), Moors and black Africans seem to be associated with wild ones. In Peele's show honoring Sir Wolstan Dixi (1585), one "apparelled like a Moore" rides on a "Luzarne," or lynx,[52] and Munday's King of Moors rides on a leopard. Webster's *Monuments of Honour* (1624) introduces a "Lyon and Cammell": "on the Camell rides a Turke, such as use to Travaile with Caravans, and [on] the Lyon a Moore or wild Numidian."[53] Whereas the great cats may be thought to introduce a note of savagery, a different iconographic significance is explicitly noted in the text. The lynx in *Wolstan Dixi* is present because the new mayor was a member of the Skinners' Company, and the lynx was valued for its pelt. Munday's character is described as "gallantly mounted on a *golden* Leopard, . . . hurling *gold and silver* every way about him."[54] Thus the animals evoke wealth and luxury rather than wildness. Even Webster's "Moore or wild Numidian" is represented on a lion because, along with the camel, it is one of the two beasts "proper to the Armes of the [Merchant-Taylors'] Company."[55] In the iconography of the Lord Mayors' Shows, the apparently "wild" animals associated with Moorish or African peoples are domesticated, even ennobled, through heraldic conventions and the activities of the guild.

"INDIAN" CHARACTERS—EAST MEETS WEST

"Indians" first appear at court in Chapman's *Masque* for the marriage of the Princess Elizabeth. The term "Indians" could refer to the inhabitants of several locales: the New World, including the American continent and the West Indies; the Spice Islands or the Moluccas (islands in the Malay archipelago between the Celebes and New Guinea); all of Indonesia including Java and New Guinea; and India proper, especially the Malabar Coast known for its wonderful black pepper.[56] Chapman's Indians appear to be Native Americans. They are identified as "Virginian priests" and "Virginian princes," but their costumes blend Eastern and Western motifs including ostrich feathers from North Africa:[57] "The ground-cloth of silver richly [was] embroidered with golden suns, and about every sun ran a trail of gold imitating Indian work . . . but betwixt every pane of embroidery went a row of white estridge feather. . . . On their heads high sprigged feathers, compassed in coronets, . . . their vizards of olive colour, but pleasantly visaged: their hair black and large, waving down to their shoulders."[58] Vizards of "olive colour" establish their complexion but do not conclusively identify which hemisphere these people inhabit. The stage set, a craggy rock that opens to reveal Plutus's golden mine, could by legend belong equally to the East or West Indies. Adding to the confusion, Strong and Orgel report that Jones based his "Indian torchbearer" on a figure in Vecellio labeled an "African Indian."[59] Indamora, "the glorious Indian Queen" in *The Temple of Love* (1634), is similarly vague; though clearly an oriental figure, she is surrounded by imagery recalling the birth of Venus, and any ethnic or geographic specificity quickly fades.[60]

Though ethnographically confused, these Indians, unlike the Moors in court masques, are high status (priests and princes), and they are splendid, and "pleasantly visaged," not savage. Their costumes, though fanciful, are presented as "authentic" ("imitating Indian work," "Indian habits all of a resemblance") to bolster the verisimilitude of the pageant *and* the expert knowledge of the pageant-makers, who, it is implied, are to be admired for possessing such precise knowledge about these exotic others.

By contrast, Indians in the Lord Mayors' Shows are clearly associated with the spice trade. Middleton's *Triumphs of Honour and Industry* (1617) honors a member of the Grocers' Company. India, depicted as "a rich personage" and "the seat of merchandise," rides upon "an illustrious chariot" holding a "wedge of gold" and flanked by Traffic and Industry.[61] She does not speak, but the scene suggests the Spice Islands, and her subjects are nothing if not industrious: "A company of Indians, attired according to the true nature of their country, seeming for the most part naked, are set at work on an Island of growing spices; some planting nutmeg-trees, some other spice-trees of all kinds. . . . These Indians are all active youths, who, ceasing in their labours, dance about the trees, both to give content to themselves and the spectators."[62] I do not know whether the inhabitants of the Moluccas or the Malabar Coast were "for the most part naked" in this era, and to a modern reader, the combination of happy industry and simple recreations uncomfortably anticipates colonialist fantasies of plantation life in the New World, but unlike the Indian settings in court masques, this one is geographically coherent. Similarly, in Middleton's *Triumphs of Honour and Virtue* (1622), "a black personage . . . the Queen of Merchandise," attended by Indians in "antique habits," is identified as "the Continent of India" and associated with the spice trade.[63]

In both court and city pageantry, Indian figures are more susceptible to religious conversion than others. Chapman's Indians worship the sun, and are "therefore called the Phoebades."[64] However, they are persuaded to turn their "devotions . . . / To this our Briton Phoebus," James I, "whose bright sky / . . . Is never subject to black Error's night."[65] Whereas the Muslim Turks in the sea fights are defeated and destroyed by James's naval might, these "pagan" Indians are won over by his Protestant faith, and thus are imagined as open to spiritual enlightenment, as the English understood it. In his Lord Mayors' Show *Honor and Virtue,* Middleton reprises the theme of conversion. Like the Moorish/Indian King and Queen in his *Triumphs of Truth* (discussed above), the Queen of India has already received Christianity from "three [figures] habited like merchants"—Commerce, Adventure, and Traffic.[66] In a speech of some forty-five lines, she, too, challenges onlookers to see beyond differences of skin color:

> This black is but my native dye,
> But view me with an intellectual eye,

> As wise men shoot their beams forth, then you'll find
> A change in the complexion of the mind:
> I'm beauteous in my blackness.[67]

She goes on to say that all the "gums and fragrant spices" of her realm cannot compare to the "odours whose scent [can] ne're decay," that is, the sweet truth of Christianity, but her modesty neatly associates the commodities she offers to the English with their own religion.

CONCLUSION

As David Bergeron has pointed out, the entertainments of court and city have much in common: they were "occasional" in nature; staged at great expense, supervised and subsidized by institutional figures (the Master of the Revels or the masters and wardens of the London companies); and often produced by long-term collaborators (a poet-playwright and a designer). Further, although the court masques were designed exclusively for the aristocracy, outdoor royal entertainments, such as the sea fights and royal entries (like that for James in 1604), were enjoyed by great and small, and thus resembled the Lord Mayors' Shows.[68] Anthony Miller, in his study of the Roman motifs in royal and civic entertainments, concludes that the city pageants "distinguish themselves from courtly idleness by teaching the virtue of industriousness" and counter "the improvidence of James's masquing" with "their scrupulous account-keeping," but like James's triumphs and masques, they "[adventure] across the globe in order to bring home the trophies of peaceful triumphs."[69]

These similarities notwithstanding, court and city entertainments represented the East in distinctive ways. Eastern characters at court are more fanciful, conflating Persia, neo-Platonism, and sun worship, and imagining Virginian priests who are simultaneously Eastern, Western, and African. In the Lord Mayors' Shows, by comparison, Easterners are seen more realistically in terms of trade and geographic space. Court masques emphasized the class status and supposed qualities of each group: Turks are warlike and powerful; Persians are benign and elegant; Moors and black Africans are usually subordinates (females or servants) and view their blackness as a defect. City pageants, not surprisingly, portray them all—even the warlike Turks—in the context of trade, and they stress the themes of mutual benefit and peaceful cooperation. As an Indian character (riding a rhinoceros) in Heywood's *Porta Pietatis* (1638) observes, a merchant like the current mayor ventures for the common good:

> The land he pierceth, and the ocean skowers,
> To make them all by free transportage ours.[70]

The pronoun "ours" suggests that global trade is imagined as creating (to borrow Barbour's phrase) a single world of "excited desire." In addition, the Easterners in city pageants are wealthy and of high status. While their rank is meant to enhance the dignity of the pageant sponsors, one can't benefit by association with others whom one demonizes or disparages.

In the matter of religious conversion, court and city also diverge somewhat. Turks are never represented as susceptible to conversion in either court or city entertainments, though Moors, Africans, and Indians are. At court, the catalyst for enlightenment is the monarch himself, whereas in the city merchant adventurers are credited with spreading the faith. City pageants treat conversion more directly and explicitly. Given the long-standing moral symbolism of the black versus white, the desire of Jonson's daughters of Niger to become "white" may imply spiritual longing, but religion (except for references to classical deities such as Neptune) is not mentioned in the text. The Persians in *The Temple of Love* worship a romantic ideal, but in this they are like their courtly audience and need no reform. The only explicit conversion imagined at court is that of the sun-worshipping Virginian/Indians in Chapman's *Masque.* Since the figures and their religion are so ambiguous, their conversion testifies to James's pious charisma but seems rather lacking in practical relevance.

Middleton's city entertainments also imagine the conversion of less threatening "Indian" Moors, rather than specifically Muslim ones, but whereas the "Virginian Indians" in Chapman's *Masque* mutely receive the light of Christianity (revising their sun-worshipping song to address James when they are so instructed), Middleton's imaginary converts articulate what Londoners might learn from *them,* namely, that what is in a person's heart should count more than visible differences. They challenge the significance of skin color more seriously than does Jonson's *Masque of Blackness,* in which the issue is precisely outward beauty, not inner light.

Missionary activity was, of course, an important feature of later colonialism, and it is now seen as a symptom of an imperialistic desire to remake others in the image of oneself and (wittingly or not) to disrupt the solidarity of indigenous peoples. At the same time, would-be missionaries have to abandon the notion that potential converts are demonic or otherwise irreconcilably alien, and, just as Muslims believed only Muslims could enter heaven, most Christians believed that only Christians could be saved. The imperial ambassador to Suleyman the Magnificent, Ogier Ghislain de Busbecq, can understand why the Turks consider conversion of Christians both a "duty" and "the greatest act of kindness" they can perform because he held the parallel opinion of Christians' duty to spread the Gospel.[71] In this period under discussion, however, English merchants and their pastors made no efforts in that direction. Cleric William Biddulph, whose letters record his experiences as pastor to a group of English merchants in the Levant, had no interest in converting Muslims. Rather, he admired their piety, envied the respect they gave their "priests," and complained about the bad behavior of the Englishmen and Europeans he met.[72] Thus, the playwrights' portrayal of "missionary" merchants seems designed not as a program for action, but as a strategy to bolster their reputations at home, to counter the charge (exemplified in Massinger's poem with which I began) that trade in Eastern luxuries weakened the moral fiber of Christendom.

Overall, court masques and Lord Mayors' Shows up to the mid-1600s suggest that, more than the courtly poets and their audiences, city playwrights and Londoners were comfortable imagining Eastern peoples as superiors or equals—not as objects, or slaves, or children. While not devoid of fantasy, Eastern characters in the Lord Mayors' Shows are seen in the context of trade and geographic space. Entertainments of both court and city flattered their sponsors and audiences, but in doing so, the court feminized and condescended (especially to Moors and sub-Saharan Africans), while the city merchants were more likely to imagine relationships of mutual benefit and respect.[73] Whether their Eastern counterparts took the same view, of course, is another question altogether.

NOTES

1. Philip Edwards and Colin Gibson, eds., *The Plays and Poems of Philip Massinger* (Oxford: Clarendon Press, 1976), 399–400, 2:13–29, 46. I have capitalized the first word of each line. Note that the sources of luxury goods include several European cities as well as Eastern ones.

2. "Homegrown" symbols are, however, often appropriated from elsewhere: the English or Damascene rose is originally from Damascus.

3. On the evolution from Medieval (religious) to Renaissance (classical) iconography, see Roy C. Strong, *Splendour at Court: Renaissance Spectacle and Illusion* (London: Weidenfeld and Nicolson, 1973), 24–31; David M. Bergeron, *English Civic Pageantry, 1558–1642* (London: Edward Arnold, 1971), 5–7.

4. Campion, *A Description of a Maske . . . Presented . . . At the Mariage of the . . . Earle of Somerset,* in Walter R. Davis, ed., *The Works of Thomas Campion* (London: Faber and Faber, 1969), 268. In this masque Campion's enchanters and enchantresses turn out to be quite familiar morality characters: Error, Rumor, Curiosity, and Credulity (271).

5. Samuel Chew, *The Crescent and the Rose: Islam and England During the Renaissance* (1937; repr. New York: Octagon Books, 1965), 457.

6. Fredson Bowers, ed., *The Dramatic Works of Thomas Dekker* (Cambridge: Cambridge University Press, 1952–58), 2:253–309, esp. 275. Dekker describes the figure of Arabia Britannica in detail; however, the extant drawing by the designer, Stephen Harrison (in *Arches of Triumph,* 1604), does not include it. See Bergeron, *Civic Pageantry,* 80–81, and plate 5.

7. For a typical statement of this view, see Daniel Vitkus, ed., *Three Turk Plays from Early Modern England* (New York: Columbia University Press, 2000), 2–3.

8. Daniel Vitkus, *Turning Turk: English Theatre and the Multicultural Mediterranean, 1570–1630* (New York: Palgrave Macmillan, 2003), 22. Vitkus here significantly complicates his previous formulation.

9. Kim F. Hall, *Things of Darkness: Economies of Race and Gender in Early Modern England* (Ithaca, NY: Cornell University Press, 1995), esp. chap. 5, 211–53.

10. Richmond Barbour, "Britain and the Great Beyond: *The Masque of Blackness* at Whitehall," in *Playing the Globe: Genre and Geography in English Renaissance Drama,* ed. John Gillies and Virginia Mason Vaughan (Madison, NJ: Fairleigh Dickinson University Press, 1998), 129–30.

11. Ibid., 130.

12. Vitkus notes that in their relations with Spain, Portugal, and Turkey, the English were largely "mimic-men . . . learning (or hoping) to imitate alien models of power, wealth, and luxury"; while they might claim as Heywood did, that "the potent Turke (although in faith adverse) / Is proud that he with England can commerce," it was the English who were proud to trade with him (*Turning Turk,* 9; qtd. on p. 32). Nabil Matar cites a series of setbacks that England suffered on the global stage between 1558 and 1603, and asserts that even "proud Britons" knew they were weak compared with imperial powers like Spain and Turkey; see his *Turks, Moors, and Englishmen in the Age of Discovery* (New York: Columbia University Press, 1999), 10–11.

13. Barbour makes his view of the similarities more explicit in his book, *Before Orientalism: London's Theatre of the East, 1576–1626* (Cambridge: Cambridge University Press, 2003), 81. In his chapter on royal and civic entertainments (68–101), which I had the pleasure of reading after this essay was submitted for publication, Barbour notes many of the details I discuss here but comes to somewhat contrary conclusions. Our positions differ chiefly on whether, if the intent is self-serving, the attribution of positive qualities and high status to Eastern figures is negated or reinforced. He takes the former view, and I the latter.

14. Hall's *Chronicle,* quoted in Chew, *Crescent and the Rose,* 454.

15. Strong, *Splendour at Court,* 49.

16. Qtd. in Chew, *Crescent and the Rose,* 454–56.

17. Ibid., 457.

18. Ibid., 452.

19. "Neptune's whale" appeared and a dolphin upon which were seated "two of his choicest Trytons . . . and personating in them the severall Genii of Corinea the Beautiful Queene of Cornewall, and Amphion, the Father of Hermonie or Musick." See John Nichols, ed., *The Progresses, Processions, and Magnificent Festivities of King James I* (London, 1828; repr., New York: AMS Press, [1968?]), 2:319–20.

20. Ibid., 2:323.

21. Ibid., 2:538.

22. Ibid., 2:539–40.

23. From a contemporary description written by the poet John Taylor, qtd. in Chew, *Crescent and the Rose,* 461.

24. Nichols, *Progresses,* 2:541.

25. Qtd. in Chew, *Crescent and the Rose,* 462. For Robert Naile's detailed description of the event, see Nichols, *Progresses,* 2:648–49.

26. *Monuments of Honour,* in F. L. Lucas, ed., *The Complete Works of John Webster* (Boston: Houghton Mifflin, 1924), 3:319–20, 323.

27. *London's Tempe,* in Bowers, *Dramatic Works,* 4:103, 106.

28. In 1584, Elizabeth I wrote to Murad III "for the restitution of the shippe, called the Jesus, and the English captives detained in Tripolie in Barbarie, and for certain other prisoners in Argiers," and he wrote to his viceroys "commanding" the same. See Hakluyt, *Principall Navigations* (Cambridge: Cambridge University Press for the Hakluyt Society and the Peabody Society of Salem, 1965), 199–201.

29. Lucas, *Complete Works,* 3: 323.

30. Anthony Parr, ed., *Three Renaissance Travel Plays* (Manchester, UK: Manchester University Press, 1995), 11.

31. On the tendency to conflate the ancient and early modern Persians, see my "'Bringing in a Persian,'" *Medieval and Renaissance Drama in England* 12 (1999): 236–67, esp. 239, 245.

32. Stephen Orgel and Roy C. Strong, *Inigo Jones and the Theatre of the Stuart Court* (London: Sotheby Parke Bernet, 1973), 621–22.

33. In James Maidment and W. H. Logan, eds., *The Dramatic Works of Sir William D'Avenant* (Edinburgh: William Paterson, 1872), 1:298.

34. Ibid., 1:286.

35. Other Eastern figures and motifs were painted on the stage "ornament," including "a naked Indian on a whitish elephant representing the Indian monarchy" and an "Asiatique in the habit of an Indian borderer, riding on a camel; his turban and coat differing from that of the Turks, figured for the Asian monarchy." The Temple of Chaste Love, however, is apparently in England ("in this Island") in the court itself (ibid., 1:286–87).

36. The painting is reproduced as Plate VIII in Orgel and Strong, *Inigo Jones*, 44.

37. Hall, *Things of Darkness*, fig. 17, p. 235.

38. In the 1760s, Turkish dress also came into fashion as "at home" clothing, as can be seen in portraits of aristocratic women by Angelica Kauffman and others.

39. Qtd. in Chew, *Crescent and the Rose*, 454–55.

40. Ibid., 455.

41. Ibid., 456 n. 6. For a study of blackface and related stage practices, see Virginia Mason Vaughan, *Performing Blackness on English Stages, 1500–1800* (Cambridge: Cambridge University Press, 2005), esp. chap. 2.

42. The figure of Oceanus appears in blue body paint. For an analysis of the functioning of skin color and cultural difference in this masque, see Barbour, "Britain and the Great Beyond," 129–53.

43. Ibid., 145–46.

44. Davis, *Works of Thomas Campion*, 271.

45. Thomas Marc Parrott, ed., *The Plays and Poems of George Chapman* (London: Routledge and Sons, 1910), 2:440.

46. Another exception might be D'Avenant's Indamora, whose name suggests "Moor" as well as "India." However, Jones's sketch does not show her as dark-skinned; see Orgel and Strong, *Inigo Jones*, 625. Henrietta Maria probably appeared as Indamora: the Argument ends with a reference to King Charles as "the last and living Hero (Indamora's Royal Lover)" (Maidment and Logan, *Dramatic Works*, 1:287).

47. David M. Bergeron, ed., *Pageants and Entertainments of Anthony Munday: A Critical Edition* (New York: Garland, 1985), 104 (lines 90–93). Munday's text describes the kings as "on horsebacke" although the extant drawing shows them on foot.

48. Barbour points out that Munday's Moors are not unambiguously African, since they are tossing "Indian treasure" (*Before Orientalism*, 91).

49. A. H. Bullen, ed., *The Works of Thomas Middleton* (Boston: Houghton Mifflin, 1884–86; repr., New York: AMS Press, 1964), 7:247–48.

50. Ibid., 7:248.

51. Ibid., 7:249.

52. George Peele, *The Device of the Pageant Borne Before Wolstan Dixi*, in David H. Horne, ed., *The Life and Minor Works of George Peele* (New Haven, CT: Yale University Press, 1952), 1:209–13. In this earliest surviving description of a Lord Mayors' Show, the Moorish presenter is royal, and he does not refer to his complexion. According to Horne, a "King of the Moors" was also presented by the Drapers for the "midsummer watch" in 1520 (see 1:160 n. 50).

53. Lucas, *Complete Works*, 4:323.

54. Horne, *Minor Works*, 1:105, emphasis added.

55. Lucas, *Complete Works*, 4:323.

56. Both Old and New World "Indians" were rumored to be custodians of fabulous riches (the "mines of the Indies").

57. They wear "turbans, stuck with several coloured feathers" and decorated with "wings of flies of extraordinary bigness, like those of their country" (Parrott, *Plays and Poems,* 2:439.

58. Ibid., 2:439–40.

59. Orgel and Strong, *Inigo Jones,* 262.

60. Her name evokes "Moor" as well as "Indian," and her kingdom borders Persia and is associated in the decor with an elephant; but she is "ent[h]roned" on "a maritime chariot . . . , the back of which was a great skallop shell"; see Maidment and Logan, *Dramatic Works,* 1:286, 300.

61. Bullen, *Works,* 7:298–99.

62. Ibid., 7:297–98.

63. Ibid., 7:358. She is "replenished with all manner of spice-plants and trees bearing odour" and "advanceth herself upon a bed of spices."

64. Parrott, *Plays and Poems,* 2:439.

65. Ibid., 2:455.

66. Bullen, *Works,* 7:358.

67. Ibid., 7:358.

68. Bergeron, *Pageants and Entertainments,* xi.

69. Anthony Miller, "Domains of Victory: Staging and Contesting the Roman Triumph in Renaissance England," in *Playing the Globe: Genre and Geography in English Renaissance Drama,* ed. John Gillies and Virginia Mason Vaughan, 260–287, esp. 278–79 (Madison, NJ: Fairleigh Dickinson University Press, 1998).

70. Thomas Heywood, *Porta Pietatis, or London's Gate of Piety,* in *The Dramatic Works of Thomas Heywood* (London: John Pearson, 1874; repr. New York: Russell and Russell, 1964), 5:269.

71. *The Four Turkish Letters of Ogier Ghislain de Busbecq,* trans. Edward Seymour Forster (1927; repr., Oxford: Oxford University Press, 1968), 120.

72. [Biddulph, William.] *The Travels of Certaine Englishmen into Africa, Asia . . . ,* ed. Theophilus Lavender (London, 1609), 62–63, 66. Barbour likewise notes that the English did not proselytize in the Levant, and that the governor of the East India Company and Sir Thomas Roe's chaplain deemed such ambitions "unreasonable" and viewed the Jesuits' evangelical efforts as ineffective (*Before Orientalism,* 92).

73. Barbour rightly notes that later Indian figures in city pageants, specifically Middleton's "Queen of Merchandise" (1617) and his "Continent of India" (1622), are feminine and, he argues, eroticized (*Before Orientalism,* 95–96).

BIBLIOGRAPHY

Barbour, Richmond. *Before Orientalism: London's Theatre of the East, 1576–1626.* Cambridge: Cambridge University Press, 2003.

———. "Britain and the Great Beyond: *The Masque of Blackness* at Whitehall." In *Playing the Globe: Genre and Geography in English Renaissance Drama,* edited by John Gillies and Virginia Mason Vaughan, 129–53. Madison, NJ: Fairleigh Dickinson University Press, 1998. 129–53.

Bergeron, David M. *English Civic Pageantry, 1558–1642.* London: Edward Arnold, 1971.

———, ed. *Pageants and Entertainments of Anthony Munday: A Critical Edition.* New York: Garland, 1985.

[Biddulph, William.] *The Travels of Certaine Englishmen into Africa, Asia, Troy, Bythinia, Thracia, and to the Black Sea.* Edited by Theophilus Lavender. London, 1609.

Bowers, Fredson, ed. *The Dramatic Works of Thomas Dekker.* 4 vols. Cambridge: Cambridge University Press, 1952–58.

Bullen, A. H., ed. *The Works of Thomas Middleton.* 8 vols. Boston: Houghton Mifflin, 1884–86. Reprint, New York: AMS Press, 1964.

Busbecq, Ogier Ghislain de. *The Four Turkish Letters of Ogier Ghislain de Busbecq.* Translated by Edward Seymour Forster. 1927. Reprint, Oxford: Oxford University Press, 1968.

Chew, Samuel. *The Crescent and the Rose: Islam and England During the Renaissance.* 1937. Reprint, New York: Octagon Books, 1965.

Davis, Walter R., ed. *The Works of Thomas Campion.* London: Faber and Faber, 1969.

Edwards, Philip, and Colin Gibson, eds. *The Plays and Poems of Philip Massinger.* 5 vols. Oxford: Clarendon Press, 1976.

[Heywood, Thomas.] *The Dramatic Works of Thomas Heywood.* 6 vols. London: John Pearson, 1874. Reprint, New York: Russell and Russell, 1964.

Hakluyt, Richard. *The Principall Navigations, Voiages, and Discoveries of the English Nation: Imprinted at London, 1589.* Cambridge: Cambridge University Press for the Hakluyt Society and the Peabody Society of Salem, 1965.

Hall, Kim F. *Things of Darkness: Economies of Race and Gender in Early Modern England.* Ithaca, NY: Cornell University Press, 1995.

Horne, David H., ed. *The Life and Minor Works of George Peele.* In *The Life and Works of George Peele.* 3 vols. New Haven, CT: Yale University Press, 1952.

Lucas, F. L., ed. *The Complete Works of John Webster.* 4 vols. Boston: Houghton Mifflin, 1924.

Maidment, James, and W. H. Logan, eds. *The Dramatic Works of Sir William D'Avenant.* 5 vols. Edinburgh: William Paterson, 1872.

Matar, Nabil. *Turks, Moors, and Englishmen in the Age of Discovery.* New York: Columbia University Press, 1999.

McJannet, Linda. "'Bringing in a Persian,'" *Medieval and Renaissance Drama in England* 12 (1999): 236–67.

Miller, Anthony. "Domains of Victory: Staging and Contesting the Roman Triumph in Renaissance England." In *Playing the Globe: Genre and Geography in English Renaissance Drama,* edited by John Gillies and Virginia Mason Vaughan, 260–87. Madison, NJ: Fairleigh Dickinson University Press, 1998.

Nichols, John, ed. *The Progresses, Processions, and Magnificent Festivities of King James I.* London. 1828. Reprint, New York: AMS Press, [1968?].

Nichols, John Gough, ed. *The Fishmongers' Pageant.* London, 1859.

Orgel, Stephen, ed. *Ben Jonson: The Complete Masques.* New Haven, CT: Yale University Press. 1969.

Orgel, Stephen, and Roy C. Strong. *Inigo Jones and the Theatre of the Stuart Court.* London: Sotheby Parke Bernet, 1973.

Parrott, Thomas Marc, ed. *The Plays and Poems of George Chapman.* 2 vols. London: Routledge and Sons, 1910.

Strong, Roy C. *Splendour at Court: Renaissance Spectacle and Illusion.* London: Weidenfeld and Nicolson, 1973.

Vitkus, Daniel, ed. *Three Turk Plays from Early Modern England.* New York: Columbia University Press, 2000.

———. *Turning Turk: English Theatre and the Multicultural Mediterranean, 1570–1630.* New York: Palgrave Macmillan, 2003.

The Strange Finding Out of Moses his Tombe: News, Travel Narrative, and Satire

Kate Loveman

IN DECEMBER 1656, THERE APPEARED ON LONDON BOOKSTALLS A PAMphlet entitled *A True and Exact Relation of the Strange Finding Out of Moses his Tombe.*[1] Foreign news and religious marvels fascinated the public in Oliver Cromwell's England, and *The Strange Finding Out of Moses his Tombe* held this double allure. The work immediately created much discussion, for its title promised readers an astonishing revelation. The Bible states that Moses died after viewing the Promised Land from Mount Nebo and that God "buried him in a valley in the land of Moab, over against Bethpeor: but no man knoweth of his sepulchre unto this day."[2] *The Strange Finding Out of Moses his Tombe* describes how a potential candidate for the patriarch's sepulchre had been discovered. The forty-page octavo narrative was anonymous but professed excellent credentials. It had been "communicated by a person of quality residing at *Constantinople,* to a person of Honour here in *England,* and by him permitted to be published, for the satisfaction of the Ingenious."[3] The pamphlet tells how, in October 1655, Maronite shepherds on Mount Nebo were puzzled by the fact that their goats disappeared for long periods and returned with "a most odiferous scent" (2). The shepherds investigated and found a cave. Suffused with perfume, it appeared "more than the work of nature" and contained a sealed sepulchre (4). Further inspection revealed an inscription in Hebrew: "MOSES *THE SERVANT OF GOD*" (6). A quarrel over who should have control of the tomb immediately ensued between the various religions resident in the Ottoman Empire: the Jews, the Maronite Christians, the Armenian and Greek Churches, the Jesuits, and the Franciscan monastery at Jerusalem. Each group attempted to ingratiate themselves with senior Ottoman officials through denouncing the other groups and offering large bribes. Professing abhorrence of the idolatry which the tomb might encourage, the French Jesuits at last succeeded in placating the various parties and persuaded the Turkish authorities that travel to the site should be forbidden. However, the Jesuits in fact intended "to steal away the body of *Moses,* and shipping it for *France,* to place it in their Colledge of *le Fleche,* whereby they propounded to themselves the gaining of infinite reputation in holiness, besides the accumulation of wealth by indulgences" (12). To this end the Jesuits used the cover of the annual Easter procession from Jerusalem to the River Jordan to get near the tomb. They employed a band of mercenary Druses to attack the caravan and stage a fake kidnapping of their own agents. In the company of the Druses, the Jesuits broke open the tomb only to find it contained no corpse. They were subsequently seized by the local governor's forces—so much for the Jesuits' plot. The final part describes the debates between the different religions and denominations over what had happened to Moses's body. The Jews looked to rabbinical works to show that the body had disappeared a thousand years ago during a raid by a devil called Asmandeus. In confutation, the Roman Catholics cited the Epistle of St. Jude and St. John's Revelation which, they said, showed that the archangel Michael had defeated the devil and still had Moses's body in his custody. The other Christian churches decried the Roman Catholics' claims, protesting that these books were not canonical. When asked their opinion, the English Protestant divines excused themselves as ignorant on this point and proposed to seek advice from home. The dispute was eventually resolved by Rabbi Jeconius Ben-Gad who presented a raft of arguments showing that this was not the biblical Moses's tomb, but that of a later namesake. Amongst other points, "he maintained it to be most unbeseeming the wisdom of God to hide the body of *Moses,* and yet to write his name upon his Sepulchre" (35–36). All the supposed miracles surrounding the discovery of the tomb had rational explanations. The corpse of this later Moses had not vanished in a supernatural combat but had been destroyed by the Christian crusaders, men infamous for pillaging tombs. The correspondent reports that the Rabbi's pragmatic and scholarly book, "though written (after the Jewish manner) with much bitternesse against the Christians, did give exceeding satisfaction. So it is thought this business hath received its full period" (39).

Any reader who was satisfied with the "true" relation of *Moses his Tombe* was making an embarrassing mistake. The scholar Anthony Wood described events following publication: "This book, at its first appearance, made a great noise, and pusled the presbyterian rabbies for a time: at length the author thereof being known, and his story found to be a meer sham, the book became ridiculous and was put to posterior uses."[4] Being an inveterate bibliophile, Wood did not put his copy to posterior uses but instead noted on the title page: "This is a meere lye, it was writt by Thomas Chaloner: esq*uire,* and inuented at a tauern: London."[5] The attribution to Thomas Chaloner (1595–1660) was also given by Wood's collaborator, John Aubrey. Since Aubrey did not refer to the piece being composed in a London tavern, it seems Wood had information about Chaloner's authorship from an additional source. Chaloner's education had included travels in France, Italy, and

Germany. In 1637 he set off on another trip abroad, this time to escape pros-
ecution for a treatise offensive to Archbishop Laud. David Scott believes that
on this occasion Chaloner probably went to stay with his brother William
in Turkey, a visit which may have helped inspire *Moses his Tombe*.[6] In 1645
Chaloner took up a seat in the Long Parliament as a recruiter member for
Richmond. A republican and a regicide, he sat on the Council of State from
February 1650 until the exclusion of the Rump by Cromwell in April
1653.[7] Chaloner was notorious for his religious principles (or lack thereof).
Wood cites him as an example of the "beastly and atheistical company"
favored by the writer Thomas May (1596–1650). Aubrey took a more
generous view of Chaloner and his publication. He found *Moses his Tombe*
to be "written very wittily," and said of its author, "He was as far from a
puritan as the East from the West. He was of the naturall religion, and of
Henry Martyn's gang, and one who loved to enjoy the pleasures of this life."[8]

Chaloner is unlikely to have been the sole perpetrator of the hoax. While
he was unable to benefit from his well-traveled brother's expertise—for
William had died over a decade earlier—there are hints that others were
involved.[9] The preface to *Moses his Tombe* implies that the publisher,
Richard Lowndes, was in on the joke. Given in the name of "the Stationer,"
the effusive preface urges readers to believe the account, stating, "the quality of the persons from whom I have received it, the particular circumstances of places and persons adde very much credit to it, so that it would
be absurd to doubt the truth of it amongst a cloud of witnesses" (A3v). "A
cloud of witnesses" is an allusion to Heb. 12:1 where St. Paul cites accounts
of the faithful in the Old Testament in vindication of Christianity. The preface appears sincere at first glance but, with knowledge that the piece is a
hoax, becomes ironic: it proves more absurd to credit these "witnesses"
than to doubt them. Given the consonance of this mocking biblical allusion
with the satire of the main narrative, Lowndes may well have had assistance in drafting the preface. It is not clear that he realized the inflam-
matory nature of the pamphlet: certainly, he seems to have been oddly
unconcerned about attaching his name to it and thereby risking the ire of
his customers and the authorities. While the preface incriminated Lowndes,
the reference to the "persons" who supplied the narrative indicates other
collaborators. Wood's comments suggest popular suspicion that Chaloner's
project was assisted by members of tavern society. The chief suspects
would have to be the ex-MP Henry Marten (1601–80) and his republican
"gang" who were meeting at the Nonsuch Tavern in Covent Garden during this period. Initially perceived as authored by a respectable gentleman
in Constantinople, *Moses his Tombe* came to be seen as a product of dis-
reputable London tavern society. Nevertheless, Aubrey tells us that
"'twas a pretty while before the shamme was detected."[10] How, then, did
Chaloner manage to convince readers that *Moses his Tombe* was a genuine

account of foreign affairs and marvellous discoveries? As we will see, the deception required knowledge of the East, manipulation of news networks, and careful exploitation of Englishmen's preoccupations and preconceptions.

For *Moses his Tombe* to appear to be genuine news from the Levant, Chaloner needed to present it as arriving via the accustomed news routes. The relation had apparently been sent as a manuscript from a well-informed gentleman in Constantinople. Foreign news was often dispersed by oral reports emanating from the Exchange in London—this was the resort of merchants who were in receipt of the latest information through their trading contacts abroad. Judging by the sources given in printed newsbooks, information from Constantinople usually traveled to London via Venice. In winter it took around thirty-eight days for reports from Venice to make it into the London newsbooks, but those in receipt of manuscript news would expect to have it in advance of print bulletins.[11] In the summer months false reports could be detected relatively quickly when confirmation failed to arrive via alternative news routes.[12] In winter, however, bad weather hampered travel and neither confirmation nor definitive refutation of *Moses his Tombe* could be obtained quickly. Chaloner could therefore have expected his sham to deceive for weeks, if not longer.

Like so much Levant news, *Moses his Tombe* seems to have first spread as hearsay. The preface remarked that readers might have heard "flying rumours" about the account (A3r). This seems likely given the author's reported method for hoaxing. Aubrey relates that Chaloner "had a trick sometimes to goe into Westminster hall in a morning in Terme time, and tell some strange [false] story (sham), and would come thither again about 11 or 12 to have the pleasure to heare how it spred; and sometimes it would be altered, with additions, he could scarce knowe it to be his owne."[13] Westminster Hall, the site of law courts and bookstalls, was a major point for the exchange of news in London. It would not be surprising if Chaloner and his co-conspirators had visited Westminster Hall or the Exchange in order to generate intriguing gossip about the pamphlet. Chaloner clearly had an acute sense for the kind of stories that would spread rapidly, and how, where, and when to initiate them. *Moses his Tombe* was issued during the parliamentary sessions, when London was at its busiest and news networks eager for information. With foreign news a valuable commodity, an exotic tale such as *Moses his Tombe* would be seized upon and quickly disseminated. Demand would be all the greater because printed newsbooks, having reached unprecedented numbers during the 1640s and early 1650s, were now strictly controlled. In 1655 Cromwell had suppressed all printed English newsbooks with the exception of the government-controlled *Mercurius Politicus* and *The Publick Intelligencer.* These two publications, edited by Marchamont Nedham, were the only regular suppliers of printed foreign news in English. Nedham had access to the government's diplomatic and intelligence network, meaning that his foreign reporting was of a high standard for the period.[14] In the case of the Ottoman Empire, readers were told of major events that might impact upon the English traders there or upon Christendom: revolts, changes of rulers, and battles with Venice. Yet Nedham's reports from the empire were usually fragmentary and often second- or third-hand, giving Chaloner room to invent his own version of Levantine intrigues. Although Chaloner did not plant false reports in the newsbooks he did succeed in infiltrating *The Publick Intelligencer* by other means. Lowndes advertised *Moses his Tombe* in this government mouthpiece alongside his more innocent publications.[15] With this advertisement in a respectable government newsbook, Chaloner and Lowndes placed a tempting bait for news-hungry readers.

Moses his Tombe appeared to have followed the accustomed pattern for Levant news arriving as rumor, in manuscript, and finally in print. To complete the deception, the pamphlet had to seem to describe accurately the topography, society, and politics of the Levant. If Chaloner did visit the Levant in the late 1630s, his experience would have been of great help in creating a credible depiction. However, he appears to have turned to others' accounts to assist him. Cyril Hackett Wilkinson, in his accomplished introduction to *Moses his Tombe,* points out that Chaloner drew on the printed narratives of travelers to the East. For example, Chaloner took his description of the mercenary Druses from George Sandys's *A Relation of a Journey Begun An. Dom: 1610* and from William Biddulph's account in *Purchas his Pilgrimes* (1625).[16] On their way to the tomb, Chaloner's Jesuits land at Jaffa, and travel past Ramallah to Jerusalem where they stay at the Franciscan monastery. This was the traditional route for Western pilgrims described in the travel narratives of Sandys and Fynes Moryson. The traveler William Lithgow had been on the annual caravan to the Jordan and had described how pilgrims were regularly attacked there.[17] Since travel narratives often show signs of being modeled upon each other—the same information is repeated by different travelers—anyone noticing Chaloner's sources would not necessarily have been alerted to the deception. Chaloner's clever borrowings meant that his sham seemed to be confirmed by travelers' accounts, masking the fact that it is actually based on these tales.

The travel narratives of Sandys and others were decades old, and so could not supply information on the Holy Land for the years 1655 and 1656 in which the story is set. To deduce Chaloner's other sources we can look in detail at a passage from *Moses his Tombe*. This extract also serves to demonstrate the intricate web of fact and fiction which Chaloner created. Here the narrator describes how the *"Sanziack* of *Jerusalem"* reacted on learning of the Jesuits' plan: "Being of a more subtle braine then Turks ordinarily are (he being in truth a *Renegado* Christian, a notable knave, and a Scottish-man borne; his right name being *Sande Murrey,* but upon his circumcision he called himself *Ram-Dam*) he gave notice of his feares to *Nazuffe* the *Sanziack* of *Saphetta,* who was also a *Renegado* of *Hungary,* and as cunning a knave as himself: advising him, that he should give notice hereof to certain troupes of *Spahees* who lay grasing of their horses on the other side of *Jordane* untill they received orders from *Morat, Bashaw* of *Damasco,* to goe against the sonne of *Ipsheer Bashaw,* the rebell *Bashaw* of *Aleppo*" (20–21). The place names would be familiar to readers of travel narratives, newsbooks, and merchants' correspondence, as would the transliterated terms used. Sandys, for example, describes "*Sanziaks*" as "gouernors of cities" and says of "*Bassas*" that "some are Generals of armies, some Vizers of the Port, the rest vice-royes of prouinces."[18] Nabil Matar has discussed how travel writers were fascinated by the figure of the Christian convert to Islam, and the wealth and status he could gain.[19] Their remarks on converts may well have prompted Chaloner to claim that Sande Murrey, alias Ram-Dam, was the governor of Jerusalem. In the 1650s the district of Jerusalem was actually under the control of the most powerful dynasty in the region: the governor in 1655 to 1656 appears to have been either Husayn Pasha Ridwān or his son Ibrahīm.[20] Chaloner evidently thought he could get away with the renegade Scotsman because Sande Murrey's role happily complied with English perceptions of both the conduct of Ottoman affairs and the Scottish character. Readers of English newsbooks were entertained with descriptions of the rapid turnover of Ottoman officials due to violent competition for places and frequent executions.[21] Sande Murrey and his superiors are similarly portrayed as devious politicians motivated by greed and ambition. The Scots' role in the Civil Wars had not endeared them to Chaloner's circle. During the mid-1640s the English Parliament was in alliance with the Scottish Covenanters. However, following the breakdown of the Solemn League and Covenant, the Scottish forces joined with Charles I, and then with his heir, to fight Parliament. Chaloner's irritation with the Scots had first surfaced publicly in 1646 when he issued a pamphlet accusing them of meddling in English affairs. His friends Henry Marten and Thomas May subsequently joined in the attack, portraying the Scots as reneging on their religious commitments in order to gain power.[22] To Parliamentarian pamphleteers of the 1650s the Scots became "barbarous" plunderers and "Unchristian Machiavells."[23] The appearance of the Scotsman Sande Murrey amongst the barbarous Turks was therefore a sly piece of propaganda and something of an in-joke.

Chaloner could afford to invent certain individuals because he was elsewhere very precise in his references to local current affairs. Mention of Sande Murrey is quickly followed by a comment on the situation prompted by "the sonne of *Ipsheer Bashaw.*" Readers of *The Publick Intelligencer* in March 1656 would have learned from Venice that "the son of the last Visier *Ibscher Bassa,* goeth on still in his Rebellion, and was advanced with 50000 men as farre as *Aleppo,* threatening to assault that place."[24] However, Chaloner's narrative could not have been pieced together solely from the fragmentary news in *Mercurius Politicus* and *The Publick Intelligencer.* He had almost certainly seen letters from English residents in the Levant describing local events in more detail. These would have been of the kind that John Thurloe, the Secretary of State, was receiving from his informants at Leghorn and Constantinople. In March 1656 Charles Longland at Leghorn wrote to Thurloe that "Ipsir Bashawe's son (the great vizier who was cut off at Constantinople) to revenge his father's death has raised a great army of 20 thousand men, and besieged Aleppo in Siria, which the bashaw of Damascus seeking to reliev has bin beaten."[25] Chaloner's access to this kind of detailed reportage was a legacy of his time in government. While a member of the Rump Parliament he had taken a leading role in formulating commercial and diplomatic policy, cultivating close ties with the merchant community. As recently as 1655 he had sat on the Committee for Trade, but had been ejected by a vote of the Protector's Council.[26] Evidently, despite Chaloner's fall from power, his government contacts and merchant friends continued to keep him apprised of developments abroad. He was thus able to construct a narrative that unwound against the background of known events in the East and that could therefore not easily be dismissed by readers.

The newsworthiness of *Moses his Tombe* was assured by appeals to a range of preoccupations concerning the mysterious and the foreign. If representations of the Turks as powerful and exotic infidels intrigued the English, the Jews held an even greater fascination because their religious mysteries were seen as intimately related to England's role as an elect nation. In discussing modern Jewish activities and ancient Jewish traditions *Moses his Tombe* appealed to the growing philo-semitism amongst England's elites. The early seventeenth century had seen a renewed interest in Jewish traditions, which, as Wilkinson points out, culminated in debates on the formal readmission of Jews into England in 1655 and 1656.[27] The pamphlet also exploited millenarian beliefs that the conversion of the Jews was imminent and would signal the End of Days. The date on which the Jews were to be called was often given as a year in the 1650s, with, for example, the fifth monarchist Mary Cary believing that the Israelites would be delivered in 1656.[28] The revelation that the tomb of Moses had been discovered could only have added fuel to millenarians' fiery convictions. Although of particular import to religious radicals, claims that Moses's tomb had been found would also, of course, intrigue more moderate Protestants. It was traditionally held that the sepulchre had been hidden by God to prevent people being tempted into idolatry.[29] For Protestants this specifically meant the threat of Roman Catholic idolatry. In 1640 John Blenkow had written a sermon on the subject dedicated to the father of Henry Marten. Blenkow imagined that, unconcealed, the tomb would have become a source of income for Catholic idolaters: "We cannot but see to what excellent purpose the body of *Moses* would have served; when we see so many armes, legges, hands, feet, & fingers of Martyrs, to be had in such reverent if not divine estimation."[30] This is exactly the scenario that Chaloner satirically describes in his tale of mercenary Jesuits. Decades of anti-Catholic propaganda had told English Protestants of nefarious and daring Jesuit conspiracies. These schemes ranged from the Gunpowder Plot to the popular notion that it was the Catholics who had provoked the Civil War by manipulating the king and Parliament into confrontation. As *"oyly-mouthed Absolons"* the Jesuits were experts in "juglings, legerdemaines, stratagemeticall plots, and combustions in state." They were, however, prone to overreaching themselves and divine providence could be relied upon to reveal their schemes.[31] *Moses his Tombe* portrayed the Jesuits in a familiar light: ambitious, manipulative, cunning, and ultimately frustrated. What appear improbable elements of the narrative to us, then, would have seemed highly credible to many seventeenth-century Englishmen. The narrator's final comment that the matter has been settled with the discrediting of the tomb must have reassured moderate Protestants. Their anti-Catholic interpretation of the biblical mystery remained unchallenged and there was no immediate call for millenarian alarm: this was not a religious document but merely a historical one.

The subsequent discovery that the pamphlet was a sham ridiculed readers' sense of complacency: the historical document proved no such thing. Instead it was a blasphemous joke. Wood and Aubrey, respectively, describe Chaloner as "atheistical" and "of the naturall religion"—labels commonly applied to deists and freethinkers. Chaloner's anticlericalism and lack of respect for revealed religion were to be found throughout *Moses his Tombe*. In presuming to continue the narrative of Moses's death in Deuteronomy Chaloner had mocked the Holy Writ. Sly digs were made at the authority of the Bible. For example, when the preface (in which one suspects Chaloner had a hand) alluded to the Old Testament's "cloud of witnesses" the implication was that the witnesses who could be known only through the Bible itself might be as fraudulent as those created through the text of *Moses his Tombe*. To make matters worse, English divines were reputed to be the most prominent victims of the sham. According to Wood the pamphlet puzzled "the presbyterian rabbies" and seemed "a great wonder to the Presbyterian Divines," while Aubrey claimed that it "sett the witts of all the Rabbis of the Assembly then to worke."[32] Wood and Aubrey were writing some years after events, and Wood had a severe bias against Presbyterians: their identifications of the pamphlet's victims must therefore be treated with caution. In any case these descriptions require some interpretation. It was an established satiric trope to describe parliamentarians and their sympathizers as

Jews, ridiculing their covenants, patriarchs, synagogues, and, of course, their rabbis.[33] Here the term "rabbis" suggested the deceived clergy's pretensions to expertise in the Pentateuch. Aubrey's reference to "the Rabbis of the Assembly" indicates the Westminster Assembly of Divines, a group dominated by Presbyterian clergy. They had been active in the 1640s but were dormant in 1657. Aubrey's dates are confused, but it is possible that surviving members of the Assembly were amongst those who noisily discussed the sham. The pamphlet itself encouraged such debates for, according to the narrator, the English at Constantinople intended to refer the whole matter to "the Assembly of Divines in *England*" (35).[34] Once the pamphlet was recognized as a deception it was English Protestants who replaced the Jesuits as the principal objects of satire. The depiction of religions in the Ottoman Empire squabbling over divine truth bore an uncomfortable resemblance to the strife between Protestant denominations under Cromwell. If, as seems likely, the English religious authorities took the pamphlet to be genuine, they exceeded the gullibility of all the religious groups described in *Moses his Tombe*. The Jesuits, Armenians, Greeks, Franciscans, and so on, were only represented as credulous and self-serving; the English divines, in crediting the pamphlet, actually provided evidence of their own foolishness. Reports that *Moses his Tombe* had humiliated Presbyterians in particular would have pleased Chaloner and his allies since Presbyterian preachers had been amongst the most vehement opponents of the republican government.[35]

At the time *Moses his Tombe* was published Chaloner and his associates had reason for particular dissatisfaction with the Protector's regime. In September 1656 the army had implemented a sweeping policy of exclusion and prevented over one hundred MPs from sitting. Those banned from the House included the obstructive republicans, amongst them Chaloner's ally Thomas Scot.[36] *Moses his Tombe* was completed by December 9th for this was the date Lowndes registered it with the Stationers' Company.[37] However, subsequent events can only have increased the satiric impact of the pamphlet. From December 5th the Commons was preoccupied with fierce debates over what it held to be the "horrid blasphemy" of the Quaker James Nayler. In October Nayler had made a triumphal entry into Bristol in the manner of Christ into Jerusalem. The Commons' debates over the nature of his offense and a suitable punishment took up the majority of December, to the hindrance of other business. Despite there being no current law against blasphemy, Nayler was sentenced to be pilloried, whipped, branded, and imprisoned.[38] When it appeared in late December Chaloner's mockery of religious zeal proved extraordinarily timely, satirizing not only the clerical authorities, but those members of the Second Protectorate parliament who claimed the rights to determine religious truth and to police worship.

To conclude, in a culture where it was proverbial that travelers might "lie by authority," *Moses his Tombe* could be regarded by readers as a contribution to a tradition of travelers' false stories.[39] Wood's and Aubrey's comments, however, show that this "sham" was also recognized—at least by some—as a subversive satire. It was a particularly expert and well orchestrated deception, involving as it did not just the manipulation of print conventions to create a credible persona, but the successful exploitation of oral and manuscript news networks. The elaborateness of the hoax was partly a response to a reading public who were unusually well-informed about foreign affairs. Unlike previous generations, readers of the 1640s and 1650s were accustomed to receiving regular and frequent foreign reports through the newsbooks: to deceive the more knowledgeable members of this audience therefore required skill and care. The elaborateness of the hoax was also essential to Chaloner's religious critique. At a time when the authorities were particularly alert to blasphemy, he was engaged in a concerted attack on revealed religion. In Chaloner's scenario representatives of all faiths were governed by superstition and worldly motives, and their holy texts were suspect. He could afford to be overt in slighting Roman Catholics, Muslims, and Jews, but his assault on the Protestant clergy had to proceed by implication. Obliqueness and subtlety were thus necessary components in his attempts to expose the English religious authorities to ridicule. Chaloner's strategy of using mystification to demystify established religion was subsequently to become a recognized method of free-thinking writers. Early eighteenth-century freethinkers, including the third Earl of Shaftesbury and Anthony Collins, defended irony, equivocation, and tacit ridicule as legitimate means of critiquing the religious orthodoxy under oppressive regimes.[40] Chaloner, with his sophisticated sham, anticipated these writers' arguments by decades. As a satire upon the religious and political authorities and all manner of authoritative texts, *Moses his Tombe* earned Chaloner contempt—yet as a prominent republican he can have been no stranger to that. However, crucially, it also won him esteem as the author of a pamphlet written, as Aubrey put it, "very wittily." The hoax amusingly advertised Chaloner's knowledge, social acumen, and ability to manipulate opinion; it demonstrated that, despite his fall from power, he remained formidable. Ostensibly an account of foreign marvels and faction, *Moses his Tombe* instead served its author's personal, political, and religious agenda in struggles far closer to home.

Notes

I would like to thank Kate Bennett and Filippo de Vivo for their comments on earlier drafts of this essay.

1. The bookseller George Thomason dated his copy December 31, 1656. British Library E.1660 (3).

2. Deut. 34:6.

3. [Chaloner, Thomas], *A True and Exact Relation of the Strange Finding Out of Moses his Tombe* (London, 1657), title page. All future references will be cited parenthetically in the text and will be to this edition unless otherwise stated.

4. Anthony Wood, *Athenae Oxonienses,* ed. Philip Bliss (London, 1813–20), 3:533.

5. Bodleian Library, Oxford, Wood 246 (3). Contractions are expanded and underlined.

6. John Aubrey, *Brief Lives,* ed. Andrew Clark (Oxford: Clarendon Press, 1898), 1:159; David Scott, "Chaloner, Thomas (1595–1660)," in *Oxford Dictionary of National Biography,* ed. H. C. G. Matthew and Brian Harrison (Oxford: Oxford University Press, 2004), http://www.oxforddnb.com/view/article/5042. The exact nature of the offending work is unclear.

7. Aubrey, *Brief Lives,* 1:159; Sarah Barber, "The People of Northern England and Attitudes towards the Scots, 1639–1651: 'The Lamb and the Dragon Cannot be Reconciled,'" *Northern History* 35 (1999): 107; *Calendar of State Papers Domestic Series, 1650,* (CSPD), ed. Mary Anne Everett Green (London: H. M Stationary Office (HMSO), 1876; repr., Vaduz, Liechtenstein: Kraus, 1965), xv; *CSPD 1652–1653* (HMSO, 1878), xxxiii.

8. Wood, *Athenae Oxonienses,* 3:810; Aubrey, *Brief Lives,* 1:159.

9. "House of Lords Journal, vol. 7: 24 December 1644," *Journal of the House of Lords: 1644* (1802), 7:112–14, http://www.british-history.ac.uk/report.asp?compid=33189.

10. Sarah Barber, *A Revolutionary Rogue: Henry Marten and the English Republic* (Thrupp, UK: Sutton, 2000), 41, 88; *CSPD 1661–1662,* (London: Longman, 1861), 86, 196; Aubrey, *Brief Lives,* 1:160.

11. The figure of thirty-eight days is based on dates for reports from Venice appearing in London newsbooks in the winters of 1654–55 and 1655–56. It includes the time from receipt to appearance in print and assumes the dates given on reports are New Style. London news writers took some of their foreign news from Continental newsbooks so the communication between Venice and London was not necessarily direct. By way of comparison, Peter Fraser reports that after the Restoration the Secretary of State's letters to Constantinople took about twenty-four days to arrive if sent via Venice. See Fraser, *The Intelligence of the Secretaries of State and their Monopoly of Licensed News, 1660–1688* (Cambridge: Cambridge University Press, 1956), 62.

12. For example, in summer 1655 reports from Roan alleged that the English at Constantinople had all been massacred; this was denied in print within days when letters from Venice and Marseilles failed to confirm it. See *Mercurius Politicus,* no. 264, June 28 to July 5, 1655: [5451], and *Certain Passages of Every Dayes Intelligence,* June 29 to July 6, 1655: [28].

13. Aubrey, *Brief Lives,* 1:160. The manuscript has "false" interlined above story (Bodleian Library, MS Aubrey 7, fol. 19r)—my thanks to Kate Bennett for this information.

14. See James Sutherland, *The Restoration Newspaper and Its Development* (Cambridge: Cambridge University Press, 1986), 123.

15. *The Publick Intelligencer,* No. 66, January 12–19, 1656/7: 1129. *Moses his Tombe* was advertised with *The Golden Fleece* (a work on the English wool trade) and William Prynne's *A Seasonable Vindication of Free Admission, and Frequent Administration of the Holy Communion.*

16. [Thomas Chaloner], *The Strange Finding Out of Moses his Tombe,* ed. C. H. Wilkinson, Luttrell Society Reprints 18 (Oxford: Luttrell Society, 1958), introduction, ix–x.

17. George Sandys, *A Relation of a Journey begun An. Dom. 1610,* 2nd ed. (London, 1615; Amsterdam: Theatrum Orbis Terrarum, 1973), 152–59; Fynes Moryson, *An Itinerary* (London, 1617), pt. 1, 215–17, 222; William Lithgow, *A Most Delectable, and True Discourse, of an Admired and Painefull Peregrination from Scotland, to the Most Famous Kingdomes in Europe, Asia and Affricke* (London, 1614), P1r–P3v.

18. Sandys, *A Relation,* 48.

19. N. I. Matar, "The Renegade in English Seventeenth-Century Imagination," *Studies in English Literature, 1500–1900* 33 (1993): 489–505.

20. Dror Ze'evi, *An Ottoman Century: The District of Jerusalem in the 1600s* (Albany: State University of New York Press, 1996), 39–41, 57.

21. For example, the newsbooks of February to August 1655 reported the installment of one grand vizier, his execution, the installment of his successor, and that successor's unnatural death.

22. Thomas Chaloner, *An Answer to the Scotch Papers* (London, 1646); Barber, "People of Northern England," 102–12. For an English account of Scottish perfidy see [Thomas May], *The Changeable Covenant* (London, 1650).

23. [May], *The Changeable Covenant*, 10; R. F., *The Scot Arraigned* (London, 1651), 4.

24. *The Publick Intelligencer,* No. 25, March 17–24, 1655/6: 418–19.

25. *A Collection of the State Papers of John Thurloe, Esq,* ed. Thomas Birch (London, 1742), 4:552. This edition gives the letter's date as "3 March 1655 [NS]," but the year must be 1656 New Style. The Protector was informed by the ambassador to Constantinople that "Morat Bassa" was the man appointed to quell the rebellion (6:257).

26. Blair Worden, *The Rump Parliament, 1648–1653* (Cambridge: Cambridge University Press, 1974), 254–59; *CSPD 1655* (HMSO, 1881), 240; *CSPD 1655–1656* (HMSO, 1882), 1.

27. [Chaloner], *Moses his Tombe,* ed. Wilkinson, Introduction, xi. See David S. Katz, *Philo-Semitism and the Readmission of the Jews to England, 1603–1655* (Oxford: Clarendon Press, 1982), particularly chap. 6.

28. Katz, *Philo-Semitism,* 98–103.

29. See, for example, *A Help to Discourse* (London, 1654), 269–70.

30. John Blenkow, *Michaels Combat with the Divel; or, Moses his Funerall* (London, 1640), 13.

31. John Gee, *The Foot Out of the Snare* (London, 1624), 9; [Thomas Heywood], *The Rat-trap; or, The Jesuites Taken in their Owne Net* ([London], 1641), 8. For details of the Jesuits' alleged schemes see also Gregory Thims's *The Protestant Informer* (London, 1643) and William Prynne's *Romes Master-peece* (London, 1643).

32. Wood, *Athenae Oxonienses,* 3:533; note inserted before Wood's copy of *Moses his Tombe,* Bodleian, Wood 246 (3); Aubrey, *Brief Lives,* 1:159–60.

33. C. John Sommerville, *The News Revolution in England: Cultural Dynamics of Daily Information* (New York: Oxford University Press, 1996), 52; Jason McElligott, "The Politics of Sexual Libel: Royalist Propaganda in the 1640s," *Huntington Library Quarterly* 67 (2004): 94–96.

34. A new assembly may have been anticipated in late 1656. In 1657 Cromwell agreed to call an assembly of divines to settle national doctrine, but did not do so. Ronald Hutton, *The British Republic, 1649–1660* (Basingstoke, UK: Macmillan, 1990), 74.

35. Toby Barnard, *The English Republic, 1649–1660,* 2nd ed. (Harlow, UK: Longman, 1997), 27.

36. See Carol S. Egloff's "The Search for a Cromwellian Settlement: Exclusions from the Second Protectorate Parliament, Part I: The Process and its Architects," *Parliamentary History* 17 (1998): 178–97, and "Part II: The Excluded Members and the Reactions to the Exclusion," *Parliamentary History* 17 (1998): 311. Wood, *Athenae Oxonienses,* 4:409–10; Worden, *The Rump Parliament,* 256.

37. G. E. Briscoe Eyre, ed., *A Transcript of the Registers of the Worshipful Company of Stationers from 1640–1708 AD* (London: privately printed, 1913–14), 2:100.

38. *Journals of the House of Commons,* (n.p., n.d.), 7:463–76. For a detailed discussion of the debates see William G. Bittle, *James Nayler, 1618–1660: The Quaker Indicted by Parliament* (Richmond, IN: Friends United Press, 1986), chaps. 5, 6.

39. *Oxford Dictionary of English Proverbs,* 3rd ed., rev. by F. P. Wilson (Oxford: Claren-don Press, 1970), 836. For a study of travelers' fibs (using examples that largely post-date *Moses his Tombe*) see Percy G. Adams, *Travelers and Travel Liars, 1660–1800* (Berkeley and Los Angeles: University of California Press, 1962).

40. See David Berman, "Deism, Immortality and the Art of Theological Lying," in *Deism, Masonry, and the Enlightenment,* ed. J. A. Leo Lemay (Newark: University of Delaware Press, 1987), 61–78; Isabel Rivers, *Reason, Grace, and Sentiment: A Study of the Language of Religion and Ethics in England, 1660–1780, Volume II: Shaftesbury to Hume* (Cambridge: Cambridge University Press, 2000), 31–50.

BIBLIOGRAPHY

Adams, Percy G. *Travelers and Travel Liars, 1660–1800.* Berkeley and Los Angeles: University of California Press, 1962.

Aubrey, John. *Brief Lives.* Edited by Andrew Clark. 2 vols. Oxford: Clarendon Press, 1898.

Barber, Sarah. "The People of Northern England and Attitudes towards the Scots, 1639–1651: 'The Lamb and the Dragon Cannot be Reconciled.'" *Northern History* 35 (1999): 93–118.

———. *A Revolutionary Rogue: Henry Marten and the English Republic.* Thrupp, UK: Sutton, 2000.

Barnard, Toby. *The English Republic, 1649–1660.* 2nd edition. Harlow, UK: Longman, 1997.

Berman, David. "Deism, Immortality and the Art of Theological Lying." In *Deism, Masonry, and the Enlightenment.* Edited by J. A. Leo Lemay, 61–78. Newark: University of Delaware Press, 1987.

Bittle, William G. *James Nayler, 1618–1660: The Quaker Indicted by Parliament.* Richmond, IN: Friends United Press, 1986.

Blenkow, John. *Michaels Combat with the Divel; or, Moses his Funerall.* London, 1640.

Calendar of State Papers Domestic Series, 1650. Edited by Mary Anne Everett Green. London: H. M. Stationery Office, 1876. Reprint, Vaduz, Liechtenstein: Kraus, 1965.

Calendar of State Papers Domestic Series, 1652–1653. Edited by Mary Anne Everett Green. London: H. M. Stationery Office, 1878. Reprint, Vaduz, Liechtenstein: Kraus, 1965.

Calendar of State Papers Domestic Series, 1655. Edited by Mary Anne Everett Green. London: H. M. Stationery Office, 1881. Reprint, Vaduz, Liechtenstein: Kraus, 1965.

Calendar of State Papers Domestic Series, 1655–1656. Edited by Mary Anne Everett Green. London: H. M. Stationery Office, 1882. Reprint, Vaduz, Liechtenstein: Kraus, 1965.

Calendar of State Papers Domestic Series, 1661–1662. Edited by Mary Anne Everett Green. London: Longman, 1861.

Certain Passages of Every Dayes Intelligence. London, June 29 to July 6, 1655.

Chaloner, Thomas. *An Answer to the Scotch Papers.* London, 1646.

[Chaloner, Thomas]. *The Strange Finding Out of Moses his Tombe.* Edited by C. H. Wilkinson. Luttrell Society Reprints 18. Oxford: Luttrell Society, 1958.

[Chaloner, Thomas]. *A True and Exact Relation of the Strange Finding Out of Moses his Tombe.* London, 1657.

Egloff, Carol S. "The Search for a Cromwellian Settlement: Exclusions from the Second Protectorate Parliament, Part I: The Process and its Architects." *Parliamentary History* 17 (1998): 178–97.

————. "The Search for a Cromwellian Settlement: Exclusions from the Second Protectorate Parliament, Part II: The Excluded Members and the Reactions to the Exclusion." *Parliamentary History* 17 (1998): 301–21.

Eyre, G. E. Briscoe, ed. *A Transcript of the Registers of the Worshipful Company of Stationers from 1640–1708 AD.* 3 vols. London: Privately printed, 1913–14.

F., R. *The Scot Arraigned.* London, 1651.

Fraser, Peter, *The Intelligence of the Secretaries of State and their Monopoly of Licensed News, 1660–1688.* Cambridge: Cambridge University Press, 1956.

Gee, John. *The Foot Out of the Snare.* London, 1624.

A Help to Discourse. London, 1654.

[Heywood, Thomas]. *The Rat-trap; or, The Jesuites Taken in their Owne Net.* [London], 1641.

"House of Lords Journal Volume 7: 24 December 1644." In *Journal of the House of Lords: 1644, vol. 7* 1802. http://www.british-history.ac.uk/report.asp?compid=33189/.

Hutton, Ronald. *The British Republic, 1649–1660.* Basingstoke, UK: Macmillan, 1990.

Journals of the House of Commons from August the 15th 1651 to March the 16th 1659. Vol. 7. n.p., n.d.

Katz, David S. *Philo-Semitism and the Readmission of the Jews to England, 1603–1655.* Oxford: Clarendon Press, 1982.

Lithgow, William. *A Most Delectable, and True Discourse, of an Admired and Painefull Peregrination from Scotland, to the Most Famous Kingdomes in Europe, Asia and Affricke.* London, 1614.

Matar, N. I. "The Renegade in English Seventeenth-Century Imagination." *Studies in English Literature, 1500–1900* 33 (1993): 489–505.

[May, Thomas]. *The Changeable Covenant.* London, 1650.

McElligott, Jason. "The Politics of Sexual Libel: Royalist Propaganda in the 1640s." *Huntington Library Quarterly* 67 (2004): 75–99.

Mercurius Politicus, No. 264, June 28 to July 5, 1655.

Moryson, Fynes. *An Itinerary.* London, 1617.

Oxford Dictionary of English Proverbs. 3rd edition. Revised by F. P. Wilson. Oxford: Clarendon Press, 1970.

Prynne, William. *Romes Master-peece.* London, 1643.

The Publick Intelligencer, No. 25, March 17–24, 1655/6.

The Publick Intelligencer, No. 66, January 12–19, 1656/7.

Rivers, Isabel. *Reason, Grace, and Sentiment: A Study of the Language of Religion and Ethics in England, 1660–1780, Volume II: Shaftesbury to Hume.* Cambridge Studies in Eighteenth-Century Literature and Thought 37. Cambridge: Cambridge University Press, 2000.

Sandys, George. *A Relation of a Journey begun An. Dom. 1610.* A facsimile of the second edition of 1615. Amsterdam: Theatrum Orbis Terrarum, 1973.

Scott, David. "Chaloner, Thomas (1595–1660)." In *Oxford Dictionary of National Biography,* edited by H. C. G. Matthew and Brian Harrison. Oxford: Oxford University Press, 2004. http://www.oxforddnb.com/view/article/5042/.

Sommerville, C. John. *The News Revolution in England: Cultural Dynamics of Daily Information.* New York: Oxford University Press, 1996.

Sutherland, James. *The Restoration Newspaper and Its Development.* Cambridge: Cambridge University Press, 1986.

Thims, Gregory. *The Protestant Informer.* London, 1643.

Thurloe, John. *A Collection of the State Papers of John Thurloe, Esq.* Edited by Thomas Birch. 7 vols. London, 1742.

Wood, Anthony. *Athenae Oxonienses.* Edited by Philip Bliss. 4 vols. London, 1813–20.

Worden, Blair. *The Rump Parliament, 1648–1653.* Cambridge: Cambridge University Press, 1974.

Ze'evi, Dror. *An Ottoman Century: The District of Jerusalem in the 1600s.* Albany: State University of New York Press, 1996.

Strangely Familiar:
Emblems in Early Modern England

Mary V. Silcox

Emblems possess a split personality in their attitude toward the mysterious and foreign. They rely utterly on the different and the strange, and yet use them in the service of the universalized and the familiar. The formal source of English emblem books was a foreign model, Andrea Alciato's *Emblematum liber,* originally published in France in 1539 and republished many times. This debt was widely known and acknowledged, though the varied ingredients that combined to make up the genre of the emblem were all present in English culture as much as in Continental cultures by the second half of the sixteenth century—the popularity of adages, proverbs, and commonplace collections; bestiaries, fables, and moralized ancient myths; the renewed interest in ancient history, especially Roman; the interpretation of the components of nature as possessing symbolic meaning related to the human world; the importance of the visual image and its relationship to the verbal in speaking pictures; and analogical and allegorical thinking. Its combination of word and image makes the emblem itself into an unusual genre. Geffrey Whitney's *A Choice of Emblemes* (1586), as one of the earliest, most referenced and representative English emblem books, provides a significant site for examining the English emblem's exploitation of the unfamiliar.

A Choice of Emblemes relied heavily on the foreign, even in its composition and the circumstances of its publication. Though very English in its preoccupations, Whitney's emblem book was published in the Netherlands, in Leiden, by Christopher Plantin's son-in-law, Francis Raphelengius. Whitney first created a manuscript version, presented to the Earl of Leicester late in 1585.[1] Then, when he traveled to the Netherlands during Leicester's stint as Lord Lieutenant of the English forces fighting against the Spanish, he adapted, rearranged, and expanded the manuscript into its print form; and therefore, while the Epistle Dedicatorie to Leicester is signed "At London the XXVIII of November. Anno M.D.LXXXV," the title page declares the book "Imprinted at Leyden, In the house of Christopher Plantyn, by Francis Raphelengius. M.D.LXXXVI" (✳✳3, ✳1). Taking advantage of the huge stock of woodblock illustrations from the Plantin Press, with a few newly made blocks, Whitney and Raphelengius were able to produce the print version in less than four months after Whitney's arrival, even though the changes to the manuscript were extensive.[2] While the manuscript was a private offering to Leicester as Whitney's patron, the printed book was a public piece, and emblems were altered to reflect that new status. John Manning has convincingly argued that the publication of *A Choice of Emblemes* was part of a concerted propaganda effort supporting Leicester's political and military campaign in the Low Countries, both from the perspective of the Dutch civilian allies and the critical English at home, hesitant to become embroiled in seemingly endless Continental religious wars.[3] The very circumstances of the book's publication thus involve the delicate and complex foreign relations of England during the 1580s, as well as the equally delicate and complex maneuvering of factions in Queen Elizabeth's court.

As for the composition of *A Choice of Emblemes,* it is an amalgamation and adaptation of 232 emblems from earlier, Continental emblem books, along with 16 of Whitney's own, totaling 248 emblems. (The total number of emblems with woodcuts is 247, since one of Whitney's is without a picture.) This reliance on Continental, particularly Dutch illustrators is typical of England at the time. As the title page reads, it is *A Choice of Emblemes, and other devises, For the most parte gathered out of sundrie writers, Englished and Moralized. and divers newly devised, by Geffrey Whitney.* These "sundrie writers" are Andrea Alciato, Joannes Sambucus, Claude Paradin, Hadrianus Junius, Gabriel Faernus, Guillaume de la Perrière, Barthélemy Aneau, and Georgette de Montenay, and Whitney's use of their emblems ranges widely from literal translation of the original motto and/or epigram to entirely new text and topic for the symbolic picture.[4] This combination of old and new, foreign and local, and what we would call derivative and original, was a perfectly respectable, indeed admired part of the period's rhetorical practice that valued the restatement of the commonplace. As Marion Trousdale explains, the commonplace in the sixteenth-century rhetorical system was "the primary matter (*res*) of the artist, and the efficacious expression of forms of common knowledge the definition of his artistry."[5] *A Choice of Emblemes* thus performs what it is meant to be, a normative model of behavior and a repository of iconographic topoi for Western culture. The emblem "came into existence at a time when conflicting systems of signs" were complicating reading practices. "Each emblem is constructed from a fragment of one of the various sign systems, or codes, available to Renaissance artists. . . . [T]he emblematist read the chosen fragment in some variant sense . . . that runs sufficiently counter to the reader's usual expectations in a given situation to produce a mild, but pleasurable and even memorable surprise."[6] Add to this mixture Whitney's marginal allusions to and quotations from other writers, especially classical, and his dedications of particular emblems to individuals such as members of his family, clergy, military officers, and noblemen, and the referential codes in this emblem book expand to draw together multiple arenas of significance.

The three parts of Whitney's emblems—motto, picture, and epigram (or four parts if you include the marginalia, or five parts with the dedications) —thus create something of a puzzle or mystery to be solved by the reader's interacting with the total of the parts, no one of which contains the entirety of the emblem's message. Whitney emphasizes this aspect of the emblem's nature by his explanation of its origin: "havinge some wittie devise expressed with cunning woorkemanship, somethinge obscure to be perceived at the first, whereby, when with further consideration it is understood, it maie the greater delighte the behoulder" (✳✳4). Although Whitney does not use the term hieroglyphic to describe emblems, it was common to do so at the time. By doing so emblematists linked contemporary emblem making with the exotic, ancient symbol writing of the Egyptians and its supposed system of natural signs, God's own language speaking to us from nature: "The emblem form was attractive to Renaissance humanists because it seemed to combine discursive with ideogrammatic communication. For Renaissance Neo-Platonists ideogrammatic hieroglyphs permitted the visual intuition of truths not otherwise accessible in their absolute form. . . . But in fact, the illusion of intuition resulted from the kind of effort the reader was obliged to make in order to solve the allegorical riddle formed by the choice and disposition of the components of the emblem."[7] Such a conception of the role of the emblem as almost hermetic (and therefore speaking to a privileged audience) is at odds with the equally strong conception of it found in most English emblem books as a teaching tool. Often these explanations of the emblem are found side by side in the prefatory material, as though no contradiction exists. Whitney, however, refers to his emblems as mirrors in which both the ignorant and the godly can view themselves, the ignorant to mend themselves and the godly to strengthen themselves in their righteous course (✳✳3). The unfamiliar people, things, animals, places, and events that comprise many of the emblems are thus not to be viewed for their own sake, but only as they can act as reflective commentary on what should be familiar to the reader as a moral member of Elizabethan society.

This trend is obvious in the treatment of nature in *A Choice of Emblemes,* particularly in the treatment of animals, those strange "Others" with which we share the world. Animals abound in the emblem book. In some instances they are engaged in their normal activities, though they are not animals Elizabethans would see often, especially in their natural settings. The interest lies not in the animals, but in how they can operate as metaphors for human qualities or actions. The picture for emblem 118 thus shows us a tall palm tree with serpents and frogs gathered at its base, and the epigram explains how sweet and fresh the "gallant Palme" is as opposed to the frogs and serpents that "do their worste" to destroy the palm, "With ercksome noise, and eke with poison fell." Just so, we are told, do envious men attempt to undermine those who "By juste deserte, doe live in honor greate." Likewise, a lion and boar are fiercely fighting each other in 119, watched by a very interested vulture, sitting safely in a tree. Again, not a common sight for Englishmen, but certainly possible animal behavior that illuminates how someone else stands to gain when "men of mighte" attack each other with deadly intent: "So, Soliman his Empire did increase, / When christian kinges exiled love, and peace."

Whitney's fables carry the comparison of human to animal even further into personification: "This tendency to see in each species some socially relevant human quality was very ancient, for men had always looked to animals to provide categories with which to describe themselves. The characters attributed to individual beasts were usually stereotypes, based less on observation than literary inheritance. They were derived from Greek, Roman and medieval compilations, not from scrutiny of life in the fields and the woods. For centuries the fox continued to be cunning, the goat lustful and the ant provident."[8] The cunning of the fox in emblems 161 and 210 is typical of fables and therefore not unfamiliar. What makes these emblems striking and memorable, however, is the human specificity of the small narratives in which the fox outsmarts the far more powerful lion. In #161 the fox is in her den, sickly, and the lion offers to use the sovereign healing power of his tongue to lick her well again. The fox's response is to acknowledge the lion's power, but decline his help until his tongue's neighbors (i.e., his teeth) are banished. In #210 an old lion, no longer able to run down his prey, pretends to be sick and stays in his den, where he eats all those who come to see how he is. When the fox comes by, "his dutie to declare," the lion invites him in, but the fox refuses to enter, "For, all I see have gone into thy denne, / But none I finde, that have retorn'd againe." The picture shows paw and hoof prints leading only into the cave.

These fables are amusing because of the jarring disjunction of human behavior and speech in animals. They thus exploit the difference between human and animal, but emblems can also be seen blurring the line dividing human from beast. To know what is human one needs the nonhuman, but when, as the preacher Thomas Wilcox argues, "God would have a lively image of virtues and vices to be in the creatures, that even in them we might be provoked to virtue and deterred from vice," the distinction can be slippery.[9] In emblem 127 we are shown the startling image of hares biting a dead lion, to comment on the activities of those who attempt to slander the great man, but have the courage to do so only after he is dead. The human activity is more than bestialized here, since the slanderers are acting in an unnatural fashion that no hare would engage in.

Because of their resemblance to us, which was recognized at the time, apes are perhaps the most disquieting animals to serve as vehicles for admonishing human behavior. The ape that catches hold of a puppy in order to use its paw to pull chestnuts from a fire is displaying humanlike reason (#58). The mother ape that holds her young one so fondly it is squeezed to death is displaying a humanlike love (#188a). Yet neither display of human qualities is admirable, even though humans are supposedly superior to animals in just these areas. Whitney develops a comparison between ape and human in several emblems, and Erica Fudge has examined #145 in her *Perceiving Animals: Humans and Beasts in Early Modern English Culture.* In this emblem an ape is shown attempting to imitate a woodworker by playing with his tools, but the ape ends up crushing his own foot in the stocks: "The ape, in typical fashion, imitates humanity and fails. The attempt to overstep natural status figured in the image is paralleled in verse by the attempt to overstep social status. The message of Whitney's emblem is apparently a conservative one: social order—the clear and limiting structure of early modern society—is in place to protect the members of that society. Knowing your own place is about knowing when you are well-off and overstepping your place is about ignorance, animality."[10] But, Fudge argues, something more is going on in the woodcut: "The workman points at the ape just as Whitney points at the apishness of social climbing. But the ape itself . . . looks out of the frame at the reader and itself gestures towards the workman. . . . The human and the ape of Whitney's woodcut are both readers: the man examines the ape, the ape examines us."[11] Not only is the ape's apishness being used to teach us about the need for each of us to remain in our social positions, but it is also reaching across the boundary separating human from nonhuman to challenge us to maintain that distinction of superior knowledge and wisdom.

Some of Whitney's emblems go further in suggesting that, far from humans being superior to animals, animals possess more knowledge than we do. The beaver in the woodcut to emblem 30 knows it is being pursued by hunter and hounds for its testicles, used in creating valuable medicines. It is therefore chewing them off to throw to the hunter, who will then leave the beaver alone. Even more amazing, "afterwarde, if anie doe him course, / He shewes his wante, to moove them to remorse." The beaver understands better than humans that sometimes it is better to give up something you value than to lose your life. Emblem 3 goes so far as to assert: "Suche providence hathe nature secret wroughte / In creatures wilde, and eeke such knowledge strange, / That man, by them in somme thinges maie be taughte." The example developed in this emblem is the crocodile pictured in the woodcut who knows how high the Nile will flood each year and lays her

Geoffrey Whitney, *A Choice of Emblemes* **(1586), Emblem 145. This item is reproduced by permission of** *The Huntington Library, San Marino, California,* **RB 79714.**

eggs at that spot: "Suche skill devine, and science to foretell, / Hath Nature lente unto this Serpent fell." Man is an outsider to nature in that he is missing "Suche skill devine" and must rely on reason instead. But lest the reader think that man is lifted beyond nature, emblem 57 reminds us that we are still subject to it. Although emblem 57 has a woodcut not of animals but of two white men attempting to wash the black from an Ethiopian's skin, its epigram is about the power of nature exceeding human control and understanding:

> Leave of with paine, the blackamore to skowre,
> With washinge ofte, and wipinge more then due:

For thou shalte finde, that Nature is of powre,
Doe what thou canste, to keepe his former hue:
Thoughe with a forke, wee Nature thruste awaie,
She turnes againe, if wee withdrawe our hande:
And thoughe, wee ofte to conquer her assaie,
Yet all in vaine, shee turnes if still wee stande:

We can, indeed we must, read the book of nature, carrying as it does so many lessons for us. But the most we can do is read, not dictate, and we are left in the uncomfortable position of being both within nature and a foreigner to it.

Just as the knowledge of nature and animal ways is not an end in itself in emblem books, so the knowledge of foreign cultures is esteemed only as it can improve the reader's own behavior. In the "Epistle Dedicatorie," as part of his praise for Leicester's support for learning, Whitney explains the value of the foreign: "by the benefit thereof, The actes of mightie Monarches & great Princes, and the matters and thinges of former time worthie memorie, done by sage Governors, and valiant Captaines. The manners and lawes of straunge nations, & customes of oulde time. The mutabillitie of worldly felicitie, and howe the wise have behaved them selves in bothe fortunes: have bin presented unto them as in a glasse, for their instruction, from which they might drawe understanding and good counsaile, to instruct and governe them selves in all their actions: and finde approoved examples for the whole course of their life, eyther to bee imitated, or eschewed" (✳✳). The foreign appears in *A Choice of Emblemes* through classical myth and ancient history, but not through other sixteenth-century cultures, except incidentally as in #22, in which the sight of the fox trapped on ice floating downriver is located in "Ravenspurge." The location, however, is not significant and has no bearing on the interpretation of the image.

Greek myths, particularly those transmitted by Ovid's *Metamorphoses,* provide the icons for many of Whitney's emblems. Mythical figures abound: to name only a few, Ullyses and the Sirens (10), Niobe (13), Hercules (16), Icarus (28), Tantalus (74), Prometheus (75), Arion (144), Apollo and Bacchus (146), Cupid (147 & 148), Narcissus (149), Orpheus (186), and Midas (218a). Most of these emblems are in the tradition of the moralized translations of Ovid such as that by Golding, and are used to warn against deceptive beauty (10), pride (13), forbidden knowledge (28), covetousness (74), self-love (149), and so on. Whitney takes care to defuse any suggestion of subversive paganism, even as he mines these tales of powerful foreign gods, by reminding his readers that these are only fiction: "The Poetes faine" the story of Danaus's daughters (12), the "Poetts first did frame" the "tragedie" of Niobe (13), and Tantalus appears "as Poettes doe devine" (74). In an emblem such as #146, Whitney actually deconstructs the godly status of Apollo and Bacchus to emphasize how important their supposed gifts are to man:

> Two sonnes of Jove that best of man deserve,
> Apollo great, and Bacchus, this impartes:
> With diet food, the one doth healthe preserve,
> With pleasante wine, the other cheares our hartes.
>   And theise, the worlde immortall Goddes would have,
>   Bicause longe life, with sweete delighte, they gave.
>
> But if theise are so sovereigne unto man,
> That here, with joye they doe increase his daies,
> And freshe doe make the carefull colour wanne:
> And keepe him longe from sicknes, and disease:
>   I graunte, they ought to be renowmed more,
>   Then all the Goddes, the Poettes did adore.

The possible reality of good health, cheerfulness, and long life takes the place of the gods as worthy of renown, and perhaps as a rarity too.

Whitney's unease with mythology shows clearly in #177, but equally clear is the value he finds in linking the foreign myth with the native. This emblem is illustrated with a woodcut of the phoenix on its nest, surrounded by flames. After eight lines rehearsing the essentials of the myth of the phoenix as apparently fact, Whitney feels it is necessary to add a disclaimer:

> And thoughe for truthe, this manie doe declare,
> Yet thereunto, I meane not for to sweare:
>   Althoughe I knowe that Aucthors witnes true,
>   What here I write, bothe of the oulde, and newe.

In spite of this doubt, he goes on to apply the longevity of the phoenix and its ability to rise from its ashes to the English town of Nampwich. This emblem is dedicated "To my countrimen of the Namptwiche in Cheshire," rebuilding their town after a fire destroyed it: "Whose buildinges brave, where cinders weare but late, / Did represente (me thought) the phoenix fate." The mysterious glory of the phoenix is lost in this comparison; what remains is simply the correlation of the two fires and Whitney's wish for a successful outcome for Nampwich.

The assimilation of non-Christian mythology in *A Choice of Emblemes* is perhaps most striking in emblem 122. Dedicated to Francis Windham and Edward Flowerdew as judges and headed by the motto "*Sine iustitia, confusio*" (Without justice, there is confusion), this emblem depends upon classical descriptions of the origins of the world and its four ages of gold, silver, brass, and iron to praise Protestant England. As John Manning has

Geoffrey Whitney, *A Choice of Emblemes* **(1586), Emblem 122. This item is reproduced by permission of** *The Huntington Library, San Marino, California,* **RB 79714.**

shown, Whitney depends far more upon Ovid's *Metamorphoses* and Virgil's *Eclogue IV* than upon the source of his picture and motto, Barthélemy Aneau's *Picta Poesis.*[12] In the 50–line verse for this emblem Whitney first describes an Ovidian chaos, "When Fire, and Aire, and Earthe, and Water, all weare one / . . . / There was no forme of thinges, but a confused masse." He then paints for us at some length the golden age of abundance and peace that began "when they [the elements] weare dispos'd, eache one into his roome." After briefly mentioning the silver and brass ages, he expands on the iron, "a fearefull cursed tyme" of armies, crime, rigor, revenge, oppression, tyranny, falsehood, and hate, in which the virtues were so mixed with vices "That nowe, into the worlde, an other Chaos came." At this point Whitney departs from Ovid and has the Christian God send the goddess

Justice down to earth, specifically to "happie England, where Justice is embrac'd" and "the land doth flourishe still, and gladnes, their doth growe: / Bicause that all, to God, and Prince, by her their dewties knowe." Whitney is here picking up on the representation of Queen Elizabeth as Astraea to build a patriotic portrait of England, its queen, its special relationship with God, and its potential exportation of peace and prosperity. Classical and Christian traditions are intertwined to form a proud English identity that finds neither foreign to it.

This process of assimilation brings up the question of just how foreign the ancient world was to the literate Englishman of the 1580s. Latin was the language of the schools, and Latin literature and history formed much of their curriculum. Sixteenth-century writers and readers certainly recognized differences between their world and the ancient world; indeed, "The discovery of 'difference'—i.e., that men varied in manners, customs, and beliefs—grew out of the Renaissance experience of classical texts. It was above all the recognition of historical difference" that awakened the Renaissance to diversity.[13] But as we have seen previously, in Whitney's *A Choice of Emblemes* difference in itself has no significance; it is always held in a state of comparison, a metaphorical state in which the sameness of transhistorical values is discovered in the midst of apparent difference. For the emblem to work, the reader has to recognize and acknowledge estrangement from the ancient past, while at the same time possess enough familiarity with that foreign world to understand what is being compared. This is perhaps why the New World and the Orient make no appearance in English emblem books. They are too far outside the familiar network of European discourse to evoke the sets of associations needed for emblems. Instead, we see in #14 Heraclitus weeping and Democritus laughing over the follies and crimes of their own time. Whitney considers what would happen if these philosophers lived in his own lifetime:

> What if they livde, and shoulde beholde this age
> Which overflowes, with swellinge seas of sinne:
> Where fooles, by swarmes, doe presse uppon the stage,
> With hellishe Impes, that like have never binne:

The difference in time gives Whitney the opportunity to emphasize the degenerate nature of the present without worrying about unfamiliar belief systems. Usually, though not always, the many emblems referring to figures from the ancient world employ those figures as paragons against which the modern world should measure itself. The emblem on silence (60) thus recalls the wisdom of Pythagoras, Lycurgus, Demaratus, Zeno, Cato, Harpocrates, and others in urging the reader to hold his tongue and speak only after much thought. The second part of Whitney's book opens with a poem

(109) praising Philip Sidney through comparison with an even longer list of ancient warriors. Subsequent emblems develop a few of these warriors more fully as guides to valiant behavior (111, 113, 114, 115, 116, 117). Another type of emblem makes use of the distance between the ancient world and the present to assert the superiority of writing as a monument and source of longevity. In #196 fame blows the reputation of poets such as Homer, Edward Dyer and Philip Sidney around the world and across time, while the spires of Egypt and the walls of Rome crumble. In emblem 131 the great cities of the past such as Troy, Carthage, Thebes, and Babel are razed to the ground. "Nothinge at all, but time doth over reache," except for books, which can preserve the great acts of great men for posterity. The chronological remoteness of antiquity becomes, in these emblems, a means to erase distance, drawing the great men and poets of the ancient past into the present, even as their physical world disappears.

It is not the past, but the world and life itself that are foreign if there is no memory of you remaining: "For, what is man in this worlde? without fame to leave behind him, but like a bubble of water, that now riseth, & anon is not knowne where it was" (✶✶2ᵛ). Home is therefore very important as the place where you are known and the anchor to your life, and travel, while it can be enriching, can also lose you everything. For every emblem in which travel to foreign shores is endorsed, three emblems deprecate it. The emblems dedicated "To M. William Harebrowne, at Constantinople" (#207) and "To Richard Drake Esquier, in praise of Sir Francis Drake Knight" (#203) are unusual in praising the traveler. Emblem 207's motto *"Imparilitas"* (Inequality) sets up the interpretation of the picture in which a "faulcon mountes alofte unto the skie," while ducks and geese "in eche diche, and muddie lake doe lighte" and "seeke their foode in puddles, and in pittes." Falcons are, of course, much nobler birds. Men also possess such differences: "Some, throughe the worlde doe passe by lande, and sea: / And by deserte are famous farre, and neare"; others refuse to travel "Beyonde the smell of native countries smoke." The praise in this emblem is subdued—the deserving traveler becomes famous—but the praise for Drake in #203 is fulsome. The epigram first stresses the danger and strangeness he faced on his voyage. Through scorching heat, cold, tempests, "By ragged rocks, by shelfes & sandes," he kept on course. He encountered "pirattes, thieves, and cruell foes, that long'd to spill his blood." He even survived "gaping gulfes" and "monsters of the flood." How? "God was on his side." The picture represents the aid of God, as his right hand descends from the clouds and holds a bridle that, attached to the ship, guides Drake around the world. Drake's circumnavigation of the globe is signaled by the belt around it. That feat, however, is not mentioned in the epigram. Instead, it concentrates on the reward that Drake achieved; *"By helpe of power devine"* he managed "to finde the goulden mine" and bring home riches. Whitney

Geoffrey Whitney, *A Choice of Emblemes* (1586), Emblem 203. This item is reproduced by permission of *The Huntington Library, San Marino, California*, RB 79714.

advises all "yee woorthie wightes, that seeke for forreine landes" to imitate Drake and "come alwaies home, by Ganges goulden sandes." Thus they will, like Drake above all others, "doe their countrie good." It seems that foreign travel is a way to gain renown and serve one's country, but the measure of success is how much gold one gathers to bring back to England.

Traveling, though, can also lose you everything. The merchant pictured in #179 swimming in the sea with a pack on his back has endured "travaile, toile, and labour voide of reste" as well as shipwreck because of his "Desire to have." In #39,

> He that poastes, to make awaie his landes,
> And credittes all, that wandringe heades reporte:
> Maye Tagus seeke, and Ganges goulden sandes,
> Yet come at lengthe, with emptie purse to courte:

The exile of #90 is in even worse straits, thrown out of his element like a dolphin cast upon the shore. Such an image, with the dolphin dying, gasp-

Geoffrey Whitney, *A Choice of Emblemes* **(1586), Emblem 89. This item is reproduced by permission of** *The Huntington Library, San Marino, California,* **RB 79714.**

ing for breath, indicates just how strong the affinity with, indeed the desperate need for one's native land could be. Another compelling image of travelers losing more than they gain develops in emblem 89. Travelers who are always on the move are like the Apodes, the bird in the picture, which have no feet and fly constantly. Such men see much, but "They ofte looke backe," like the man in the picture turning his head to see the idyllic scene behind him, "and doe theire fortune rue, / Since that therin, they have no seate to set: / Thus, passe they throughe theire longe unquiet life." Peace eludes these travelers until death ends their "worldlie strife." The need to travel is questioned even further by emblem 178, which points out, "No forren soile, hath anie force to change the inward minde." The fool sent far away to find wisdom will return a fool still, and those who are malicious

in nature will return the same. Travel is not a way to improve or alter oneself; in no emblem in *A Choice of Emblemes* does the traveler find happiness
or even knowledge. Rather, travel to strange parts is likely to diminish if
not destroy you.

Experiencing the diversity of foreign travel could be seen as a way to
expand horizons and question the familiar perspectives of one's own culture, but Whitney does not use it so. Emblem 200 puts travel to foreign
lands in its place outside an ordered, hierarchical, golden society. The icon
pictured is a hive, with bees returning to it. The bees work together all day
sucking flowers and gathering honey, until each returns to her proper hive
at night. The "maister bee, within the midst dothe live, / . . . / And everie
one to him dothe reverence give, / And in the hive with him doe live in
blisse." This, Whitney tells us, is the perfect expression of a commonwealth.
He then narrows his focus to a particular estate in England, belonging to
Richard Cotton, to whom the emblem is addressed.[14] Cumbermaire is described in glowing terms as fertile, beautiful, and well ordered: "This is the
hive; your tennaunts, are the bees: / And in the same, have places by degrees." And this is what Whitney longs to return to, his homeland, though he
has been absent many years attempting to gather "goulden honie" to bring
back. The outside world is valuable only as it can enrich the unchanging,
safe, orderly community of home, where standards are understood by all,
degree is respected, and all work for the greater good. Rather than challenging his own culture, Whitney is affirming cultural certainties.

This assurance of familiarity and safety remaining somewhere, if not
with the traveler, is lost in some emblems. Danger does not have to enter
from outside; it can lurk beside you, or even within: "at the national as well
as at the domestic level, [early modern] English culture located threat in
the familiar as much as in the strange."[15] The foe disguised as a friend turns
up time and again in English emblem books. Here in *A Choice of Emblemes*
such an enemy appears in emblem 24 as the viper hidden under the straw-
berry plant, ready to use "flattringe speeche, with sugred wordes" to trick
the unsuspecting: "No foe so fell, nor yet soe harde to scape, / As is the foe,
that fawns with freindlie shape." Worse are those who betray their own kin-
dred or those kind enough to take them into their homes. The tame duck
who lures wild ducks into a net (#27) is just such a traitor to her kind. In
#33 those who hate their own kindred are compared to Medea, who killed
her own children. The unsuspecting swallow, nesting on Medea's statue, is
warned not to entrust her young to such a tyrant. If she could slaughter her
own, how can she be trusted with anyone else? Even more striking, because
of the unusual image, is emblem 49. A goat, forced to feed the wolf cub
which is sucking on her teat, is the speaker of the epigram and the subject of
the picture. Eventually, in spite of the goat's care for it, the wolf "Bewray'de
his harte" and killed her, "a warninge good to those, / Whoe in theire howse,

doe foster up theire foes." The fear of domestic betrayal and danger from the familiar rings through these emblems. It is not necessary to seek outside one's home to find an intruder.

The most intimate betrayal is of oneself, a possibility brought up in emblem 25. "[G]riping greifes" may "harbour in thie breste, / And pining cares, laie seige unto the same," making you unable to care for your own interests. "Or straunge conceiptes" may "reave thee of thie rest, / And daie and nighte" may "bringe thee out of frame," ending in your own "untimelie grave." The cure for such self-loss is to share your grief and "secret sighes" with a friend, who can free your heart from its confinement. Enclosed within oneself or exposed to the wild seas and unknown shores, the foreign is present.

Why is this so? Because, Whitney suggests, the entire world is a strange and foreign place, and we are all merely travelers through it. As a metaphor for our lives, traveling provides Whitney with a large field to describe our spiritual journey. The seaman, steering "his course to countries farre" "dothe ever keepe his eie" upon the polestar and makes his compass "agree" with it (emblem 43). Just so should we use the compass of "our inward vertues" and "shape our course" by the "heavenlie starre." In this way, "Scylla, and Charybdis, wee maie misse, / And winne at lengthe, the porte of endlesse blisse." In emblem 2 we are advised to learn from the traveling man in the picture (not named in the emblem, though he is Hercules) who, faced with multiple paths, follows Mercury's guidance to "the perfect path." This tale

> doth tell our wanderinge state,
> Before whose face, and eeke on everye side,
> Bypathes, and wayes, appeare amidd our gate,
> That if the Lorde bee not our onlie guide:
>   We stumble, fall, and dailie goe astraye,
>   Then happie those, whome God doth shew the waye.

Not only can God show us the way through this world, but as emblem 225 explains, "here wee are but straungers," and "when that this life is donne, / Wee shall bee sure our countrie right to see." In the picture the pilgrim, identifiable as such by his staff and hat, kicks the world aside and keeps his eyes on heaven. Happy are those who join him and, while they are still on earth, "Resigne this worlde: and marche with all their mighte / Within that pathe, that leades where joyes shall last." Whitney even maintains the same goals for this metaphoric journey as he does for the actual journeys in his emblems—gaining riches to take home: "And whilst they maye, there [in heaven], treasure up their store, / Where, without rust, it lastes for evermore."

In Whitney's *A Choice of Emblemes,* as in all English emblem books, his emblems become sites for the double metamorphosis of the foreign into

Geoffrey Whitney, *A Choice of Emblemes* **(1586), Emblem 225. This item is reproduced by permission of** *The Huntington Library, San Marino, California,* **RB 79714.**

the familiar and the familiar into the foreign. While it is obvious that the unknown can pose physical and psychological challenges to early modern English men and women, the boundaries between known and unknown are more porous and fluid than modernists often admit. What is strange and what is familiar depend as much on perspective as on actuality. The hybrid nature of the emblem form and of its purpose embodies these sometimes unsettling shifts and, in the end, as in Whitney's *Choice,* creates readers who have mastered both through their unlocking of the mystery residing at the heart of each emblem.

NOTES

1. The manuscript is in the Houghton Library, MS. Typ 14.
2. For discussions of the relationship of the manuscript to the print version of *A Choice of Emblemes* see Mason Tung, "Whitney's *A Choice of Emblemes* revisited: A comparative

study of the manuscript and the printed versions," *Studies in Bibliography* 29 (1976): 32–101; John Manning, "Unpublished and Unedited Emblems by Geffrey Whitney: Further evidence of the English adaptation of continental traditions," in *English Emblems and the Continental Tradition,* ed. Peter M. Daly (New York: AMS Press, 1988): 83–107.

3. John Manning, "Whitney's *Choice of Emblemes:* a reassessment," *Renaissance Studies* 4 (1990): 155–200.

4. See Tung, "Whitney's' *Choice of Emblemes;* and Manning, "Unpublished," for discussions of Whitney's adaptations from other emblem books.

5. Marion Trousdale, *Shakespeare and the Rhetoricians* (Aldershot, UK: Scolar Press, 1982), 49.

6. Daniel S. Russell, *The Emblem and Device in France* (Lexington, KY: French Form, 1985), 172.

7. Ibid., 89.

8. Keith Thomas, *Man and the Natural World: Changing Attitudes in England 1500–1800* (London: Allen Lane, 1983), 64.

9. Thomas Wilcox, *A Short, yet sound Commentarie; written on that woorthie worke called; the Proverbes of Salomon; and newly published for the profite of Gods people* (London: Printed by Thomas Orwin for Thomas Man, 1589), 18.

10. Erica Fudge, *Perceiving Animals: Humans and Beasts in Early Modern English Culture* (New York: St. Martin's Press, 2000), 30.

11. Ibid., 30.

12. Manning, "Whitney's *Choice,*" 169–76.

13. Michael T. Ryan, "Assimilating New Worlds in the Sixteenth and Seventeenth Centuries," *Comparative Studies in Society and History* 23 (1981): 520.

14. For a discussion of this emblem as a country-house poem see Kathryn Hunter, "Geoffrey Whitney's 'To Richard Cotton, Esq.': An Early English Country-House Poem," *Review of English Studies* 28 (1977): 438–41.

15. Frances E. Dolan, *Catholicism, Gender, and Seventeenth-Century Print Culture* (Ithaca, NY: Cornell University Press, 1999), 1.

BIBLIOGRAPHY

Boehrer, Bruce. *Shakespeare Among the Animals: Nature and Society in the Drama of Early Modern England.* New York: Palgrave, 2002.

Dolan, Frances E. *Catholicism, Gender, and Seventeenth-Century Print Culture.* Ithaca, NY: Cornell University Press, 1999.

Fudge, Erica. *Perceiving Animals: Humans and Beasts in Early Modern English Culture.* New York: St. Martin's Press, 2000.

Hunter, Kathryn. "Geoffrey Whitney's 'To Richard Cotton, Esq.': An Early English Country-House Poem." *Review of English Studies* 28 (1977): 438–41.

Janson, H. W. *Apes and Ape Lore in the Middle Ages and the Renaissance.* London: Warburg Institute, University of London, 1952.

Manning, John. "Unpublished and Unedited Emblems by Geffrey Whitney: Further evidence of the English adaptation of continental traditions." In *English Emblems and the Continental Tradition.* Edited by Peter M. Daly, 83–107. New York: AMS Press, 1988. 83–107.

Manning, John. "Whitney's *Choice of Emblemes:* A reassessment." *Renaissance Studies* 4 (1990): 155–200.

Russell, Daniel S. *The Emblem and Device in France.* Lexington, KY: French Form, 1985.

Ryan, Michael T. "Assimilating New Worlds in the Sixteenth and Seventeenth Centuries." *Comparative Studies in Society and History* 23 (1981): 519–38.

Thomas, Keith. *Man and the Natural World: Changing Attitudes in England 1500–1800.* London: Allen Lane, 1983.

Trousdale, Marion. *Shakespeare and the Rhetoricians.* Aldershot, UK: Scolar Press, 1982.

Tung, Mason. "Whitney's *A Choice of Emblemes* revisited: A comparative study of the manuscript and the printed versions." *Studies in Bibliography* 29 (1976): 32–101.

Varty, Kenneth. *Reynard, Renart, Reinaert, and Other Foxes in Medieval England. The Iconographic Evidence.* Amsterdam: Amsterdam University Press, 1999.

Whitney, Geffrey. *A Choice of Emblemes.* Leiden: Francis Raphelengius, 1586.

Wilcox, Thomas. *A Short, yet sound Commentarie; written on that woorthie worke called; the Proverbes of Salomon; and newly published for the profite of Gods people.* London: Printed by Thomas Orwin for Thomas Man, 1589.

Contributors

SANDRA BELL is an associate professor of Renaissance Literature at University of New Brunswick, Saint John. She has published articles on the writings of James VI and I, and is co-editor with Marie Loughlin and Patti Brace of the *Broadview Anthology of Sixteenth-Century Prose and Poetry* (forthcoming).

Born in France to British parents, STEPHEN BUICK grew up in Europe, the United Kingdom, and North America. His numerous encounters with the mysterious and the foreign include teaching in departments of English and History at universities in Canada and Turkey. Buick has published articles on the Elizabethan Settlement, the Reformation Bible, and Tudor lexicography. He is completing a critical edition of *The Second Tome of Homilies,* a collection of twenty sermons published in 1563 for unlicensed preachers to read to their congregations as the Elizabethan regime attempted to enforce the orthodoxy of its Settlement of Religion.

PHILIP D. COLLINGTON completed his PhD in English at the University of Toronto (1998), and a postdoctoral fellowship at the University of Michigan – Ann Arbor (1999–2000). He is currently an assistant professor of English at Niagara University in New York State. He has published articles in *ELR, Shakespeare Quarterly,* and *Medieval and Renaissance Drama in England,* and has essays forthcoming in *Studies in Philology* and *Early Theatre.*

JANE FARNSWORTH is an associate professor at Cape Breton University, Nova Scotia. Her areas of scholarly interest include English emblems, early modern English poetry and prose, and women's studies. She has published articles in *SEL* and *Emblematica* and is currently editing an anthology of new criticism on the seventeenth-century English emblematist, George Wither.

COLLEEN FRANKLIN is an assistant professor in the Department of English Studies at Nipissing University, North Bay, Ontario, Canada. Her publications include essays on Thomas James, Edward Umfreville, Mary Shelley and John Barrow, and British representations of the Canadian north.

She is currently preparing a scholarly edition of *The Strange and Danger-ous Voyage of Captaine Thomas James.*

JONATHAN GIL HARRIS is professor of English at George Washington University. He is the author of *Foreign Bodies and the Body Politic: Dis-courses of Social Pathology in Early Modern England* (1998) and *Sick Economies: Drama, Mercantilism, and Disease in Shakespeare's England* (2004), and the co-editor, with Natasha Korda, of *Staged Properties in Early Modern English Drama* (2002). He is currently working on a book manuscript, *Untimely Matter: Reworking Material Culture in Shakespeare's England,* and the New Mermaids critical edition of Thomas Dekker's *The Shoemaker's Holiday.*

KATE LOVEMAN is a junior research fellow at St. Anne's College, Ox-ford. In 2004 she completed a PhD at Cambridge University on deception in English literary and political culture, 1640–1740. She is currently a lec-turer at Leicester University and is working on reading and news-gathering in Samuel Pepys's circle.

BINDU MALIECKAL is an assistant professor in the English Department of Saint Anselm College, New Hampshire. She specializes in early mod-ern literature and contact studies, specifically European encounters with the Jews and Muslims of India, Turkey, and North Africa. Her publications appear in *The Upstart Crow, The Muslim World, Shakespeare Yearbook,* and *Essays in Arts and Sciences.* At present, she is completing a book on the black pepper trade of the early modern era.

MATHEW R. MARTIN is associate professor at Brock University. Author of *Between Theater and Philosophy: Skepticism in the Major City Come-dies of Ben Jonson and Thomas Middleton* (University of Delaware Press, 2001), he is currently working on a book-length project on Marlowe's plays and the aesthetics of trauma.

LINDA MCJANNET, professor of English at Bentley College in Waltham, Mass., has published essays in *Shakespeare Quarterly, Theatre Research International, The Journal of Theatre and Drama,* and *MaRDiE.* She is the author of *The Voice of Elizabethan Stage Directions: The Evolution of a Theatrical Code* (University of Delaware Press, 1999) and *The Sultan Speaks,* a study of dialogue in Western discourse about the Ottomans (forthcoming).

MARIANNE MONTGOMERY is an assistant professor of English at the East Carolina University. She is currently working on a study of foreign ver-naculars on the early modern stage.

SCOTT OLDENBURG received an MA in English Literature from San Francisco State University and is completing a PhD in English at SUNY Buffalo. His publications have appeared in such journals as *The Journal for Early Modern Cultural Studies, Radical Teacher, Renaissance Quarterly,* and *The Sixteenth-Century Journal.*

HELEN OSTOVICH, professor of English at McMaster University, has published articles on Shakespeare and Jonson, and several modern critical editions of Jonson's comedies, most recently *Every Man Out of His Humour* for Revels Plays (2001). She has just completed an edition of Jonson's *The Magnetic Lady* for the Cambridge Works of Ben Jonson (2007). With Elizabeth Sauer, she co-edited *Reading Early Modern Women* (2004), and with Karen Bamford is co-editing Shakespeare's *All's Well that Ends Well* for Internet Shakespeare Editions; and editing Heywood and Brome's *The Late Lancashire Witches* for the Richard Brome electronic project at Royal Holloway University of London. She is the editor of the journal *Early Theatre;* a general editor of the Revels Plays; series editor of Studies in Performance and Early Modern Drama for Ashgate Publishing, and with Alexandra Johnston (REED, University of Toronto) is leading a SSHRC-funded performance project (2005–8) called "Shakespeare and the Queen's Men."

PATRICIA PARKER is professor of English at Stanford University. Her research interests include Shakespeare, early modern studies, feminist theory, and literary theory. She is the author of three books: *Inescapable Romance, a study of romance from Ariosto to Wallace Stevens; Literary Fat Ladies: Rhetoric, Gender, Property;* and *Shakespeare from the Margins: Language, Culture, Context.* She has co-edited five collections of essays, including *Shakespeare and the Question of Theory and Women, "Race" and Writing in the Early Modern Period,* and is currently completing three new books on Shakespeare, race, and gender in the early modern period and editing the new Arden edition of *A Midsummer's Night Dream.*

GRAHAM ROEBUCK is professor emeritus at McMaster University. He has published widely on early modern literature including the literature of science and mathematics, historiography, Civil War pamphlets and propaganda, and the drama. He is past president of the John Donne Society, past president of the Toronto Renaissance and Reformation Colloquium, and director of McMaster Stratford Seminars on Shakespeare and the Theatre.

MARY SILCOX is professor of English at McMaster University, with interests in sixteenth- and seventeenth-century nondramatic literature, particularly emblem books and poetry. As one of the leading scholars in English emblem studies she has published several books, including *The English*

Emblem: Bibliography of Secondary Literature (1990), *The Modern Critical Reception of the English Emblem* (1991), and three volumes of *The English Emblem Tradition* (1988, 1993, 1998), a foundational series setting up the parameters of English emblematic studies. Over the past few years she has also published articles on a number of emblematists, such as Whitney, Combe, Wither, and Alciato, and is in the process of preparing an edition of Robert Farley's seventeenth-century emblem books. Her current major project is a book on the intersection of death, the self, and symbolic universes in early modern emblems.

Index

Page numbers in italics refer to illustrations

acephalism. *See* Ewaipanoma; headless peoples
Actes and Monuments (Foxe), 209, 221, 235
Admonition Controversy, 242
Adventures of Brusanus, Prince of Hungaria, The (Riche), 210, 224
Africa: European views of, 188; historical works on, 192; Othello's inaccuracy about, 188–90; in Pliny's *Natural History,* 44–45. *See also* Africans
Africans: portrayed as villains on English stage, 192; in Ottoman seraglios, 59, 61–63. *See also* Africa; "Moors" and sub-Saharan African characters; *Othello*
Alciato, Andrea: *Emblematum liber,* 281
Amazons, 40
Amurath II, 214, 220, 222
Anatomy of Melancholy (Burton), 189
Andrewes, Lancelot, 98–99
Aneau, Barthélemy: *Picta Poesis,* 289
Anglicus, Bartholomaeus: *Batman vppon Bartholome,* 221
animals: in court and civic entertainments, 253, 256–57; illustrations of, *286;* as metaphor for humans, 283–86, 294
Anne (of Denmark), 255
anthropophagi: in *Othello,* 188
anti-feminist literature, 52
anti-Semitism. See under *The Unfortunate Traveller;* and *The Merchant of Venice. See also* Jews
Arcadia, (Sidney), 91
Archbishop of Canterbury, 235, 238, 241, 246 n. 29
Arithmetick made easie, in two Bookes (Wingate), 110–11, 114–15
Arnold, Matthew, 242
artists: Renaissance, 282–83. *See also* illustrations

Athenae Oxonienses (Wood), 267, 273, 275
Aubrey, John: role in creation of *A True and Exact Relation of the Strange Finding Out of Moses his Tombe,* 267–69, 273, 275
Auden, W.H.: analysis of *The Merchant of Venice,* 134
Augustine, Saint, 49; *De Mendacio* (*On Lying* [c.395]), 191
Augustus (Caesar), 210

Bacon, Sir Francis: advice to travelers, 10; on natural order, 31–32; *Of Travel,* 197; *Of Truth,* 196; "On Usurie" 128–29, 131–32. *See also* "Of Simulation and Dissimulation"
Bacon, Sir Nicholas, 237, 238
Bahamas, 53
Baiazet I, 215–17, 220, 222
Baiazet II, 213, 214, 217, 221, 222
Barclay, William: *Nepenthes, or the Vertues of Tabacco,* 155
Barlow, William: *A Briefe Discovery of the Idle Animadversions of Marke Ridley Doctor in Phisicke upon a Treatise entituled, Magneticall Advertisements,* 118; *Magneticall Advertisements,* 117
Barleti, Marin, 217–18
Basle, 235
Batman vppon Bartholome (Anglicus), 221
Beaumont, Sir John, *The Metamorphosis of Tabacco,* 156, 162, 165 n. 16, 166 n. 21
Becon, Thomas: *The New Pollecye of Warre,* 213
Bedford, Francis, Earl of, 239
Bible: *Geneva,* 211, 243, 244 n. 6; Illyria in, 211; parables from in *The Merchant of Venice,* 128–29, 132–34; in literary

303

Bible (*continued*)
hoaxes (see *A True and Exact Relation of the Strange Finding Out of Moses his Tombe*); and "monstrous" peoples, 45–46
Biddulph, William: *Purchas his Pilgrimes,* 270; *The Travels of Certaine English- men into Africa, Asia . . . ,* 63, 260–61
Bird Trappers (Bolswert), *206*
Blenkow, John, 272
Blount, Thomas, 13
Bolswert, Schelte Adams: *Bird Trappers, 206*
Bon, Ottaviano, 60: *The Sultan's Seraglio: An Intimate Portrait of Life at the Ottoman Court,* 60, 61, 63
Bonnesemaine, Dr., 179–80
Book of Common Prayer, 239, 241, 242, 245 n. 21
Book of the Courtier, The (Castiglione), 197
Boorde, Andrew, *Breuiary of Helthe,* 125
Bosnia. *See* Illyria
botanical treatises, 173. *See also* trees
Botero, Giovanni, 30–31
Boyle, Robert: *New Experiments and Observations Touching Cold,* 32
Braithwait, Richard: *The Smoking Age, or the Life and Death of Tobacco,* 161, 167 n. 49
Breuiary of Helthe (Boorde), 125
Briefe and True Report of the New Found Land of Virginia, A (Harriot): 171, 173, 181
Briefe relation of the Discovery and Plantation of New England, A, (Anon.), 181
Briggs, Henry, 110
Brouwer, Adriaen: *Taste, 2*
Browne, Sir Thomas, 11
Bullinger, Heinrich, 236
Burton, Robert: *Anatomy of Melancholy,* 189

Calvin, John, 236
Cambini, Andrea: *Two very notable commentaries . . . Turkes,* 212, 215
Camden, William, 140
Campion, Thomas: *A Description of a Maske . . . Presented . . . At the Marriage of the . . . Earle of Somerset,* 250, 253–55, 261 n. 4

Canada: in exploration narratives, 27, 29–33; postmodern representations of, 33. *See also* Hudson's Bay Company; Inuit; Northwest Passage
Carew, George, 238
Carew, Richard: "The Excellency of the English Tongue," 140–42
Carr, Ralph: *Mahumetane or Turkish Historie,* 211, 220, 221
Cary, Mary, 272
Castiglione, Count Baldassare: *The Book of the Courtier,* 197
Castor and Pollux (ship), 179–80
Catholics: and Mary Tudor, 234; negative portrayal of Franciscans in literature, 266, 267. *See also* Jesuits; Protestants
Caxton, William (printer), *The most pleasaunt history of Blanchardine . . . & . . . Eglantine Queene of Tormaday,* 210
Cecil, Sir Robert, 170, 171
Cecil, Sir William, 235, 237, 238
Chaloner, Thomas. See *A True and Exact Relation of the Strange Finding Out of Moses his Tombe*
Chancellor, Richard: "The newe Navigation and discoverie of the kingdome of Moscovia 1553," 74
Chapman, George: *Masque of the Middle Temple,* 255, 257, 258, 260
Charles I: and Scottish forces, 271
Charles II: and political use of fashion, 254
Chaucer: *The Prioress's Tale,* 96
Cherseogles, 213, 214, 220, 223
Chew, Samuel: *The Crescent and the Rose,* 220
Choice of Emblemes, A (Whitney), 20, 281–96; ancient world depicted in, 287–90; animals as metaphors for humans, 283–86, 294; Christian references in, 289–91; components of, 283; foreign cultures depicted in, 287, 291–92, 295; Greek mythology in, 287–89; illustrations in, 281–82, *286, 289, 292, 293, 296;* nature's relationship to man in, 286–87; origins of, 282–83; as teaching tool, 283; travel in, 291–94; writers of, 282
Christian Turned Turk, A (Daborne), 66, 67
Christs Tears over Jerusalem (Nashe), 91, 100 n. 32

Chrysanaleia, or the Golden Fishing (Munday), 255, 256, *256,* 257

Circles of Proportion and the Horizontal Instrument (Oughtred), 119

classical imagery, 150; regarding the North, 32 n. 7; in emblem books, 287, 288; in entertainments, 250, 260; in *Tragicall Tales* (Turberville), 81, 83–85. *See also* mythology, Greek; mythology, Roman

Coleridge, Samuel Taylor: "Rime of the Ancient Mariner," use of exploration narratives in, 32

Colet, Claude: *The famous, pleasant, and variable historie, of Palladine of England,* 210

colonization: European rationalization of, 50–53; promotion of, 181, 182; and sassafras trade, 170, 171. *See also under individual place names*

colonization: reverse, and tobacco, 157, 163

Columbus, Christopher, 77

Consent of Time, The (Lloyd), 217

Constantinople: in literature, 269

Cooke, Sir Anthony, 236, 237

Cooper, Thomas, *Thesaurus Linguae Romanae et Britannicae,* 209–10

costumes: "Indian," 257–58; "Moorish" and sub-Saharan African, 254, 255, *256;* Ottoman, 251; Persian, 253. *See also* fashion

Cotton, Sir Dodmore, 254

Counterblaste to Tobacco, A (James I), 153, *154,* 158–62

Cox, Richard, 237

Cradock, Governor, 181–82

Crescent and the Rose, The (Chew), 220

Croatia. *See* Illyria

Cromwell, Oliver: exclusion of Rump, 268; suppression of newsbooks, 269

Curio, Augustine: *Notable historie of the Saracens,* 215–16, 220

Cymbeline (Shakespeare), 29

Daborne, William: *A Christian Turned Turk,* 66, 67

Dallam, Thomas: *The Diary of Thomas Dallam,* 66

Dalmatia. *See* Illyria

Daniel, Samuel: *The Poeticall Essayes,* 210; *The Queenes Arcadia,* 163–64

D'Avenent, William: *The Temple of Love,* 253–54, 257, 260

Davies, William, 14

D'Avity, Pierre: *The estates, empires, & principalities of the world* (transl. Grimestone), 227 n. 27

Deacon, John: *Tobacco Tortured, Or The Filthie Fume of Tobacco Refined,* 136, 161–62

De Busbecq, Ogier Ghislain, 260

de Dominis, Marc'Antonio, 210

Dee, John: *Mathematicall Praeface,* 29, 108–9, 120 n. 3

Defence of Tobacco, A (Marbecke), 156, 162, 165 n. 12

Defence of Trade (Digges), 178

Dekker, Thomas: *London's Tempe,* 253, 254; *Magnificent Entertainment for James I,* 250, 253; *Patient Grissil,* 189. See also *Shoemaker's Holiday, The*

Delamain, Richard: *Grammelogia, or the Mathematicall ring,* 118–19

Deloney, Thomas: *The Gentle Craft,* 144–45, 148

De Magnete (Gilbert), 117

de Quadra, Bishop, 241

Descartes, René: on natural order, 32

Description of a Maske . . . Presented . . . At the Marriage of the . . . Earle of Somerset, A (Campion), 250, 253–55, 261 n. 4

Description of the Turkish Empire, The (George Sandys), 66

de Vera, Ibargoyen Domingo, 47

Device of the Pageant Borne Before Wolstan Dixi, The (Peele), 257

Diary of Thomas Dallam (Dallam), 66

dictionaries, 13

Diocletian, 210, 225 n. 4

Digges, Dudley: *The Defence of Trade,* 178

Discovery of Guiana, The (Ralegh): accuracy of, 39–41, 43, 45; fabulous elements in, 40–53; plagiarization, 48; relation to de Vera's account, 47–48; relation to Mandeville's *Travels,* 43, 44, 48; relation to Pliny's *Natural History,* 44–47, 49. *See also* Ewaipanoma

disease: exogenous model of, 125–26; humoral imbalance as cause of, 124–25; politicization of pathological

disease (*continued*)
  terms, 126; spread via trade routes, 126;
  terminology for used metaphorically
  in literature, 126, 130, 133–34; xenophobic view of, 126–27, 130. *See also*
  hysteria; plague; syphilis; Galenic
  theory; medicines and medicinal herbs;
  medical tracts
Dixi, Sir Wolstan, 256
Donne, John, 183 n. 7
Drake, Sir Francis: dedications to,
  291–92
Dürer, Albrecht: *A Burgundian Standard-
  bearer, 104*
Dutch (language), 141; and German
  language, 145; in literature, 139–41,
  144–49
Dutch (people): artists, 141; in literature,
  145, 146, 149
Dyer, Sir Edward, 174, 291

East: English trade with, 250; as subject of
  travel narratives, 270. *See also* motifs,
  Oriental
East India Company, 178, 249, 264 n. 72
Ecclesiastical Visitation (1559), 239–41
Eclogue IV (Virgil), 289
ecological impact of Europeans on New
  World, 182
economics. *See names of individual
  economists;* mercantilism; trade
Edward II (Marlowe), 189,
Edward VI, 245 n. 19
Egypt, 220
El Dorado, 39–41, 48–50, 173
Elizabeth I: attempted poisoning of, 97;
  classical representations of, 290;
  correspondence with Safiye (wife of
  Murad III), 64–65; and return of Marian
  exiles, 234, 237; policy during
  Protestant Reformation, 238; and
  iconoclasm, 240–41; and Sir Walter
  Ralegh, 39, 49, 52; reaction to accession
  to throne, 242
Elizabethan Settlement, 234–48; as
  compromise between Roman
  Catholicism and Protestantism, 238;
  and Ecclesiastical Visitation (1559),
  239–41; and iconoclasm, 239–41. *See
  also* Marian exiles
Emblematum liber, 281

emblem books, 20, 281–83, 295. *See also
  A Choice of Emblemes*
Endicott, Captain, 181
English (language): and character of
  English people, 140–41; influence of
  foreign languages on, 141–42; origins
  of, 140
English (people): familiarity with "Illyria,"
  209–33; identity in relation to
  Jewishness, 89–90, 94–95, 97–99;
  knowledge of foreign affairs, 275;
  observations on by Venetian
  ambassador, 9
English-Illyrian relations, 218–20, 222,
  229 nn. 51 and 53
English-Jewish relations, 89, 272; in
  literature (see *Merchant of Venice, The;
  Unfortunate Traveller, The*). *See also
  under* English (people)
English-Persian relations, 253
English-Russian relations, 74, 81. *See also
  Tragicall Tales*
English-Scottish relations, 271
English-Spanish relations, 27, 48, 167 n.
  37, 172, 174–75, 179–80
entertainments, court: animals in, 253;
  comparisons to civic entertainments,
  250–51, 259–61; Eastern characters in,
  250, 259; "Indian" characters in, 257–60;
  "Moors" and sub-Saharan African
  characters in, 254–56; Native American
  characters in, 257, 260; Ottoman
  characters in, 251–52; Persian characters
  in, 253–54; religious conversion in, 251,
  258–60. *See also* Lord Mayors' Shows;
  naval battles, mock
Essais (Montaigne), 10
Epitaphes, Epigrams, Songs and Sonets
  (Turberville), 75
Epitome of chronicles (Lanquet), 215
Erasmus: advice to authors, 188, 189
Essex, Earl of: costume in court
  entertainments, 251, 254
*Estates, empires, & principalities of the
  world, The* (D'Avity, transl. Grimestone), 227 n. 27
Every Man In His Humour (Jonson),
  satirical references to tobacco in, 157,
  162; Illyria in, 210
Ewaipanoma, 39–57; de Vera's report
  of, 47–48; illustrations of *40,* 48–49;

Kemys's report of, 46; and Pliny's "dog-headed" people, 46–47; Ralegh's report of, 40–52. *See also* "headless" peoples
"The Excellency of the English Tongue" (Richard Carew), 140–42
exploration narratives, 27–33. *See also individual titles and under individual place names*

Faerie Queene, The (Spenser): and English national identity, 89; tobacco in, 156, 165 n. 10
Færpæ, & Færoa Referata (Storpin), 32
Famous, pleasant, and variable historie, of Palladine of England, The (Colet, transl. Munday), 210
fashion, English: Persian influence, 254; Turkish influence, 263 n. 38; used to parody traveller, 90. *See also* costume
First and Second Volumes of Chronicles, The (Holinshed), 210
First Blast of the Trumpet against the Monstrous Regiment of Women, The (Knox), 52
First Part of Henry VI, The (Shakespeare): fall of Lucifer in, 29
First Part of the Institutes of the Laws of England, or a Commentary Upon Littleton, The (Littleton), 141–42
Fletcher, Giles, 74
Fletcher, John: *The Knight of Malta,* 62, 66; *The Loyal Subject,* 86 n. 6
Florida, 179
Florio, John, 13
Ford, Emmanuel: *Parismus, the renoumed prince of Bohemia,* 211
forests. *See* trees
Forster, William, 118
Fougasses, Thomas de, *Historie of the magnificent state of Venice* (transl. Shute), 213
Foure-Footed Beastes, Of (Topsell), 211
Foxe, John: letters of, 237; relations with Elizabethan Church, 242; *Actes and Monuments,* 209, 221, 235; *A Sermon of Christ Crucified,* 221–24
Fracastoro, Girolamo, 125
Frampton, John, (transl.), 173–75. See also *Joyful News out of the New World*
France, 90–92; in literature, 142, 143; in New World, 179

Frankenstein (Shelley): vilification of north in, 32
Frankfort, 236, 237
French language, 141–43
French people: English view of, 144; in English literature, 142–43
Freud, Sigmund, 50
Friar Bacon and Friar Bungay (Greene), 29
Frobisher, Martin, 29

Galenic theory, 125, 126, 130, 155, 158, 175. *See also* disease; medicines and medicinal herbs
Game at Chess (Middleton), 210
game books. *See* mathematical game books
Gardiner, Stephen, 235
Generall Historie of the Turkes, The (Knolles), 209, 212, 213
Geneva, 235, 244 n. 6
Gentle Craft, The (Deloney), 144–45, 148
Georgijević, Bartolomej: *Ofspring of the house of Ottomanno* (transl. Hugh Goughe), 212, 215
Geuffroy, Antoine: *Order of the great Turckes courte,* 213–24
Gheeraerts, Marcus: "Lady attired as a Persian Virgin," 254
Gilbert, Bartholomew, 172, 173
Gilbert, Sir Humphrey, 29
Gilbert, William: *De Magnete,* 117
Giovio, Paulo: *A Shorte Treatise vpon the Turkes chronicles,* 212, 214, 215
gold: in Guiana, 48. *See also* El Dorado
Gorges, Sir Ferdinando, 182
Gosnold, Bartholomew, 171, 172
Goughe, Hugh (transl.): *Ofspring of the house of Ottomanno,* 212, 215
Grammelogia, or the Mathematicall ring (Oughtred), 118–19
Greece, and Illyria, 217, 218
Greek language, and trade, 145
Greene, Robert: *Friar Bacon and Friar Bungay,* 29; *Pandosto,* 211
Grindal, Edmund, 235, 246 n. 29
guaiacum: in literature, 175–76; as panacea, 174; and syphilis, 176, 177; price of, 172, 176; botanical source of, 177–78
Gualter, Rudolph, 238

Guiana: and El Dorado, 48, 173; 1599 map of, *40,* 48–49; in exploration narratives, 46, 47. See also *Discovery of Guiana* (Ralegh)
guilds: and "foreigners," 144; and Lord Mayors' Shows, 253, 255, 257, 258
Gunpowder Plot, 273
Guylforde, Richard: *This is the begynnynge, and contynuance of the pylgrymage of Sir Richarde Guylforde Knyght,* 213

Hakluyt, Richard, 30, 32, 35 n. 22, 74, 181; *The principall nauigations,* 65, 75–76, 78, 171, 173, 218, 219, 224
Hakluytus posthumus, or, Purchas his Pilgrimes (Purchas), 30–32
harems. *See* seraglios, Ottoman
Harriot, Thomas, 181; *A Briefe and True Report of the New Found Land of Virginia,* 171, 173, 181
Harvey, Gabriel, 174
Hatton, Sir Christopher, 174
"headless" peoples, 39–57; in *Othello,* 49, 188; Pliny on, 188; in *The Tempest,* 49, 189; symbolizing anarchy, 51–52; symbolizing irrationality and brutality, 50–51; in travel narratives, 40. *See also* Ewaipanoma; "monstrous" peoples
hell: north as location of, 27–31, 33
Henry, Prince of Wales (1594–1613): speech in praise of, 253
Henry VIII: costume of in court entertainments, 251, 254; and first royal visitation, 245 n. 19
heresy: during Marian regime, 236
Herodotus, 45
Heylyn, Peter: *Microcosmvs, or a Little Description of the Great World,* 179–80
Heywood, Thomas: *Porta Pietatis, or London's Gate of Piety,* 259
Historie of George Castriot, surnamed Scanderbeg, 217–18
Historie of Serpents (Topsell), 211
Historie of the magnificent state of Venice, 213
History of Trauayle in the West and East Indies, The (Martyr), 212
History of the World (Pliny the Elder), 188, 189
hoaxes, literary: *A True and Exact Relation of the Strange Finding Out of Moses his Tombe,* 266–80
Hobbes, Thomas, 32, 51
Holinshed, Raphael: *The First and Second Volumes of Chronicles,* 210
Homer, 291
Hondius, Jodocus, the Elder, *40*
Horsey, Jerome, 74
Howell, James: *Instructions for Forreine Travell,* 11
Hudson, Henry, 30
Hudson's Bay Company, 27, 32, 35 n. 35
humors. *See* Galenic theory
Hurrem, 64
hysteria, 12–13

iconoclasm: and Elizabethan Settlement, 239–41
illustrated books. *See* emblem books
illustrations, 254; broadside, *154;* in emblem books *286, 289, 292, 293, 296* (see also *A Choice of Emblemes*); engravings, *24, 40, 104, 256;* maps, *24, 40;* paintings, *2, 206;* woodcuts, *24, 154, 286, 289, 292, 293, 296. See also* artists, Renaissance
Illyria: Christianity in, 223–24; relations with Ottoman Empire and the "Turk," 212–24; associated with romance and retirement, 210–11; and Christian/Turk relations, 221–22; familiarity to English people, 209–33; language of, 211–12, 223; mentioned in Shakespearean works, 209; physical description of Illyrians, 216–17; relations with England, 218–20; strategic location of, 217; in *Twelfth Night,* 209–12, 224. *See also* Ragusans
India. *See* "Indian" characters
"Indian" characters: ethnographic ambiguity of, 257; in court entertainments, 257–58; feminization of, 261, 264 n. 73; in Lord Mayors' Shows, 258–59; positive portrayals of, 258; religious conversion of, 258
indigenous peoples: and missionary activity, 260; mythical (*see* Ewaipanoma); purported links to devil, 166 n. 30; as purported source of illness, 160; use of tobacco by, 157, 159–60. *See also* Amazons; Inuit; Native Americans

Instructions for Forreine Travell (Howell), 11

intellectual property: emergence of concept, 117–19. *See also* plagiarism: and mathematics

Inuit: in exploration narratives, 29–30; recent writings by, 33

Italian language, 141, 142

Italy, 14–15, 91, 107; Jews in, 133; in literature (see *The Merchant of Venice*); in travel narratives, 14–15. *See also* Venice

James I: *A Counterblaste to Tobacco,* 153, *154,* 158–62; court entertainment written for, 250; dedications to, 163; letter from regarding dangers of tobacco use, 165 n. 12; mentioned in Chapman's *Masque of the Middle Temple,* 258

James VI: court entertainment of, 250

James, Thomas: *Strange and Dangerous Voyage of Captaine Thomas James,* 31–32; *Voyage, The Dangerous Voyage of Capt. Thomas James,* 32

Jenkinson, Anthony, 74

Jerome, Saint, 210, 211, 219, 221

Jerusalem, 271

Jesuits: in literature, 270; negative portrayal of in literature, 266, 267. *See also* Catholics

Jewel, John, 234, 237, 239, 240, 243; *A replie,* 211, *Zurich Letters,* 237

Jews: English attitude towards, 89, 272; English expulsion of in 1290, 89, 96, 128; negative portrayal of in literature, 266, 267; usury associated with, 127–28, 131–32. See also under *Unfortunate Traveller, The; Merchant of Venice, The*

Jones, Inigo: as costume designer for *The Masque of Blackness* (Jonson); *Temple of Love,* 253–54, 257, 260

Jonson, Ben: on authority of ancients, 117; as empiric, 108, 117; *Every Man In His Humour,* 157, 162, 210; *Masque of Queens,* 253, 254; *Timber,* 117, 199; *Volpone,* 175–76. See also *The Magnetic Lady; Or Humors Recondil'd; Masque of Blackness*

Jorden, Edward, 12

Josslyn, John, 182

Joyful Newes out of the New World (Monardes), 155; editions of, 173; guaiacum curing syphilis in, 176; influence on later writings, 173–74; popularity of, 180–81; sassafras in, 176–77, 179–81; tobacco in, 155; translator's role in success of, 174

Julius Caesar, 210, 218

Kemys, Lawrence: *A Relation of the Second Voyage to Guiana,* 46

Kingston, Sir Anthony, 244 n. 4

Knight of Malta, The (Fletcher), 62, 66

Knolles, Richard: *The Generall Historie of the Turkes,* 209, 212, 213

Knollys, Sir Francis, 239

Knox, John: *The First Blast of the Trumpet against the Monstrous Regiment of Women,* 52

Lady attired as a Persian Virgin (Gheeraerts), 254

Lane, Ralph: account on Virginia, 171–72

language: of Illyria, 211–12. *See also names of individual languages*

language, "foreign" in literature: as object of derision, 146–47, 148; representing economic success, 146–49; representing transnational trade, 139–40, 142–44, 146, 149; denoting untrustworthiness, 141; in Shakespearean works, 142–43. *See also Shoemaker's Holiday, The; names of individual languages*

Lanquet, Thomas, *Epitome of chronicles,* 215

Las Casas, Bartolome de, 53

Laud, William, 268

Lavardin, Jacques de, (transl.): *Historie of George Castriot, surnamed Scanderbeg,* 217–18

Leicester, Earl of, 281–82

Lenten Stuffe (Nashe), 98, 99

Leo, Johannes (Leo Africanus), 192

Leroy, Louis: *Of the interchangeable course or variety of things in the whole world,* 217

Levant Company, 249

literacy: emblem books as teaching tools, 283; of women in Ottoman seraglios, 61

Lithgow, William: *A Most Delectable and True Discourse, of an Admired and Painefull Peregrination from Scotland to . . . Europe, Asia and Affricke,* 270

Littleton, Sir Thomas: *The First Part of the Institutes of the Laws of England, or a Commentary Upon Littleton,* 141–42

Lloyd, Lodowick: *The Consent of Time,* 217

London: anti-immigrant riots in, 144; audiences, 143, 250, 260, 261; availability of exotic goods in, 149; fictionalized, 130; "foreign" language used in theatres, 143–44, 149; "foreigners" accepted in, 19, 144; "foreigners" stereotyped in, 146; Jews attacked in, 132; marginality of, 250; merchant society in, 91, 139–41, 144, 148–49; news transmitted and exchanged in, 269; in poetry, 249; sassafras in, 170; satirized, 91; social mobility in, 148–49; tavern society, 267, 268; tobacco sales in, 143. *See also* guilds

"London's Lamentable Estate," 249, 261

London's Tempe (Dekker), 253, 254

London's Triumph (Tatham), 254

Longland, Charles, 272

Lopez, Doctor, 97

Lord Mayors' Shows: animals in, 256–67; comparisons to court entertainments, 250–51, 259–61; earliest description of, 263 n. 52; Eastern characters in, 250, 259; "Indian" characters in, 257–60; "Moors" and sub-Saharan African characters in, 256–57; Persian characters in, 254; Ottoman characters in, 252–53; religious conversion in, 251, 258–60; association with spice trade, 258. *See also under* guilds

Lowndes, Richard, 268, 270

Loyal Subject, The, (Fletcher), 86 n. 6

Lucan, 218

Macbeth (Shakespeare), 28

Mace, Samuel, 173

magic. *See* witchcraft

Magnete, De, 117

Magnetic Lady; Or Humors Recondil'd, The (Jonson): and mathematical game books, 111–16; mathematical problems in, 112–16; and *Mathematicall*

Recreations, 113–15; Wingate's *Arithmetick made easie, in two Bookes* as source, 110–11, 114–15

Magneticall Advertisements (Barlow), 117

Magneticall Animadversions. Upon certaine Magneticall Advertisements lately published by Maister William Barlow (Ridley), 118

magnetism (science): and intellectual property dispute, 117–18; in *Mathematical Recreations,* 115–16; in Jonson's *The Magnetic Lady,* 119–20

Magnificent Entertainment for James I (Dekker), 250, 253

Mahumetane or Turkish Historie (Carr), 211, 220, 221

Maine, 182

Malynes, Gerard, 126, 127, 130–32; and Jonson's *The Magnetic Lady,* 122 n. 21. See also *Saint George for England Allegorically Described*

Mandeville, Sir John. See *Voiage and Travaile of Sir John Maundeville, The*

maps, *24, 40*

Marbecke, Roger: *A Defence of Tabacco,* 156, 162, 165 n. 12

Marian exiles: alienation of after repatriation, 234–48; as commissioners for royal visitation, 239; and conflict in establishment of Elizabethan church, 238–39, 242–43; exclusion from decisions of Elizabeth regime, 237; facilitation of exile, 235; financial hardship on return to England, 237; and Nicodemites, 238; reaction to executions during Marian regime, 236; religious freedom of, in Europe, 236; work and living conditions of during exile, 235–36. *See also* Elizabethan Settlement

Marlowe, Christopher: *Edward II,* 189, *Tamburlaine the Great,* 68, 212, 220; *The Tragicall History of Dr. Faustus,* 28

Marprelate controversy, 91

Martire d'Anghiera, Pietro. *See* Martyr, Peter

Marten, Henry, 268, 271, 272

Martyr, Peter, 236, 240; *The History of Trauayle in the West and East Indies,* 212

Mary Tudor, 234, 235, 237

Masque of Blackness (Jonson): conversion

in, 260; negative portrayal of Eastern characters in, 250; "Moors" and sub-Saharan African characters in, 254–55, 260; racial differences in, 260

Masque of the Middle Temple (Chapman), 255, 257, 258, 260

Masque of Queens (Jonson), 253, 254

masques. *See* entertainments, court

Massinger, Philip, "London's Lamentable Estate," 249, 261; *The Renegado,* 66–67

mathematical games and game books, 111–16

mathematical instruments, 109–10, 118–19

Mathematicall Praeface (Dee), 29, 108–9, 120 n. 3

Mathematicall Recreations (Van Etten), 112–14; magnetism in, 115–16, 119–20; and plagiarism 116–17; and prefatory poem, 112–13. *See also Récréations Mathématiques; The Magnetic Lady* (Jonson)

mathematics, 18; as framework for other knowledge and arts, 108–9, 119–20; Jonson's use of for understanding universe, 109; history of in England, 107–9, 116–20; in literature, 107–22; and mercantilism, 120 n. 3; and plagiarism 116–19; as recreational pursuit, 110; religious groups' reaction to, 108

Maxims of State (Ralegh), 51

May, Edward, 12

May, Thomas, 268, 271

Measure for Measure (Shakespeare): Illyria in, 209; source for, 210

medicines and medicinal herbs: sourced from New World, 174, 175, 178; price of, 175–76. *See also* diseases; Galenic theory; guaiacum; medical tracts; sassafras; syphilis; tobacco

medical tracts, 12–13. *See also* diseases; medicines and medicinal herbs

Mehmed III, 65

Mehmet I, 216, 220

Mehmet II (Mehmet the Conqueror), 59, 60, 213–14, 217, 220, 222

Melton, Sir John, *A Sixe-Folde Politician,* 167 n. 49

mercantilism, English: and trade loss to Spain, 174–75; and discourse on transnational trade depleting English

wealth, 126, 128–30, 136, 175, 181; in literature, 139–52; and mathematical knowledge, 120 n. 3; and usury in literature, 127–37. *See also Merchant of Venice, The. See also under* missionary activity

Merchant of Venice, The (Shakespeare), 89, 124–38; and Bacon's "On Usurie," 128; biblical parables in, 128–29, 132–34; and diseases, metaphorical applications, 130, 133, 134; and diseases, nationalized nomenclature, 126; Jewish usury in, 128–37; and Malynes's *Saint George for England Allegorically Described,* 127; Shylock as symbol of Venetian moral state, 135; Shylock's effect on other characters, 135; Shylock as "other," 134; Shylock's parable, 133; stereotyping of nationalities in, 135–36; W.H. Auden's analysis of, 134

Mercurius Politicus, 269, 272

Metamorphoses (Ovid), 287–89

Metamorphosis of Tabacco, The (Beaumont), 156, 165 n. 16, 166 n. 21

Meziriac, sieur de, Claude-Gaspar Bachet, 116

Microcosmvs, or a Little Description of the Great World (Heylyn), 179–80

Middleton, Thomas, 260: *Game at Chess,* 210; *The Triumphs of Honour and Industry,* 252, 258; *Triumphs of Honor and Virtue,* 258; *The Triumphs of Truth,* 255–56, 258

Midsummer Night's Dream, A (Shakespeare), 28

Milles, Thomas, 131

Misselden, Edward, 126

missionary activity, 260; merchants' participation in, 261. *See also* Jesuits

Moluccas. *See* "Indian" characters

Monardes, Nicolas: *Dos libros . . . las cosas que se traen de nuestras Indias Occidentales, que sirven al uso de la medicina* and *Segunda parte del libro . . . do se trata del Tabaco, y de la Sassafras. See Joyfull Newes out of the new founde worlde*

"monstrous" peoples: Biblical associations, 45–46; in travel narratives, 44–46, 49–50; projecting Europeans' view of

"monstrous" peoples (*continued*)
themselves, 52–53; reported wealth of,
47, 48. *See also* Ewaipanoma; "headless"
peoples

Montague, Lady Mary Wortley: *The
Turkish Embassy Letters,* 58

Montaigne, Michel de, 187, 188, 190;
Essais, 10

Monuments of Honour (Webster), 252–53,
256, 257

"Moors" and sub-Saharan African
characters: in court entertainments,
254–56, *256;* in Lord Mayors' Shows,
256–57; negative portrayal of, 254–56;
portrayed as slaves and servants, 255;
positive portrayal of, 255, 257; See also
Africa; *Othello;* and Othello (character)

Moryson, Fynes, 144, 270

*Most Delectable and True Discourse, of an
Admired and Painefull Peregrination
from Scotland to . . . Europe, Asia and
Affricke, A* (Lithgow), 270

*Most pleasaunt history of Blanchardine . . .
& . . . Eglantine Queene of Tormaday . . .*
(Caxton, William, printer), 210

Mun, Thomas, 126

Munday, Anthony: *Chrysanaleia, or the
Golden Fishing,* 255, 256, *256,* 257; *The
famous, pleasant, and variable historie,
of Palladine of England* (transl.), 210

Munster, Sebastion: *Typus Orbis
Universalis, 24*

Murad III, 64, 65, 213

Muscovy Company, 74, 76

mythical cities. *See* El Dorado

mythology, Germanic, 34 n. 7

mythology, Greek: in civic and court
entertainments, 250; in emblem books,
287–89

mythology, Roman: in civic and court
entertainments, 250

Nashe, Thomas: exiled from London for
sedition, 98; Marprelate controversy,
91; *Christs Tears over Jerusalem,* 91,
100 n. 32; *Lenten Stuffe,* 98, 99; *Pierce
Penilesse His Supplication to the Divell,*
91. See also *Unfortunate Traveller, The*

Native Americans: portrayal of in court
entertainments, 257, 260; encounters
with European voyagers, 47–48,
172–73; 181; Europeans' rationalization
for conquest of, 50–53; health of, 178;
treatment of disease, 179, 185 n. 27.
See also indigenous peoples; Inuit

Natural History (Pliny), 44–46, 49, 50,
116, 193, 197

*Nauigations, peregrinations and voyages,
made into Turkie* (Nicolay), 60, 61, 216

Naunton, Sir Robert, 242

naval battles, mock, 251–52

Nayler, James, 274

Nedham, Marchamont, 269, 270

Nepenthes, or the Vertues of Tabacco
(Barclay), 155

New England, 181, 182

New Englands Prospect (Wood), 182

*New Experiments and Observations
Touching Cold* (Boyle), 32

"The newe Navigation and discoverie of
the kingdome of Moscovia 1553"
(Chancellor), 74

New Pollecye of Warre, The (Becon), 213

New World. *See* exploration narratives;
indigenous peoples; language, "foreign";
trade; travel narratives. *See also* individual place names.

newsbooks, 269

Nicodemites, 238

Nicolay, Nicolas de: *Nauigations,
peregrinations and voyages, made into
Turkie,* 60, 61, 216

Nipping or Snipping of Abvses, The
(Taylor), 163

Norfolk, Duke of, 237

North: exploration of, 27–33; in literature,
27–33; postmodern representations of,
33, 36 n. 44; as purported location of
hell, 27–31, 33 n. 1, 34 n. 7; 34 n. 11, 78;
scientific treatises on, 32

Northern Act Book, 240

Northwest Passage, search for, 27, 31–33.
See also North; Hudson's Bay Company

Norton, Thomas, *Orations,* 228 n. 35

Notable historie of the Saracens (Curio),
215–16, 220

Nowell, Alexander, 239

Nur Banu (Kalè Kartánou), political power
of, 64, 65

Of Foure-Footed Beasts (Topsell), 211

"Of simulation and dissimulation"

(Bacon): and heuristic categories applied to *Othello,* 187, 190–98

Ofspring of the house of Ottomanno (Georgijević, transl. Goughe), 212, 215

Of the interchangeable course or variety of things in the whole world (Leroy), 217

Of Travel (Bacon), 197

Of Truth (Bacon), 196

"On Usurie" (Bacon), 128–29, 131–32

Orations (Norton), 228 n. 35

Order of the greate Turckes courte (Geuffroy, transl. Grafton), 213–24

Oriental motifs in literature, 249–61

Orientalism (Said), 250

Ortelius, Abraham: *The Theatre of the Whole World/Theatrum Orbis Terrarum,* 211–13

Othello: dissimulation in, 187, 191–95; editorial emendations and misinterpretation of, 196; handkerchief as symbol of dishonesty, 187, 195–97; "headless" people in, 49, 188; Indian/Judean character in, 187, 198; Pliny as possible source, 188; simulation in, 187; theme of honesty in, 187–205; Venetian/Ottoman conflict in, 216. *See also* Othello (character)

Othello (character); dishonesty of, 187–88, 193–98; exotic adventures of, 188; false modesty of, 192–93; misrepresentation of Africa by, 188–90; exaggeration of own foreignness to gain acceptance, 187, 189, 190; false pretences of, 193–94; rhetorical skills of, 192; self-contradiction, 194–95; secrecy of, 187, 190–91; siege of Vienna, 223; as soldier, 198; weakness of character, 190

Ottoman characters: in court entertainments, 251–52; in Lord Mayor's Shows, 252–53; negative portrayal of, 250, 251; portrayed as pirates, 251–52; positive portrayal of, 68, 250–53, 272; as symbol of commerce, 253. *See also* seraglios, Ottoman

Ottoman Empire: relationship with Illyria, 212–13, 220; relationship with England, 218–20, 222; conflict with Venice, 216, 220–21, 223; as subject of travel narratives, 58, 59, 61, 66, 216 (*see also* individual titles of travel narratives). *See also* seraglios, Ottoman

Orientalism (Said), 250

Oughtred, William, 118–9; *Circles of Proportion and the Horizontal Instrument,* 119

Ovid: *Metamorphoses,* 287–89

pageantry. *See* entertainments, court; Lord Mayors' Shows

Panciroli, Guido: *Rerum memorabilium jam olim depærditarum,* 173–76, 184 n. 15

Pandosto (Greene), 211

parable: in *The Merchant of Venice,* 128–29, 132–34

Paracelsus, 125

Parismus, the renoumed prince of Bohemia (Ford), 211

Parker, Matthew, Archbishop of Canterbury, 238, 241

Parsons, Robert: *The Warn-word to Sir Francis Hastinges Wast-Word,* 211, 226

Patient Grissil (Dekker), 189

Peele, George, *The Device of the Pageant Borne Before Wolstan Dixi,* 257

Persia: relations with England, 253

Persian characters: in court entertainments, 253–54, 260; in Lord Mayors' Shows, 254; positive portrayal of, 253–54

Petrarchism: connection to colonial and travel narratives, 77; in Turberville's *Tragicall Tales,* 76–86

Philaretes (pseud.): *Work for Chimny-sweepers: Or A warning for Tabacconists,* 158–61

Picta Poesis (Aneau), 289

Pierce Penilesse His Supplication to the Divell (Nashe), 91

pirates, 126, 132, 136, 209, 251–52

plagiarism: and mathematics, 116–19

plague: importation of exotic goods as cause of, 249

Plantin, Christopher, 281

Paul, Saint, 211, 221, 268

Plantin Press, 282

Plautus, 214

Pliny the Elder: *History of the World,* 188, 189; *Natural History,* 44–46, 49, 50, 116, 193, 197

Poeticall Essayes, The (Daniel), 210

poetry: topographic, 35 n. 37

Popham, Captain George, 47, 48

Porta Pietatis, or London's Gate of Piety
   (Heywood), 259
Presbyterians, 273–74
Principall nauigations,The (Hakluyt), 65,
   75, 171, 218, 219, 224
Pring, Martin, 172
Prioress's Tale, The (Chaucer), 96
Protestants: negative portrayal of in
   literature, 267, 272, 274; and English
   Jews, 89; *See also* Elizabethan
   Settlement; Marian exiles
Publick Intelligencer, The, 269–72
Purchas his Pilgrimes (Purchas), 30–32
Purchas, Samuel: *Purchas his Pilgrimes*
   (Purchas), 30–32, 270
puzzles. *See* emblem books; mathematical
   game books

Quakers, 274
Queenes Arcadia (Daniel), 163–64

Rabelais, 92–93
Ramus, Peter, 118
Ralegh, Sir Walter: condemned as traitor,
   161; and Elizabeth I, 39, 49, 52;
   imprisonment of, 170; monopoly on
   trade of goods from Americas, 170–72;
   and sassafras trade, 170–73, 175, 181;
   and tobacco, 161, 183 n. 9; *Maxims of
   State,* 51. See also *Discovery of Guiana,
   The*
Randolph, Sir Thomas, 74, 75, 78, 80–81
Raphelengius, Francis, 281–82
Recorde, Robert: work of, 118; *The
   Whetstone of Witte,* 107–10
Reformation. *See* Elizabethan Settlement;
   Marian exiles; See *also* Protestants
*Relation of a Journey Begun An. Dom:
   1610, A* (George Sandys), 212, 270
*Relation of the Second Voyage to Guiana,
   A* (Kemys), 46
*Relation, Or Rather a True Account of the
   Island of England, A* (anon.), 9–10
religion. *See* Elizabethan Settlement;
   Marian exiles; *see also names of
   individual religions*
religion and science, 108
religious conversion: to Christianity in
   literature, 258–60; to Islam, 60, 61, 66,
   67; to Islam in literature, 213, 251, 260.
   See also missionary activity

Renegado, The (Massinger), 66–67
Replie, A (Jewel), 211
*Rerum memorabilium jam olim
   depærditarum* (Panciroli), 173–76
Richard I (Richard the Lionheart): travels
   in Illyria, 218, 222
Richard II: in literature, 210
Riche, Barnaby: *The Adventures of
   Brusanus, Prince of Hungaria,* 210, 224
Ridley, Mark: *Magneticall Animad-
   versions. Upon certaine Magneticall
   Advertisements lately published by
   Maister William Barlow,* 118; *A Short
   Treatise of Magneticall Bodies and
   Motions,* 117
"Rime of the Ancient Mariner": use of
   exploration narratives in, 32
romance: medieval revival of, 250
Rome: in emblem books, 291; Jews in, 95,
   96, 100 n. 25, 133
Roxelana. *See* Hurrem
Russia: Thomas Randolph's confinement
   by Tsar in, 80–81; as subject of poetic
   travel narrative, 74–88; trade with
   England, 74. *See also* Muscovy
   Company; *Tragicall Tales* (Turberville)
Rymer, Thomas, 196

Safiye, 64–65
Said, Edward: *Orientalism,* 250
*Saint George for England Allegorically
   Described* (Malynes): and Jewish usury,
   127; mercantilist criticism of transnational trade in, 127, 129–32, 134, 136
Sandys, Edwine, 237–41
Sandys, George: *Description of the Turkish
   Empire,* 66; A *Relation of a Journey
   Begun An. Dom: 1610,* 212, 270
sassafras: as cure for syphilis, 176–77,
   180, 181; as food, 172; Hakluyt's view
   of, 171; and colonization, 171–76, 182;
   last English voyage to procure, 173;
   in literature, 175–76; market value of,
   172, 180, 181; misuse of, 180; Native
   American use of, 179; and New World
   adventurers, 171–72, 179; as medicine
   or panacea, 171, 176–77, 179–82;
   subsidizing timber trade; 178–79,
   181–82; trade of, 170–86. *See also*
   Ralegh, Sir Walter; *Joyful Newes out
   of the New World*

Scanderbeg, 214, 215, 217–18
science and religion, 108
scientific treatises: on north, 32. *See also*
    botanical treatises; magnetism;
    mathematics; medical tracts
Scot, Thomas, 274
Scots: negative portrayal in English
    literature, 270–71
Scott, Sir Walter: *Waverley,* 34
Scottish Covenant, 271
Segunda parte del libro (Monardes), 155
Selim II, 64, 213
Selimus (Greene), 214, 215
seraglios, Ottoman, 58–73: daily life in,
    60–61; ethnic origins of women in, 58,
    59, 61, 62, 68; freedom in, 58, 63;
    informing portrayal of "Turkish" women
    in literature, 59, 66–69; historical
    accounts of, 60; philanthropy of women
    in, 65; political influence of women in,
    59, 63–65; religious conversion in, 60,
    61; and slavery, 59–63; social status in,
    63; in travel narratives, 58, 59, 61, 66
Sermon of Christ Crucified, A (Foxe),
    221–24
Settle, Dionyse, 29–31
Settlement of Religion. *See* Elizabethan
    Settlement
Shakespeare: *1 Henry IV,* 142; *1 Henry VI,*
    29; *2 Henry VI,* 209; *The Comedy of
    Errors,* 209; *Cymbeline,* 29; *Henry V,*
    142, 143; *Love's Labours Lost,* 86 n. 6;
    Macbeth, weather in, 28; *Measure for
    Measure,* Illyria in, 209; source for, 210;
    The Merry Wives of Windsor, 142; *A
    Midsummer Night's Dream,* 28; *The
    Tempest,* 49, 189. See also *Othello;
    Merchant of Venice, The; Twelfth Night*
Shelley, Mary: *Frankenstein,* 32
Sherley, Anthony, 220; *Travels of the
    Three English Brothers, The,* 253
shipbuilding, 178–79
Shoemaker's Holiday, The (Dekker),
    139–52: Dekker's *The Gentle Craft*
    as source, 144–45; Dutch language
    symbolizing commerce in, 143–44; plot
    summary, 143
*Short Treatise of Magneticall Bodies and
    Motions* (Ridley), 117
*Shorte Treatise vpon the Turkes chronicles,
    A* (Giovio), 212, 214, 215

Sidney, Sir Philip, 174, 291; *Arcadia,* 91
Sixe-Folde Politician, A (Melton), 167 n. 49
slavery: of Bahamians, 53; depicted in
    court entertainments, 255. *See also*
    seraglios, Ottoman
Smith, John (captain), 14, 220
*Smoking Age, or the Life and Death of
    Tobacco, The* (Braithwait), 161, 167 n. 49
social mobility, in London, 148–49
Somerset, Earl of, masque written for, 250,
    253, 261 n. 4
Southampton, Earl of, 172
Spain: colonization of New World, 179;
    and spread of syphilis, 126; trade
    competition with England, 167 n. 37,
    172, 174–75, 180; travel narratives
    emanating from, 47–48. *See also*
    Spanish (language)
Spanish (language), 141, 142. *See also*
    Spain
Spenser, Edmund: *The Faerie Queene:* and
    English national identity, 89; tobacco in,
    156, 165 n. 10
spice trade, in literature, 258
*Statelie tragedie of Claudius Tiberius
    Nero, The* (Anon.), 225
Storpin, John: *Færpæ, & Færoa Referata,*
    32
*Strange and Dangerous Voyage of Captaine
    Thomas James, The* (James), 31–32
Strasbourg, 235
Strype, John, 237
Suffolk, Duchess of, 235
Süleyman I, 60, 64, 213
*Sultan's Seraglio: An Intimate Portrait of
    Life at the Ottoman Court, The* (Bon),
    60, 61, 63
Sylvester, Joshua, *Tobacco Battered and
    the Pipes Shattered,* 161
syphilis: first occurrence of in Europe,
    177; and guaiacum, 176, 177; and
    sassafras, 176–77, 180, 181; regional
    names for, 126; and tobacco, 160. *See
    also* disease

Tamburlaine the Great (Marlowe), 68,
    212, 220
Taste (Brouwer), 2
Tatham, John: *London's Triumph,* 254
Taylor, John, *The Nipping or Snipping of
    Abvses,* 163

Tempest, The (Shakespeare): headless peoples in, 49, 189

Temple of Love, The (D'Avenant), 253–54, 257, 260

Theatre of the Whole World, The/Theatrum Orbis Terrarum (Ortelius), 211–13

Thesaurus Linguae Romanae et Britannicae (Cooper), 209–10

This is the begynnynge, and contynuance of the pylgrymage of Sir Richarde Guylforde Knyght (Guylforde), 213

Throckmorton, Sir Nicholas, 235

Thurloe, John, 272

Tiberius (Caesar), 210

timber trade: sassafras trade subsidizing, 178–79, 181–82

Timber (Jonson), 199

Timberlake, Henry, 13

tobacco: as fashionable, 156, 165 n. 14; anti-tobacco tracts (see *A Counterblaste to Tobacco; Smoking Age, or the Life and Death of Tobacco; Tobacco Battered and the Pipes Shattered; Work for Chimny-sweepers: Or A warning for Tabacconists*); Hakluyt's use of, 171; illustration depicting use of, *154;* in literature, 163–64, 176–76; Native Americans' use of, 157, 159–60, 166 n. 30; as mental and creative stimulant, 156–57, 163, 167 n. 49; medical community's advocacy of, 155–56; as medicinal herb or panacea, 155–57, 160, 165 n. 12; pro-tobacco tracts (see *A Defence of Tabacco; The Metamorphosis of Tabacco*); and reverse colonization, 157, 163; sales revenues, 153; satirical representations of, 157, 159, 162, 163; as threat to English character, 153–55, 159–63, 165 n. 12; as threat to English sovereignty, 153, 159, 160–62, 167 n. 37; as threat to health, 157–60, 162; trade of, 153, 179. See also Ralegh, Sir Walter; *Faerie Queene, The; Every Man In His Humour*

Tobacco Battered and the Pipes Shattered (Sylvester), 161

Tobacco Tortured, Or The Filthie Fume of Tobacco Refined (Deacon), 161–62

Topsell, Edward, 211

Tottel's Miscellany: influence on Turberville's work, 75, 79

tracts: anti-tobacco, 153, *154,* 155, 158–62; medical, 12–13

trade, English: competition with Spain, 174–75; depleting English wealth (mercantilist view), 126, 128–30, 136, 175, 181; with "East" in literature, 250; as indicator of English power, 262 n. 12; with Ottoman Empire, in literature, 252; and spread of disease, 126. *See also* mercantilism, spice trade; timber trade. *See also under* guaiacum; sassafras; tobacco

Tragedy of Caesar's Revenge, The (anon.), 210

Tragicall History of Dr. Faustus, The (Marlowe), weather in, 28;

Tragicall Tales (Turberville), 74–88: classical imagery in, 81, 83–85; comparisons between Russia and England in, 77–78, 81–84; critical view of Russia in, 77–86; landscape in, 83–85; rationale for use of verse form, 76–77; Petrarchism in, 77–86; publication history of, 75; women as metaphor for Russia in, 81–82; weather in, 78–80, 82–85

travel, foreign: dangers of, 291–94; as metaphor for life, 295; transforming traveller, 90

travel narratives: anti-literary style of, 74; false, 274–75; dishonesty in, 188–89; fictional, 89–102; on Ottoman Empire, 58, 59, 61, 66, 216; Petrarchism in, 77–86; in poetic form, 74–88. *See also* exploration narratives; travel, foreign; *and individual titles. See also under* "monstrous" peoples; *and under individual place names*

Travels of Certaine Englishmen into Africa, Asia . . . , The (Biddulph), 63, 260–61

Travels of the Three English Brothers, The (Sherley), 253

trees, 177–79; as source of medicines, 177–78; deforestation of Europe causing ill health, 178; as enticement to prospective colonists, 181, 182; New World as source of, 177–78, 181; for shipbuilding, 178; timber trade, 178–79

Triumphs of Honour and Industry, The (Middleton), 252, 258

Triumphs of Honor and Virtue (Middleton), 258

Triumphs of Truth, The (Middleton), 255–56, 258

True and Exact Relation of the Strange Finding Out of Moses his Tombe, A ([Chaloner]), 266–80: anti-Catholic sentiment in, 266, 267, 273; anti-Protestant sentiment in, 274, 275; authorship of, 267–68; background of, 267–68; and censorship, 269; credibility of, 268–73; negative portrayal of Jews in, 266, 267, 272; negative portrayal of Jesuits in, 266, 267, 273, 274; political and religious leanings of author, 268, 272, 273; preface, 268; role of John Aubrey in creation of, 267–69; reaction to, 275; travel narratives as source for, 270

True Reporte of the last Voyage . . . by Captaine Frobisher, 29–31

Turberville, George, 75: epistles, 75; poetry reproduced in Hakluyt's *The Principall Nauigations,* 75–76; political ramifications of work, 75–76; *Epitaphes, Epigrams, Songs and Sonets,* 75. See also *Tragicall Tales*

"turning Turk." *See* religious conversion, to Islam

Turkish Embassy Letters, The, (Montague) 58

"Turks": in England, 224, 229 nn. 51 and 53; in literature (*see* Ottoman characters); history of, 212–18, 220–24; in travel narratives, 218–20; women, in literature, 59, 66–69. *See also* religious conversion, to Islam; Ottoman Empire; seraglios, Ottoman

Twelfth Night, 209–33: and Illyria, 209–12, 215, 217, 219, 224; sources for, 211. *See also under* Illyria

Two very notable commentaries . . . Turkes (Cambini), 212, 215

Typus Orbis Universalis (Munster), *24*

Unfortunate Traveller, The (Nashe), 89–102; Anabaptists in, 91, 93–94; anti-Semitism in, 89–90, 94–99; caricatures of French and Swiss in, 92, 93; English identity as theme, 89–90, 94–95, 97–99; exiles in, 94–95; foreigners portrayed as grotesque or violent in, 92–94; Oedipal theme in, 94–95, 97; Rabelaisian allusions in, 92–93; travel as undesirable in, 90–91

Urania (Wroth), 211

Van Etten, Henry: *Récréations Mathématiques Composées De plusiers Problems, plaisans & facetiues,* 111–12. See also translation, *Mathematical Recreations*

Venice: conflict with Ottoman Empire, 216, 220–21, 223; Marian exiles in, 244 n. 2; as news source, 269; in *Othello,* 190; in *The Merchant of Venice,* 135

Vienna: siege of, 223

Virgil: *Eclogue IV,* 289

Virginia: and sassafras trade, 170–73, 179, 180; Native peoples of, 171–72; and timber for shipbuilding, 178

Volpone (Jonson), 175–76

Voiage and Travaile of Sir John Maundeville, The (Mandeville): accuracy of, 43; and Ralegh's *Discovery of Guiana,* 41, 44–49

"Voyage of M. Henry Austell by Venice to Ragusa then over-land to Constantinople . . . anno 1586," 219

"Voyage of M. John Locke to Jerusalem, Anno 1553," 219

Voyage, The Dangerous Voyage of Capt. Thomas James (James), 32

Warn-word to Sir Francis Hastinges Wast-Word, The (Parsons), 211, 226

weather: in literature, 28. *See also* North, as purported location of hell; see also under *Tragicall Tales*

Webbe, Edward, 13

Webster, John: *Monuments of Honour,* 252–53, 256, 257

Westminster Hall, 269

Whetstone of Witte (Recorde), 107–10

Whitney, Geffrey. See *A Choice of Emblemes,* 20, 281–96

Wilcox, Thomas, 284

Wingate, Edmund: *Arithmetick made easie, in two Bookes,* 110–11, 114–15

witchcraft, 28, 29, 67

women: authors, 125; (*see also* described in travel narratives, 14–15, 29–30;

women (*continued*)
  education of, in literature, 119; Inuit,
  29–30. See also *Tragicall Tales. See
  also* seraglios, Ottoman; Montague,
  Lady Mary Wortley; witchcraft; Wroth,
  Mary
Wood, Anthony: *Athenae Oxonienses,* 267,
  273, 275

Wood, William: *New Englands Prospect,*
  182
*Work for Chimny-sweepers: Or A warning
  for Tabacconists* (Philaretes), 158–61
Wroth, Mary: *Urania,* 211
Wyatt, Sir Thomas, 77

Zurich, 237